Wild Ones
アラクレ

Vol. 3

Story & Art by
Kiyo Fujiwara

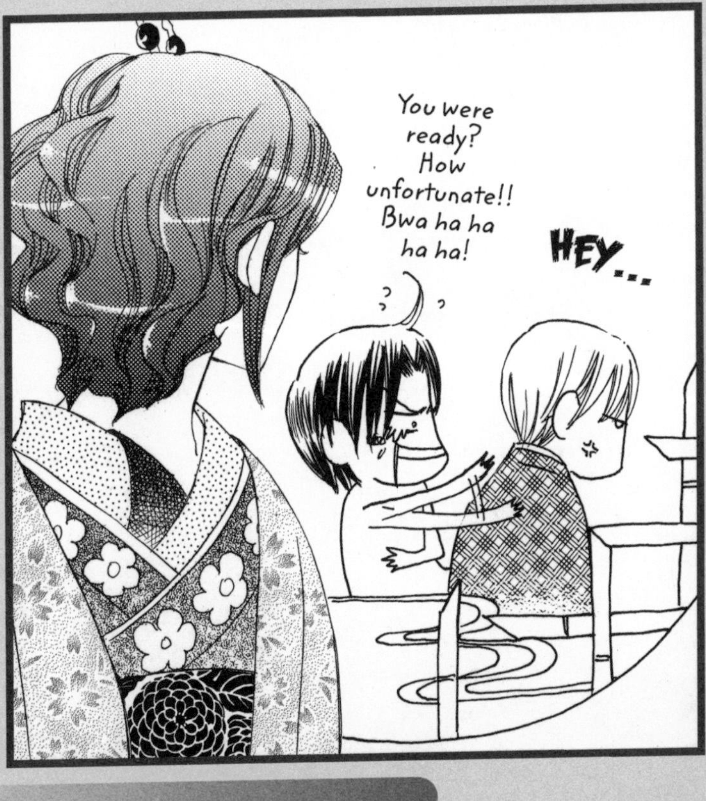
You were ready? How unfortunate!! Bwa ha ha ha ha!
HEY...

Wild Ones アラクレ

Volume 3

CONTENTS

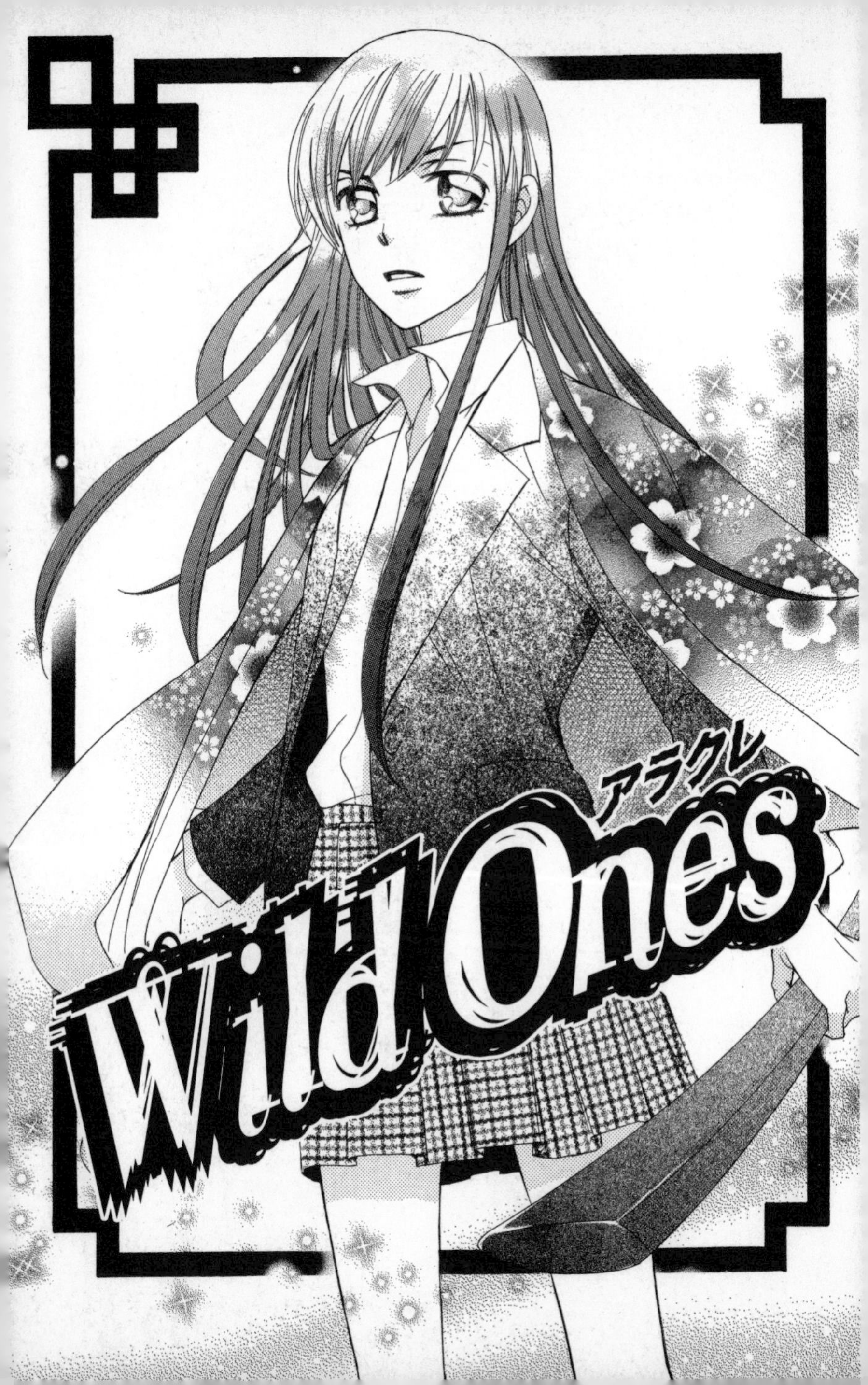
アラクレ
Wild Ones

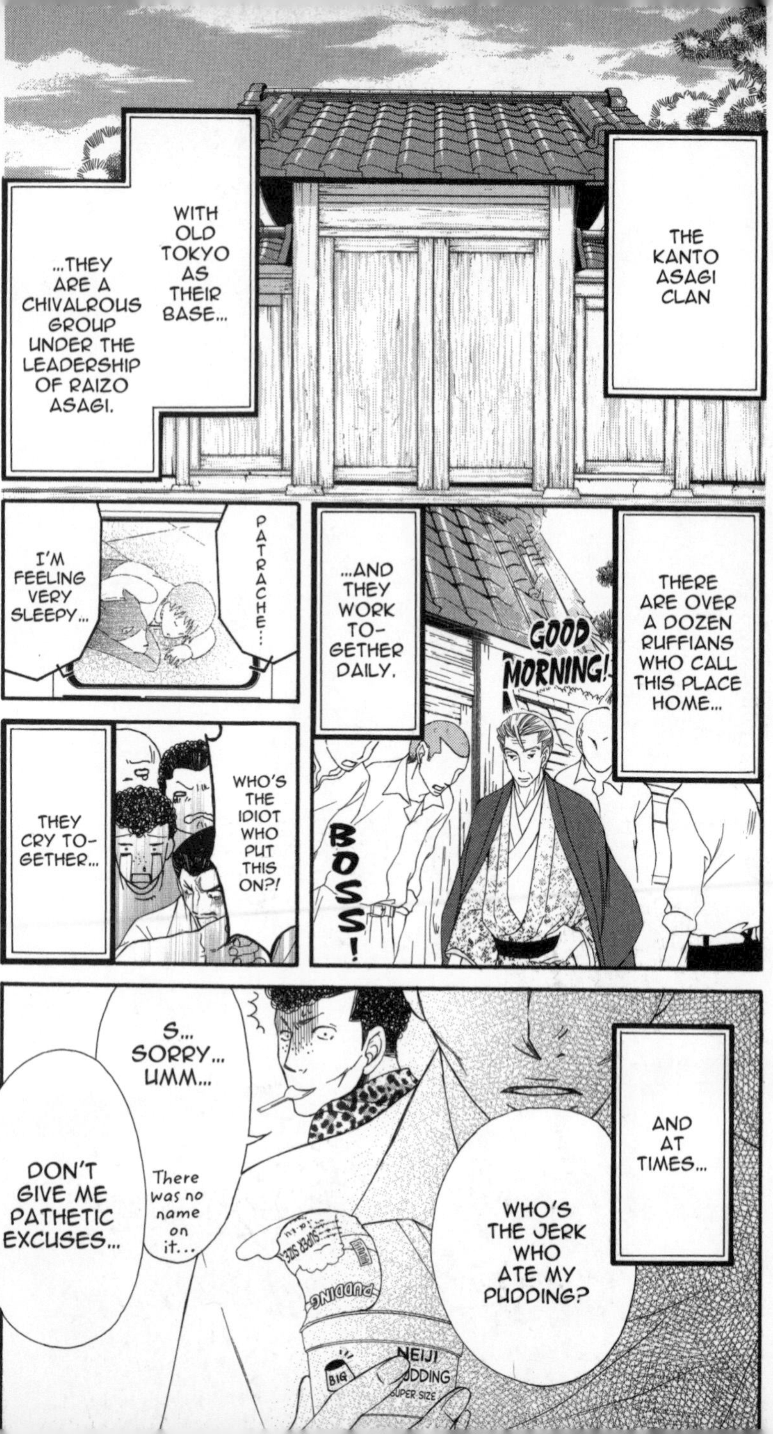
THE KANTO ASAGI CLAN
WITH OLD TOKYO AS THEIR BASE...
...THEY ARE A CHIVALROUS GROUP UNDER THE LEADERSHIP OF RAIZO ASAGI.
THERE ARE OVER A DOZEN RUFFIANS WHO CALL THIS PLACE HOME...
GOOD MORNING!
...AND THEY WORK TOGETHER DAILY.
BOSS!
PATRACHE...
I'M FEELING VERY SLEEPY...
WHO'S THE IDIOT WHO PUT THIS ON?!
THEY CRY TOGETHER...
AND AT TIMES...
WHO'S THE JERK WHO ATE MY PUDDING?
S... SORRY... UMM...
There was no name on it...
DON'T GIVE ME PATHETIC EXCUSES...
PUDDING
SUPER SIZE
NEIJI
PUDDING
SUPER SIZE
BIG

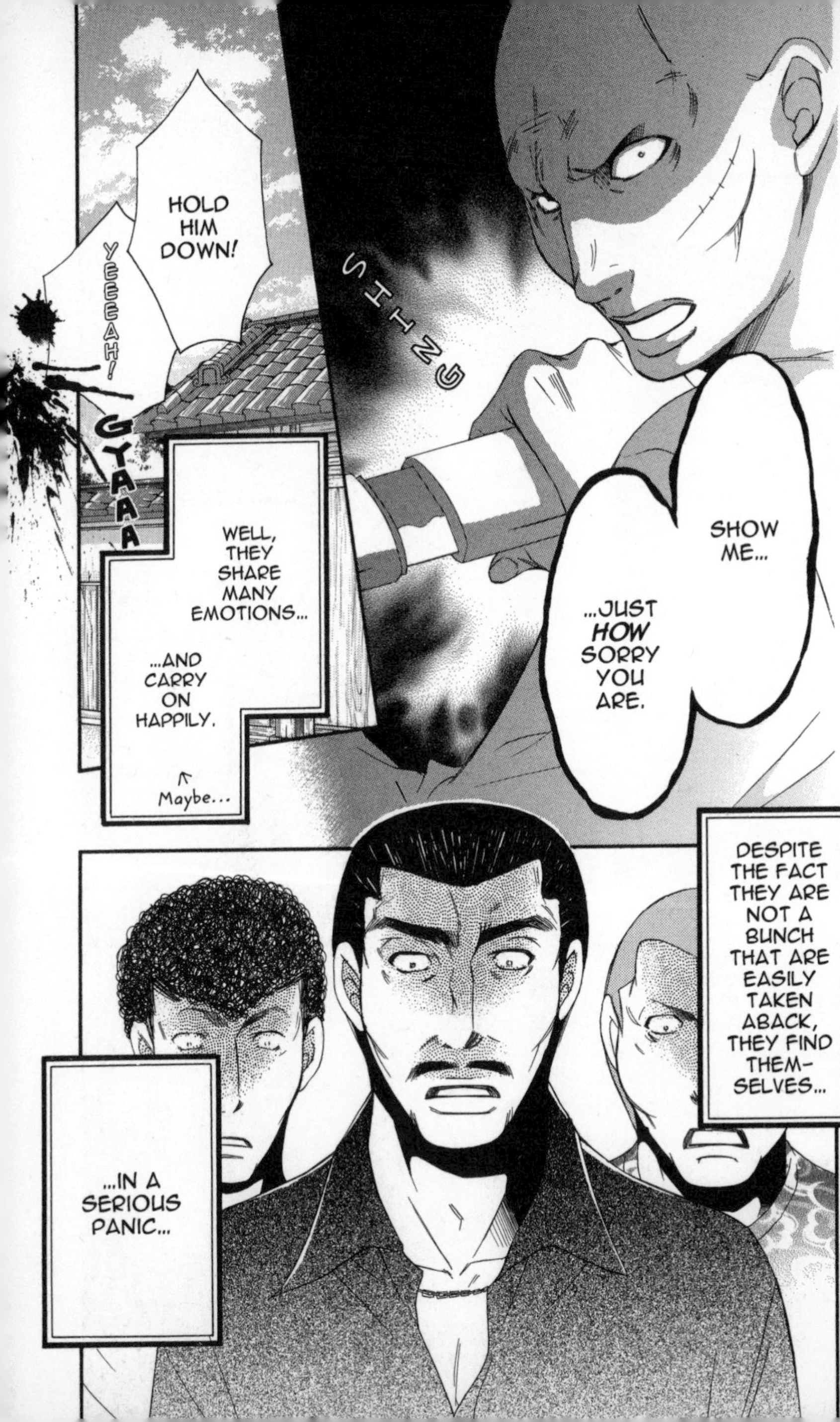
SHOW ME...
...JUST *HOW* SORRY YOU ARE.
SHING
HOLD HIM DOWN!
YEEEAH!
GYAAA
WELL, THEY SHARE MANY EMOTIONS...
...AND CARRY ON HAPPILY.
Maybe...
DESPITE THE FACT THEY ARE NOT A BUNCH THAT ARE EASILY TAKEN ABACK, THEY FIND THEM-SELVES...
...IN A SERIOUS PANIC...

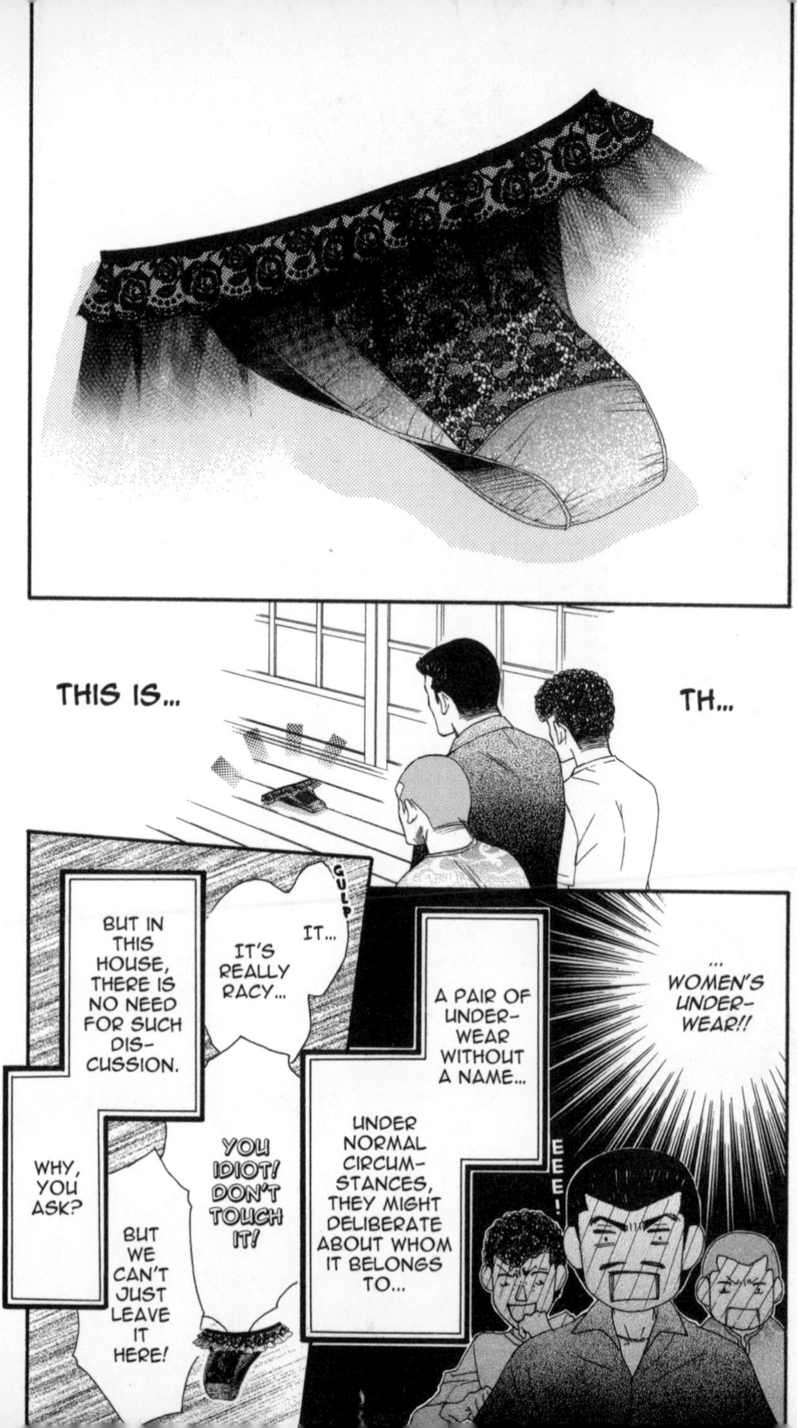
TH...
THIS IS...
... WOMEN'S UNDER-WEAR!!
EEE!
A PAIR OF UNDER-WEAR WITHOUT A NAME...
UNDER NORMAL CIRCUM-STANCES, THEY MIGHT DELIBERATE ABOUT WHOM IT BELONGS TO...
GULP
IT...
IT'S REALLY RACY...
BUT IN THIS HOUSE, THERE IS NO NEED FOR SUCH DIS-CUSSION.
YOU IDIOT! DON'T TOUCH IT!
WHY, YOU ASK?
BUT WE CAN'T JUST LEAVE IT HERE!

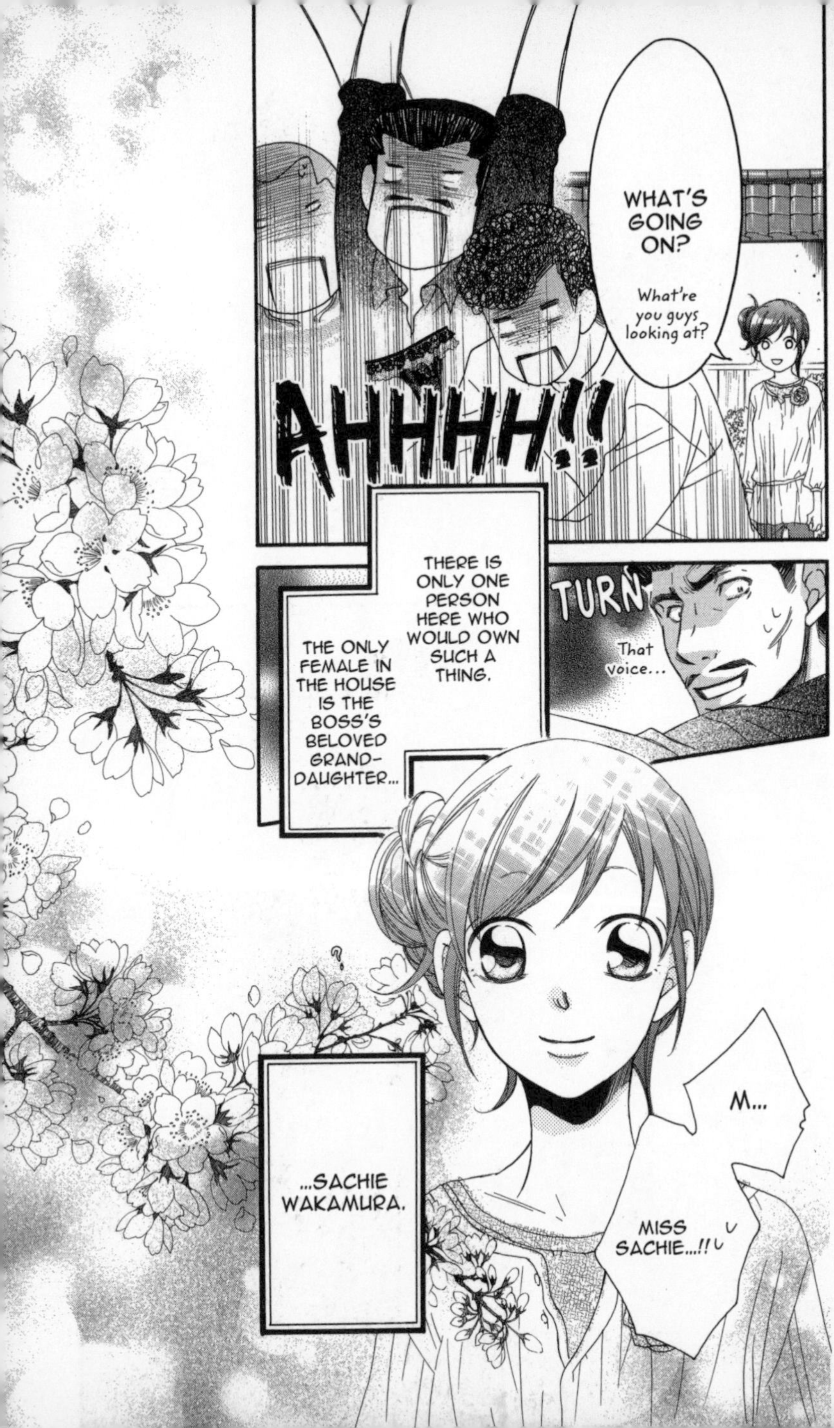
WHAT'S GOING ON?
What're you guys looking at?
AHHHH!!
TURN
That voice...
THERE IS ONLY ONE PERSON HERE WHO WOULD OWN SUCH A THING.
THE ONLY FEMALE IN THE HOUSE IS THE BOSS'S BELOVED GRAND-DAUGHTER...
M...
MISS SACHIE...!!
...SACHIE WAKAMURA.

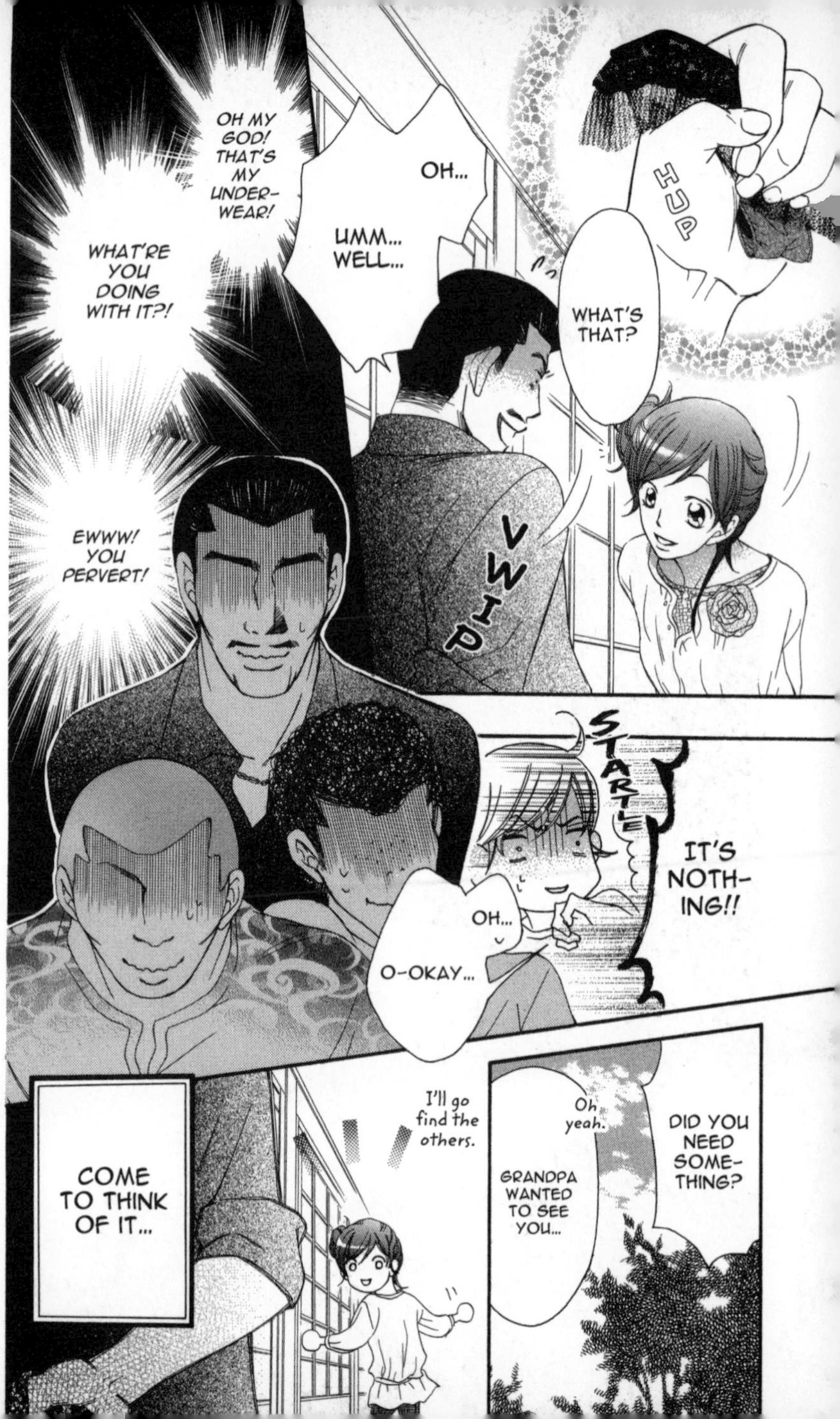
HUP
WHAT'S THAT?
VWIP
OH...
UMM... WELL...
STARTLE
IT'S NOTHING!!
OH...
O-OKAY...
OH MY GOD! THAT'S MY UNDERWEAR!
WHAT'RE YOU DOING WITH IT?!
EWWW! YOU PERVERT!
DID YOU NEED SOMETHING?
Oh yeah.
GRANDPA WANTED TO SEE YOU...
I'll go find the others.
COME TO THINK OF IT...

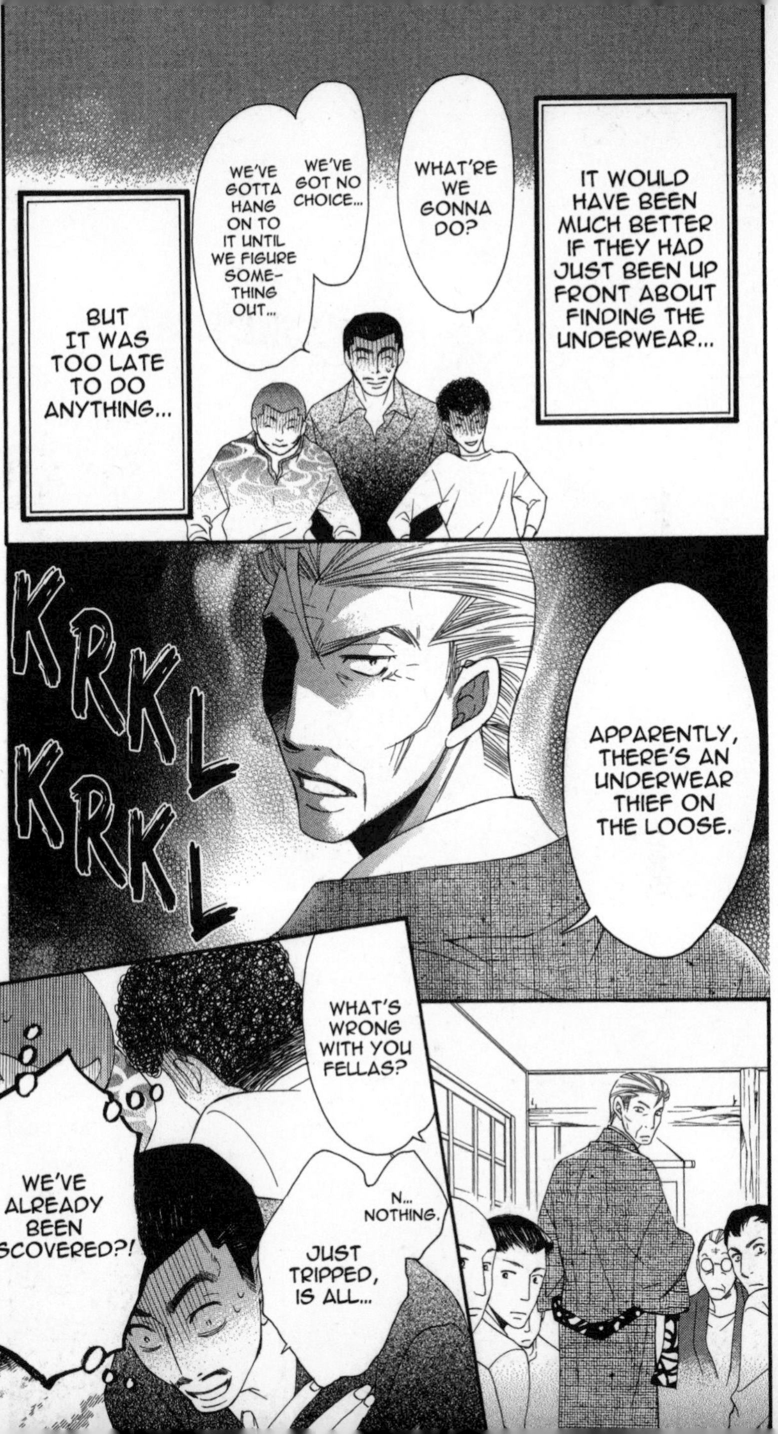
IT WOULD HAVE BEEN MUCH BETTER IF THEY HAD JUST BEEN UP FRONT ABOUT FINDING THE UNDERWEAR...
WHAT'RE WE GONNA DO?
WE'VE GOT NO CHOICE...
WE'VE GOTTA HANG ON TO IT UNTIL WE FIGURE SOME-THING OUT...
BUT IT WAS TOO LATE TO DO ANYTHING...
APPARENTLY, THERE'S AN UNDERWEAR THIEF ON THE LOOSE.
KRKL KRKL
WHAT'S WRONG WITH YOU FELLAS?
N... NOTHING.
JUST TRIPPED, IS ALL...
WE'VE ALREADY BEEN DISCOVERED?!

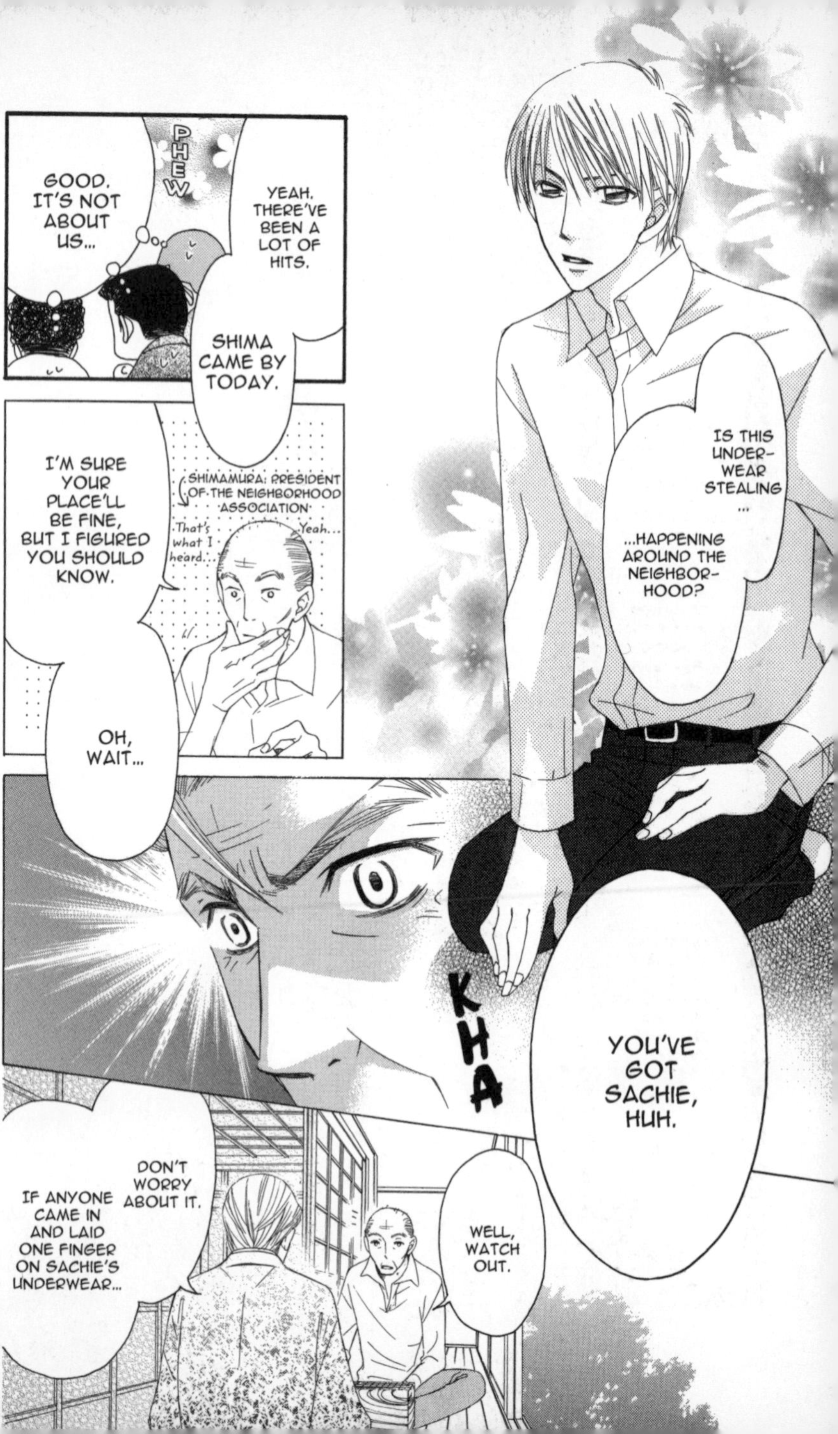
IS THIS UNDERWEAR STEALING...
...HAPPENING AROUND THE NEIGHBORHOOD?
YEAH. THERE'VE BEEN A LOT OF HITS.
PHEW
GOOD. IT'S NOT ABOUT US...
SHIMA CAME BY TODAY.
SHIMAMURA: PRESIDENT OF THE NEIGHBORHOOD ASSOCIATION
Yeah...
That's what I heard...
I'M SURE YOUR PLACE'LL BE FINE, BUT I FIGURED YOU SHOULD KNOW.
OH, WAIT...
YOU'VE GOT SACHIE, HUH.
KHA
WELL, WATCH OUT.
DON'T WORRY ABOUT IT.
IF ANYONE CAME IN AND LAID ONE FINGER ON SACHIE'S UNDERWEAR...

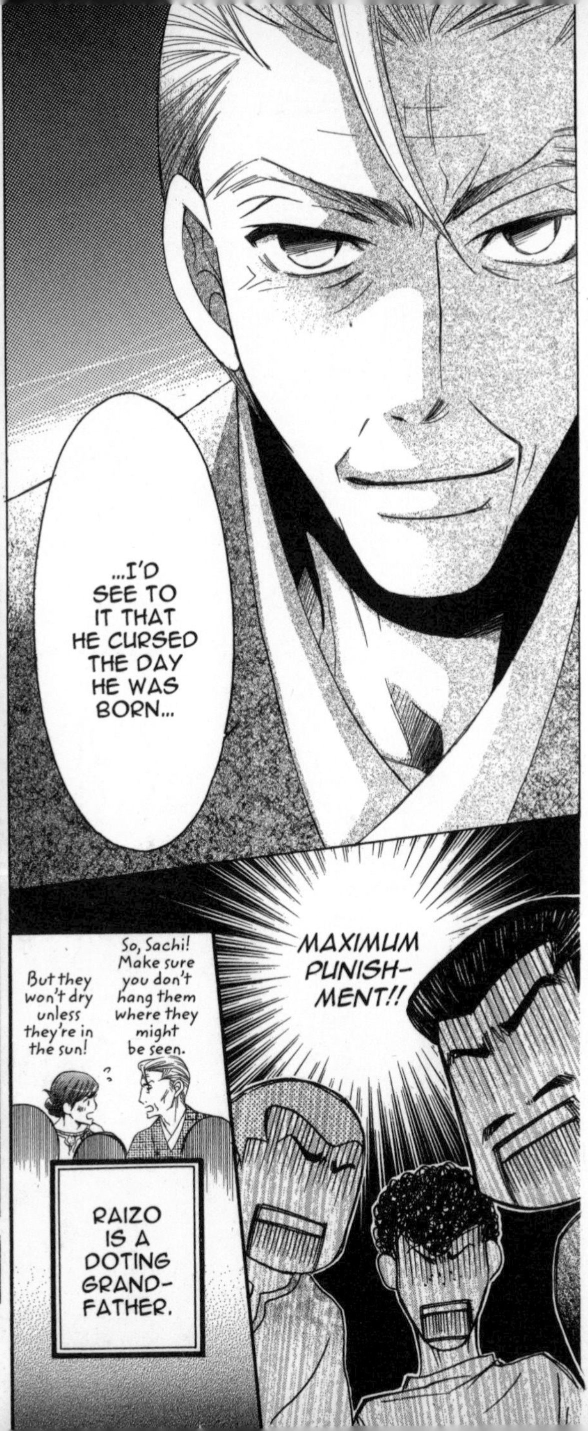
...I'D SEE TO IT THAT HE CURSED THE DAY HE WAS BORN...
MAXIMUM PUNISH-MENT!!
So, Sachi! Make sure you don't hang them where they might be seen.
But they won't dry unless they're in the sun!
?
RAIZO IS A DOTING GRAND-FATHER.

THIS IS VOLUME 3 OF ***WILD ONES!*** HOW QUICKLY TIME FLIES! IT WAS ONLY THIS MARCH THAT VOLUME 2 CAME OUT, RIGHT?!

GOLD RUSH 21 COMES OUT THIS JUNE TOO!

WOW... HOW WONDERFUL... I JUST FEEL SO BLESSED.

AROUND THE MIDDLE OF THIS VOLUME, I WAS GIVEN SIX MORE CHAPTERS TO WORK ON. I HAVEN'T DONE SIX CHAPTERS IN A ROW SINCE I DID ***HELP!!*** ALTHOUGH I'VE DONE IT BEFORE, WORKING ON A DIFFERENT SERIES IS A TOTALLY DIFFERENT EXPERIENCE. I WAS IN HYSTERICS TRYING TO KEEP UP WITH THE PACE!

WHEN I THOUGHT ABOUT HOW SERIALIZED AUTHORS HAVE TO CONTINUE THIS FOR YEARS, I WAS REALLY, REALLY IMPRESSED. AND THEN, I HAD THE OPPORTUNITY TO MEET ONE OF THOSE TRULY GREAT AUTHORS...

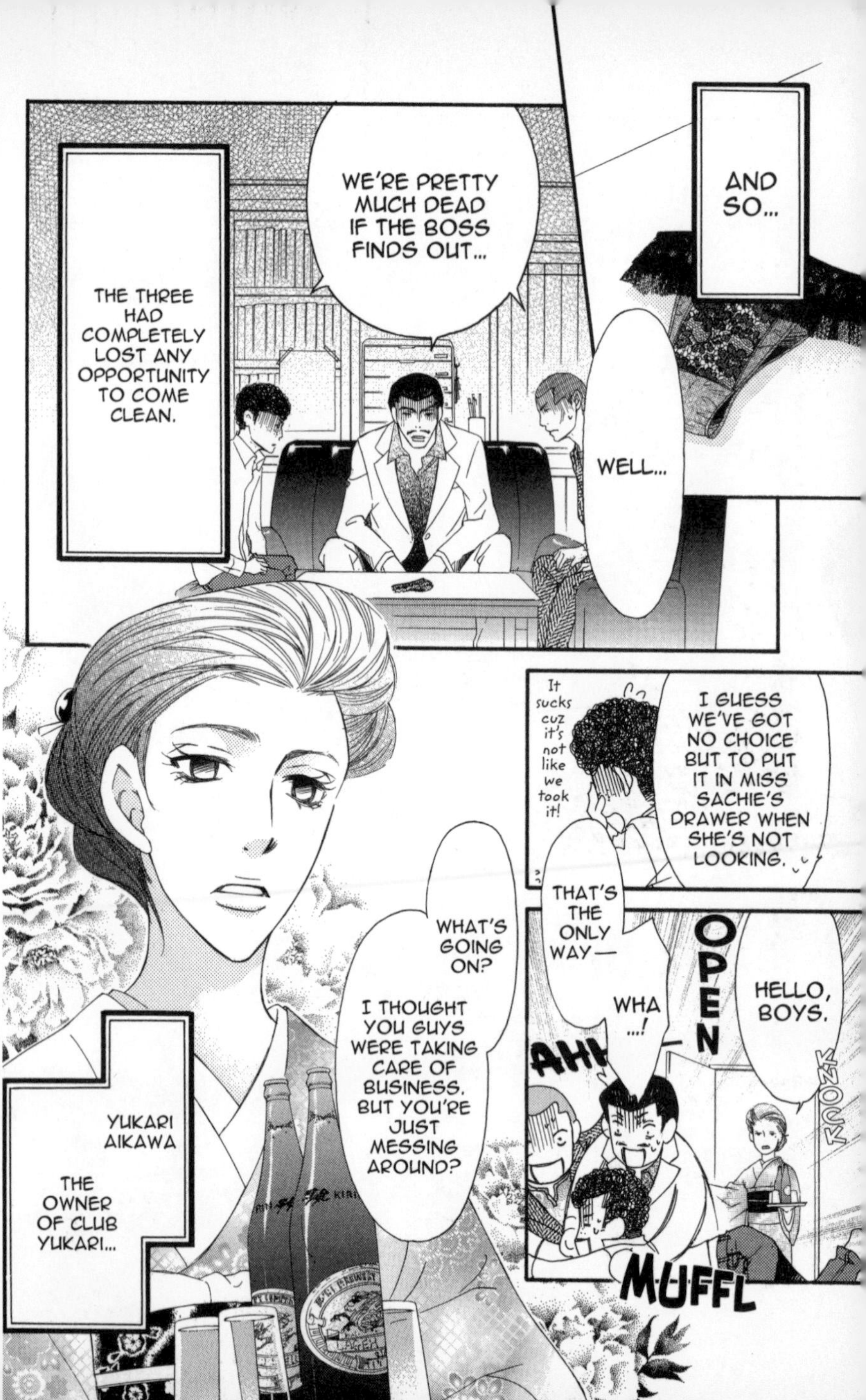
AND SO...
WELL...
WE'RE PRETTY MUCH DEAD IF THE BOSS FINDS OUT...
THE THREE HAD COMPLETELY LOST ANY OPPORTUNITY TO COME CLEAN.
I GUESS WE'VE GOT NO CHOICE BUT TO PUT IT IN MISS SACHIE'S DRAWER WHEN SHE'S NOT LOOKING.
It sucks cuz it's not like we took it!
THAT'S THE ONLY WAY—
KNOCK
HELLO, BOYS.
OPEN
WHA ...!
AHH
MUFFL
WHAT'S GOING ON?
I THOUGHT YOU GUYS WERE TAKING CARE OF BUSINESS. BUT YOU'RE JUST MESSING AROUND?
YUKARI AIKAWA
THE OWNER OF CLUB YUKARI...

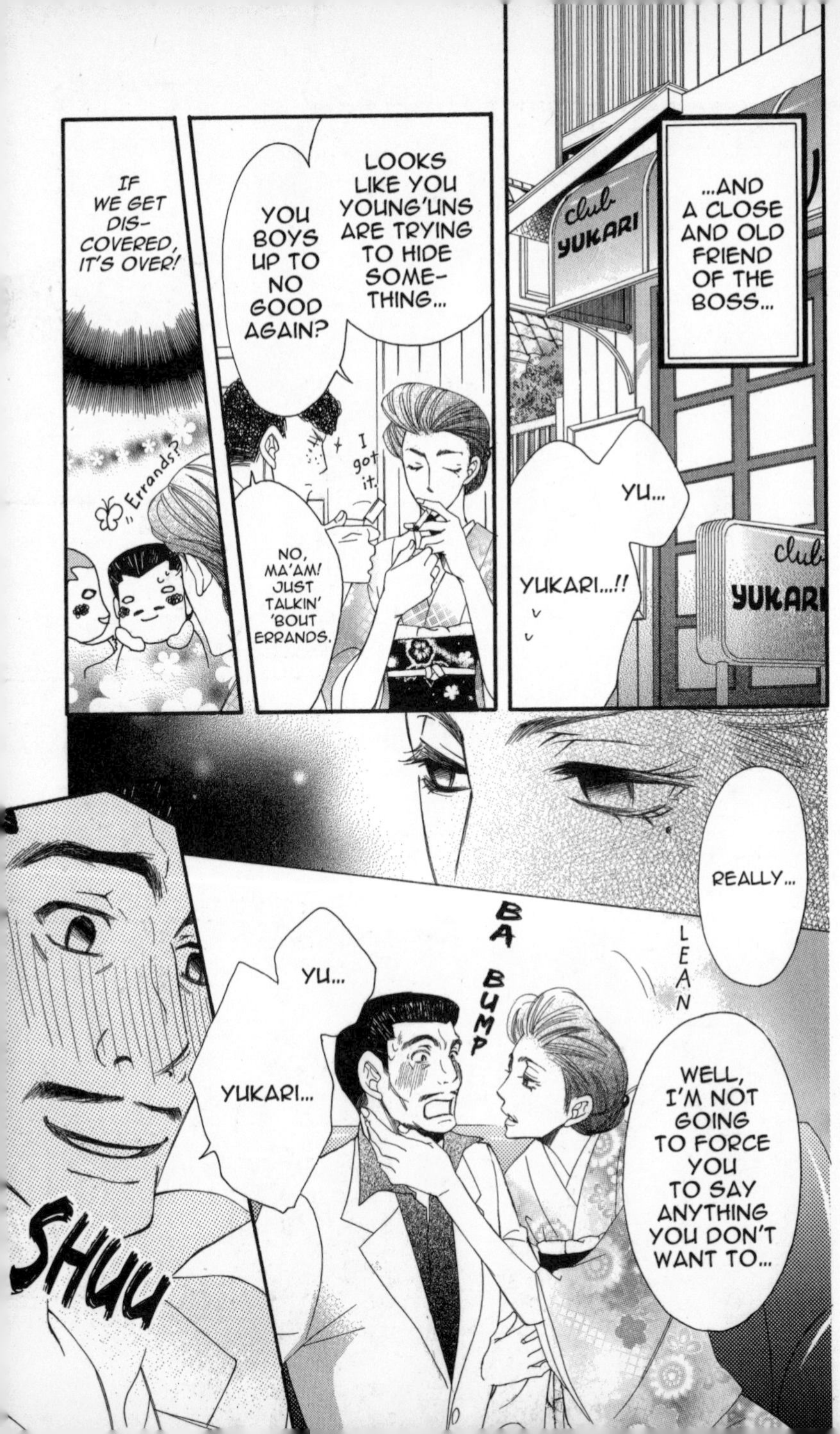
club YUKARI
...AND A CLOSE AND OLD FRIEND OF THE BOSS...
YU...
YUKARI...!!
club YUKARI
LOOKS LIKE YOU YOUNG'UNS ARE TRYING TO HIDE SOME-THING...
YOU BOYS UP TO NO GOOD AGAIN?
I got it.
NO, MA'AM! JUST TALKIN' 'BOUT ERRANDS.
IF WE GET DIS-COVERED, IT'S OVER!
Errands?
REALLY...
LEAN
WELL, I'M NOT GOING TO FORCE YOU TO SAY ANYTHING YOU DON'T WANT TO...
BA BUMP
YU...
YUKARI...
SHUU

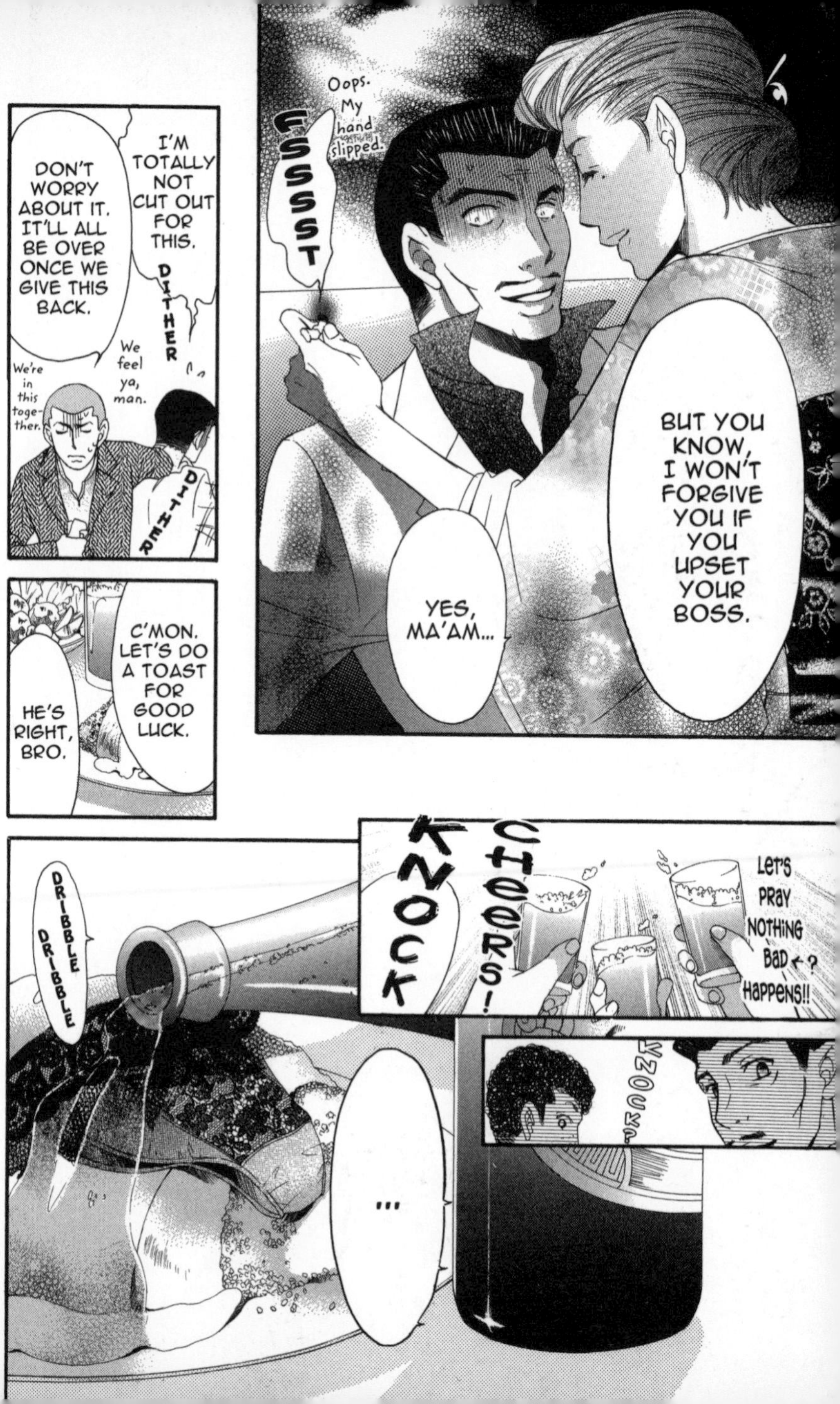
Oops. My hand slipped.
FSSSST
BUT YOU KNOW, I WON'T FORGIVE YOU IF YOU UPSET YOUR BOSS.
YES, MA'AM...
I'M TOTALLY NOT CUT OUT FOR THIS.
DON'T WORRY ABOUT IT. IT'LL ALL BE OVER ONCE WE GIVE THIS BACK.
DITHER
We feel ya, man.
We're in this toge-ther.
DITHER
C'MON. LET'S DO A TOAST FOR GOOD LUCK.
HE'S RIGHT, BRO.
Let's pray NOTHING BAD ←? Happens!!
CHEERS!
KNOCK
KNOCK
DRIBBLE DRIBBLE
...

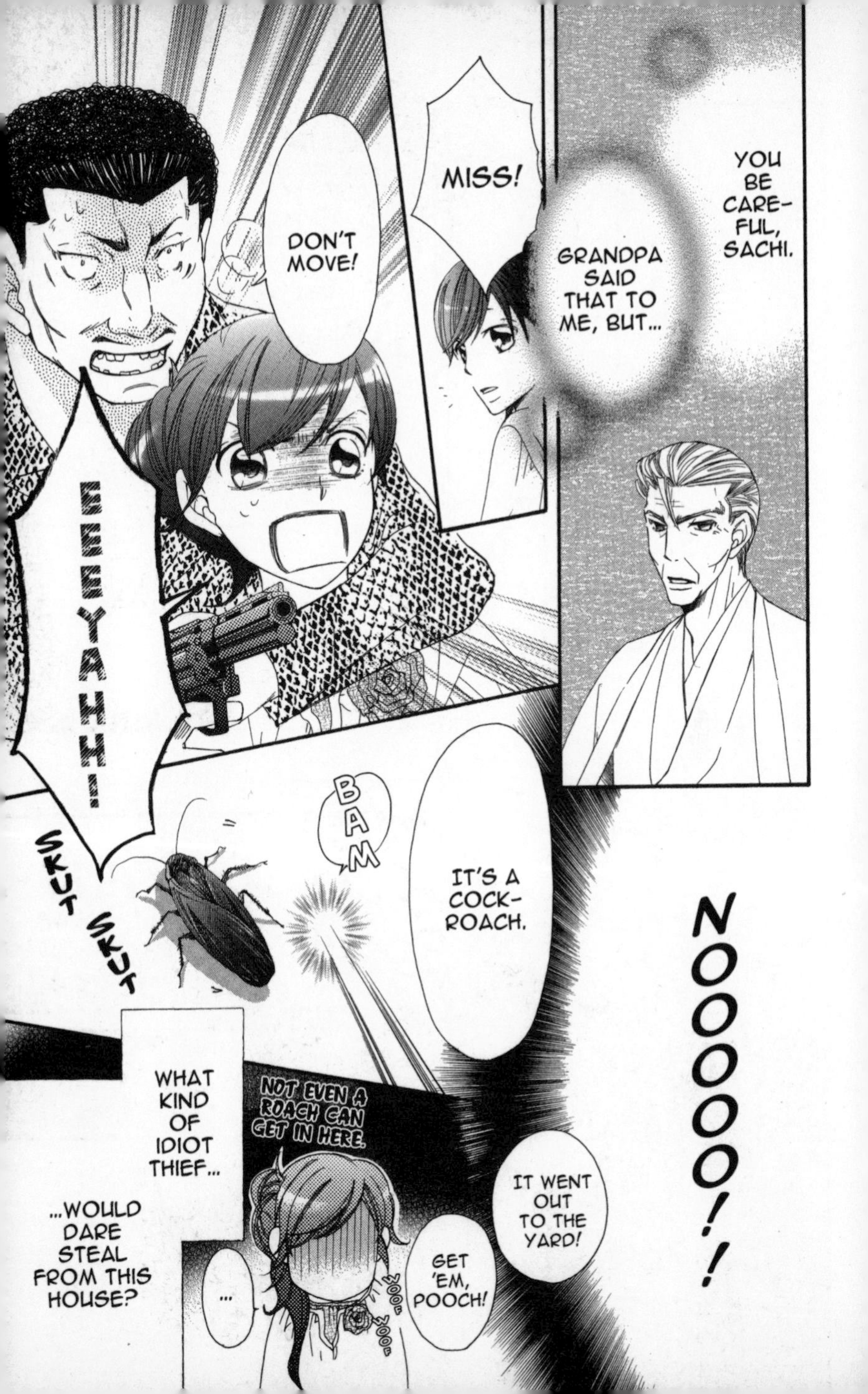
YOU BE CAREFUL, SACHI.
GRANDPA SAID THAT TO ME, BUT...
MISS!
DON'T MOVE!
EEEYAHH!
NOOOOO!!
IT'S A COCK-ROACH.
BAM
SKUT SKUT
WHAT KIND OF IDIOT THIEF...
NOT EVEN A ROACH CAN GET IN HERE.
IT WENT OUT TO THE YARD!
GET 'EM, POOCH!
WOOF WOOF
...WOULD DARE STEAL FROM THIS HOUSE?
...

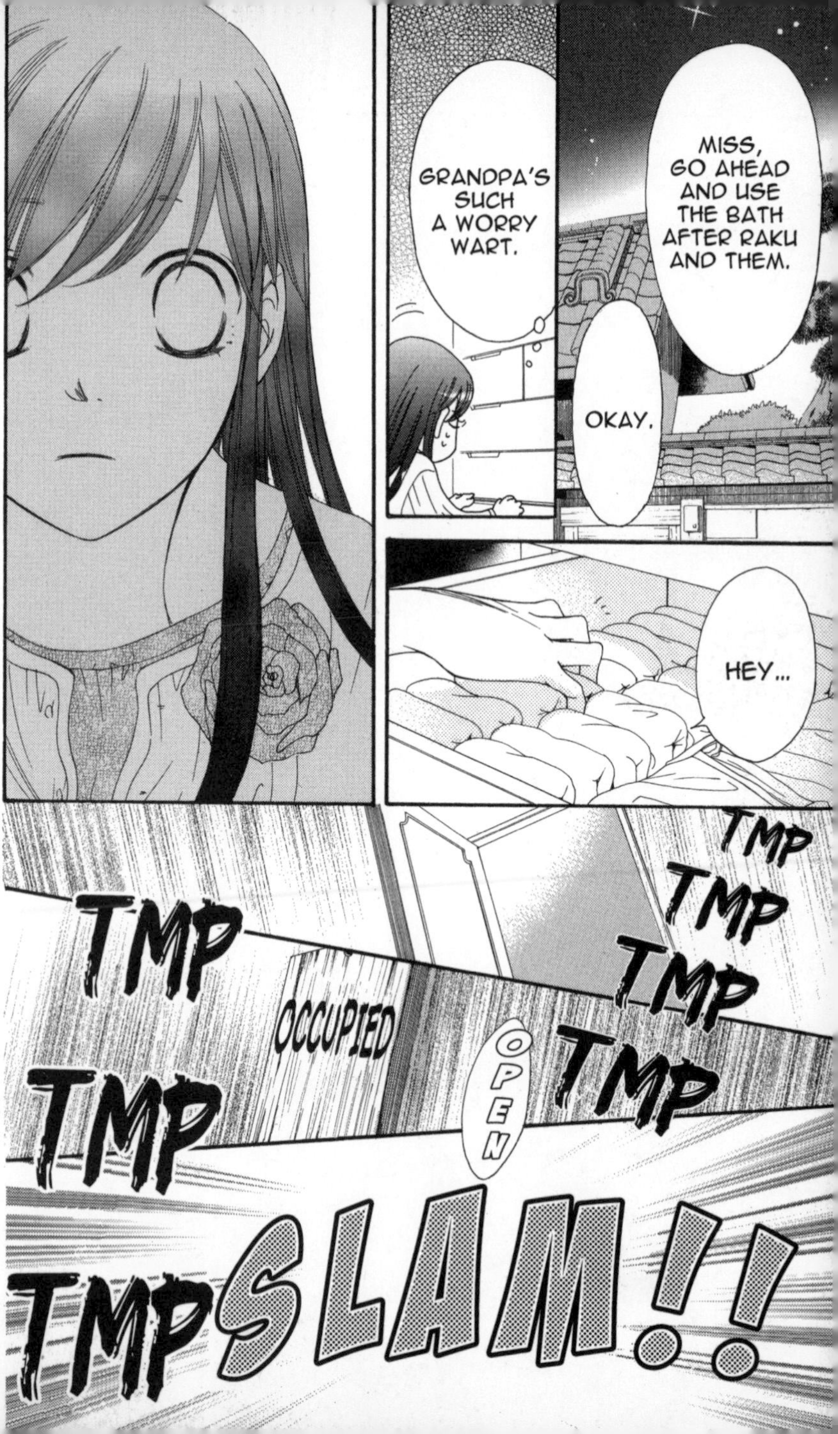
MISS, GO AHEAD AND USE THE BATH AFTER RAKU AND THEM.
OKAY.
GRANDPA'S SUCH A WORRY WART.
HEY...
TMP
TMP
TMP
TMP
OPEN
OCCUPIED
TMP
TMP
TMP
SLAM!!

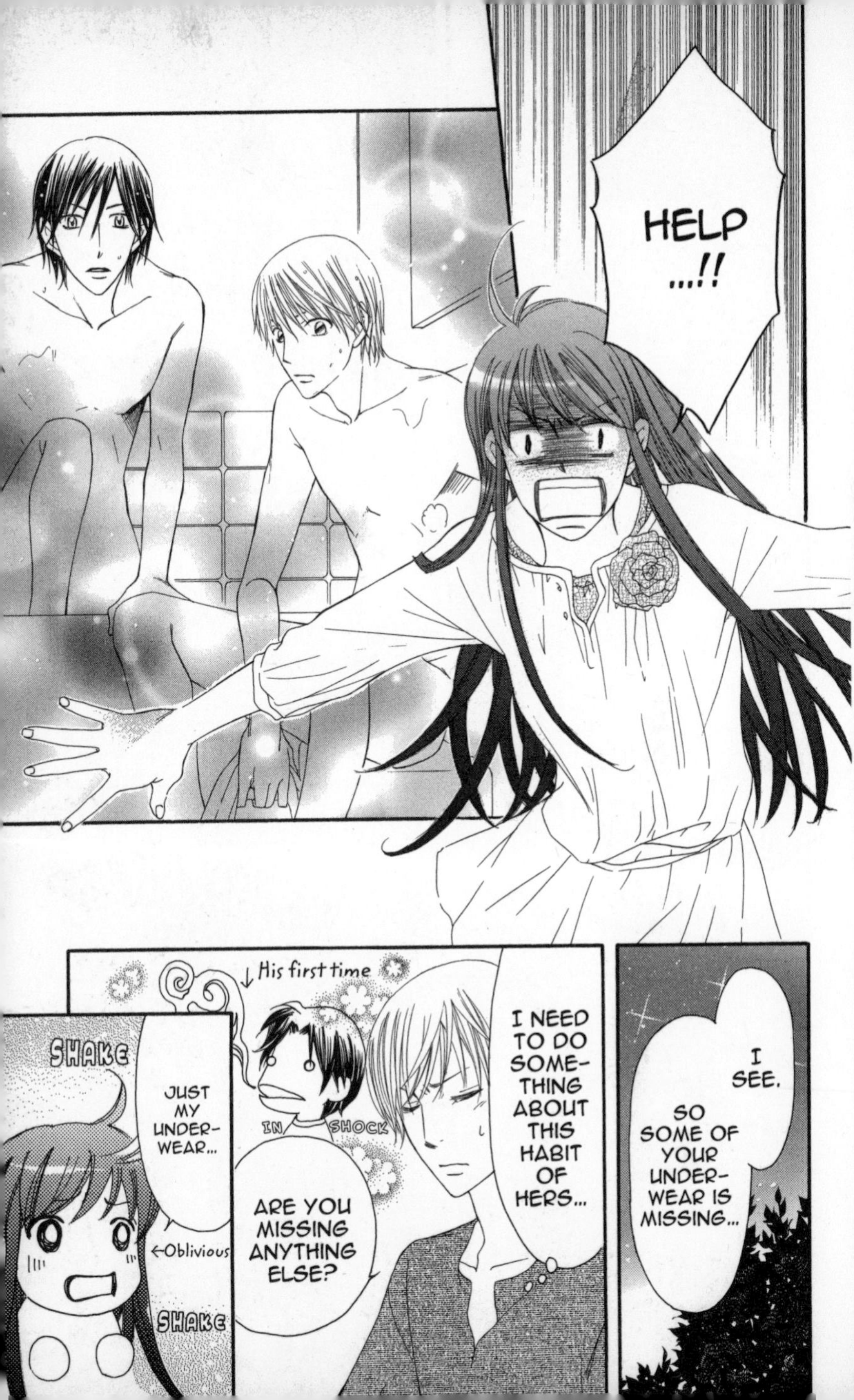
HELP ...!!
I SEE.
SO SOME OF YOUR UNDERWEAR IS MISSING...
I NEED TO DO SOMETHING ABOUT THIS HABIT OF HERS...
↓His first time
IN SHOCK
ARE YOU MISSING ANYTHING ELSE?
JUST MY UNDERWEAR...
SHAKE
←Oblivious
SHAKE

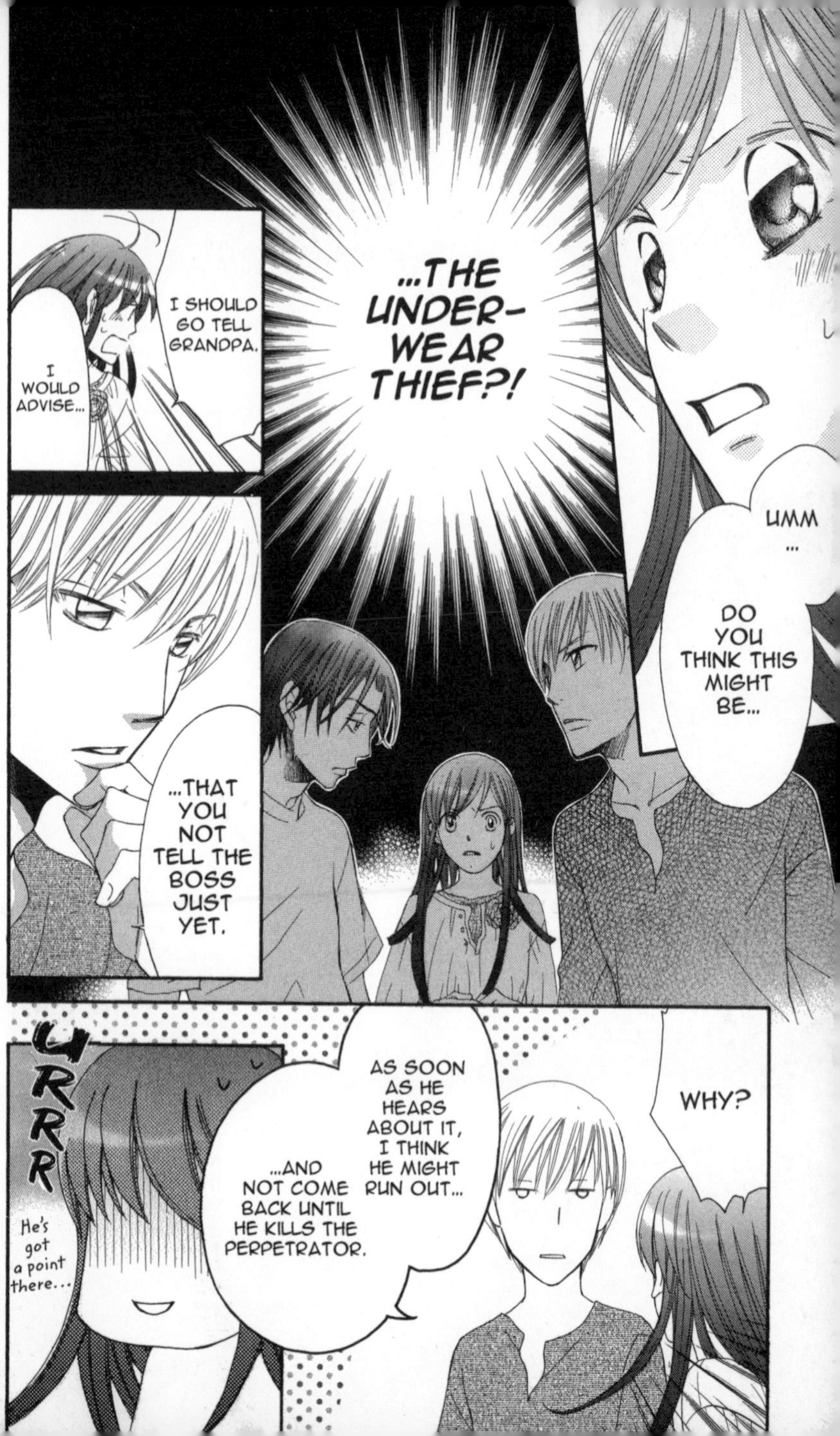
UMM...
DO YOU THINK THIS MIGHT BE...
...THE UNDER-WEAR THIEF?!
I SHOULD GO TELL GRANDPA.
I WOULD ADVISE...
...THAT YOU NOT TELL THE BOSS JUST YET.
WHY?
AS SOON AS HE HEARS ABOUT IT, I THINK HE MIGHT RUN OUT...
...AND NOT COME BACK UNTIL HE KILLS THE PERPETRATOR.
URRR
He's got a point there...

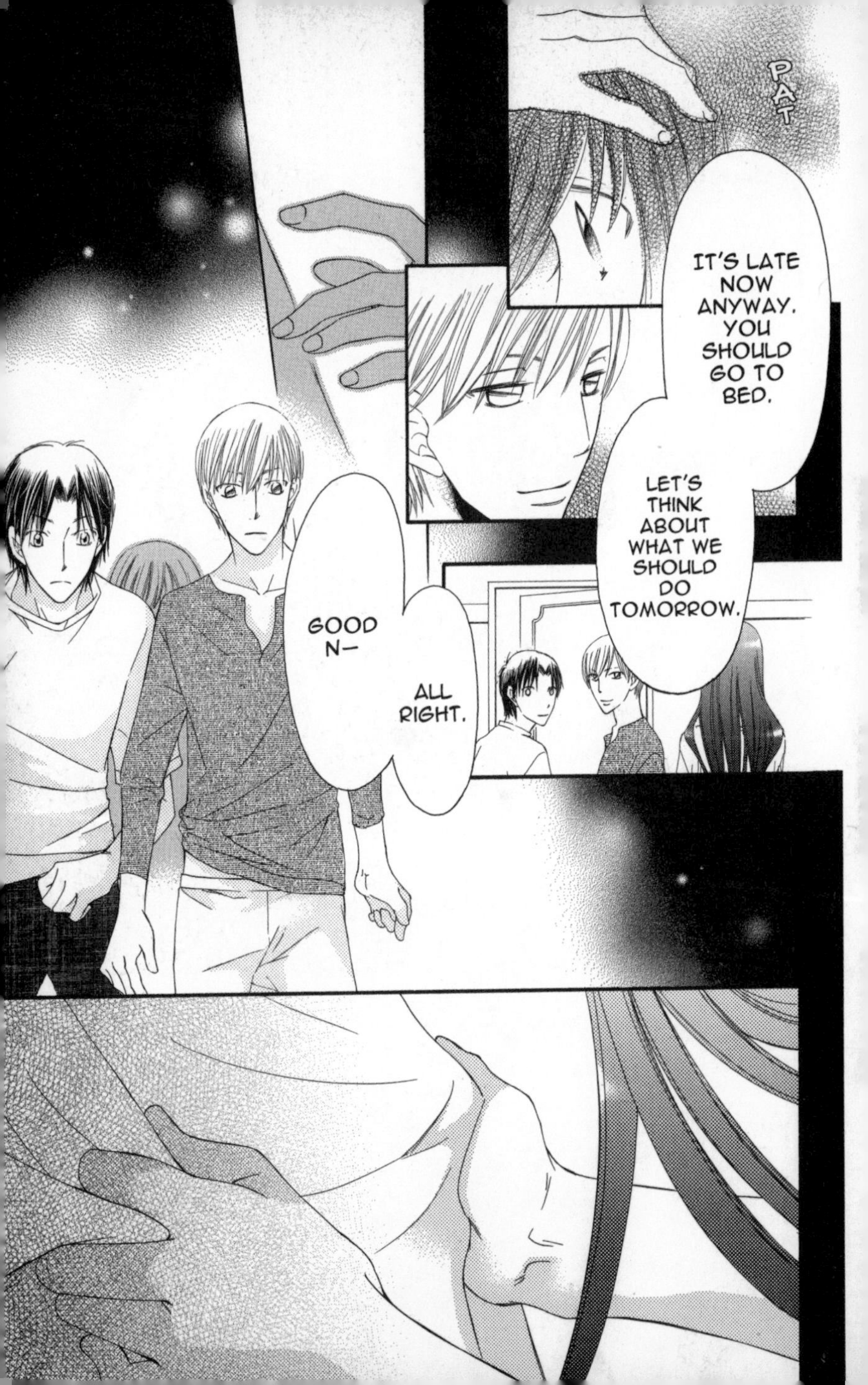
PAT
IT'S LATE NOW ANYWAY. YOU SHOULD GO TO BED.
LET'S THINK ABOUT WHAT WE SHOULD DO TOMORROW.
ALL RIGHT.
GOOD N—

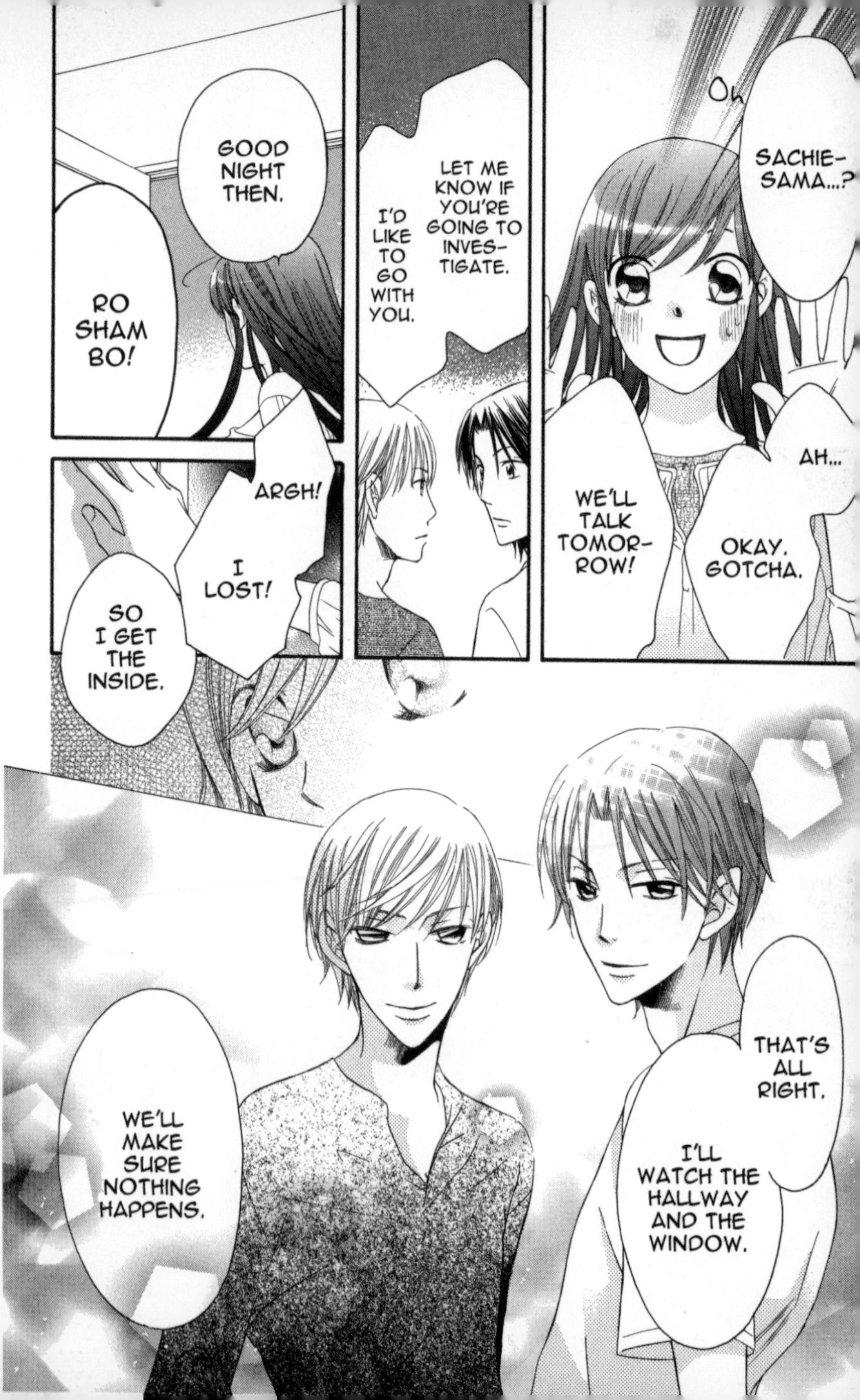
Oh
SACHIE-SAMA...?
AH...
OKAY. GOTCHA.
WE'LL TALK TOMOR-ROW!
LET ME KNOW IF YOU'RE GOING TO INVES-TIGATE.
I'D LIKE TO GO WITH YOU.
GOOD NIGHT THEN.
RO SHAM BO!
ARGH!
I LOST!
SO I GET THE INSIDE.
THAT'S ALL RIGHT.
I'LL WATCH THE HALLWAY AND THE WINDOW.
WE'LL MAKE SURE NOTHING HAPPENS.

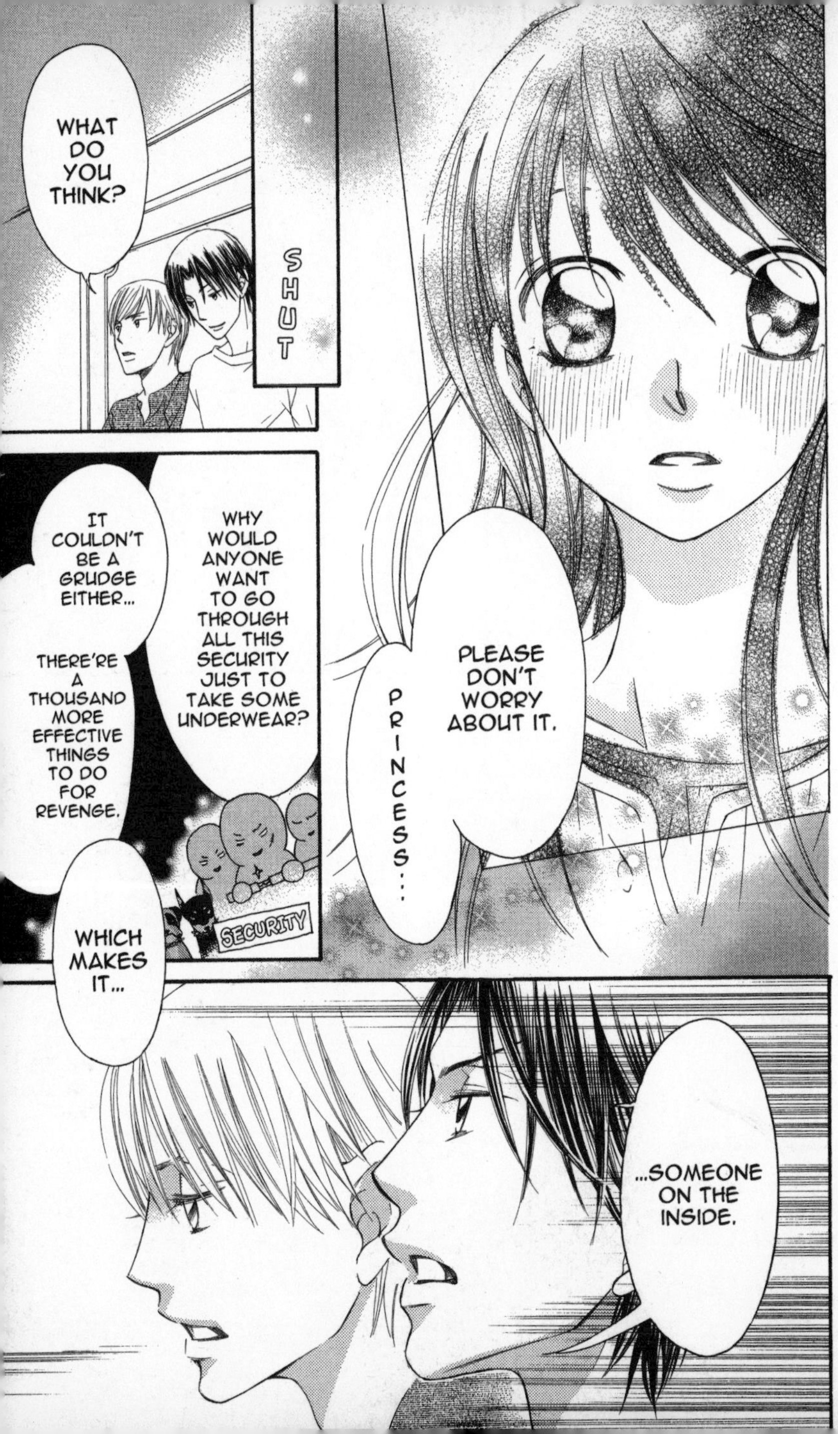
PLEASE DON'T WORRY ABOUT IT.
PRINCESS...
SHUT
WHAT DO YOU THINK?
WHY WOULD ANYONE WANT TO GO THROUGH ALL THIS SECURITY JUST TO TAKE SOME UNDERWEAR?
IT COULDN'T BE A GRUDGE EITHER...
THERE'RE A THOUSAND MORE EFFECTIVE THINGS TO DO FOR REVENGE.
SECURITY
WHICH MAKES IT...
...SOMEONE ON THE INSIDE.

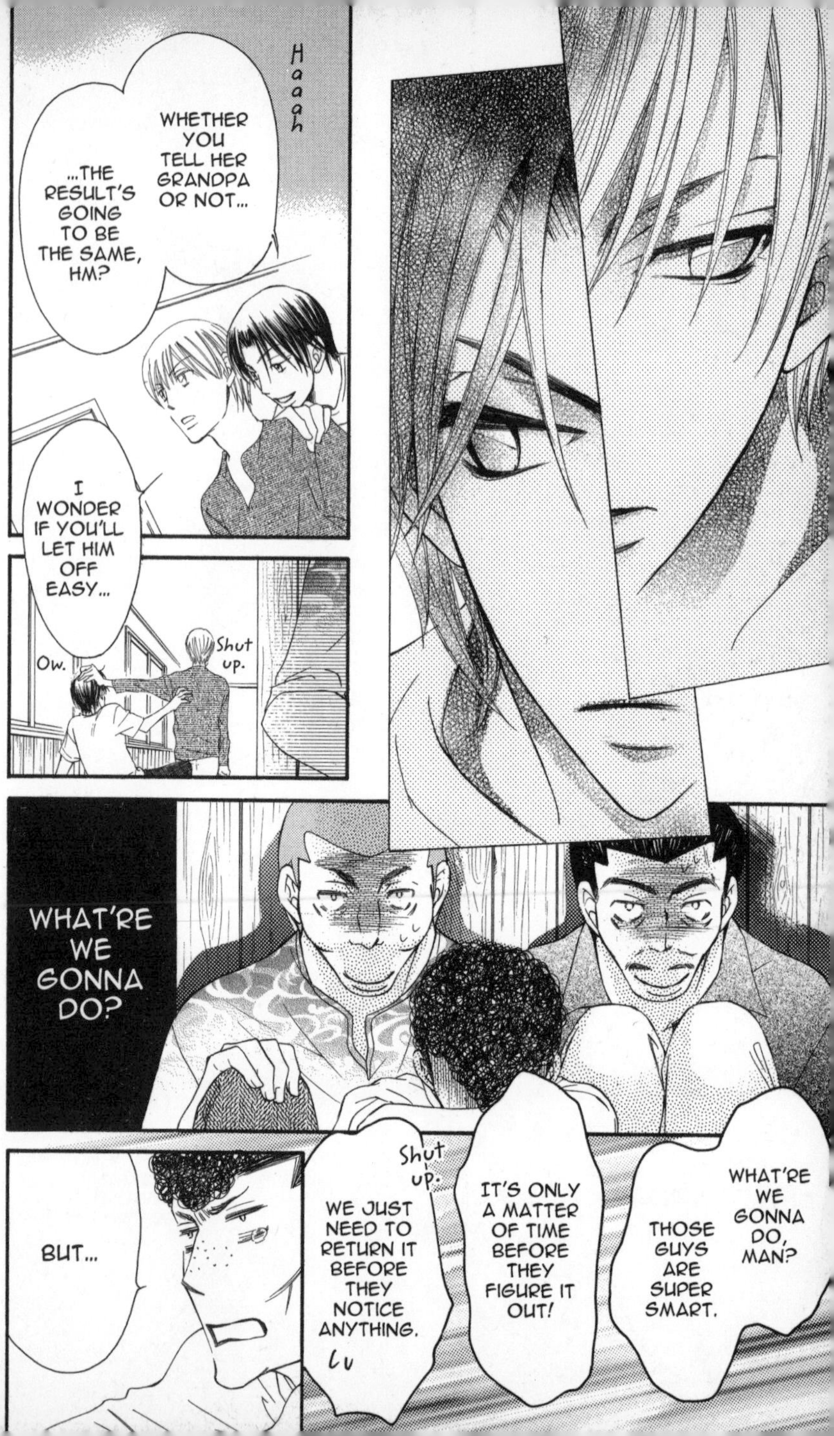
Haaah
WHETHER YOU TELL HER GRANDPA OR NOT...
...THE RESULT'S GOING TO BE THE SAME, HM?
I WONDER IF YOU'LL LET HIM OFF EASY...
Shut up.
Ow.
WHAT'RE WE GONNA DO?
WHAT'RE WE GONNA DO, MAN?
THOSE GUYS ARE SUPER SMART.
IT'S ONLY A MATTER OF TIME BEFORE THEY FIGURE IT OUT!
Shut up.
WE JUST NEED TO RETURN IT BEFORE THEY NOTICE ANYTHING.
BUT...

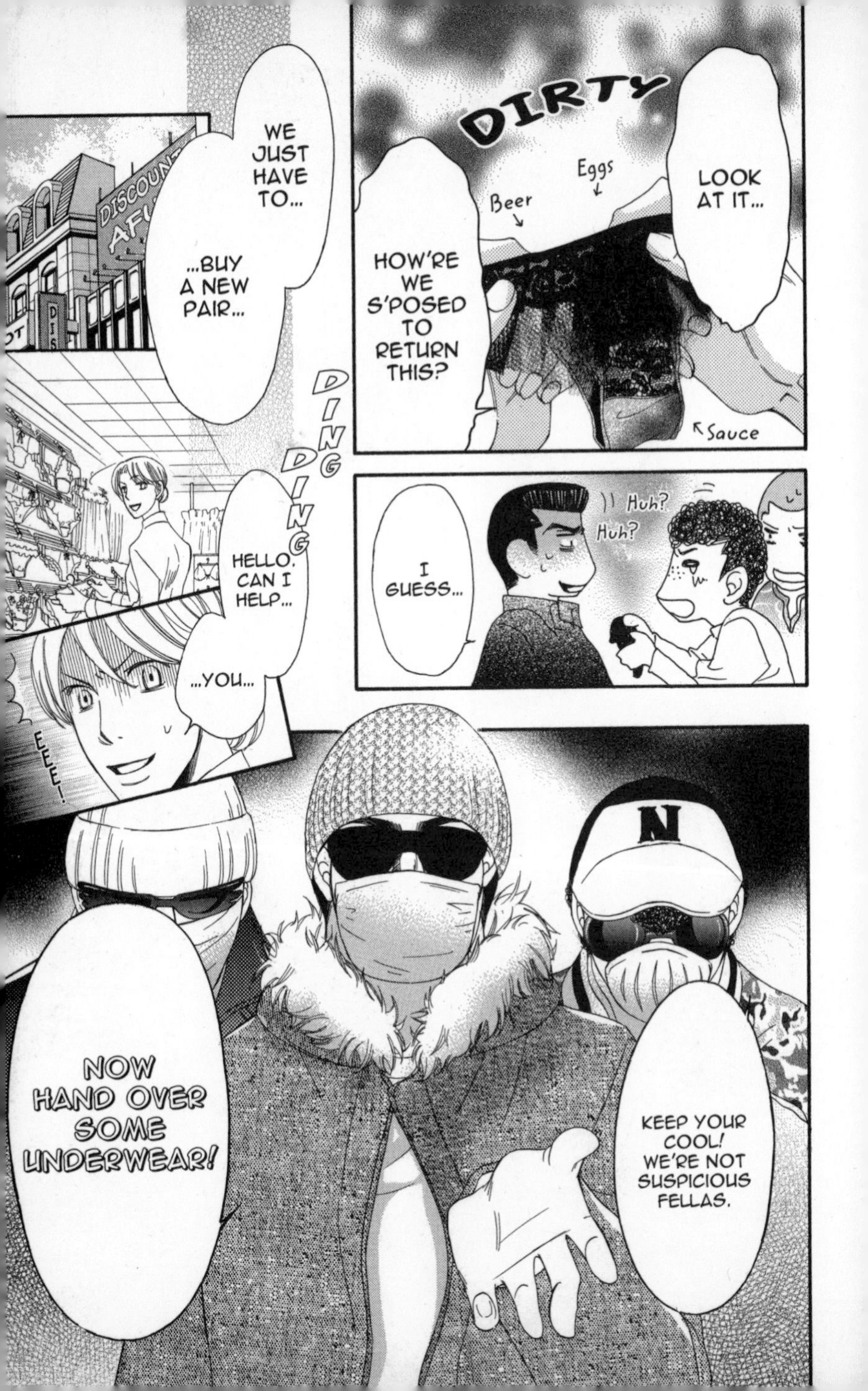
LOOK AT IT...
DIRTY
Eggs
Beer
Sauce
HOW'RE WE S'POSED TO RETURN THIS?
Huh? Huh?
I GUESS...
WE JUST HAVE TO...
...BUY A NEW PAIR...
DISCOUNT
DING DING
HELLO. CAN I HELP...
...YOU...
EEEE!
KEEP YOUR COOL! WE'RE NOT SUSPICIOUS FELLAS.
NOW HAND OVER SOME UNDERWEAR!

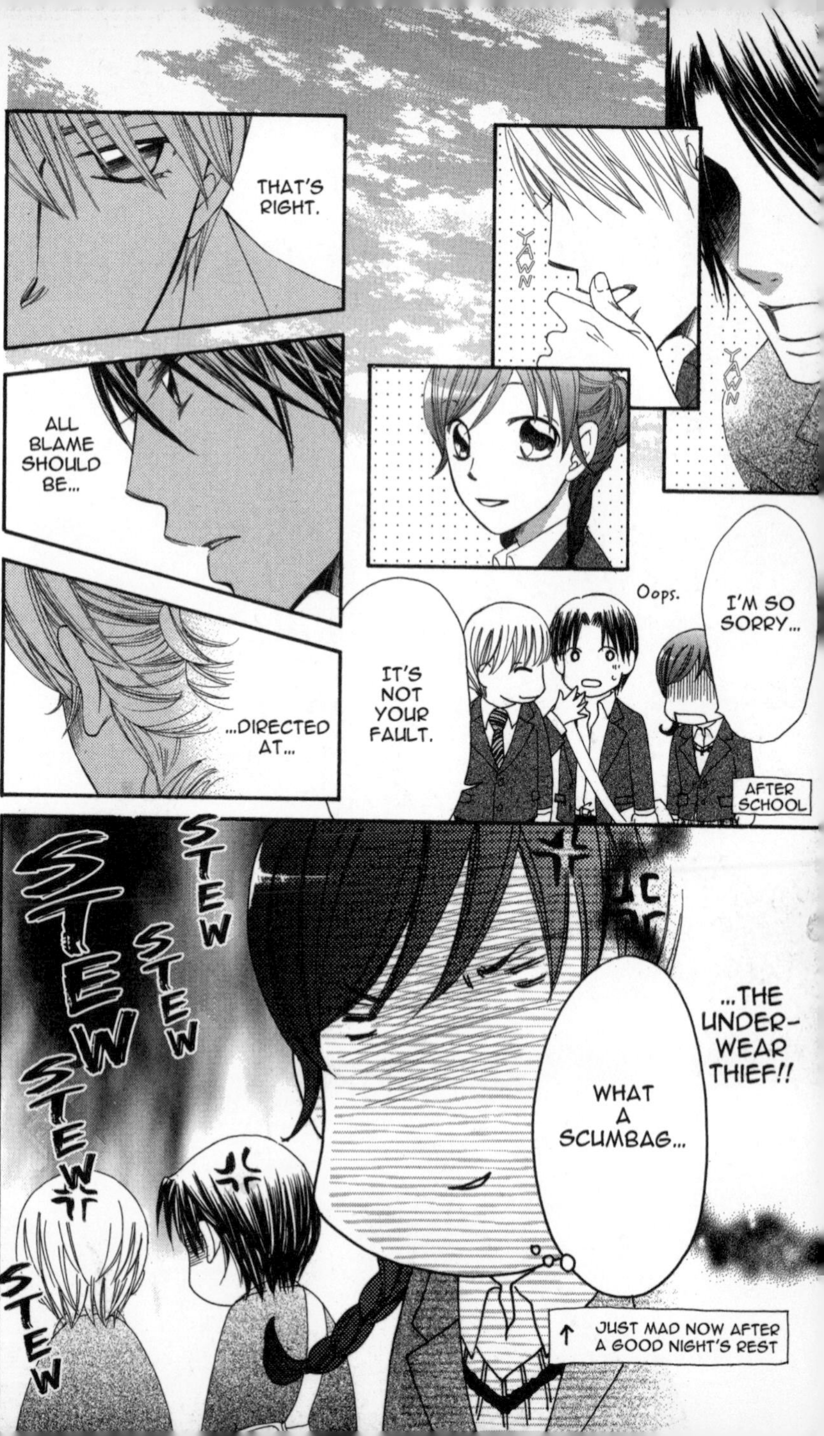
YAWN
YAWN
I'M SO SORRY...
Oops.
IT'S NOT YOUR FAULT.
AFTER SCHOOL
THAT'S RIGHT.
ALL BLAME SHOULD BE...
...DIRECTED AT...
...THE UNDER-WEAR THIEF!!
WHAT A SCUMBAG...
STEW STEW STEW STEW STEW STEW STEW
↑ JUST MAD NOW AFTER A GOOD NIGHT'S REST

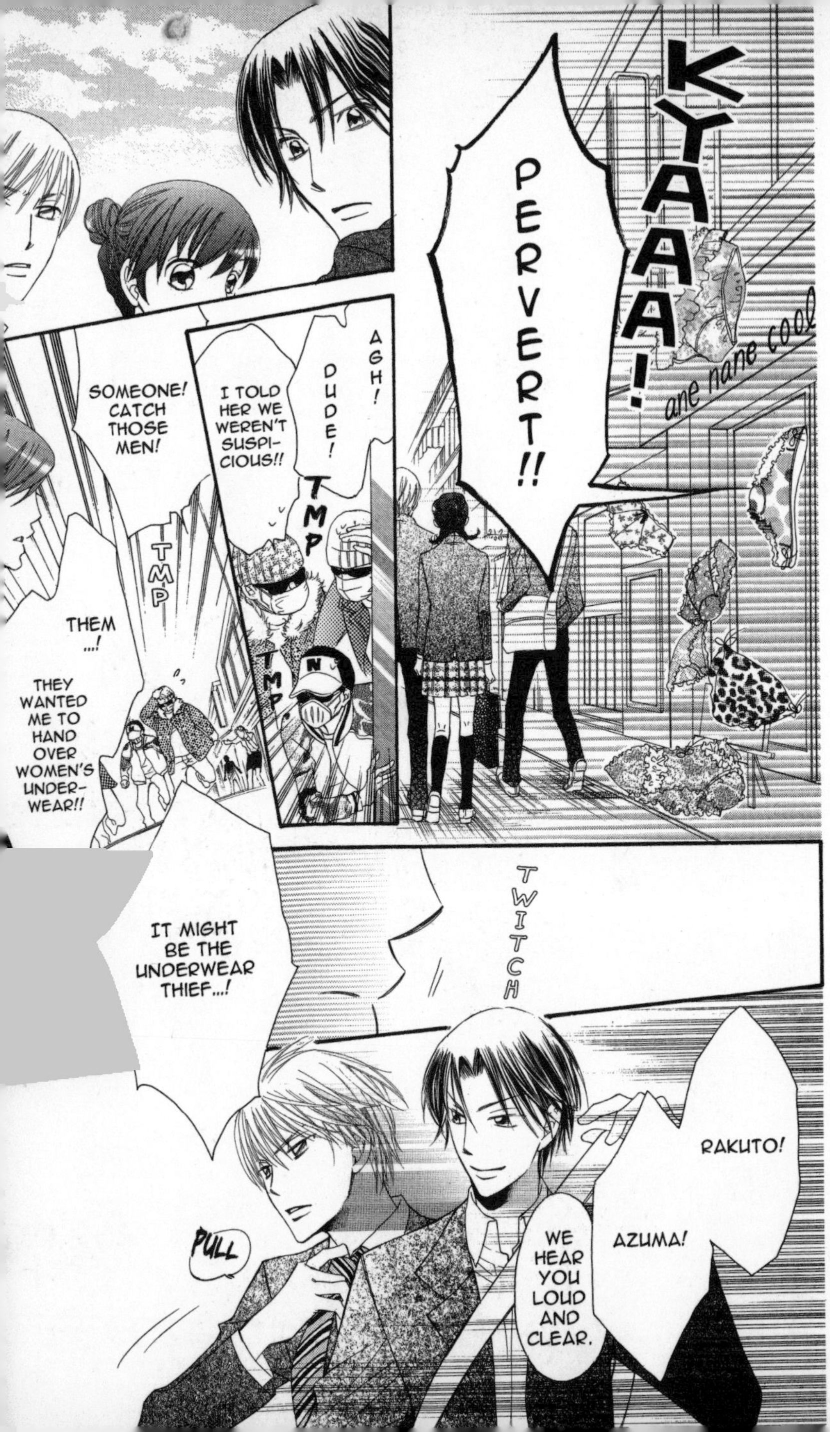
KYAAAA!
PERVERT!!
ane nane cool
AGH!
DUDE!
I TOLD HER WE WEREN'T SUSPICIOUS!!
TMP
TMP
SOMEONE! CATCH THOSE MEN!
TMP
THEM ...!
THEY WANTED ME TO HAND OVER WOMEN'S UNDERWEAR!!
TWITCH
IT MIGHT BE THE UNDERWEAR THIEF...!
RAKUTO!
AZUMA!
WE HEAR YOU LOUD AND CLEAR.
PULL

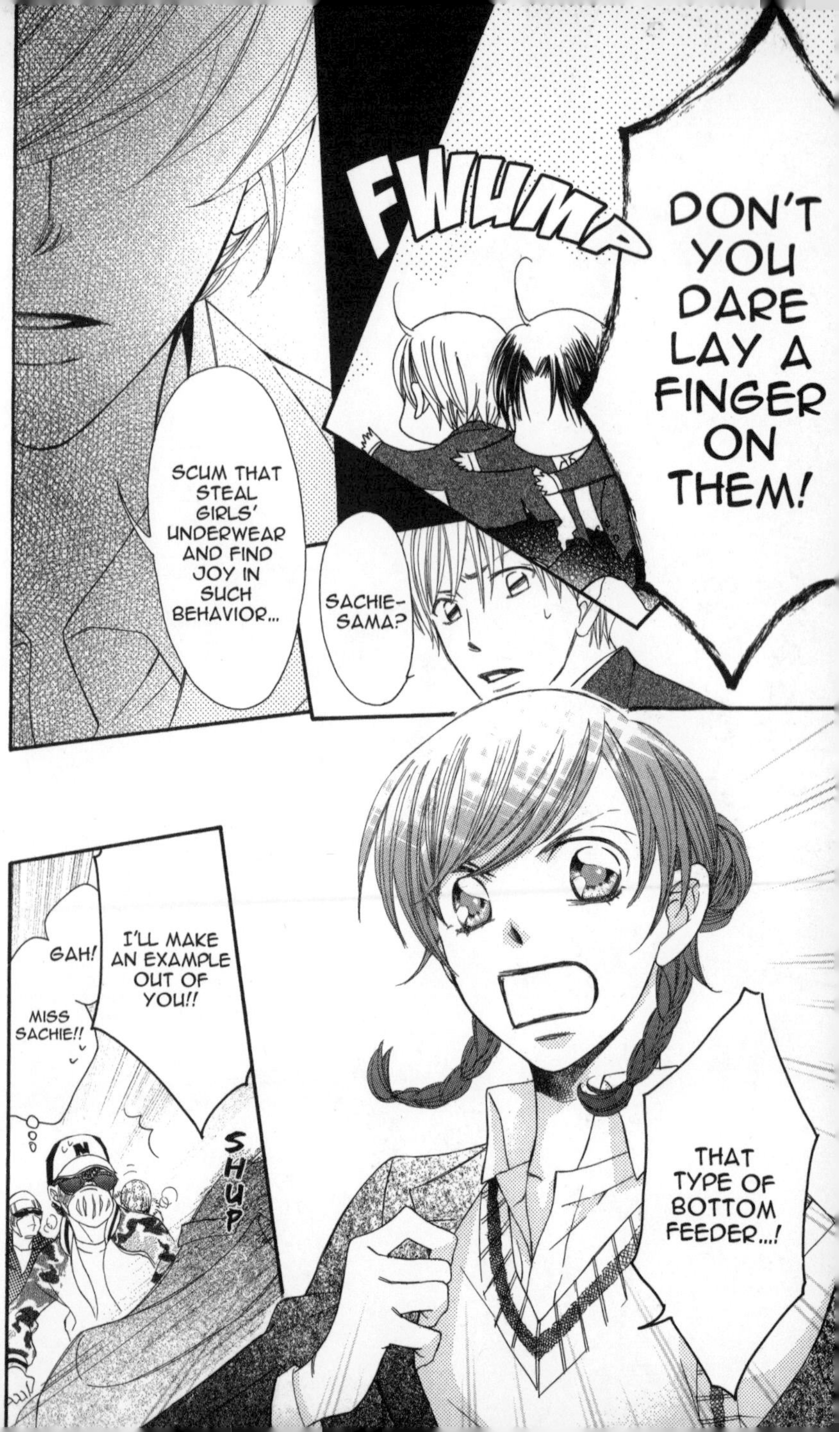
DON'T YOU DARE LAY A FINGER ON THEM!
FWUMP
SACHIE-SAMA?
SCUM THAT STEAL GIRLS' UNDERWEAR AND FIND JOY IN SUCH BEHAVIOR...
THAT TYPE OF BOTTOM FEEDER...!
I'LL MAKE AN EXAMPLE OUT OF YOU!!
GAH!
MISS SACHIE!!
SHUP

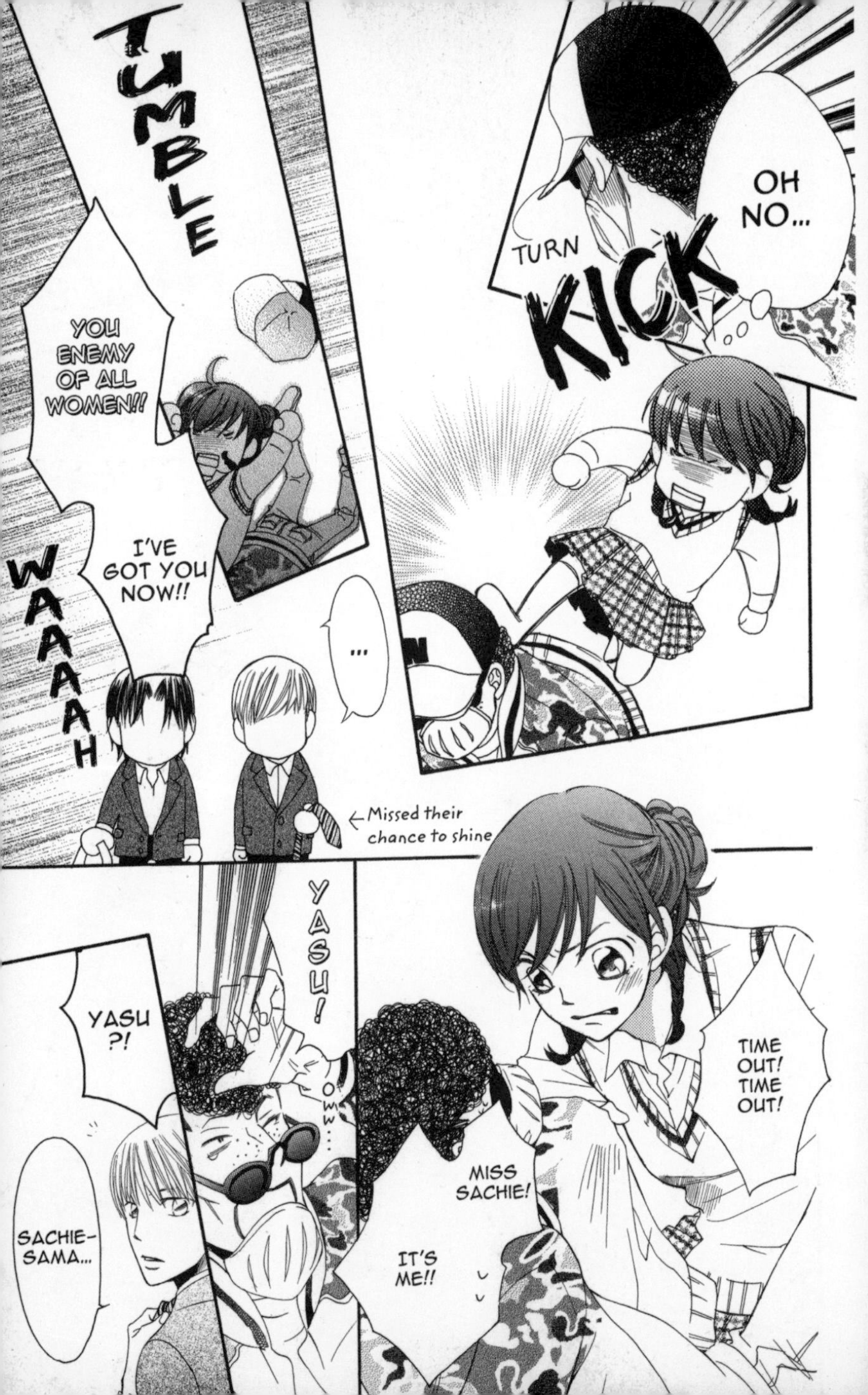
OH NO...
TURN
KICK
TUMBLE
YOU ENEMY OF ALL WOMEN!!
I'VE GOT YOU NOW!!
WAAAAAH
...
← Missed their chance to shine
TIME OUT! TIME OUT!
MISS SACHIE!
IT'S ME!!
YASU!
OWW...
YASU ?!
SACHIE-SAMA...

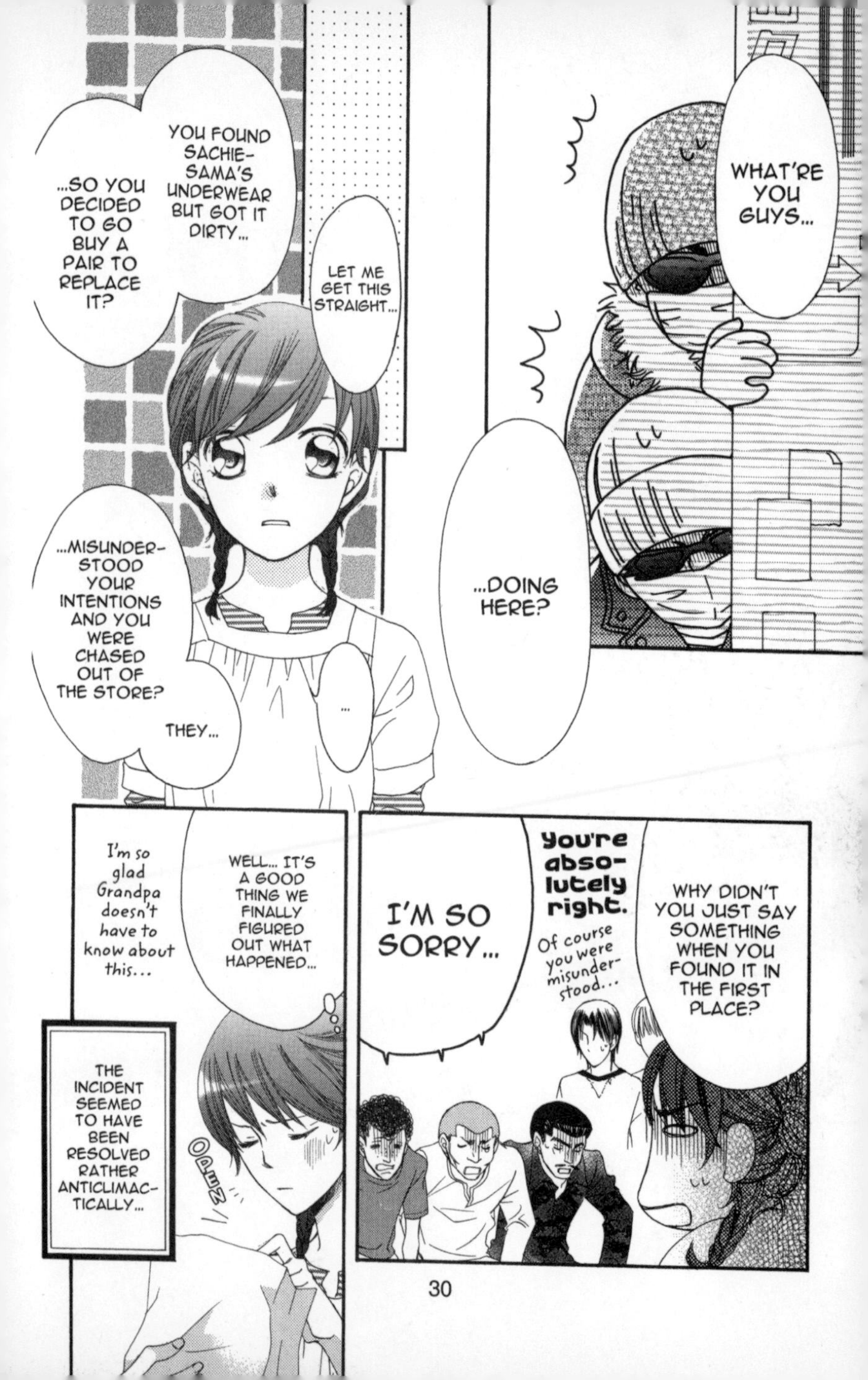
WHAT'RE YOU GUYS...
...DOING HERE?
LET ME GET THIS STRAIGHT...
YOU FOUND SACHIE-SAMA'S UNDERWEAR BUT GOT IT DIRTY...
...SO YOU DECIDED TO GO BUY A PAIR TO REPLACE IT?
...
THEY...
...MISUNDERSTOOD YOUR INTENTIONS AND YOU WERE CHASED OUT OF THE STORE?
WHY DIDN'T YOU JUST SAY SOMETHING WHEN YOU FOUND IT IN THE FIRST PLACE?
You're absolutely right.
Of course you were misunderstood...
I'M SO SORRY...
WELL... IT'S A GOOD THING WE FINALLY FIGURED OUT WHAT HAPPENED...
I'm so glad Grandpa doesn't have to know about this...
THE INCIDENT SEEMED TO HAVE BEEN RESOLVED RATHER ANTICLIMACTICALLY...
OPEN

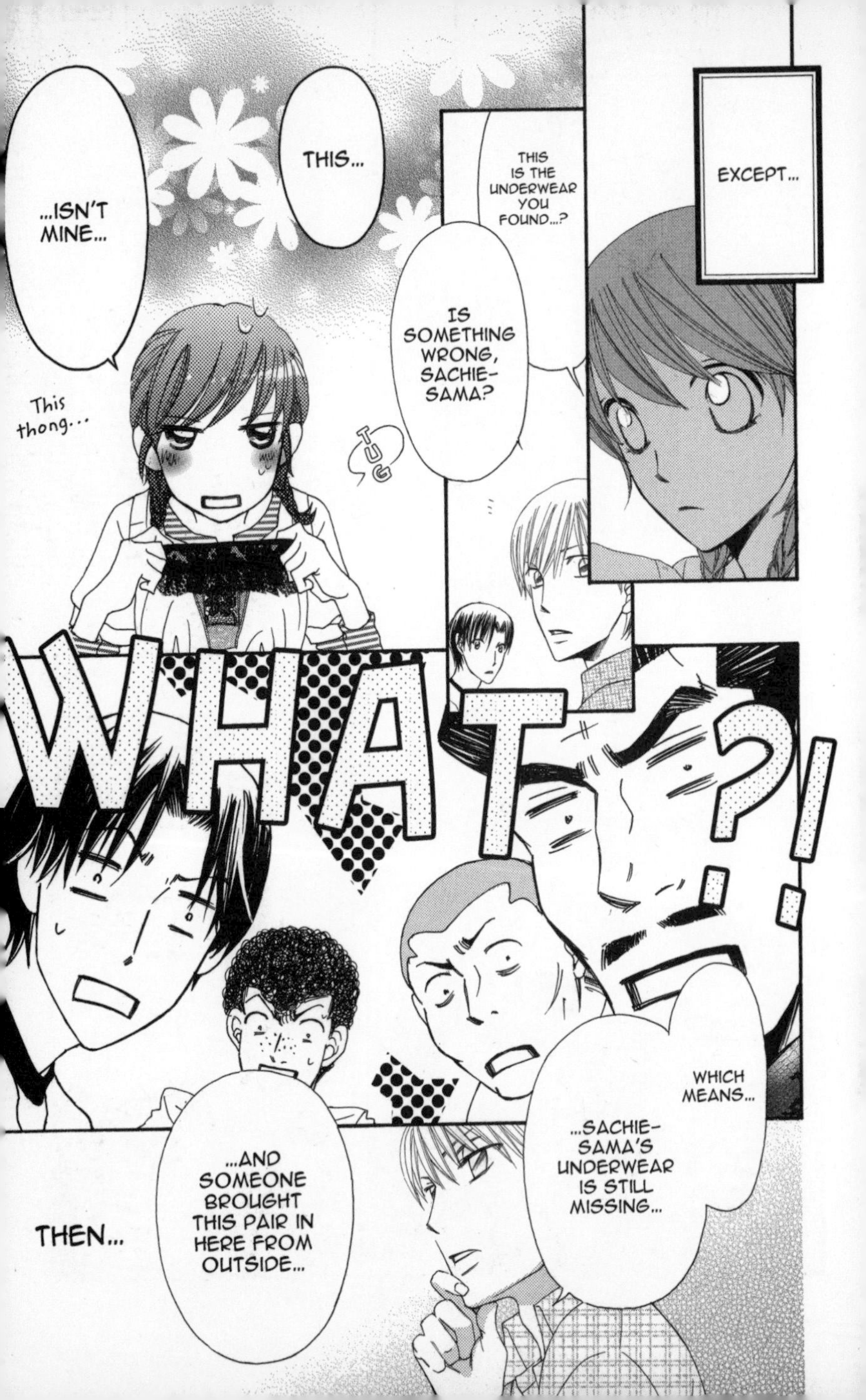
EXCEPT...
THIS IS THE UNDERWEAR YOU FOUND...?
IS SOMETHING WRONG, SACHIE-SAMA?
TUG
THIS...
...ISN'T MINE...
This thong...
WHAT?!
WHICH MEANS...
...SACHIE-SAMA'S UNDERWEAR IS STILL MISSING...
...AND SOMEONE BROUGHT THIS PAIR IN HERE FROM OUTSIDE...
THEN...

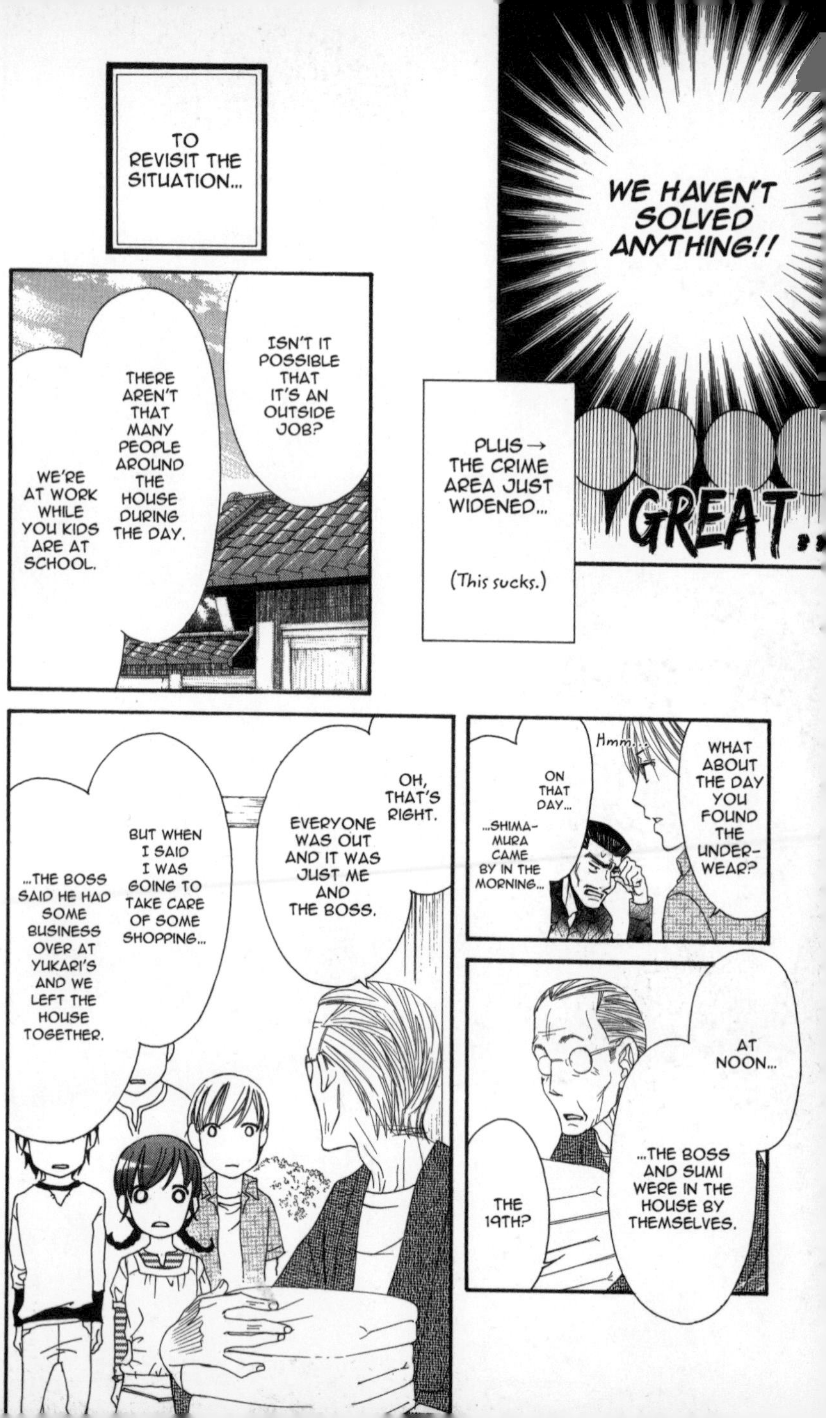
WE HAVEN'T SOLVED ANYTHING!!
GREAT..
PLUS → THE CRIME AREA JUST WIDENED...
(This sucks.)
TO REVISIT THE SITUATION...
ISN'T IT POSSIBLE THAT IT'S AN OUTSIDE JOB?
THERE AREN'T THAT MANY PEOPLE AROUND THE HOUSE DURING THE DAY.
WE'RE AT WORK WHILE YOU KIDS ARE AT SCHOOL.
WHAT ABOUT THE DAY YOU FOUND THE UNDER-WEAR?
Hmm...
ON THAT DAY...
...SHIMA-MURA CAME BY IN THE MORNING...
AT NOON...
...THE BOSS AND SUMI WERE IN THE HOUSE BY THEMSELVES.
THE 19TH?
OH, THAT'S RIGHT.
EVERYONE WAS OUT AND IT WAS JUST ME AND THE BOSS.
BUT WHEN I SAID I WAS GOING TO TAKE CARE OF SOME SHOPPING...
...THE BOSS SAID HE HAD SOME BUSINESS OVER AT YUKARI'S AND WE LEFT THE HOUSE TOGETHER.

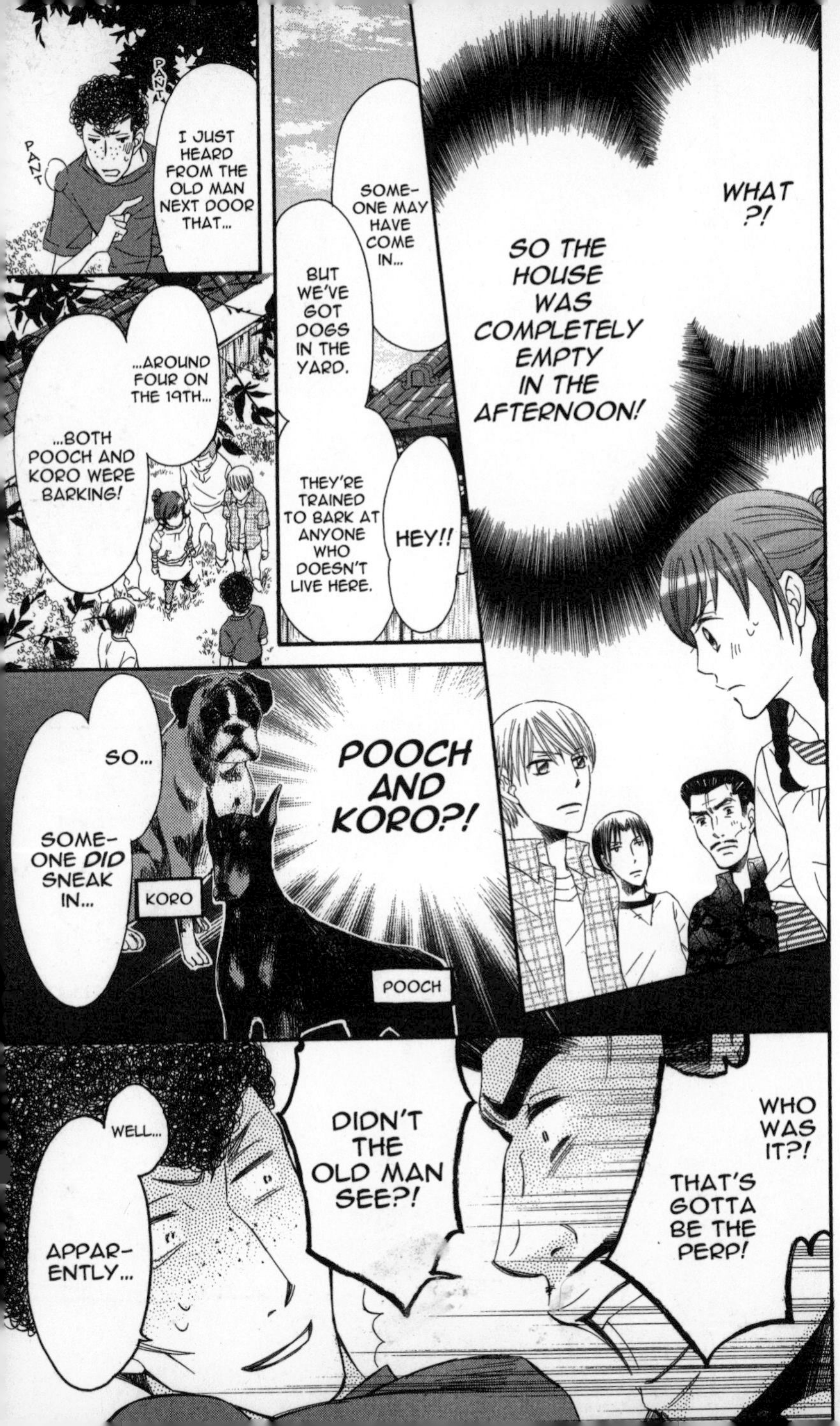
WHAT?!
SO THE HOUSE WAS COMPLETELY EMPTY IN THE AFTERNOON!
SOME-ONE MAY HAVE COME IN...
BUT WE'VE GOT DOGS IN THE YARD.
THEY'RE TRAINED TO BARK AT ANYONE WHO DOESN'T LIVE HERE.
HEY!!
PANT
PANT
I JUST HEARD FROM THE OLD MAN NEXT DOOR THAT...
...AROUND FOUR ON THE 19TH...
...BOTH POOCH AND KORO WERE BARKING!
POOCH AND KORO?!
SO...
SOME-ONE DID SNEAK IN...
KORO
POOCH
WHO WAS IT?!
THAT'S GOTTA BE THE PERP!
DIDN'T THE OLD MAN SEE?!
WELL...
APPAR-ENTLY...

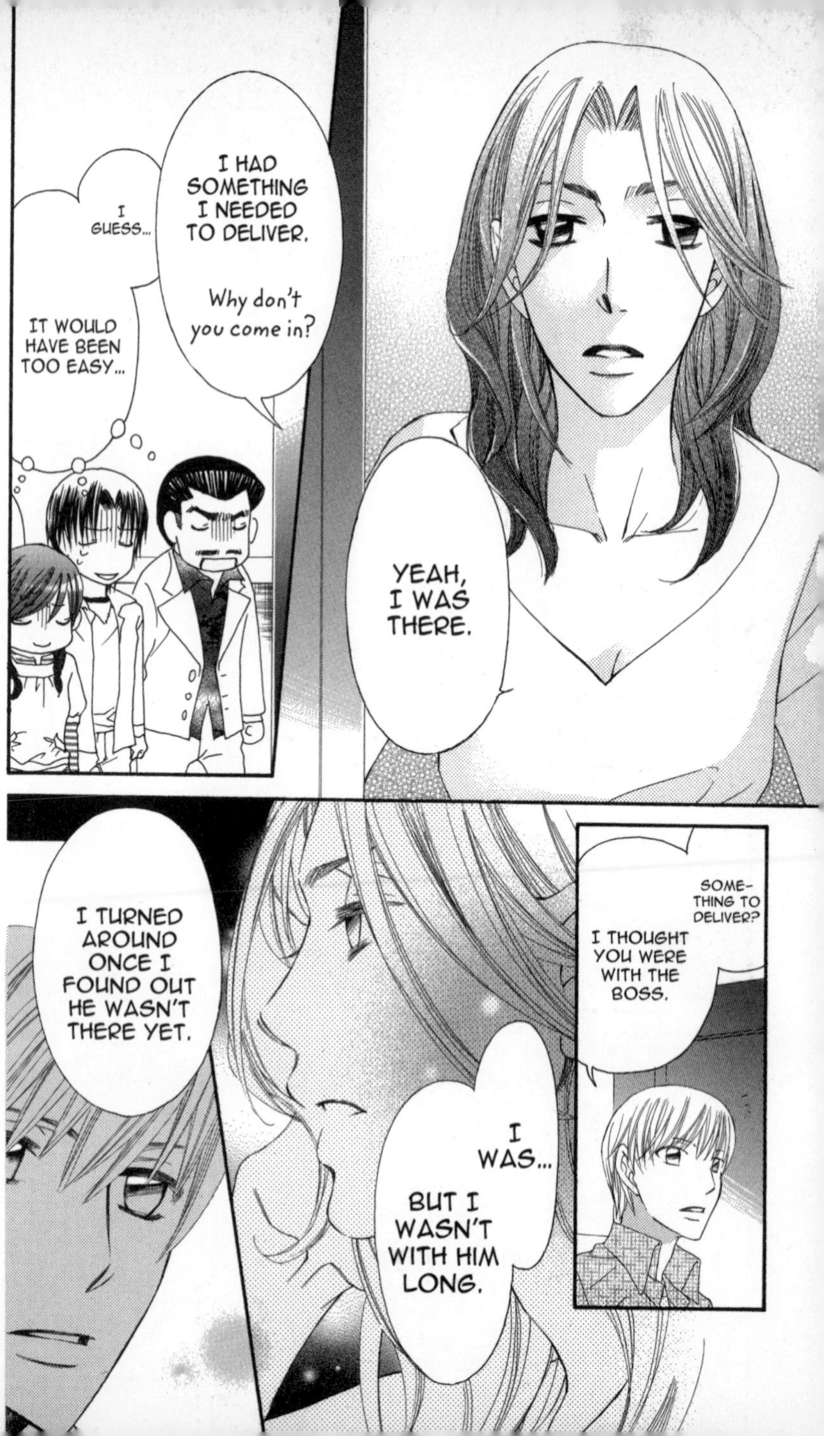
YEAH, I WAS THERE.
I HAD SOMETHING I NEEDED TO DELIVER.
Why don't you come in?
I GUESS...
IT WOULD HAVE BEEN TOO EASY...
SOME-THING TO DELIVER?
I THOUGHT YOU WERE WITH THE BOSS.
I WAS...
BUT I WASN'T WITH HIM LONG.
I TURNED AROUND ONCE I FOUND OUT HE WASN'T THERE YET.

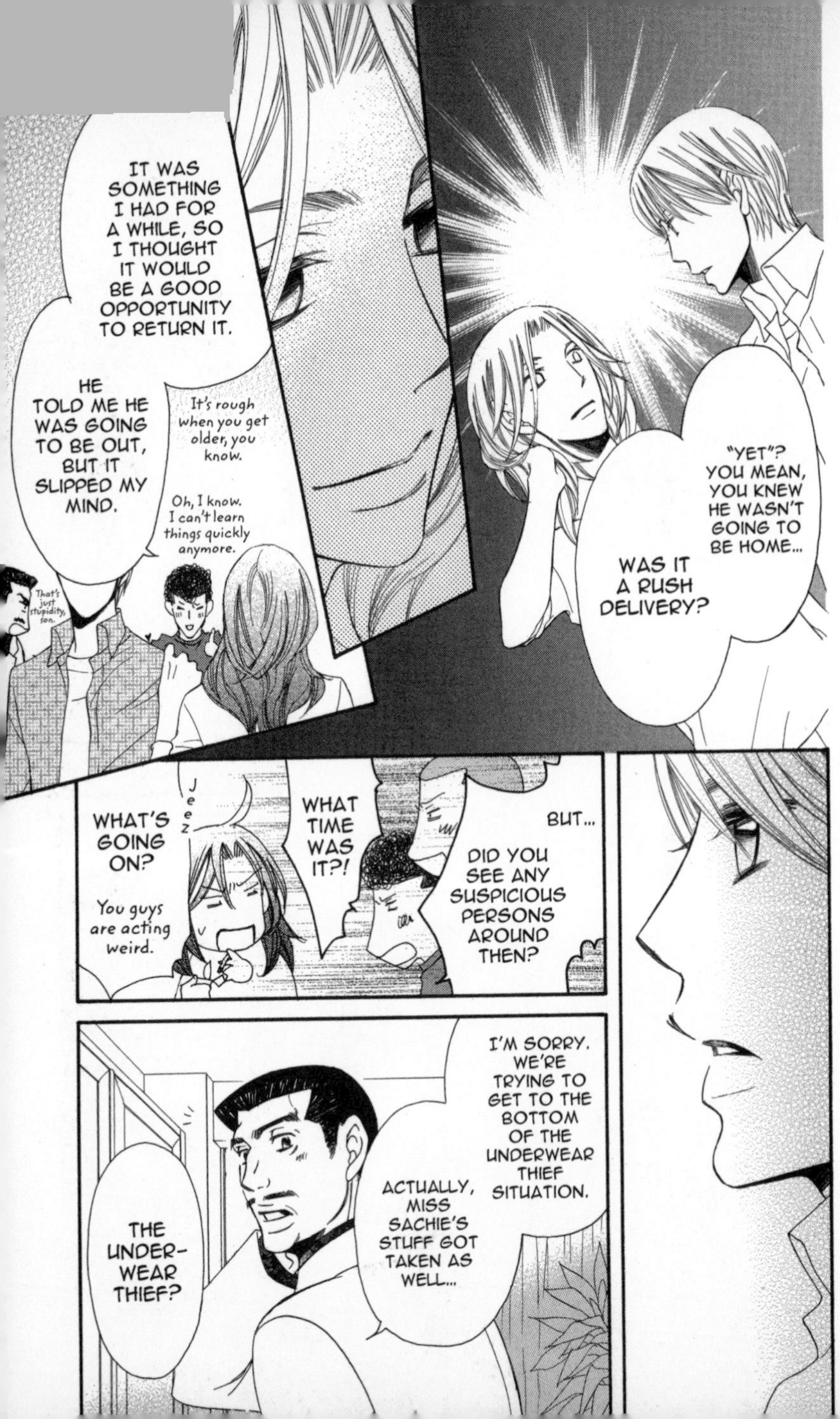
"YET"? YOU MEAN, YOU KNEW HE WASN'T GOING TO BE HOME...
WAS IT A RUSH DELIVERY?
IT WAS SOMETHING I HAD FOR A WHILE, SO I THOUGHT IT WOULD BE A GOOD OPPORTUNITY TO RETURN IT.
HE TOLD ME HE WAS GOING TO BE OUT, BUT IT SLIPPED MY MIND.
It's rough when you get older, you know.
Oh, I know. I can't learn things quickly anymore.
That's just stupidity, son.
BUT...
DID YOU SEE ANY SUSPICIOUS PERSONS AROUND THEN?
WHAT TIME WAS IT?!
Jeez
WHAT'S GOING ON?
You guys are acting weird.
I'M SORRY. WE'RE TRYING TO GET TO THE BOTTOM OF THE UNDERWEAR THIEF SITUATION.
ACTUALLY, MISS SACHIE'S STUFF GOT TAKEN AS WELL...
THE UNDER-WEAR THIEF?

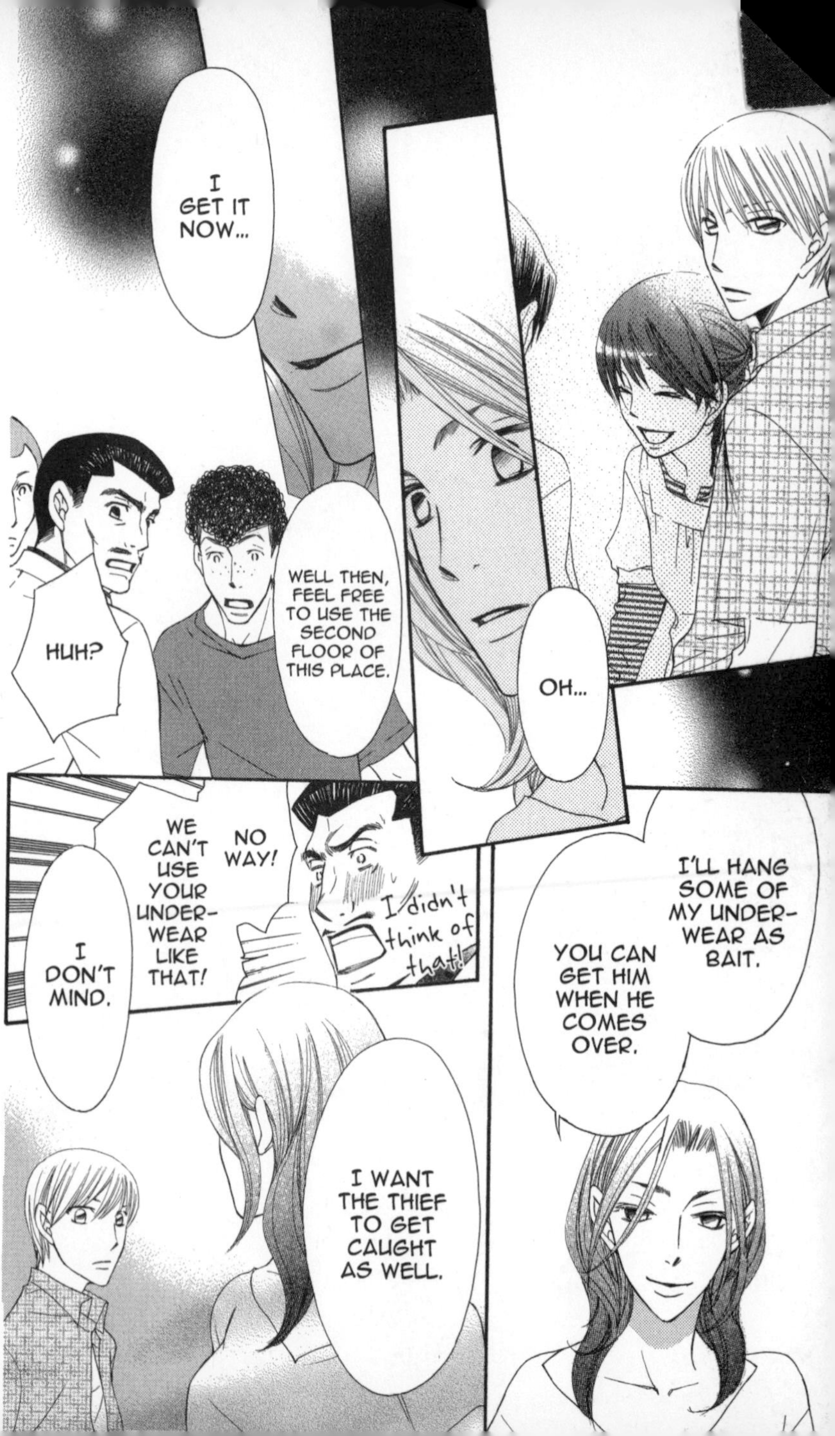
OH...
I GET IT NOW...
WELL THEN, FEEL FREE TO USE THE SECOND FLOOR OF THIS PLACE.
HUH?
I'LL HANG SOME OF MY UNDER-WEAR AS BAIT.
YOU CAN GET HIM WHEN HE COMES OVER.
NO WAY!
WE CAN'T USE YOUR UNDER-WEAR LIKE THAT!
I didn't think of that!
I DON'T MIND.
I WANT THE THIEF TO GET CAUGHT AS WELL.

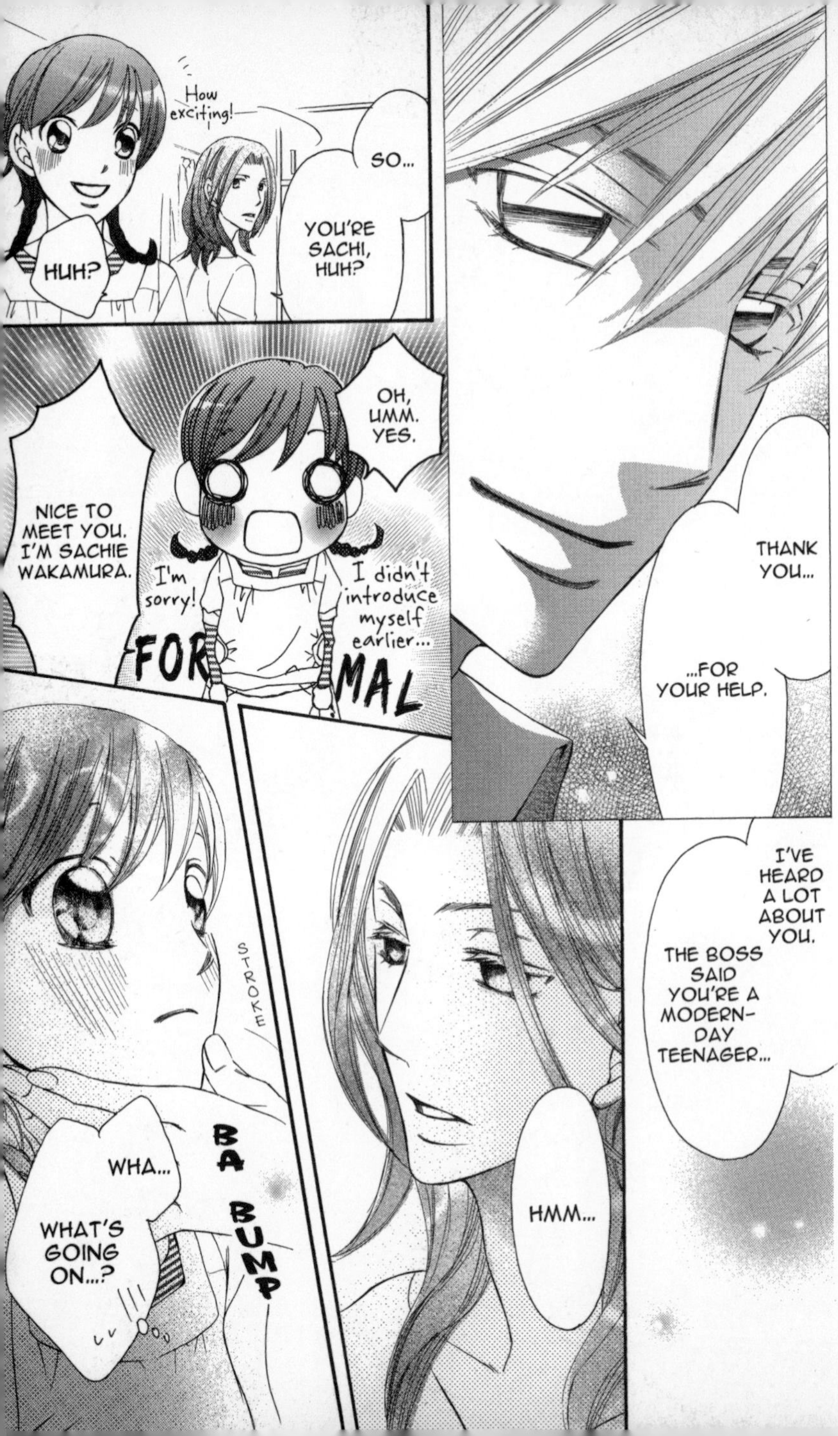
THANK YOU...
...FOR YOUR HELP.
SO...
YOU'RE SACHI, HUH?
How exciting!
HUH?
OH, UMM. YES.
I didn't introduce myself earlier...
I'm sorry!
FORMAL
NICE TO MEET YOU. I'M SACHIE WAKAMURA.
I'VE HEARD A LOT ABOUT YOU.
THE BOSS SAID YOU'RE A MODERN-DAY TEENAGER...
HMM...
STROKE
BA BUMP
WHA...
WHAT'S GOING ON...?

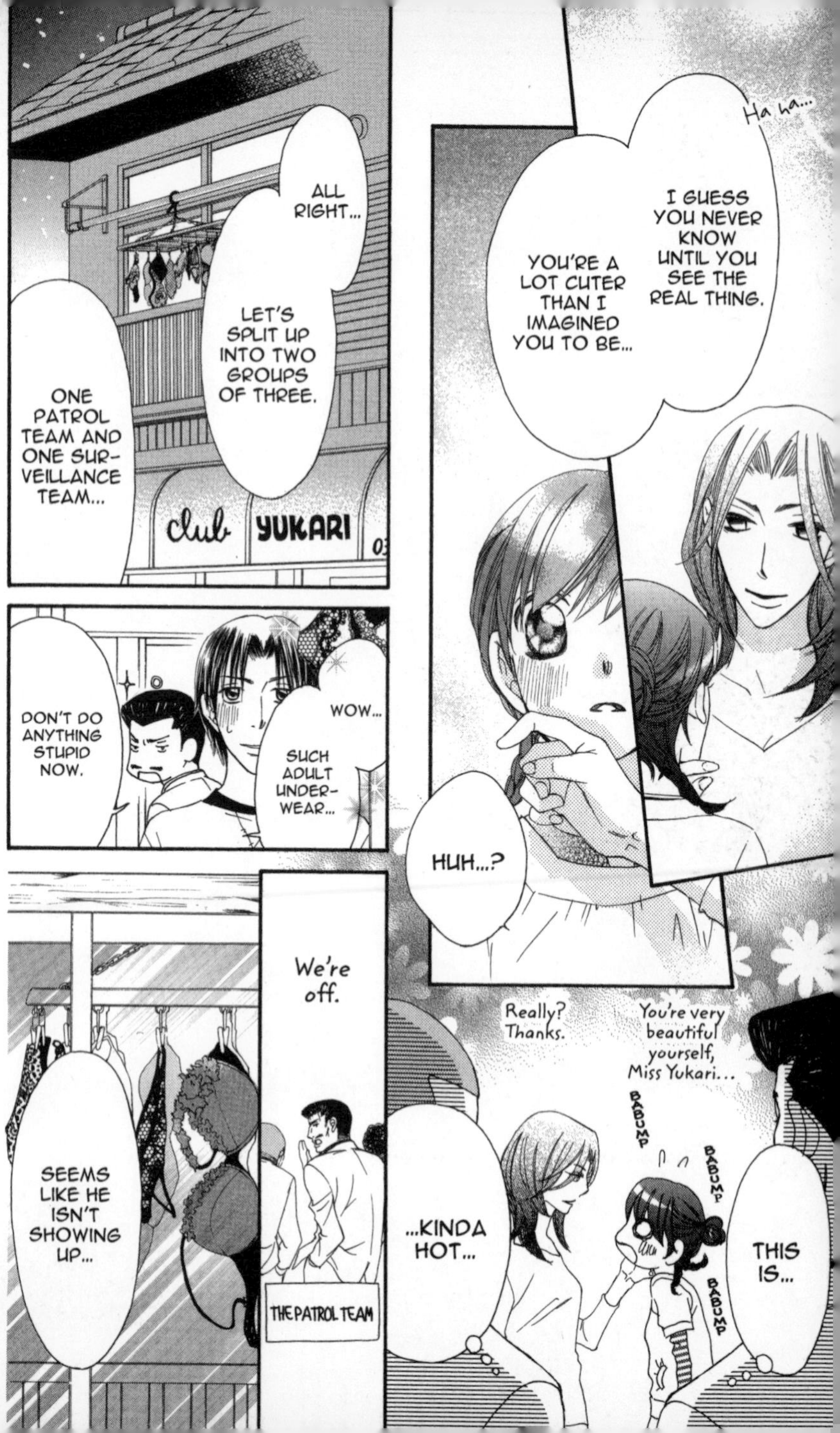

Ha ha...
I GUESS YOU NEVER KNOW UNTIL YOU SEE THE REAL THING.
YOU'RE A LOT CUTER THAN I IMAGINED YOU TO BE...
HUH...?
You're very beautiful yourself, Miss Yukari...
Really? Thanks.
BABUMP
BABUMP
BABUMP
THIS IS...
...KINDA HOT...
ALL RIGHT...
LET'S SPLIT UP INTO TWO GROUPS OF THREE.
ONE PATROL TEAM AND ONE SURVEILLANCE TEAM...
club YUKARI
WOW...
SUCH ADULT UNDERWEAR...
DON'T DO ANYTHING STUPID NOW.
We're off.
THE PATROL TEAM
SEEMS LIKE HE ISN'T SHOWING UP...

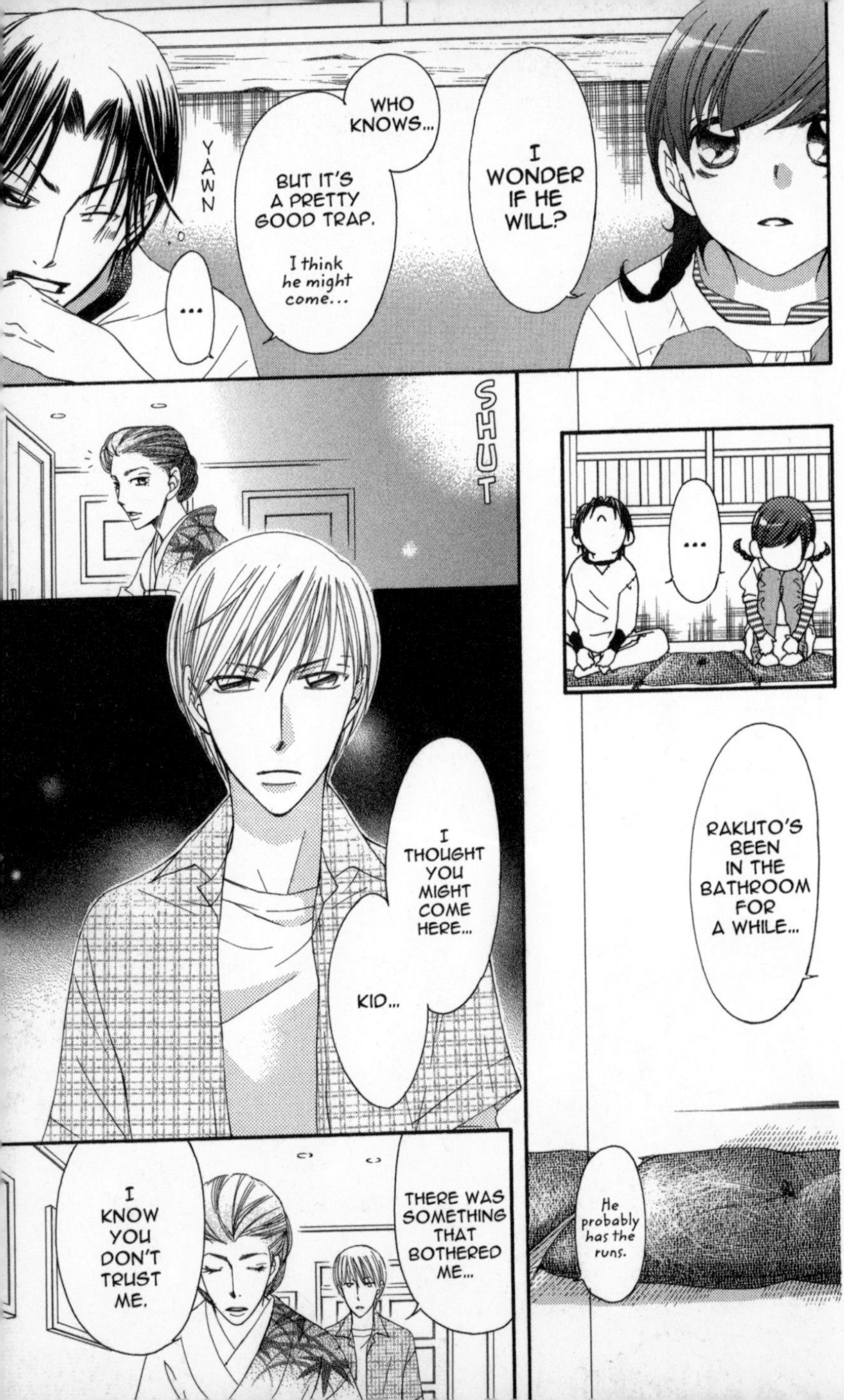
I WONDER IF HE WILL?
WHO KNOWS...
BUT IT'S A PRETTY GOOD TRAP.
I think he might come...
YAWN
...
...
RAKUTO'S BEEN IN THE BATHROOM FOR A WHILE...
He probably has the runs.
SHUT
I THOUGHT YOU MIGHT COME HERE...
KID...
THERE WAS SOMETHING THAT BOTHERED ME...
I KNOW YOU DON'T TRUST ME.

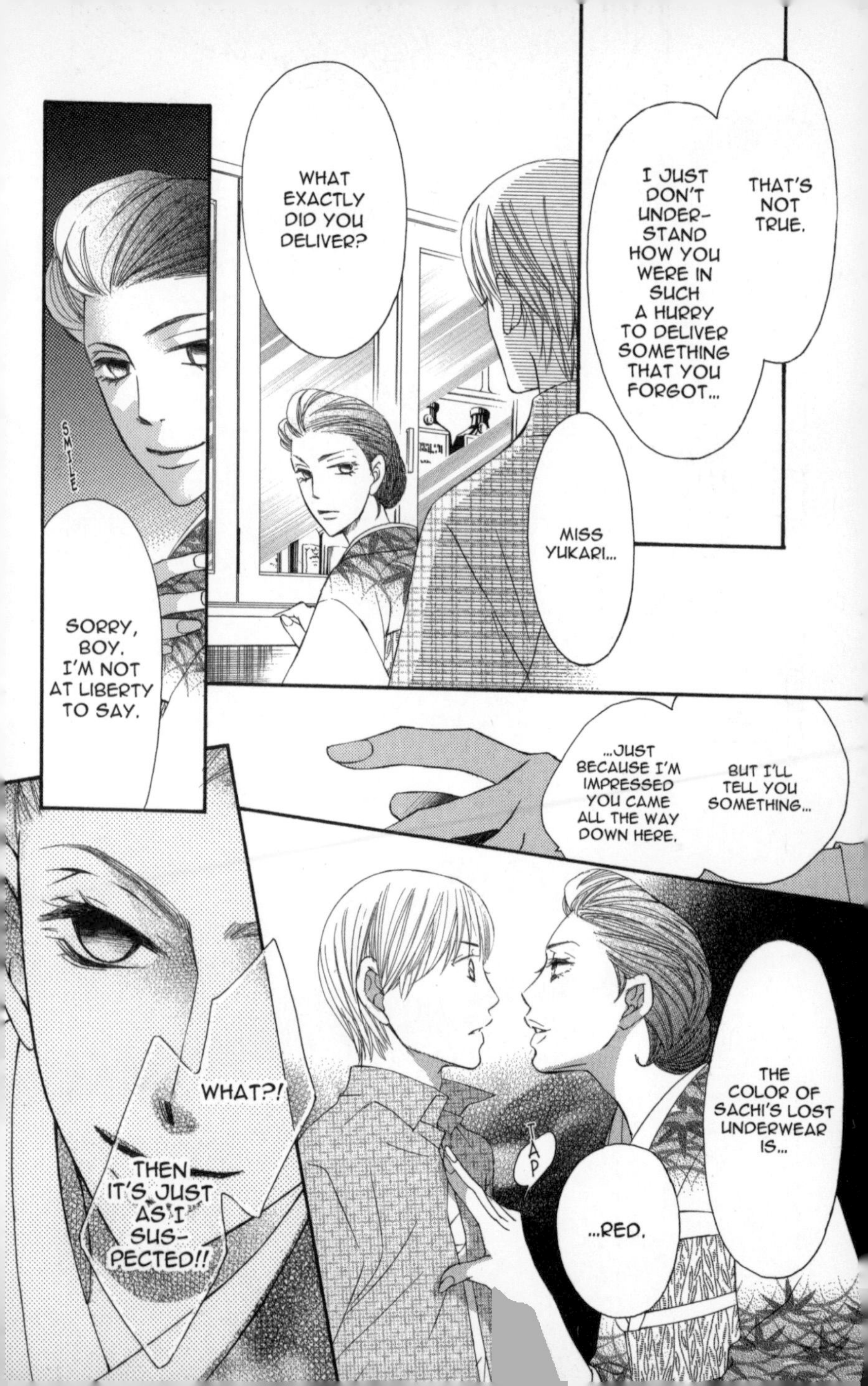
THAT'S NOT TRUE.
I JUST DON'T UNDER-STAND HOW YOU WERE IN SUCH A HURRY TO DELIVER SOMETHING THAT YOU FORGOT...
MISS YUKARI...
WHAT EXACTLY DID YOU DELIVER?
SMILE
SORRY, BOY. I'M NOT AT LIBERTY TO SAY.
BUT I'LL TELL YOU SOMETHING...
...JUST BECAUSE I'M IMPRESSED YOU CAME ALL THE WAY DOWN HERE.
THE COLOR OF SACHI'S LOST UNDERWEAR IS...
TAP
...RED.
WHAT?!
THEN IT'S JUST AS I SUS-PECTED!!

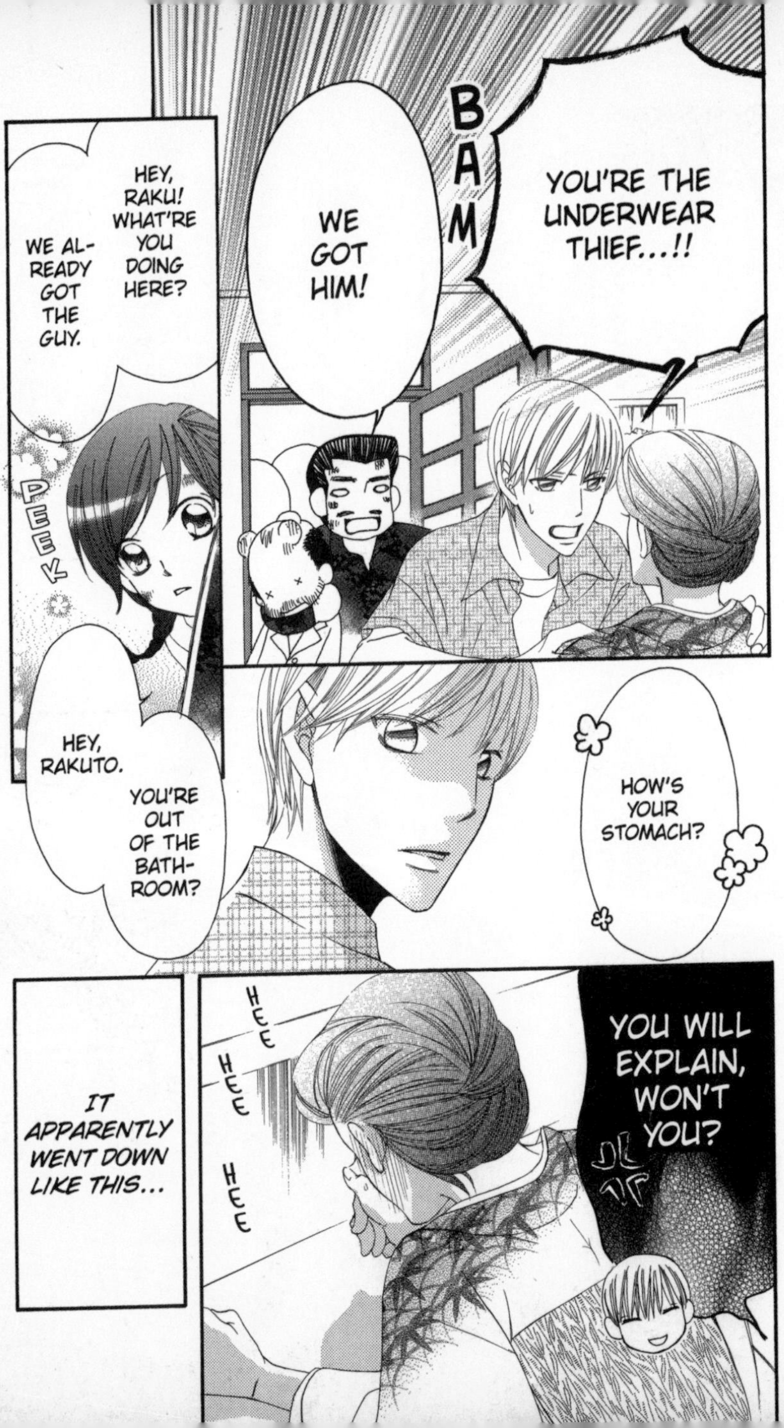
BAM
YOU'RE THE UNDERWEAR THIEF...!!
WE GOT HIM!
HOW'S YOUR STOMACH?
HEY, RAKU! WHAT'RE YOU DOING HERE?
WE AL-READY GOT THE GUY.
PEEK
HEY, RAKUTO.
YOU'RE OUT OF THE BATH-ROOM?
YOU WILL EXPLAIN, WON'T YOU?
HEE HEE HEE
IT APPARENTLY WENT DOWN LIKE THIS...

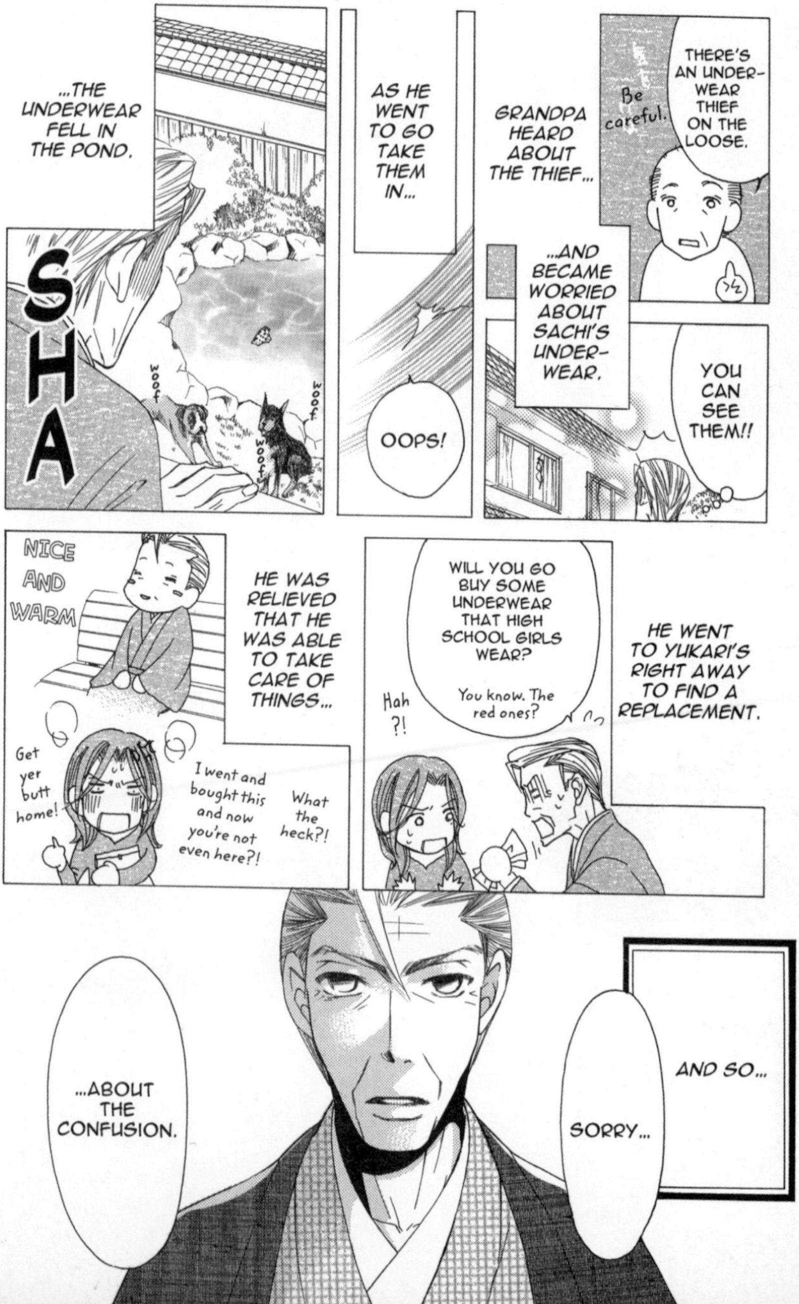
THERE'S AN UNDER-WEAR THIEF ON THE LOOSE.
Be careful.
GRANDPA HEARD ABOUT THE THIEF...
...AND BECAME WORRIED ABOUT SACHI'S UNDER-WEAR.
YOU CAN SEE THEM!!
AS HE WENT TO GO TAKE THEM IN...
OOPS!
...THE UNDERWEAR FELL IN THE POND.
SHA
woof
woof
woof
HE WENT TO YUKARI'S RIGHT AWAY TO FIND A REPLACEMENT.
WILL YOU GO BUY SOME UNDERWEAR THAT HIGH SCHOOL GIRLS WEAR?
You know. The red ones?
Hah ?!
HE WAS RELIEVED THAT HE WAS ABLE TO TAKE CARE OF THINGS...
NICE AND WARM
What the heck?!
I went and bought this and now you're not even here?!
Get yer butt home!
AND SO...
SORRY...
...ABOUT THE CONFUSION.

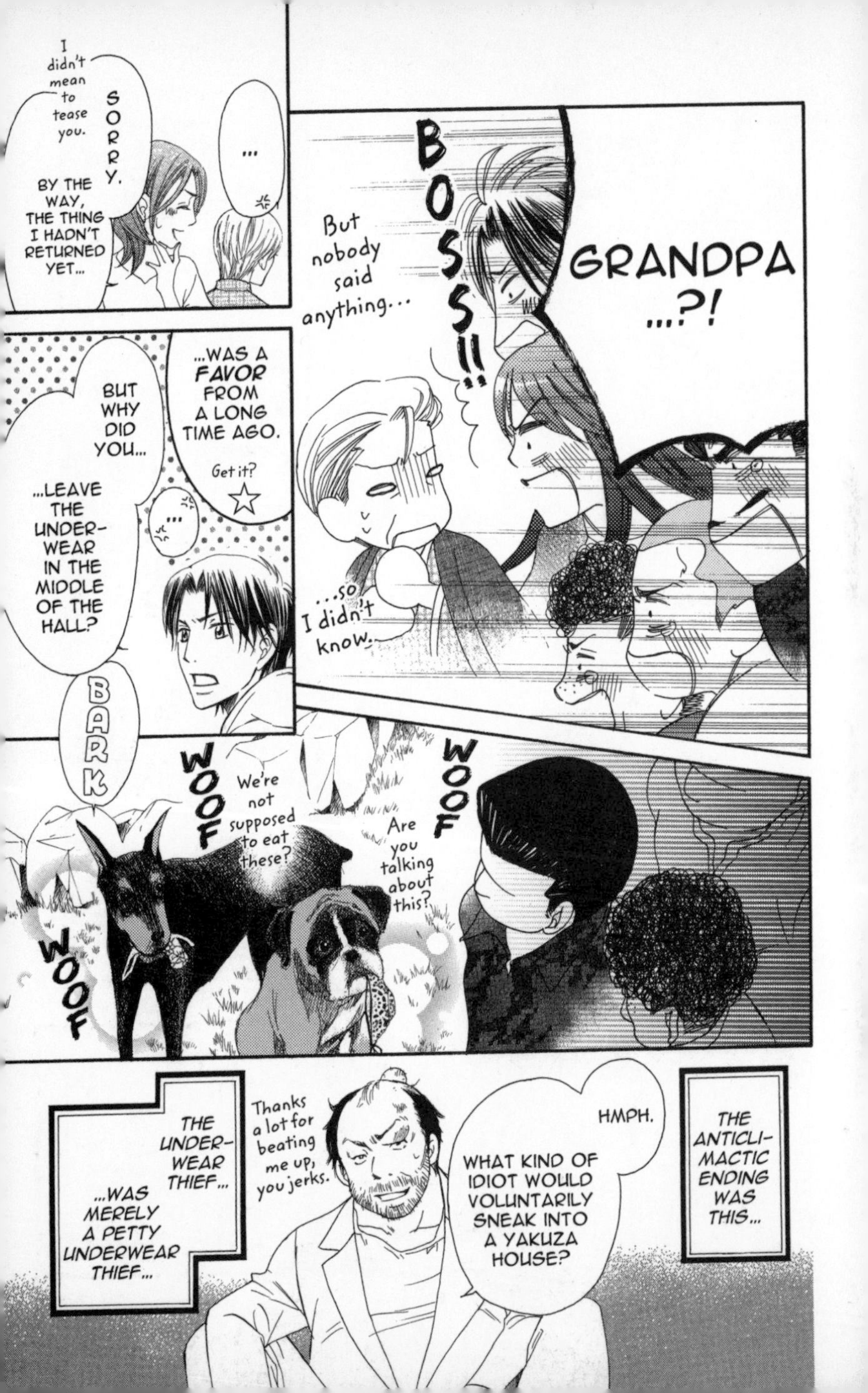
I didn't mean to tease you.
SORRY.
...
BY THE WAY, THE THING I HADN'T RETURNED YET...
GRANDPA ...?!
BOSS!!
But nobody said anything...
...so I didn't know.
...WAS A FAVOR FROM A LONG TIME AGO.
Get it? ☆
...
BUT WHY DID YOU...
...LEAVE THE UNDERWEAR IN THE MIDDLE OF THE HALL?
WOOF
Are you talking about this?
WOOF
We're not supposed to eat these?
BARK
WOOF
THE ANTICLIMACTIC ENDING WAS THIS...
HMPH.
WHAT KIND OF IDIOT WOULD VOLUNTARILY SNEAK INTO A YAKUZA HOUSE?
Thanks a lot for beating me up, you jerks.
THE UNDERWEAR THIEF...
...WAS MERELY A PETTY UNDERWEAR THIEF...

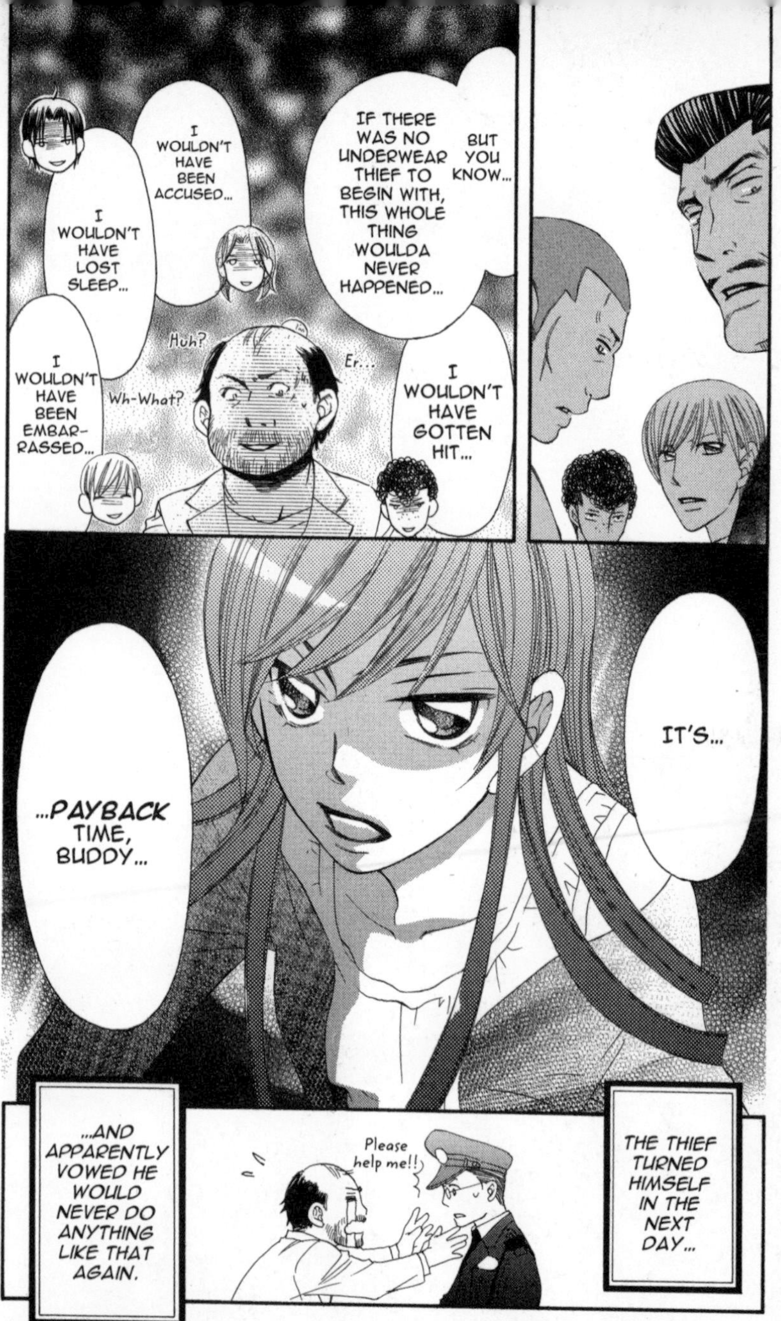
BUT YOU KNOW...
IF THERE WAS NO UNDERWEAR THIEF TO BEGIN WITH, THIS WHOLE THING WOULDA NEVER HAPPENED...
I WOULDN'T HAVE GOTTEN HIT...
I WOULDN'T HAVE BEEN ACCUSED...
Er...
Huh?
I WOULDN'T HAVE LOST SLEEP...
Wh-What?
I WOULDN'T HAVE BEEN EMBARRASSED...
IT'S...
...PAYBACK TIME, BUDDY...
THE THIEF TURNED HIMSELF IN THE NEXT DAY...
Please help me!!
...AND APPARENTLY VOWED HE WOULD NEVER DO ANYTHING LIKE THAT AGAIN.

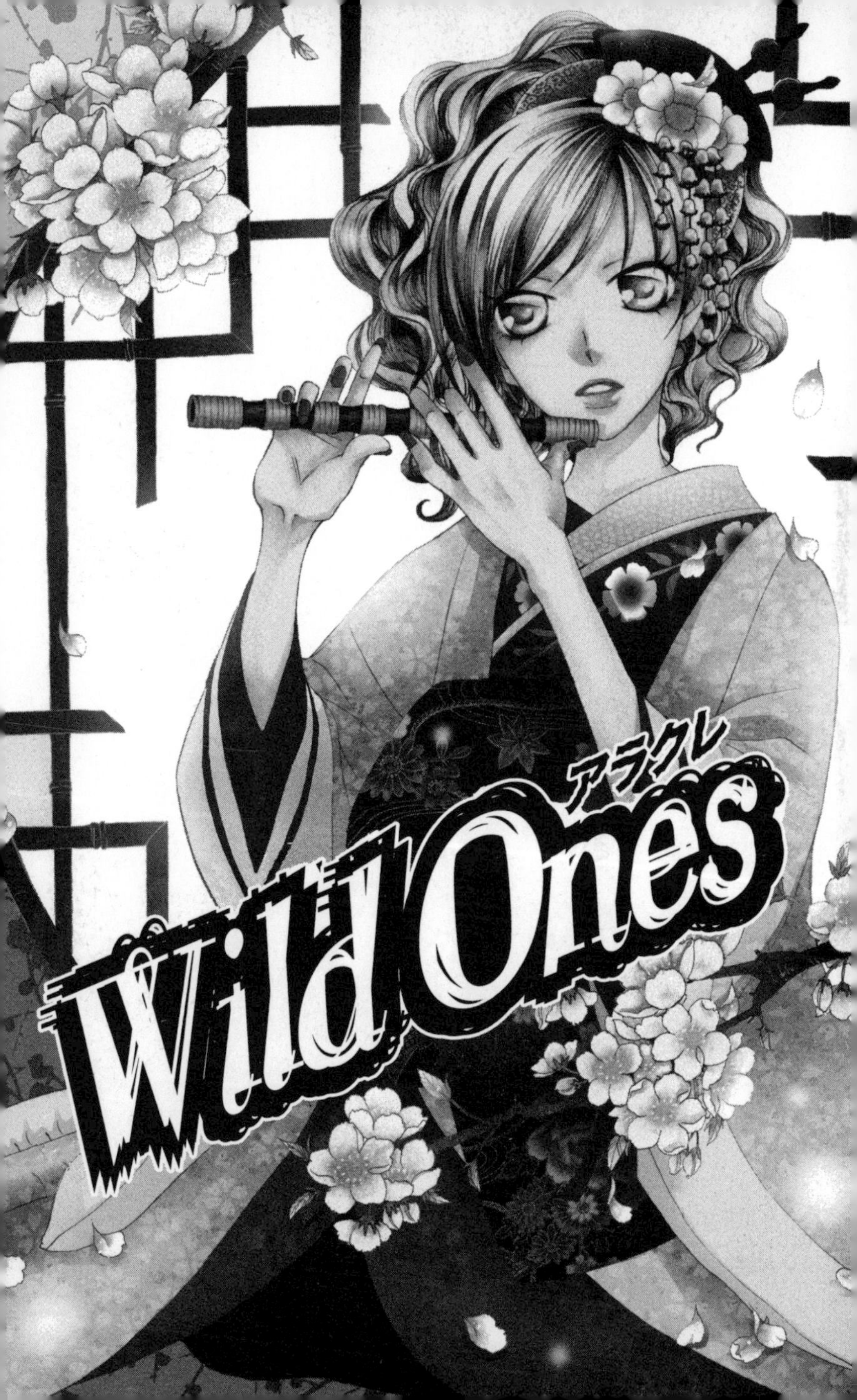
アラクレ
Wild Ones

WILD ONES CHARACTER INTRODUCTION

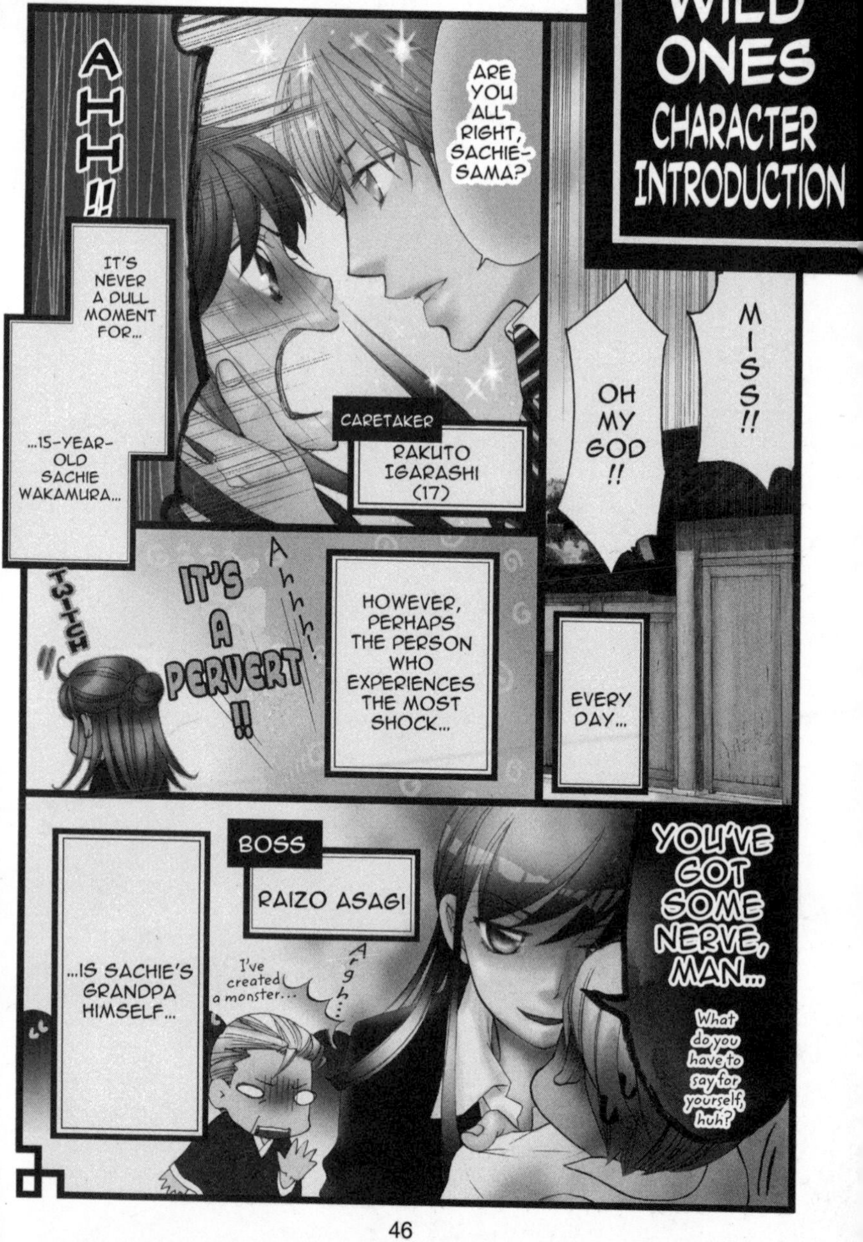
MISS!!
OH MY GOD!!
ARE YOU ALL RIGHT, SACHIE-SAMA?
AHHH!!
IT'S NEVER A DULL MOMENT FOR...
...15-YEAR-OLD SACHIE WAKAMURA...
CARETAKER
RAKUTO IGARASHI (17)
EVERY DAY...
HOWEVER, PERHAPS THE PERSON WHO EXPERIENCES THE MOST SHOCK...
Ahhh!
IT'S A PERVERT!!
TWITCH
YOU'VE GOT SOME NERVE, MAN...
What do you have to say for yourself, huh?
BOSS
RAIZO ASAGI
Argh...
I've created a monster...
...IS SACHIE'S GRANDPA HIMSELF...

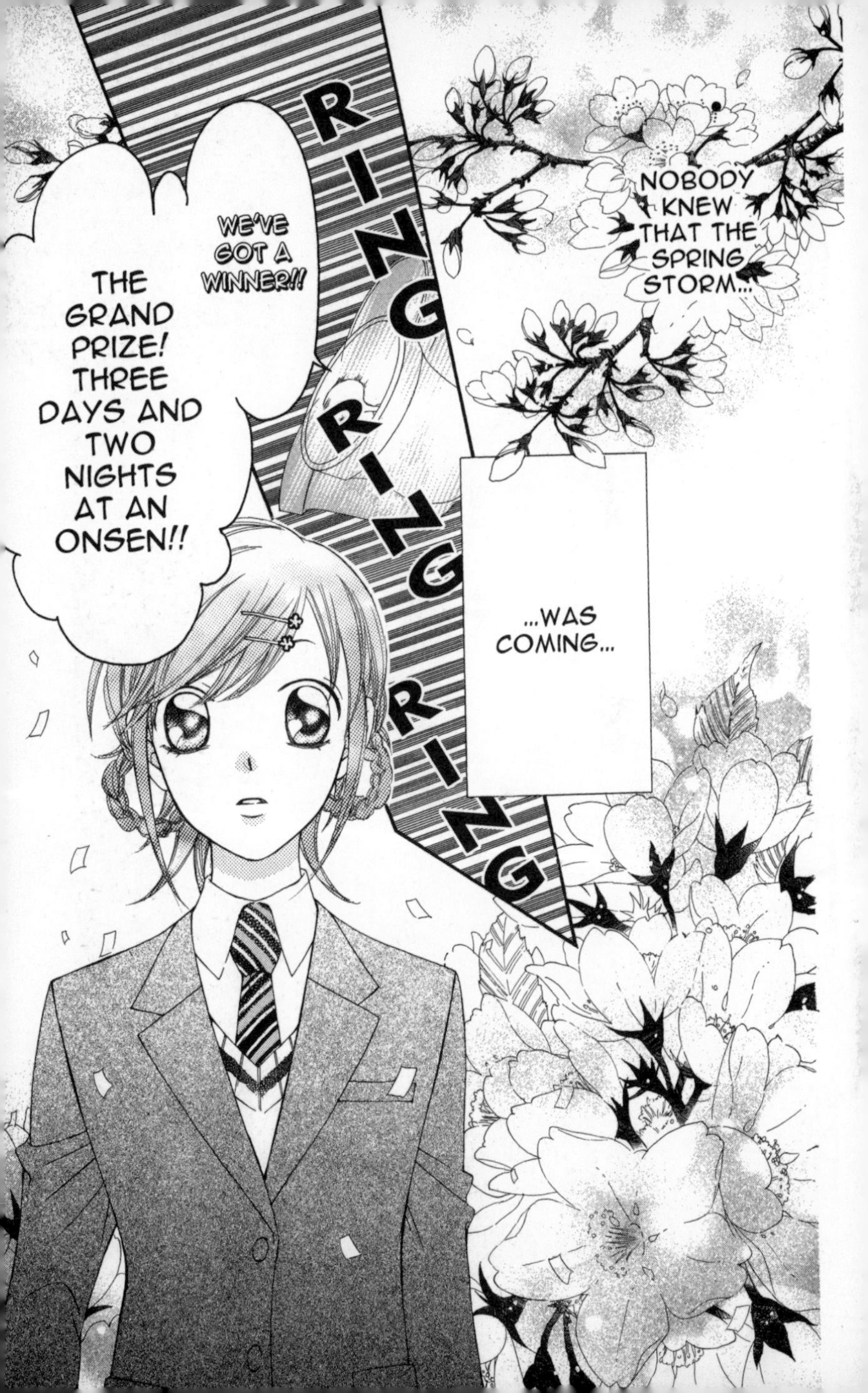
NOBODY KNEW THAT THE SPRING STORM...
WE'VE GOT A WINNER!!
THE GRAND PRIZE! THREE DAYS AND TWO NIGHTS AT AN ONSEN!!
RING RING RING
...WAS COMING...

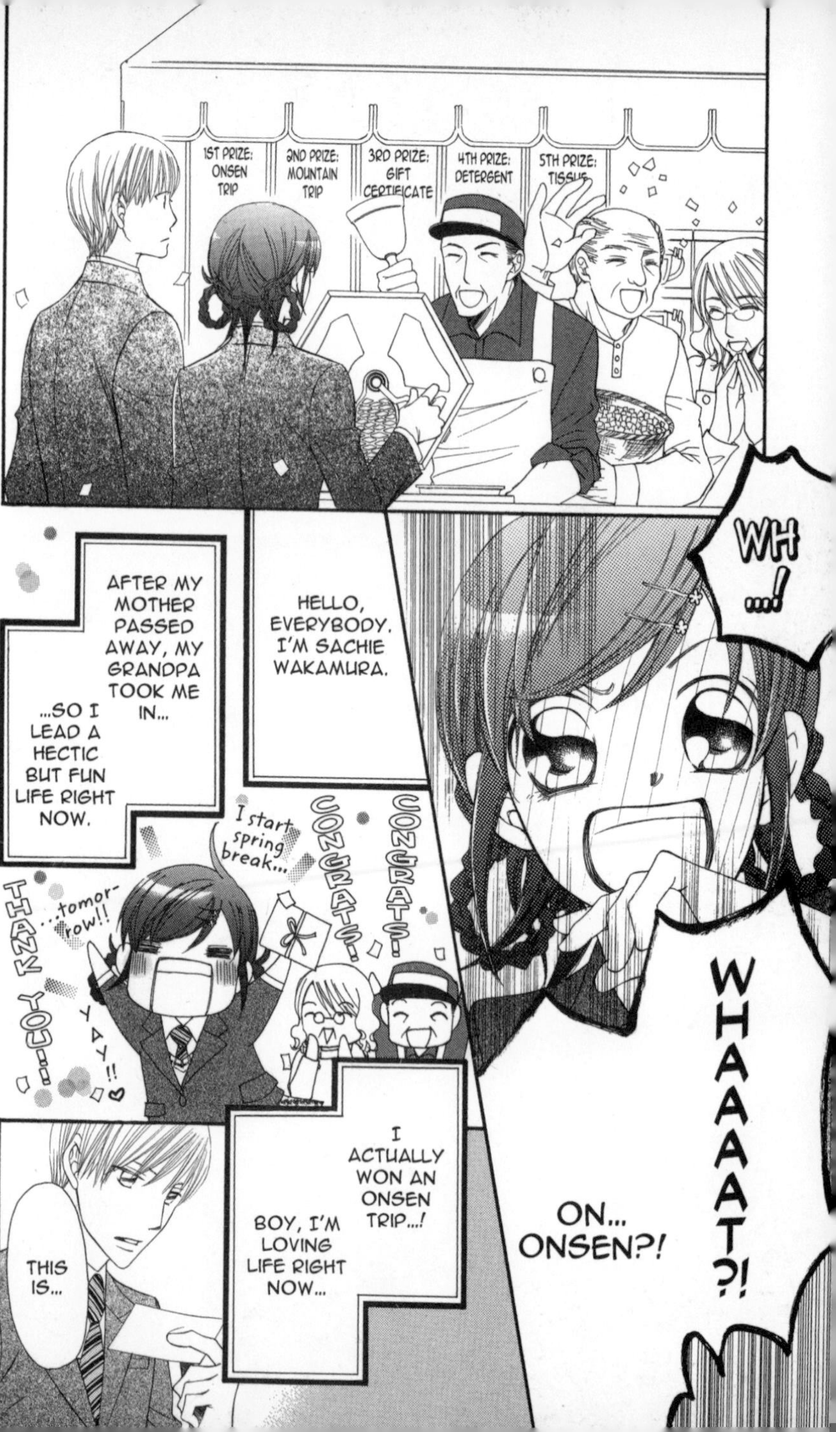
1ST PRIZE: ONSEN TRIP
2ND PRIZE: MOUNTAIN TRIP
3RD PRIZE: GIFT CERTIFICATE
4TH PRIZE: DETERGENT
5TH PRIZE: TISSUE
WH ...!
WHAAAAAT?!
ON... ONSEN?!
HELLO, EVERYBODY. I'M SACHIE WAKAMURA.
AFTER MY MOTHER PASSED AWAY, MY GRANDPA TOOK ME IN...
...SO I LEAD A HECTIC BUT FUN LIFE RIGHT NOW.
CONGRATS!
CONGRATS!
I start spring break...
...tomor-row!!
THANK YOU!!
YAY!!
I ACTUALLY WON AN ONSEN TRIP...!
BOY, I'M LOVING LIFE RIGHT NOW...
THIS IS...

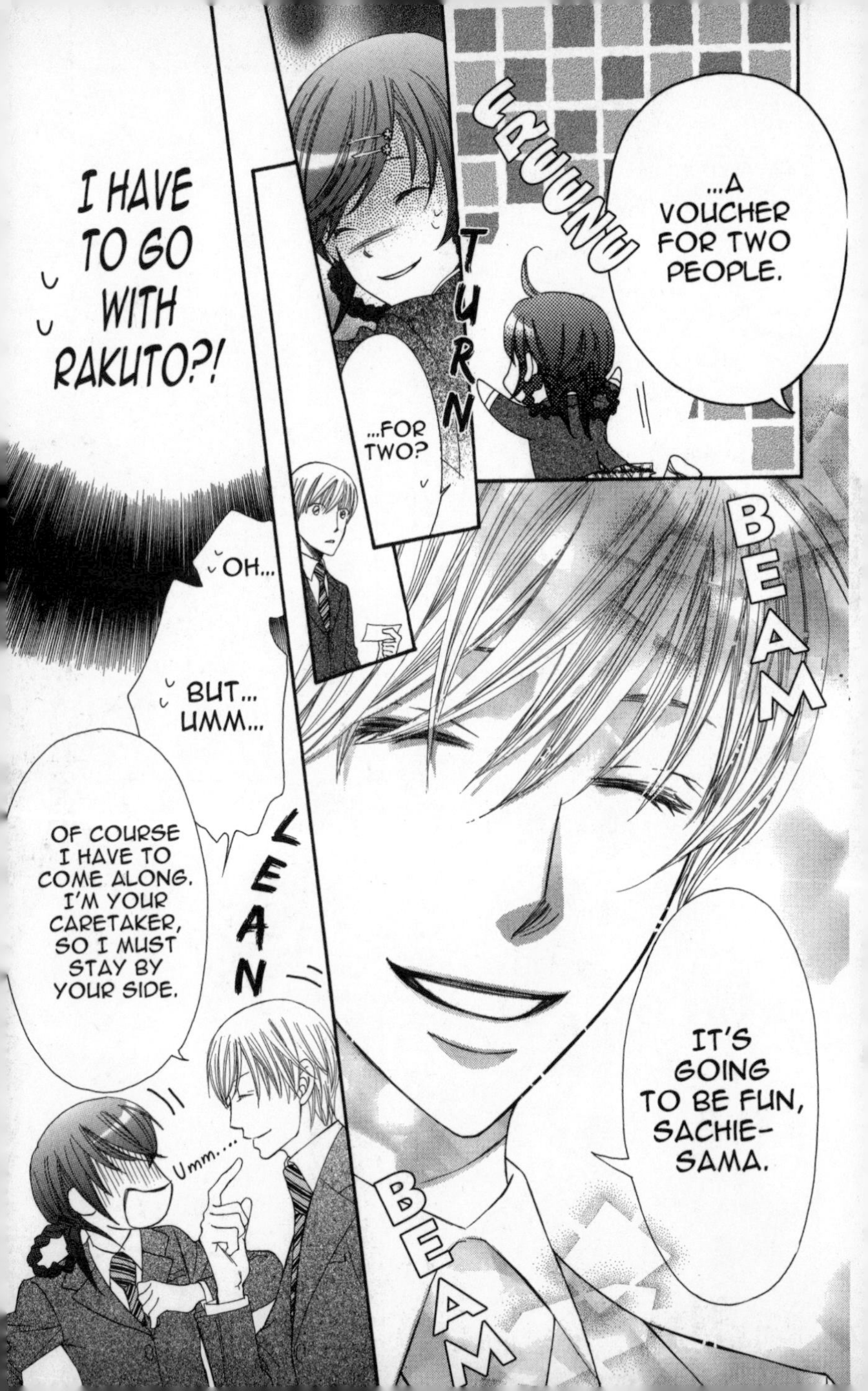
UGUUNU
...A VOUCHER FOR TWO PEOPLE.
TURN
...FOR TWO?
I HAVE TO GO WITH RAKUTO?!
OH...
BEAM
IT'S GOING TO BE FUN, SACHIE-SAMA.
BEAM
BUT... UMM...
OF COURSE I HAVE TO COME ALONG. I'M YOUR CARETAKER, SO I MUST STAY BY YOUR SIDE.
LEAN
Umm....

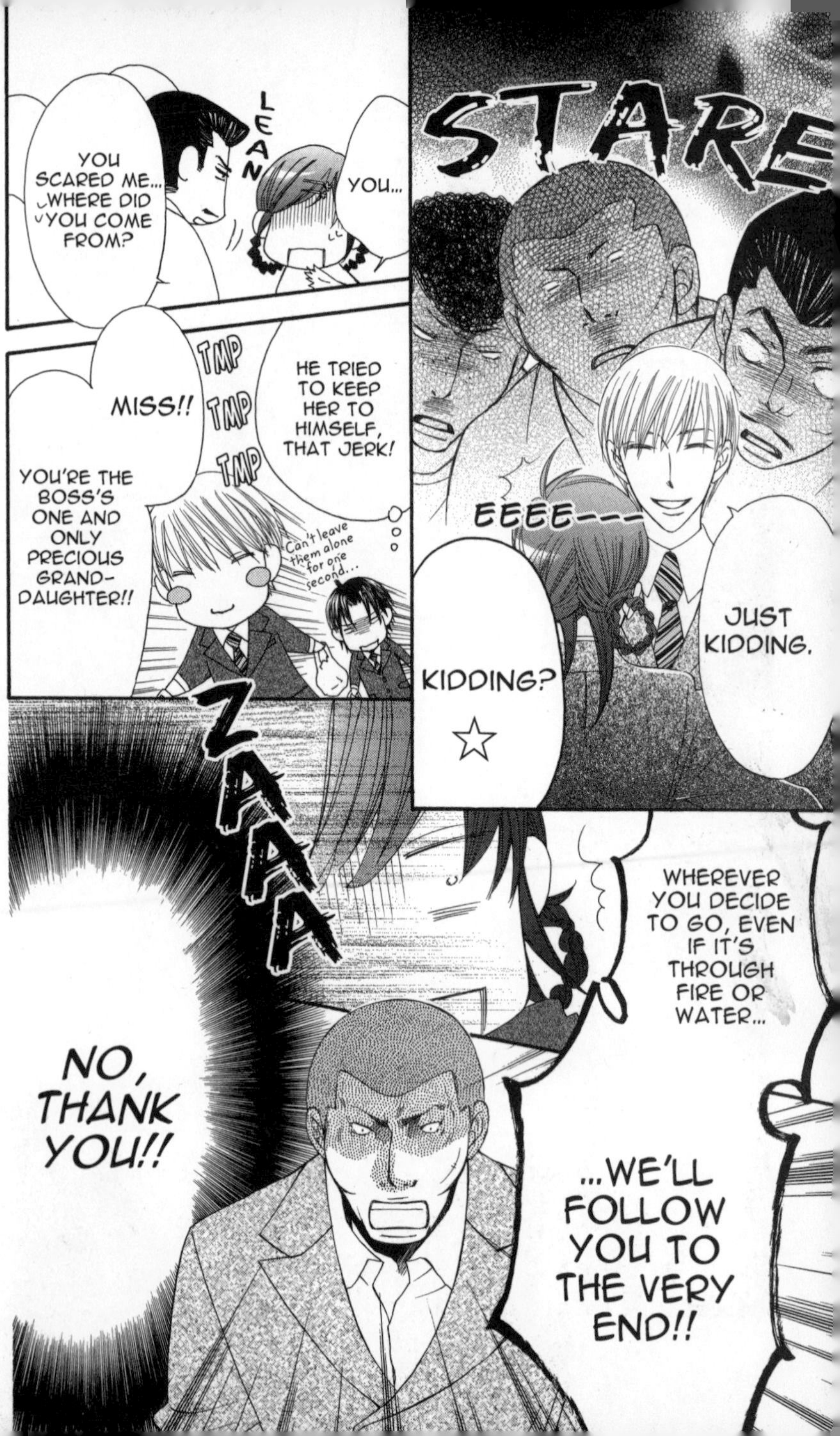
STARE
JUST KIDDING.
EEEE---
KIDDING? ☆
YOU...
LEAN
YOU SCARED ME... WHERE DID YOU COME FROM?
HE TRIED TO KEEP HER TO HIMSELF, THAT JERK!
TMP TMP TMP
MISS!!
YOU'RE THE BOSS'S ONE AND ONLY PRECIOUS GRAND-DAUGHTER!!
Can't leave them alone for one second...
WHEREVER YOU DECIDE TO GO, EVEN IF IT'S THROUGH FIRE OR WATER...
...WE'LL FOLLOW YOU TO THE VERY END!!
ZAAA
NO, THANK YOU!!

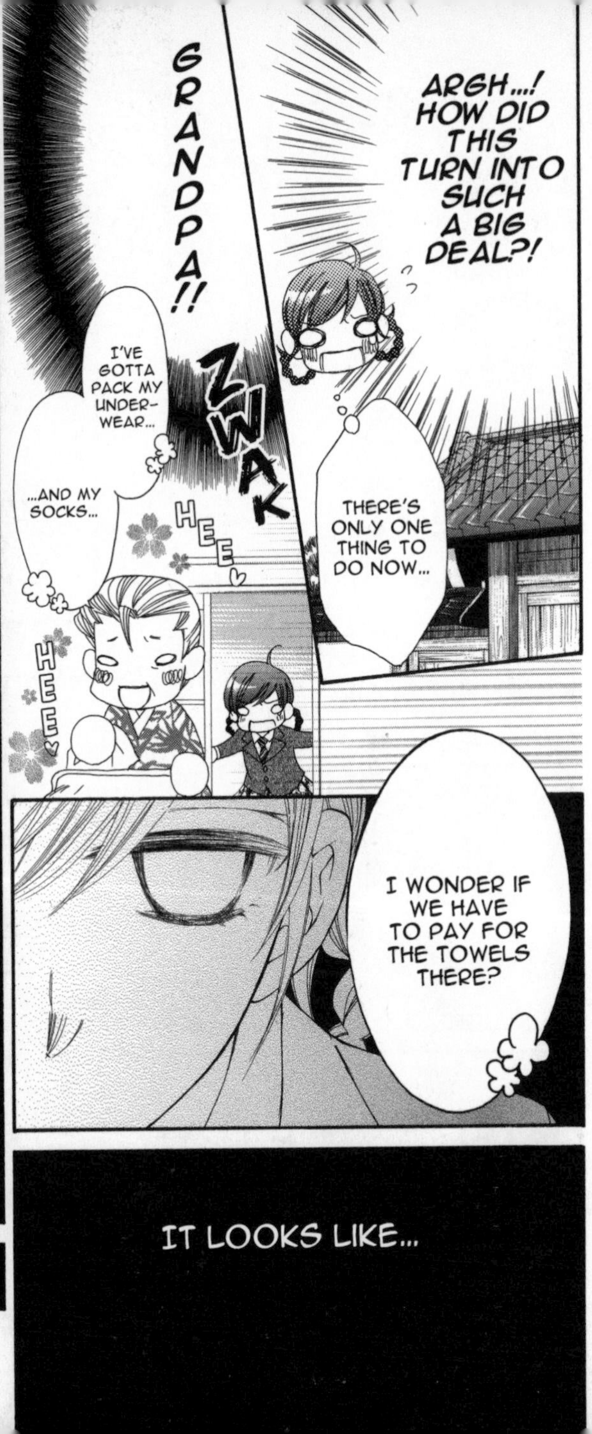
ARGH...! HOW DID THIS TURN INTO SUCH A BIG DEAL?!
GRANDPA!!
THERE'S ONLY ONE THING TO DO NOW...
ZWAK
I'VE GOTTA PACK MY UNDER-WEAR...
...AND MY SOCKS...
HEE
HEE
HEE
HEE
I WONDER IF WE HAVE TO PAY FOR THE TOWELS THERE?
IT LOOKS LIKE...

RAGAWA-SENSEI... ++

YOU HAVE NO IDEA HOW HAPPY I WAS...

I FELT THIS WAY WHEN I MET YUKI-SENSEI TOO, BUT MANGAKA WHO'VE BEEN IN THE BUSINESS FOR A LONG TIME JUST EMIT A DIFFERENT AURA.

I CAN'T BELIEVE I WAS STANDING NEXT TO SOMEONE OF HER CALIBER (I'VE BEEN READING HER WORK SINCE THE 6TH GRADE!!), LET ALONE FINDING OUT HOW DOWN-TO-EARTH SHE IS AND HEARING HER STORIES!!

I WAS IN HEAVEN.

I WAS ALSO REALLY NERVOUS, BUT MEETING HER WAS ENCOURAGING AND GAVE ME SOMETHING TO STRIVE FOR.

PRACTICE MAKES PERFECT!!

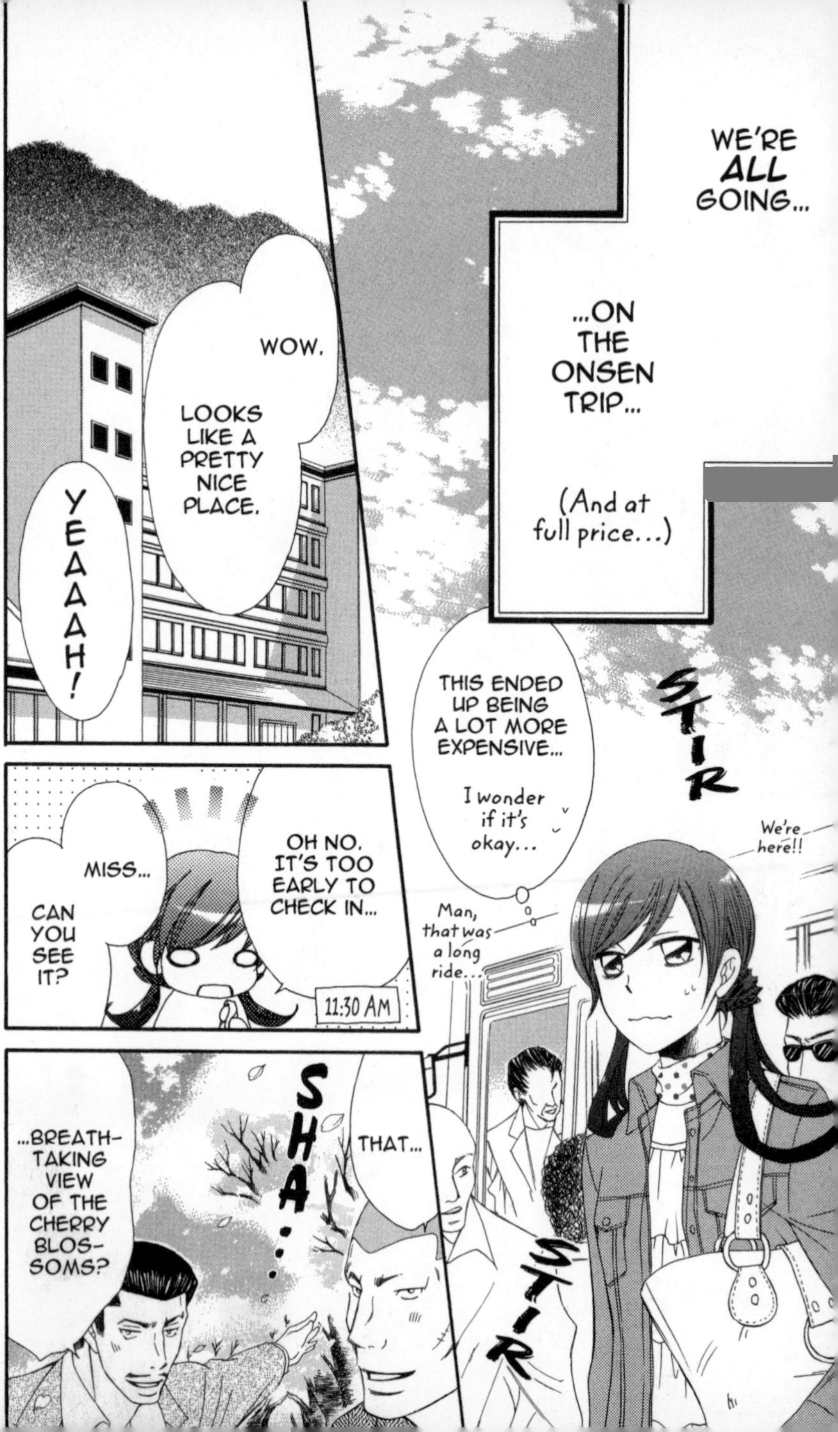
WE'RE ALL GOING...
...ON THE ONSEN TRIP...
(And at full price...)
THIS ENDED UP BEING A LOT MORE EXPENSIVE...
I wonder if it's okay...
STIR
We're here!!
Man, that was a long ride...
STIR
WOW.
LOOKS LIKE A PRETTY NICE PLACE.
YEAAAAH!
OH NO. IT'S TOO EARLY TO CHECK IN...
MISS...
CAN YOU SEE IT?
11:30 AM
THAT...
SHA...
...BREATH-TAKING VIEW OF THE CHERRY BLOS-SOMS?

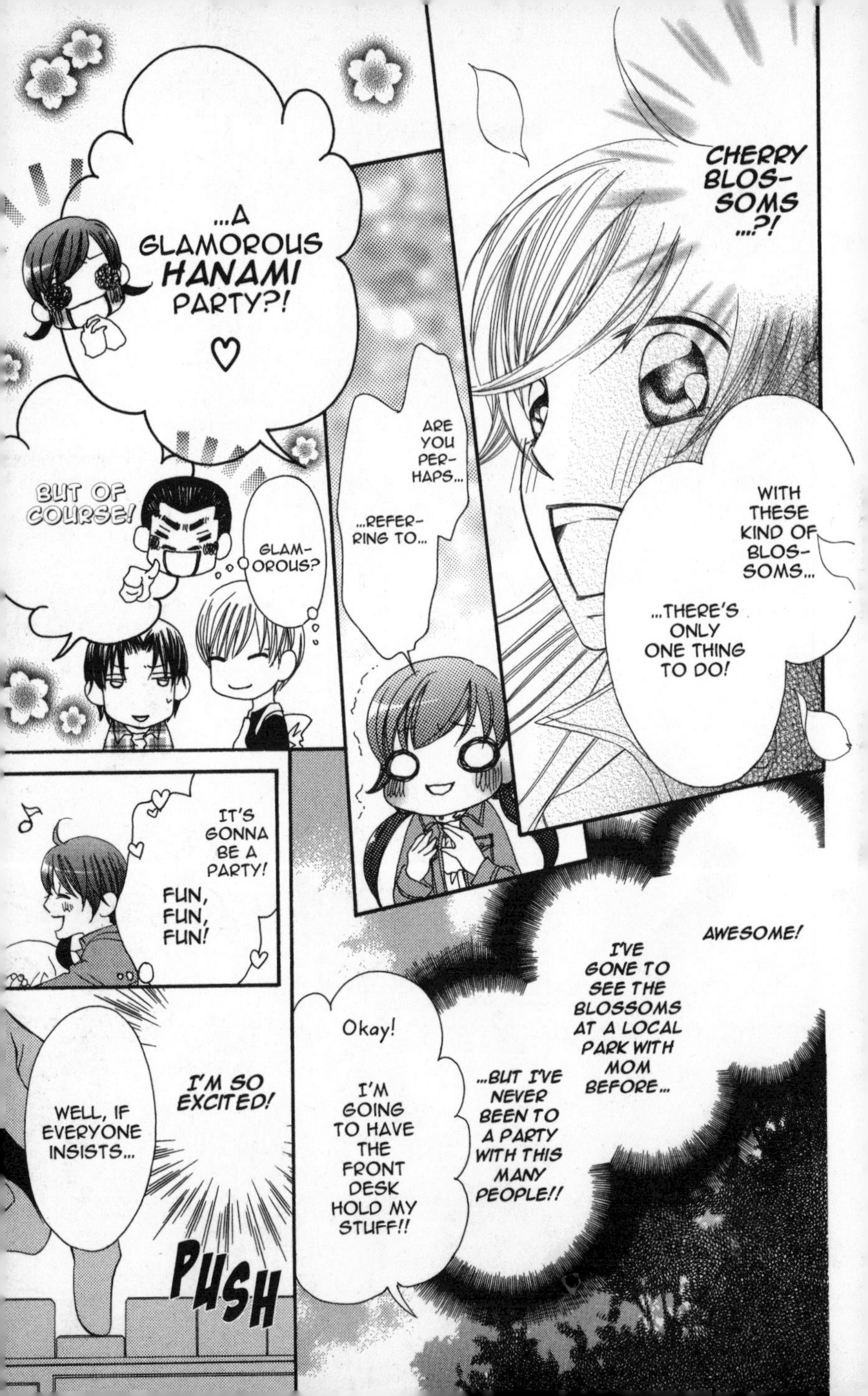
CHERRY BLOSSOMS ...?!
WITH THESE KIND OF BLOSSOMS...
...THERE'S ONLY ONE THING TO DO!
ARE YOU PERHAPS...
...REFERRING TO...
...A GLAMOROUS HANAMI PARTY?! ♡
BUT OF COURSE!
GLAMOROUS?
AWESOME!
I'VE GONE TO SEE THE BLOSSOMS AT A LOCAL PARK WITH MOM BEFORE...
...BUT I'VE NEVER BEEN TO A PARTY WITH THIS MANY PEOPLE!!
Okay!
I'M GOING TO HAVE THE FRONT DESK HOLD MY STUFF!!
IT'S GONNA BE A PARTY!
FUN, FUN, FUN!
I'M SO EXCITED!
WELL, IF EVERYONE INSISTS...
PUSH

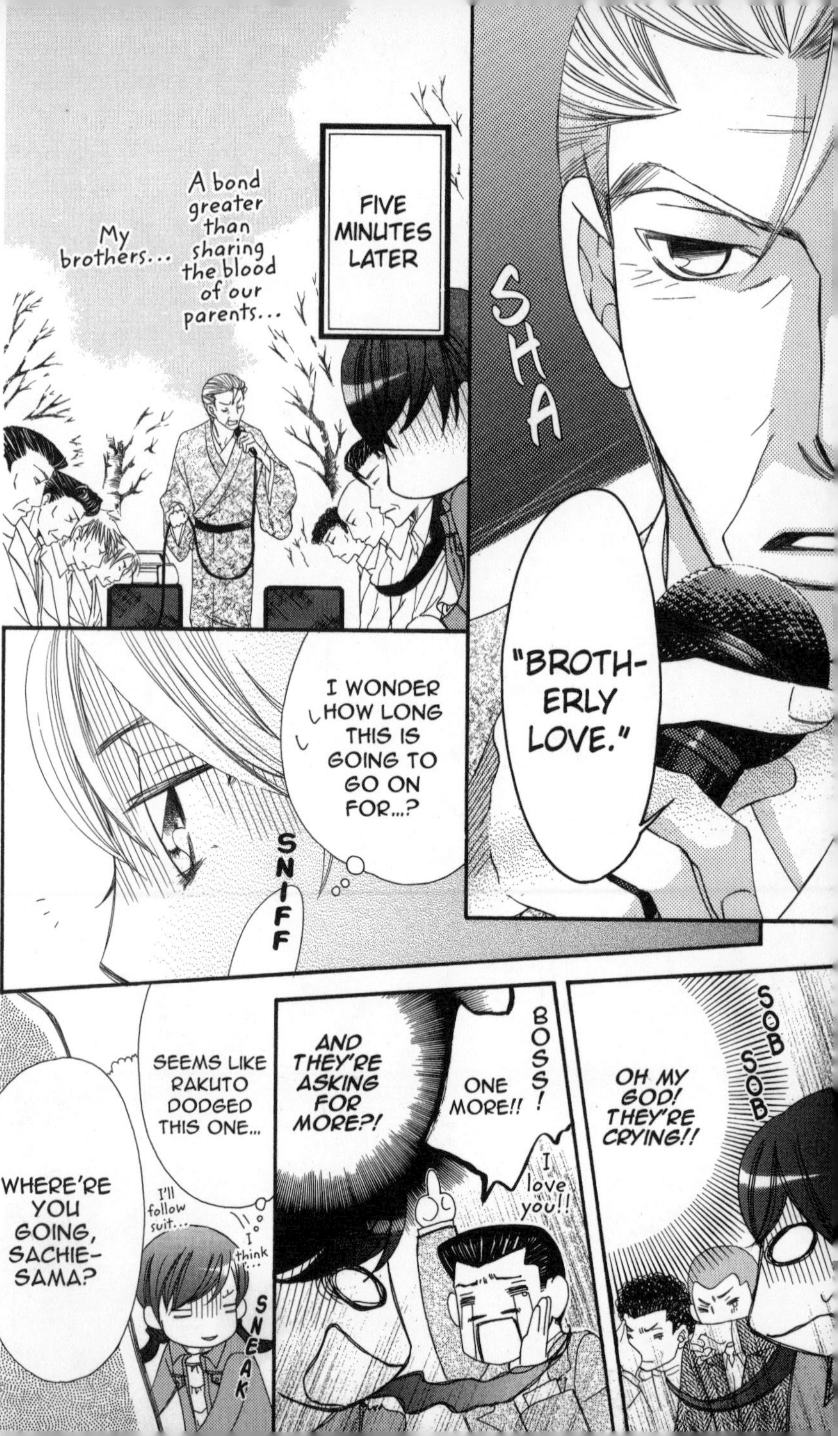
SHA
"BROTHERLY LOVE."
FIVE MINUTES LATER
A bond greater than sharing the blood of our parents...
My brothers...
I WONDER HOW LONG THIS IS GOING TO GO ON FOR...?
SNIFF
SOB SOB SOB
OH MY GOD! THEY'RE CRYING!!
BOSS!
ONE MORE!!
I love you!!
AND THEY'RE ASKING FOR MORE?!
SEEMS LIKE RAKUTO DODGED THIS ONE...
I'll follow suit...
I think I...
WHERE'RE YOU GOING, SACHIE-SAMA?
SNEAK

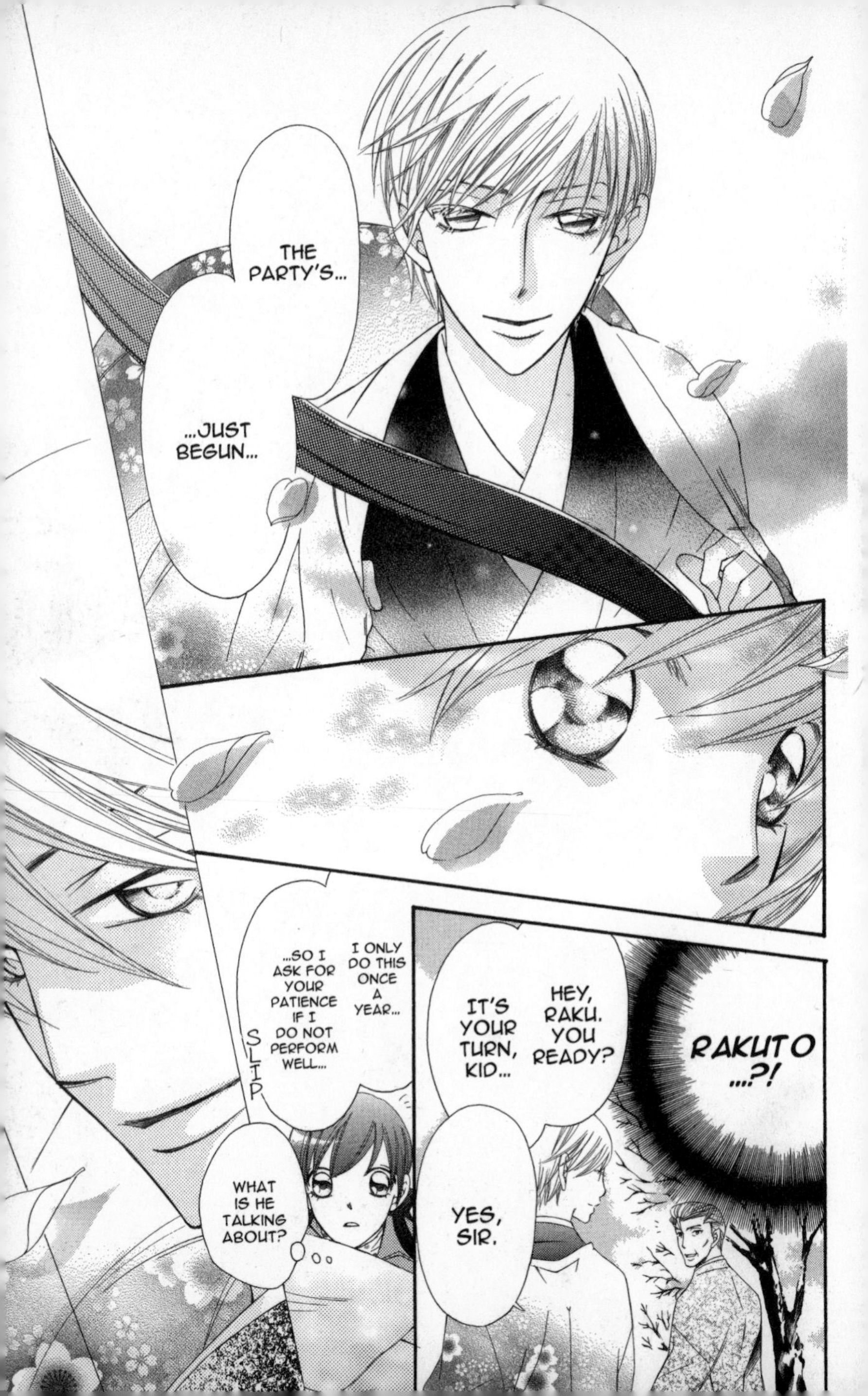
THE PARTY'S...
...JUST BEGUN...
RAKUTO ...?!
HEY, RAKU. YOU READY?
IT'S YOUR TURN, KID...
YES, SIR.
I ONLY DO THIS ONCE A YEAR...
...SO I ASK FOR YOUR PATIENCE IF I DO NOT PERFORM WELL...
SLIP
WHAT IS HE TALKING ABOUT?

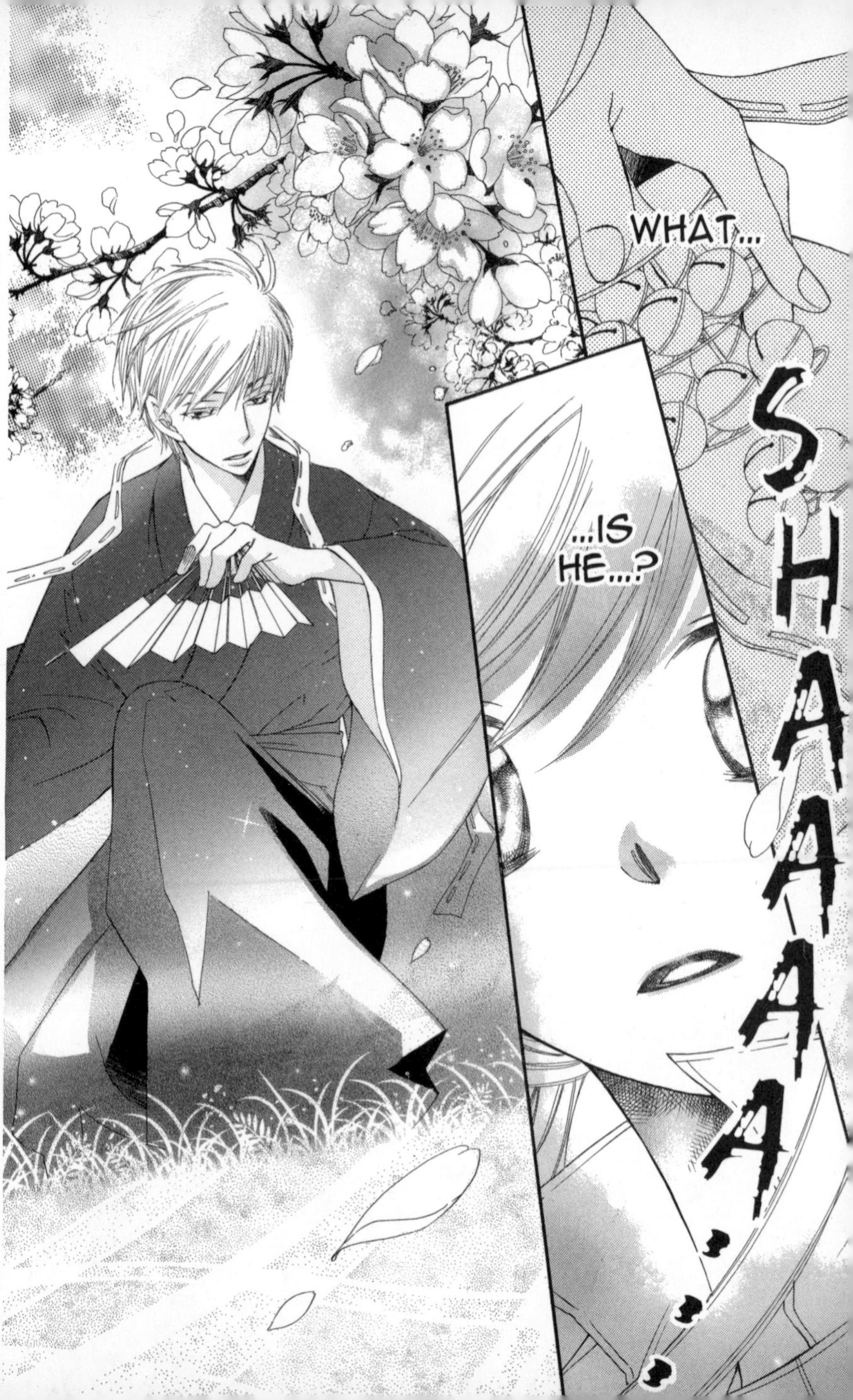
WHAT...
...IS HE...?
SHAAA...

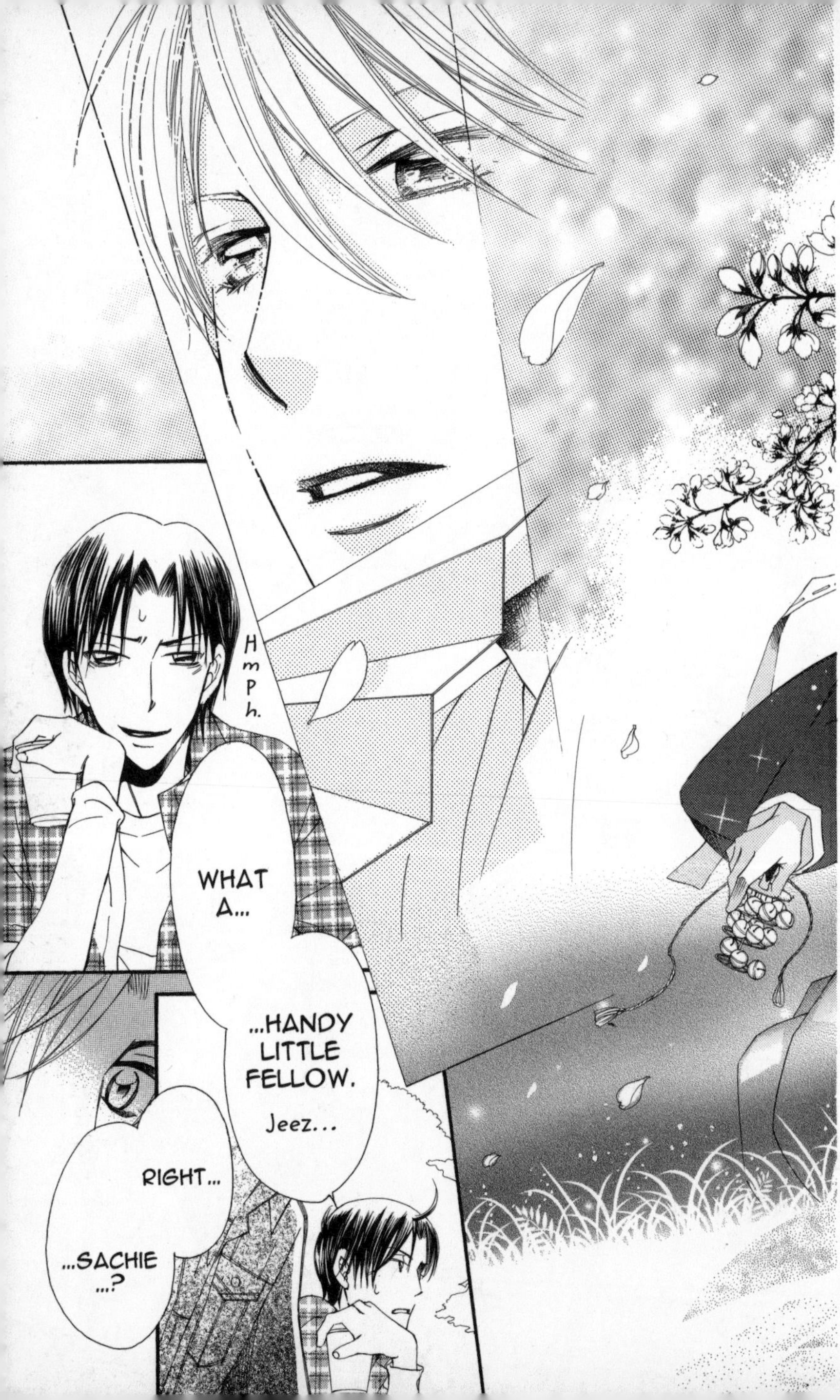
Hmph.
WHAT A...
...HANDY LITTLE FELLOW.
Jeez...
RIGHT...
...SACHIE ...?

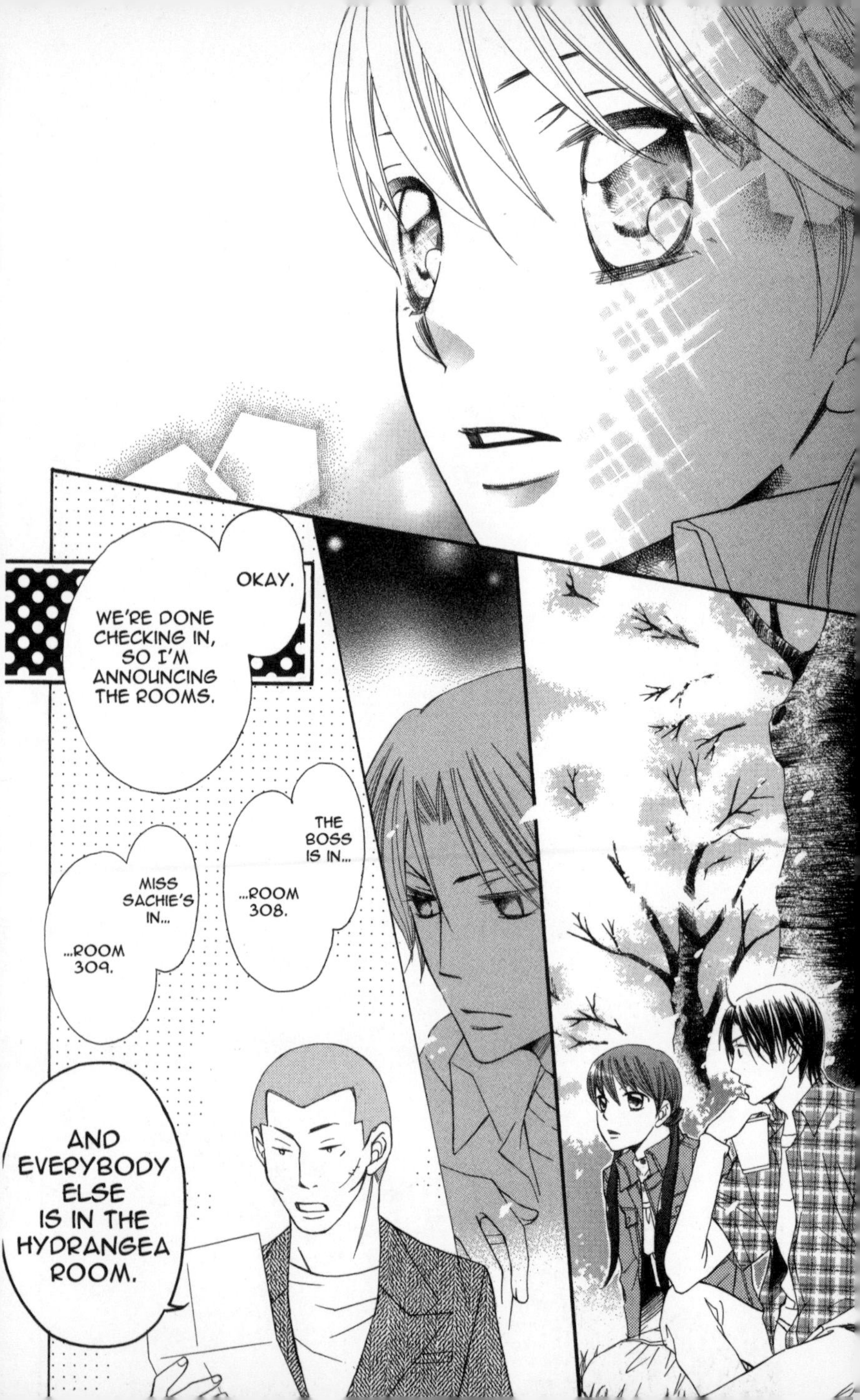
OKAY.
WE'RE DONE CHECKING IN, SO I'M ANNOUNCING THE ROOMS.
THE BOSS IS IN...
...ROOM 308.
MISS SACHIE'S IN...
...ROOM 309.
AND EVERYBODY ELSE IS IN THE HYDRANGEA ROOM.

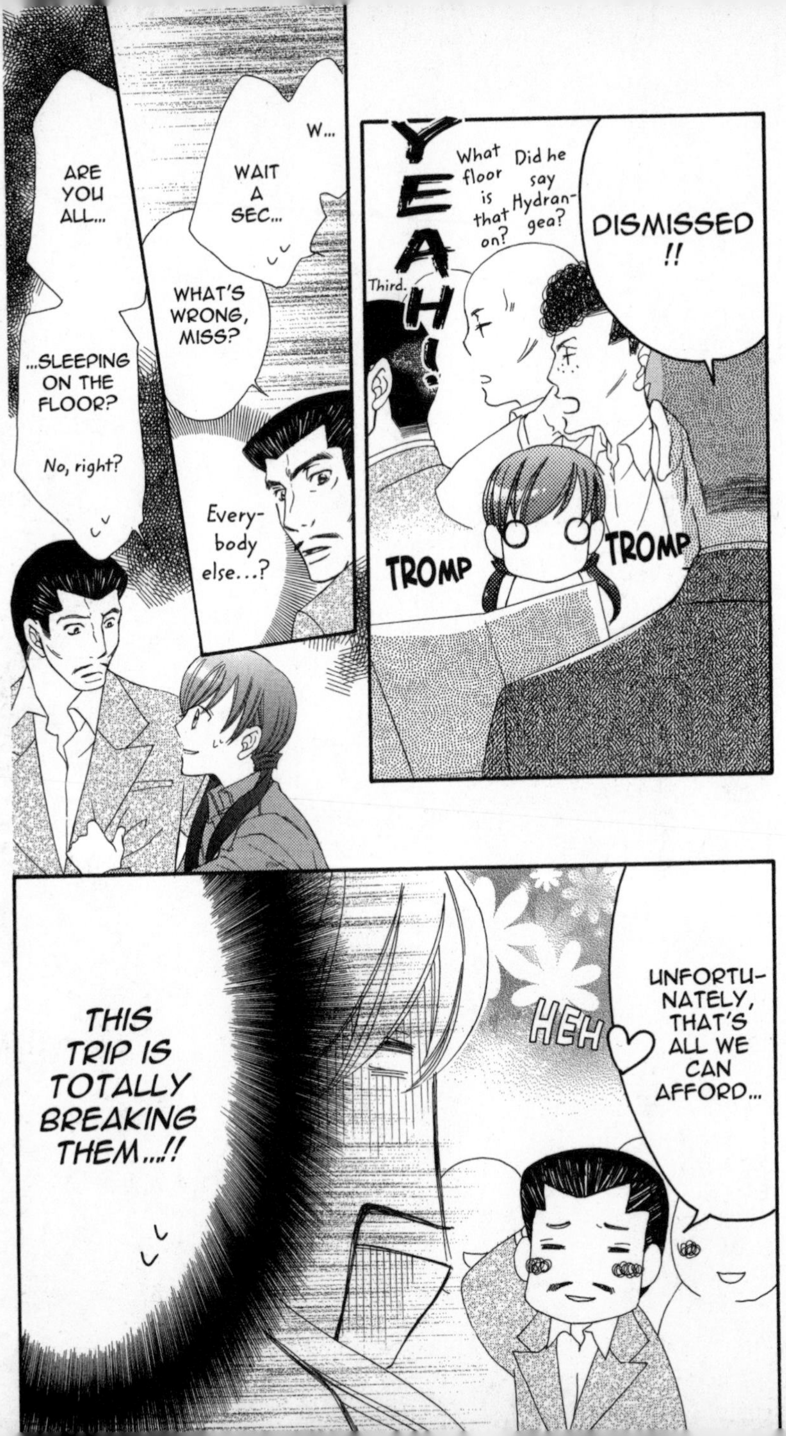
DISMISSED!!
Did he say Hydrangea?
What floor is that on?
Third.
YEAH!!
TROMP
TROMP
W...
WAIT A SEC...
WHAT'S WRONG, MISS?
Everybody else...?
ARE YOU ALL...
...SLEEPING ON THE FLOOR?
No, right?
UNFORTUNATELY, THAT'S ALL WE CAN AFFORD...
HEH
THIS TRIP IS TOTALLY BREAKING THEM...!!

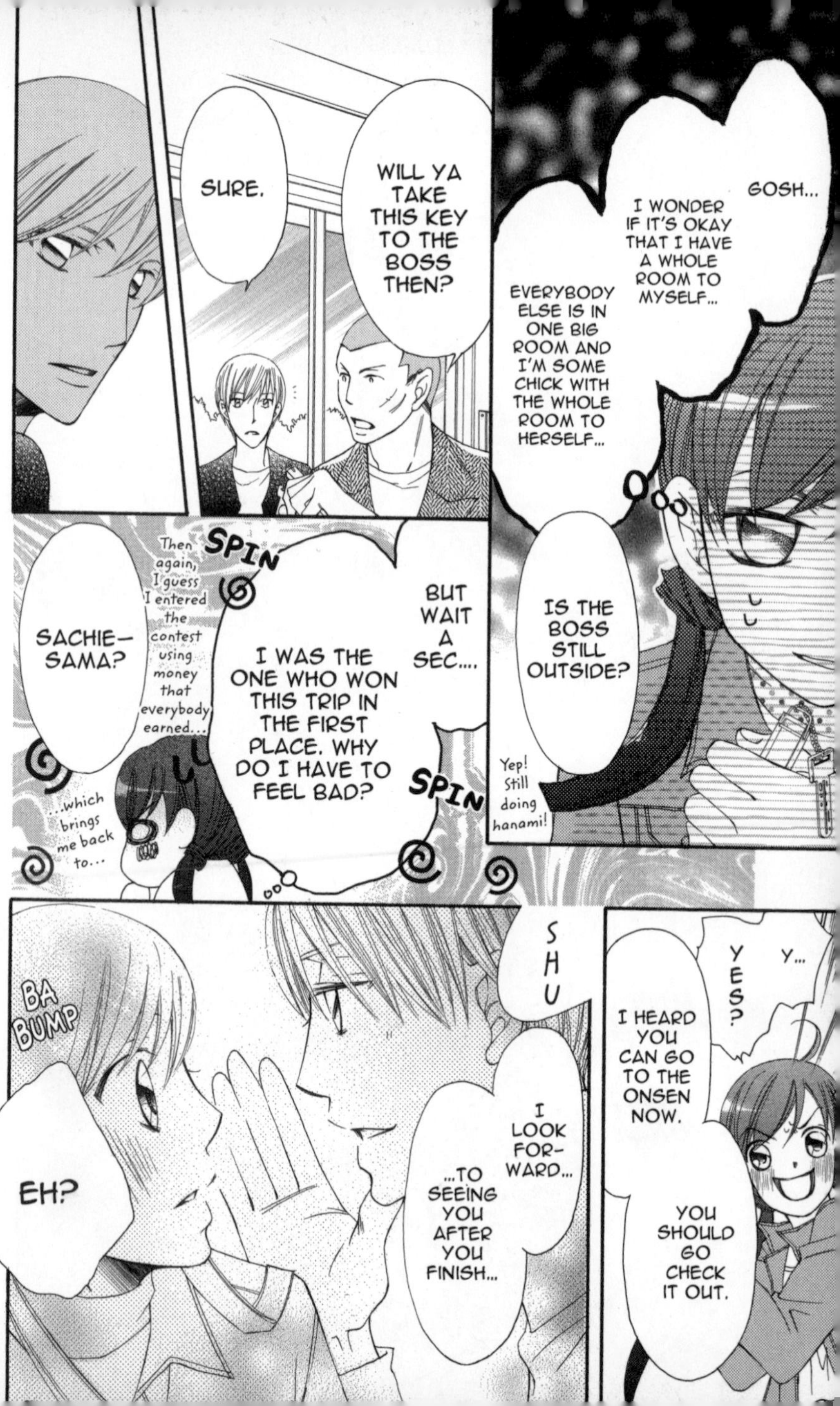
GOSH...
I WONDER IF IT'S OKAY THAT I HAVE A WHOLE ROOM TO MYSELF...
EVERYBODY ELSE IS IN ONE BIG ROOM AND I'M SOME CHICK WITH THE WHOLE ROOM TO HERSELF...
IS THE BOSS STILL OUTSIDE?
Yep! Still doing hanami!
WILL YA TAKE THIS KEY TO THE BOSS THEN?
SURE.
BUT WAIT A SEC....
I WAS THE ONE WHO WON THIS TRIP IN THE FIRST PLACE. WHY DO I HAVE TO FEEL BAD?
SPIN
SPIN
Then again, I guess I entered the contest using money that everybody earned...
SACHIE-SAMA?
...which brings me back to...
Y...
YES?
I HEARD YOU CAN GO TO THE ONSEN NOW.
YOU SHOULD GO CHECK IT OUT.
SHU
I LOOK FOR-WARD...
...TO SEEING YOU AFTER YOU FINISH...
BA BUMP
EH?

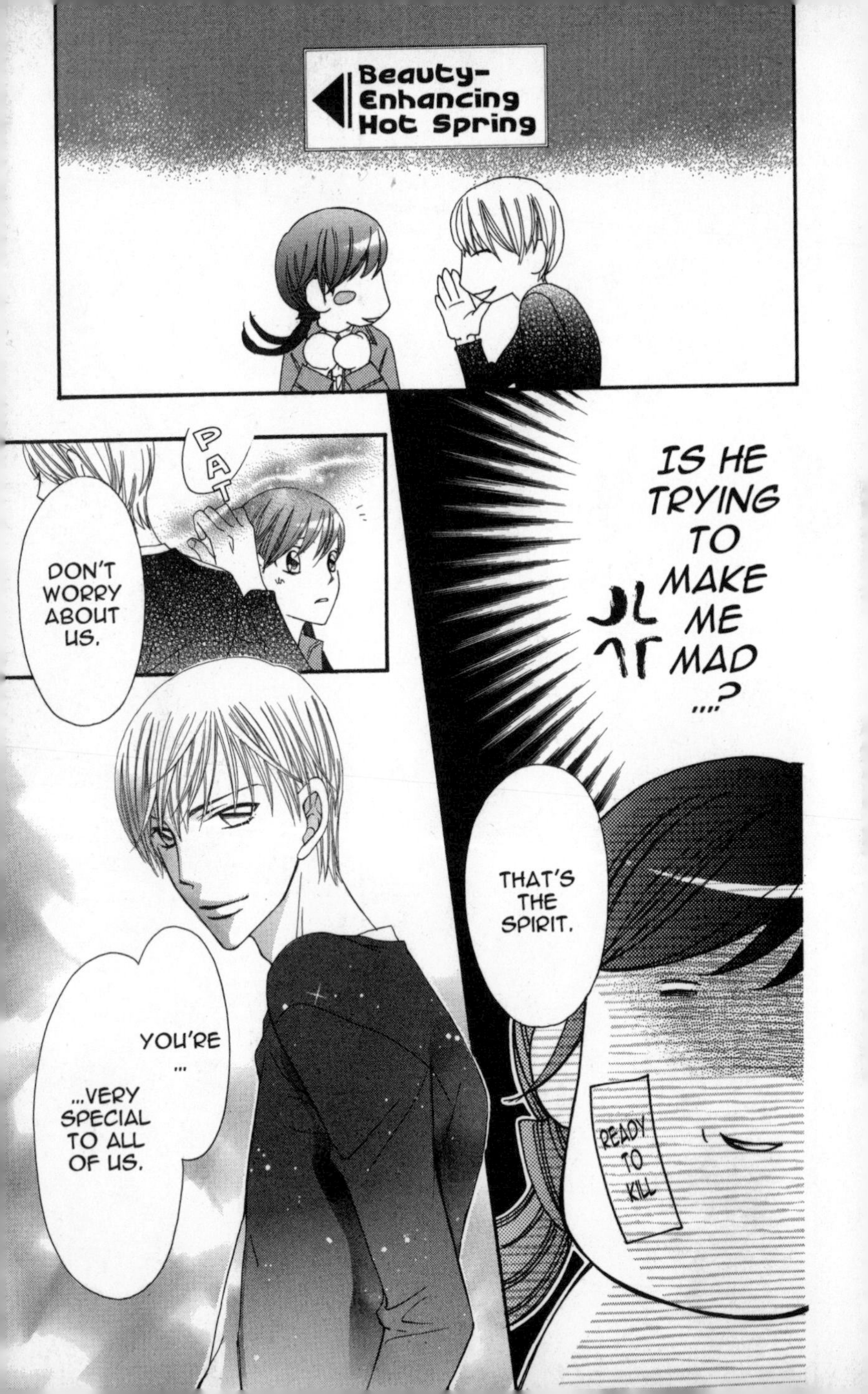

Beauty-Enhancing Hot Spring
PAT
DON'T WORRY ABOUT US.
YOU'RE ...
...VERY SPECIAL TO ALL OF US.
IS HE TRYING TO MAKE ME MAD ...?
THAT'S THE SPIRIT.
READY TO KILL

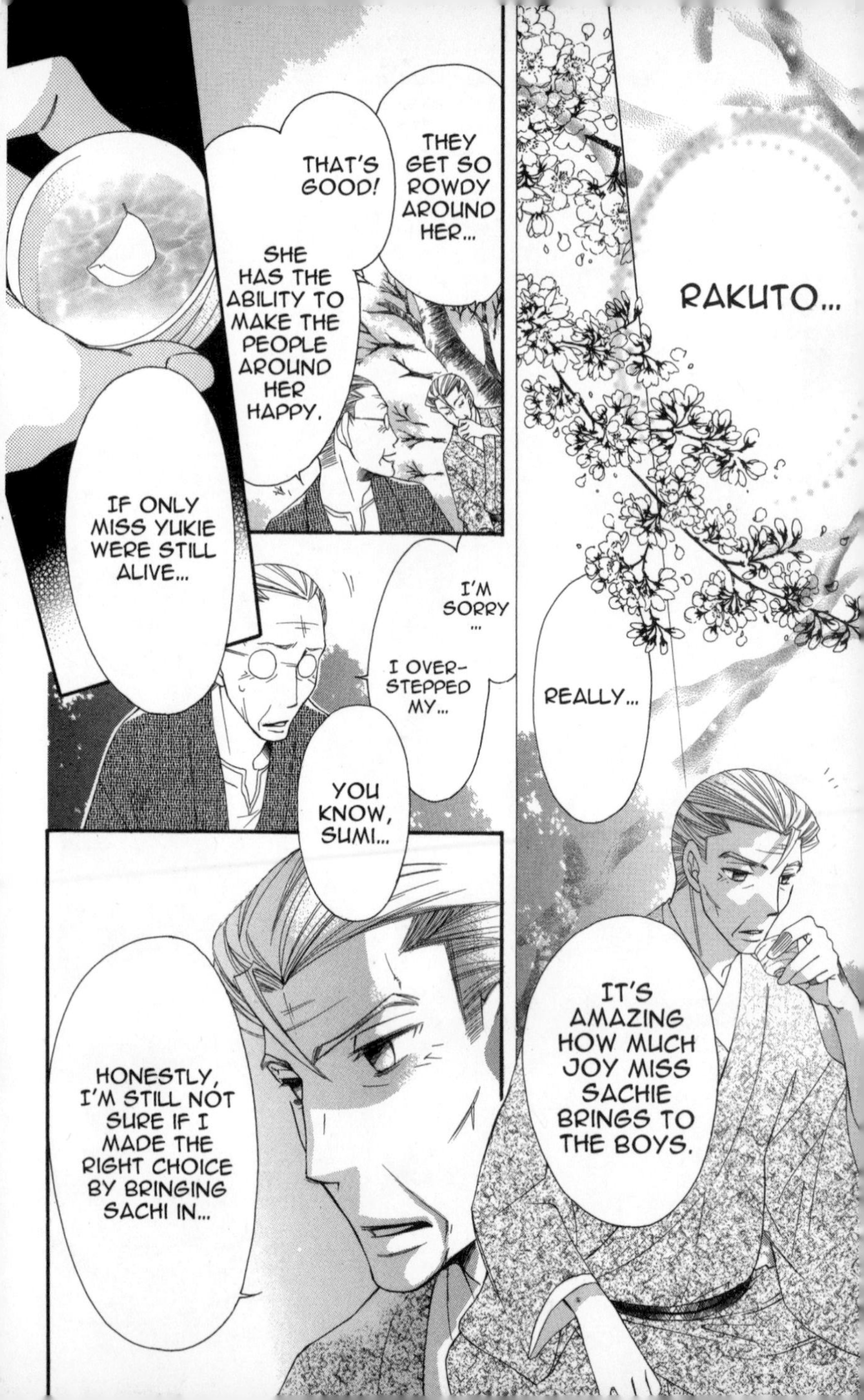

RAKUTO...
IT'S AMAZING HOW MUCH JOY MISS SACHIE BRINGS TO THE BOYS.
REALLY...
THEY GET SO ROWDY AROUND HER...
THAT'S GOOD!
SHE HAS THE ABILITY TO MAKE THE PEOPLE AROUND HER HAPPY.
IF ONLY MISS YUKIE WERE STILL ALIVE...
I'M SORRY...
I OVER-STEPPED MY...
YOU KNOW, SUMI...
HONESTLY, I'M STILL NOT SURE IF I MADE THE RIGHT CHOICE BY BRINGING SACHI IN...

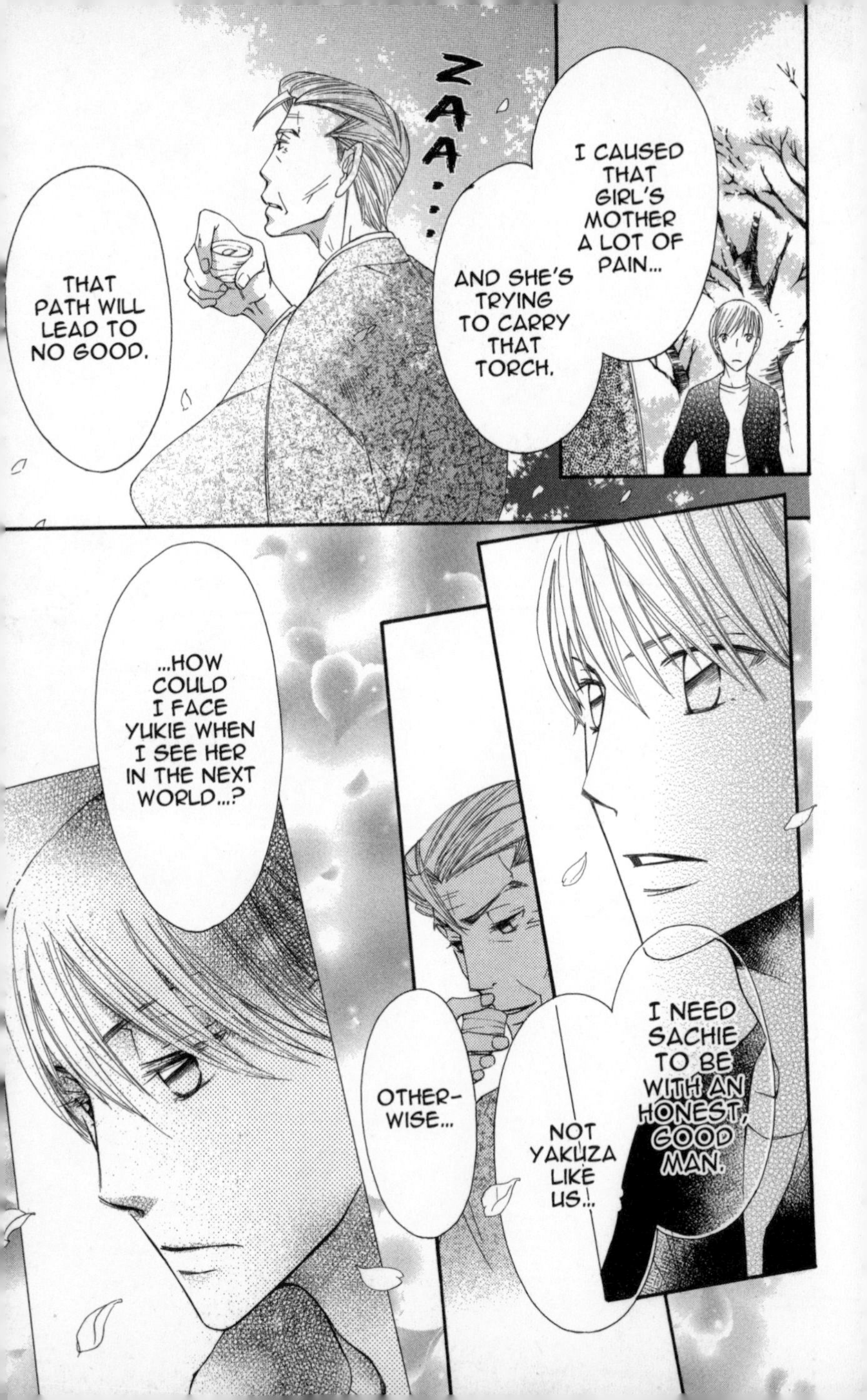
ZAA...
I CAUSED THAT GIRL'S MOTHER A LOT OF PAIN...
AND SHE'S TRYING TO CARRY THAT TORCH.
THAT PATH WILL LEAD TO NO GOOD.
I NEED SACHIE TO BE WITH AN HONEST, GOOD MAN.
NOT YAKUZA LIKE US...
OTHER-WISE...
...HOW COULD I FACE YUKIE WHEN I SEE HER IN THE NEXT WORLD...?

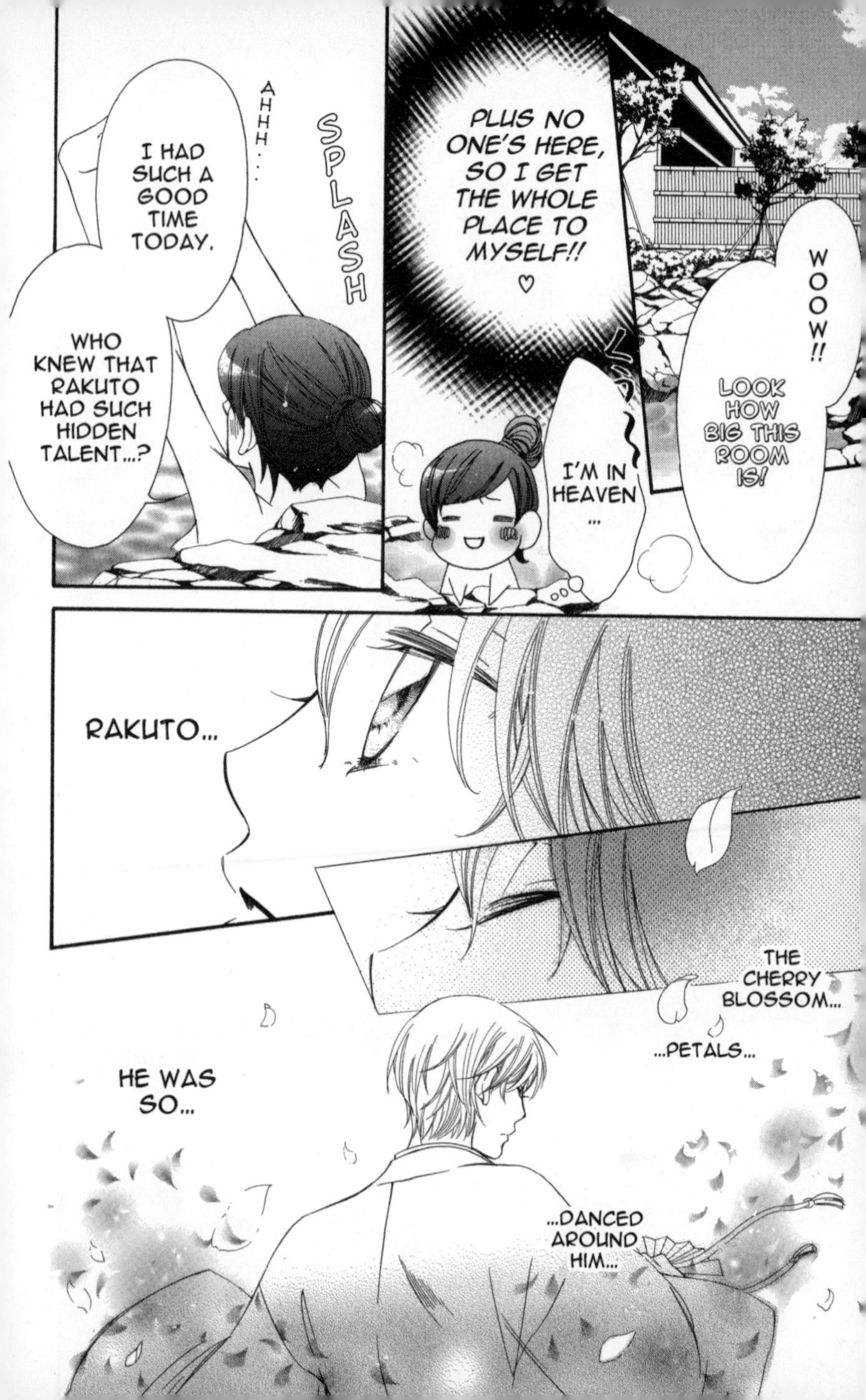
WOOOW!!
LOOK HOW BIG THIS ROOM IS!
PLUS NO ONE'S HERE, SO I GET THE WHOLE PLACE TO MYSELF!! ♡
I'M IN HEAVEN ...
SPLASH
AHHH...
I HAD SUCH A GOOD TIME TODAY.
WHO KNEW THAT RAKUTO HAD SUCH HIDDEN TALENT...?
RAKUTO...
THE CHERRY BLOSSOM...
...PETALS...
...DANCED AROUND HIM...
HE WAS SO...

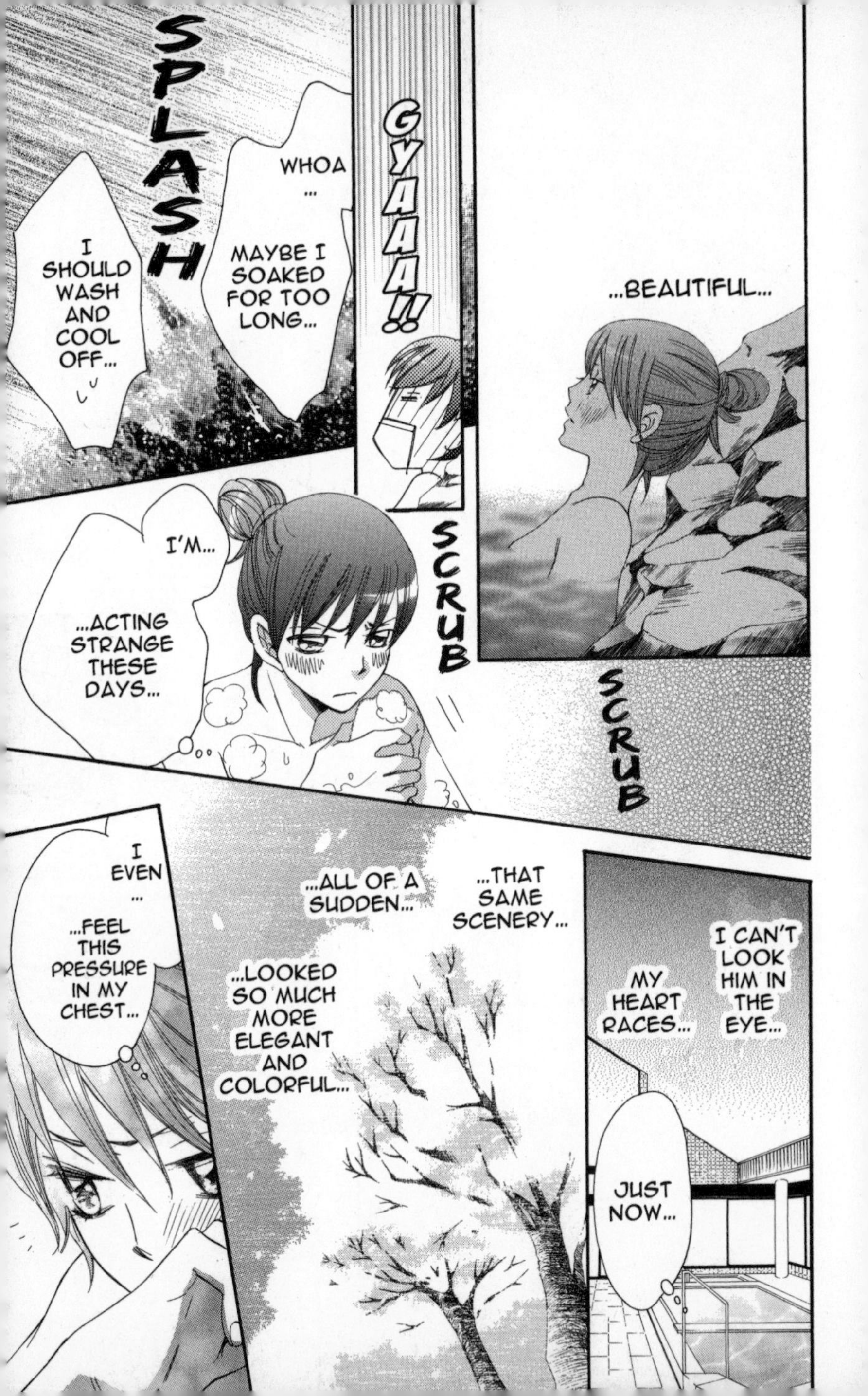
...BEAUTIFUL...
GYAAAA!!
WHOA ... MAYBE I SOAKED FOR TOO LONG...
I SHOULD WASH AND COOL OFF...
SPLASH
SCRUB
SCRUB
I'M...
...ACTING STRANGE THESE DAYS...
I CAN'T LOOK HIM IN THE EYE...
MY HEART RACES...
JUST NOW...
...THAT SAME SCENERY...
...ALL OF A SUDDEN...
...LOOKED SO MUCH MORE ELEGANT AND COLORFUL...
I EVEN ... ...FEEL THIS PRESSURE IN MY CHEST...

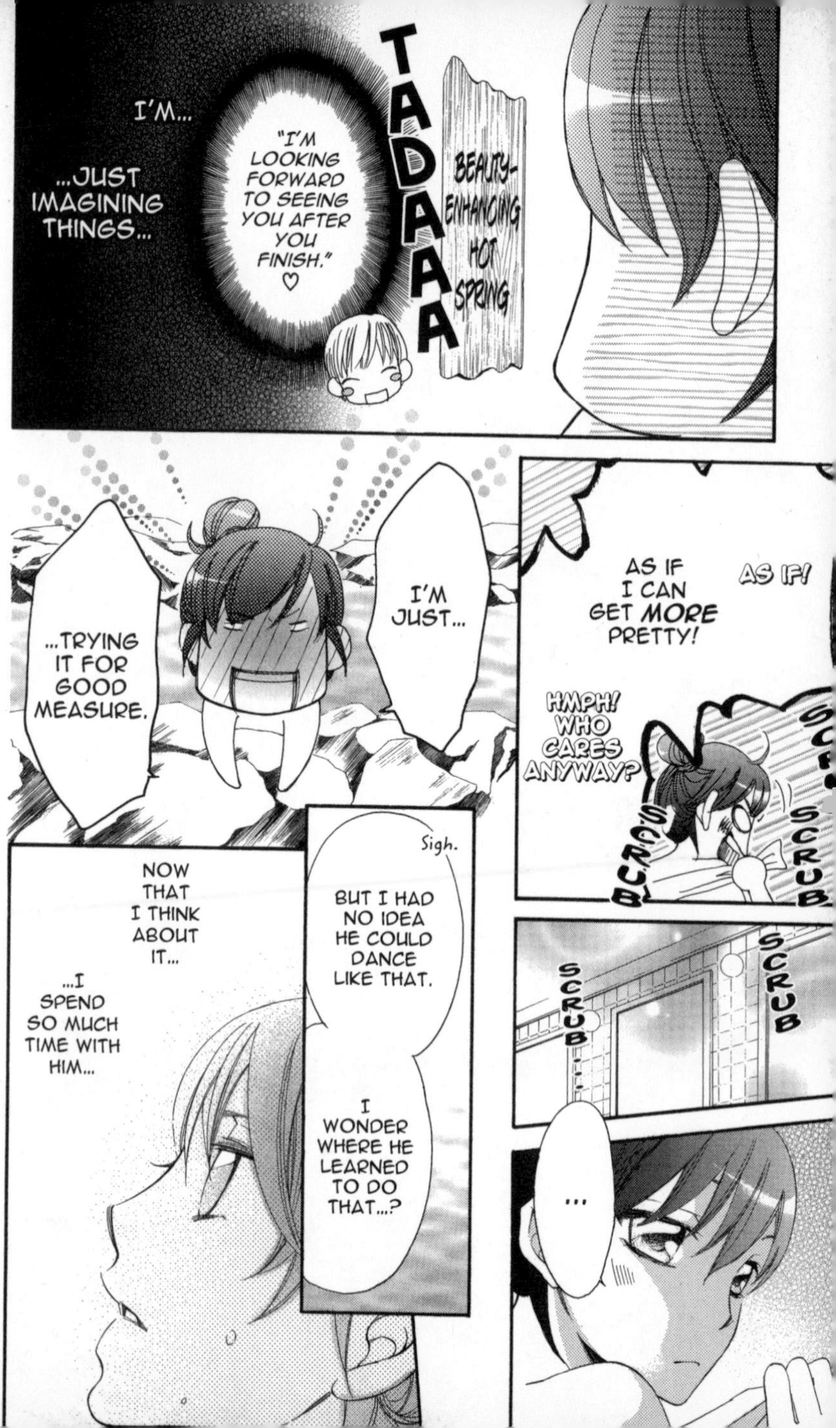
BEAUTY-ENHANCING HOT SPRING
TADAAA
"I'M LOOKING FORWARD TO SEEING YOU AFTER YOU FINISH." ♡
I'M...
...JUST IMAGINING THINGS...
AS IF!
AS IF I CAN GET MORE PRETTY!
HMPH! WHO CARES ANYWAY?
SCRUB
SCRUB
SCRUB
I'M JUST...
...TRYING IT FOR GOOD MEASURE.
SCRUB
SCRUB
...
Sigh.
BUT I HAD NO IDEA HE COULD DANCE LIKE THAT.
I WONDER WHERE HE LEARNED TO DO THAT...?
NOW THAT I THINK ABOUT IT...
...I SPEND SO MUCH TIME WITH HIM...

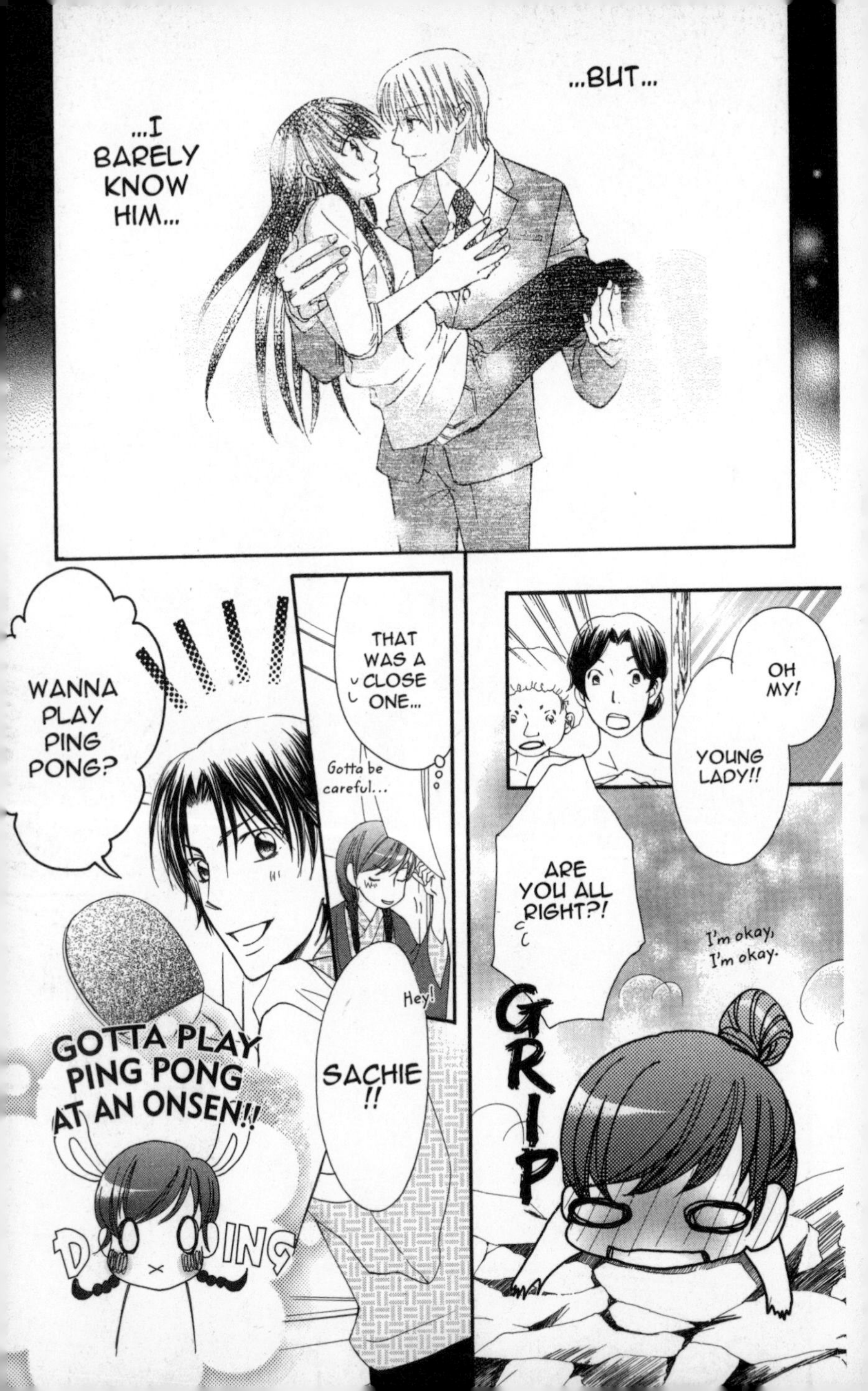
...BUT...
...I BARELY KNOW HIM...
OH MY!
YOUNG LADY!!
ARE YOU ALL RIGHT?!
I'm okay, I'm okay.
GRIP
THAT WAS A CLOSE ONE...
Gotta be careful...
Hey!
SACHIE!!
WANNA PLAY PING PONG?
GOTTA PLAY PING PONG AT AN ONSEN!!

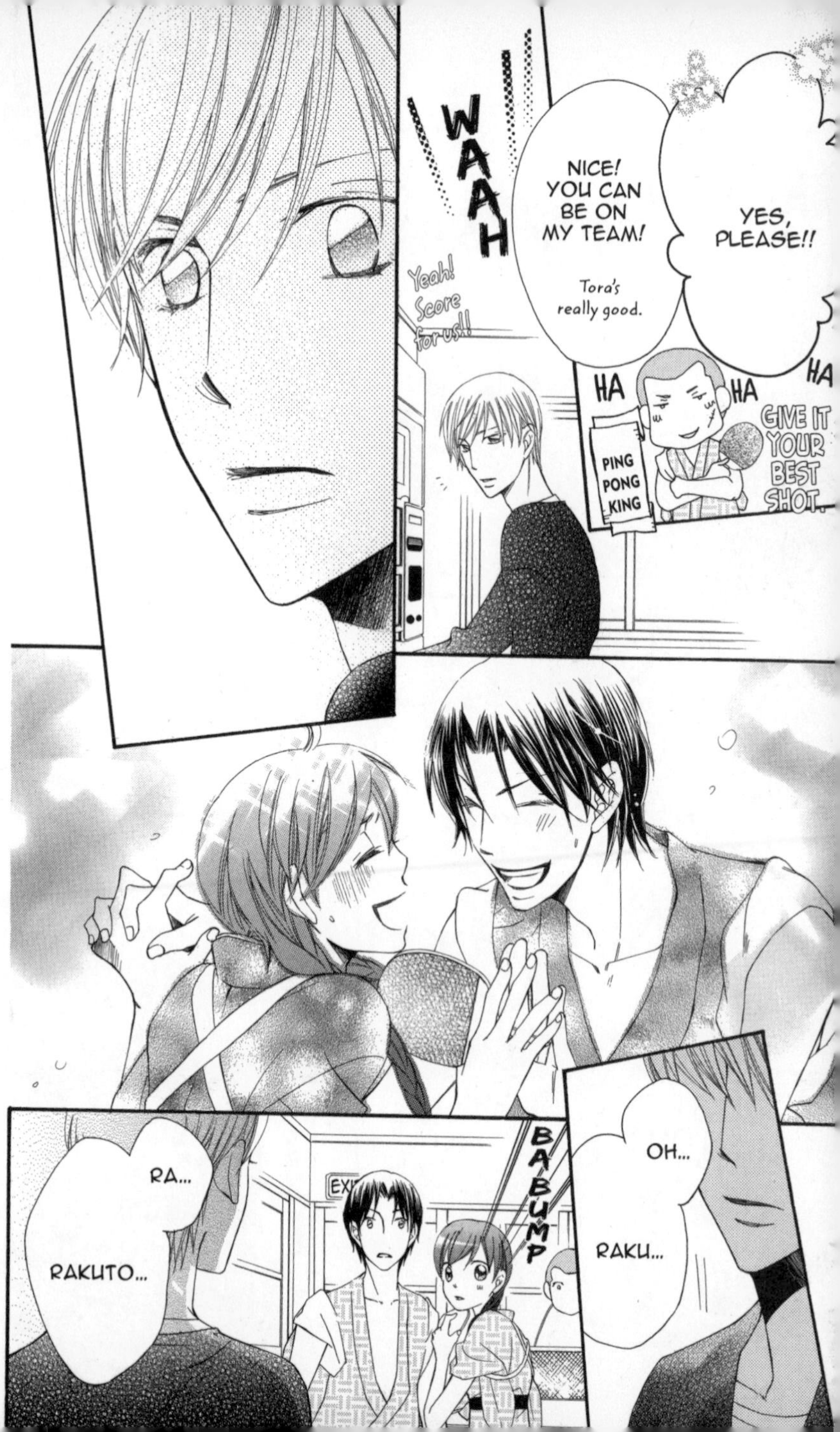
YES, PLEASE!!
NICE! YOU CAN BE ON MY TEAM!
Tora's really good.
WAAH
Yeah! Score for us!!
HA HA HA
GIVE IT YOUR BEST SHOT.
PING PONG KING
OH...
RAKU...
BABUMP
RA...
RAKUTO...

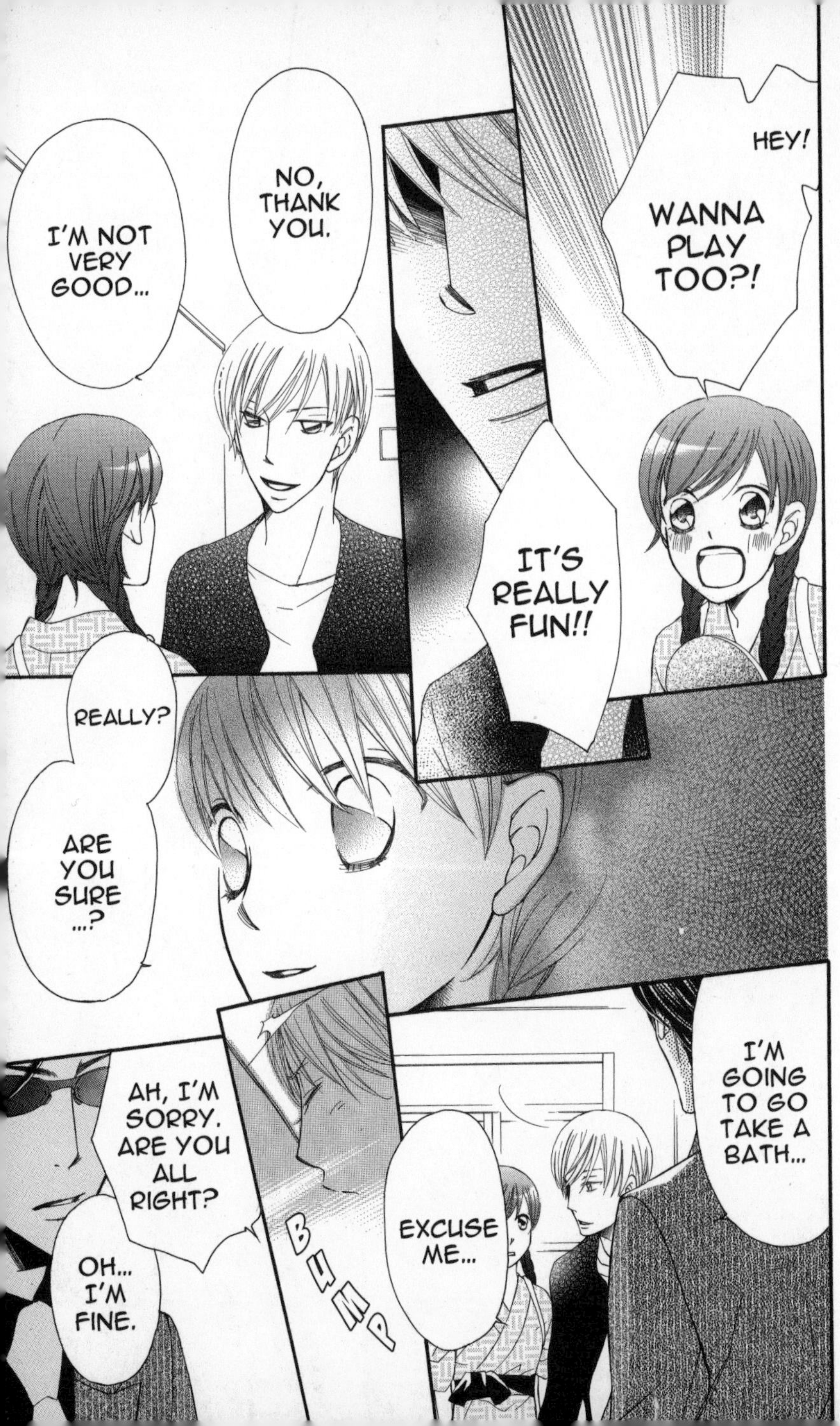
HEY!
WANNA PLAY TOO?!
IT'S REALLY FUN!!
NO, THANK YOU.
I'M NOT VERY GOOD...
REALLY?
ARE YOU SURE ...?
I'M GOING TO GO TAKE A BATH...
EXCUSE ME...
BUMP
AH, I'M SORRY. ARE YOU ALL RIGHT?
OH... I'M FINE.

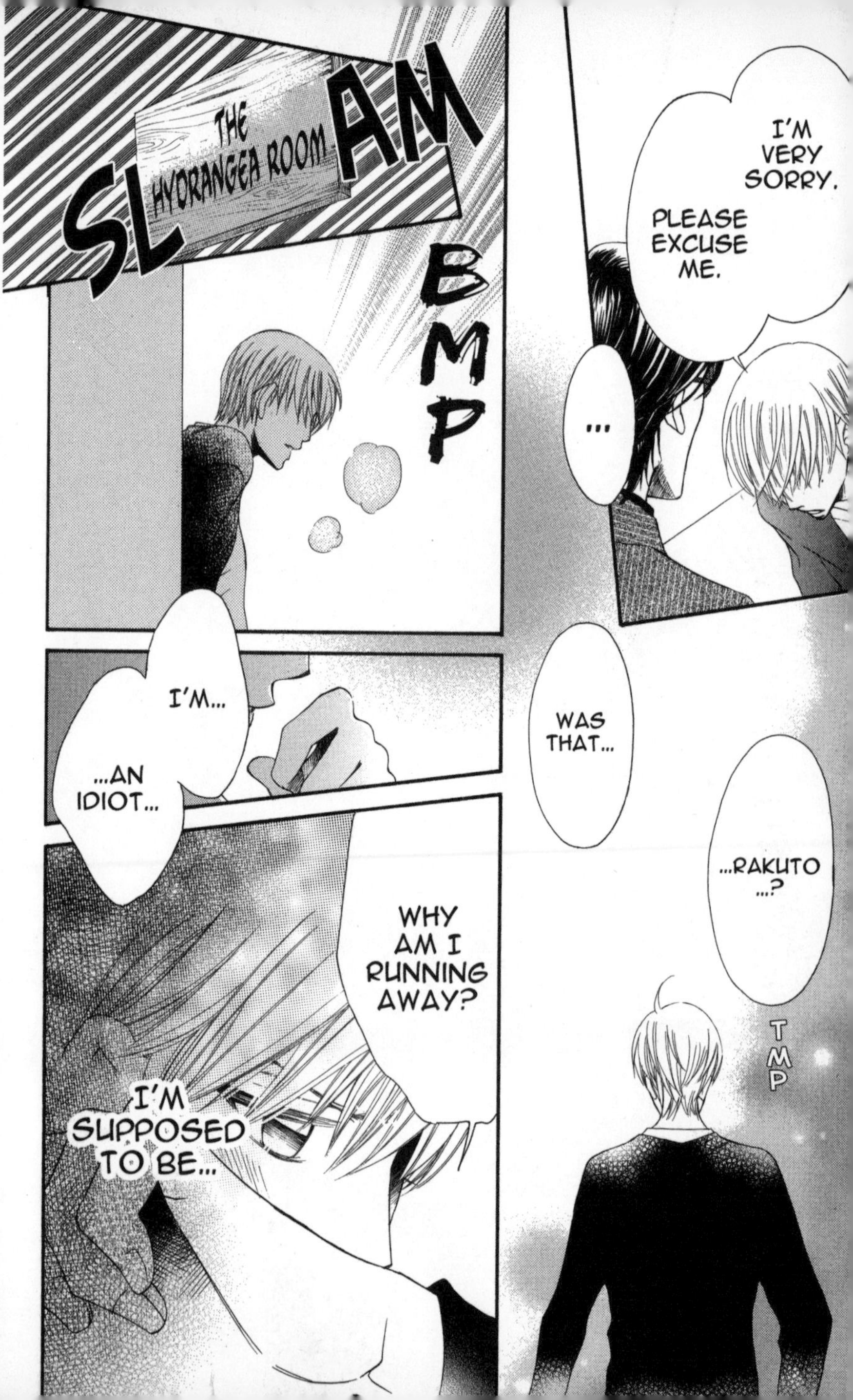
I'M VERY SORRY.
PLEASE EXCUSE ME.
...
THE HYDRANGEA ROOM
SLAM
BMP
WAS THAT...
...RAKUTO ...?
TMP
I'M...
...AN IDIOT...
WHY AM I RUNNING AWAY?
I'M SUPPOSED TO BE...

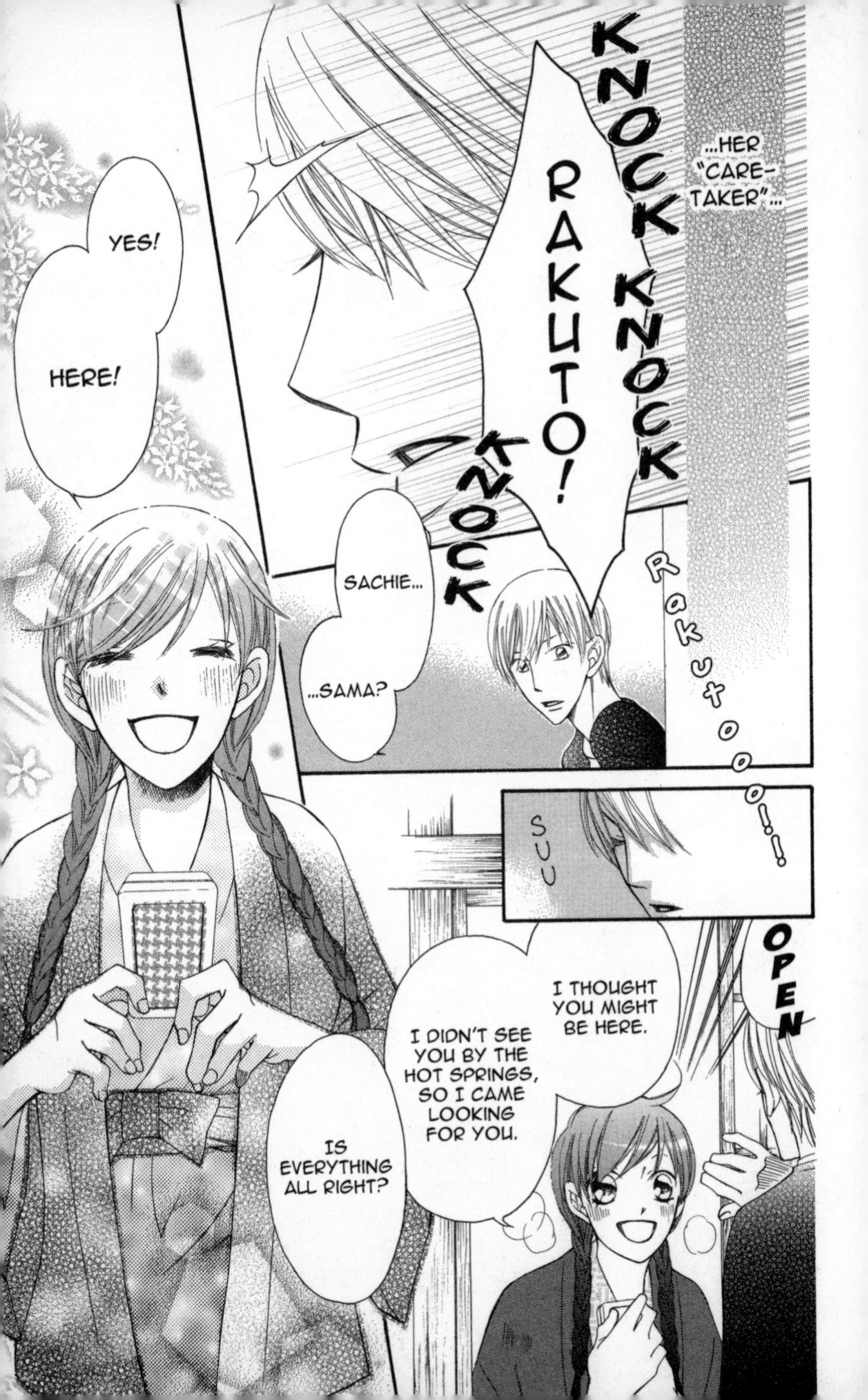
...HER "CARE-TAKER"...
KNOCK KNOCK
RAKUTO!
KNOCK KNOCK
RAKUTOOOO!!!
SACHIE...
...SAMA?
SUU
OPEN
I THOUGHT YOU MIGHT BE HERE.
I DIDN'T SEE YOU BY THE HOT SPRINGS, SO I CAME LOOKING FOR YOU.
IS EVERYTHING ALL RIGHT?
YES!
HERE!

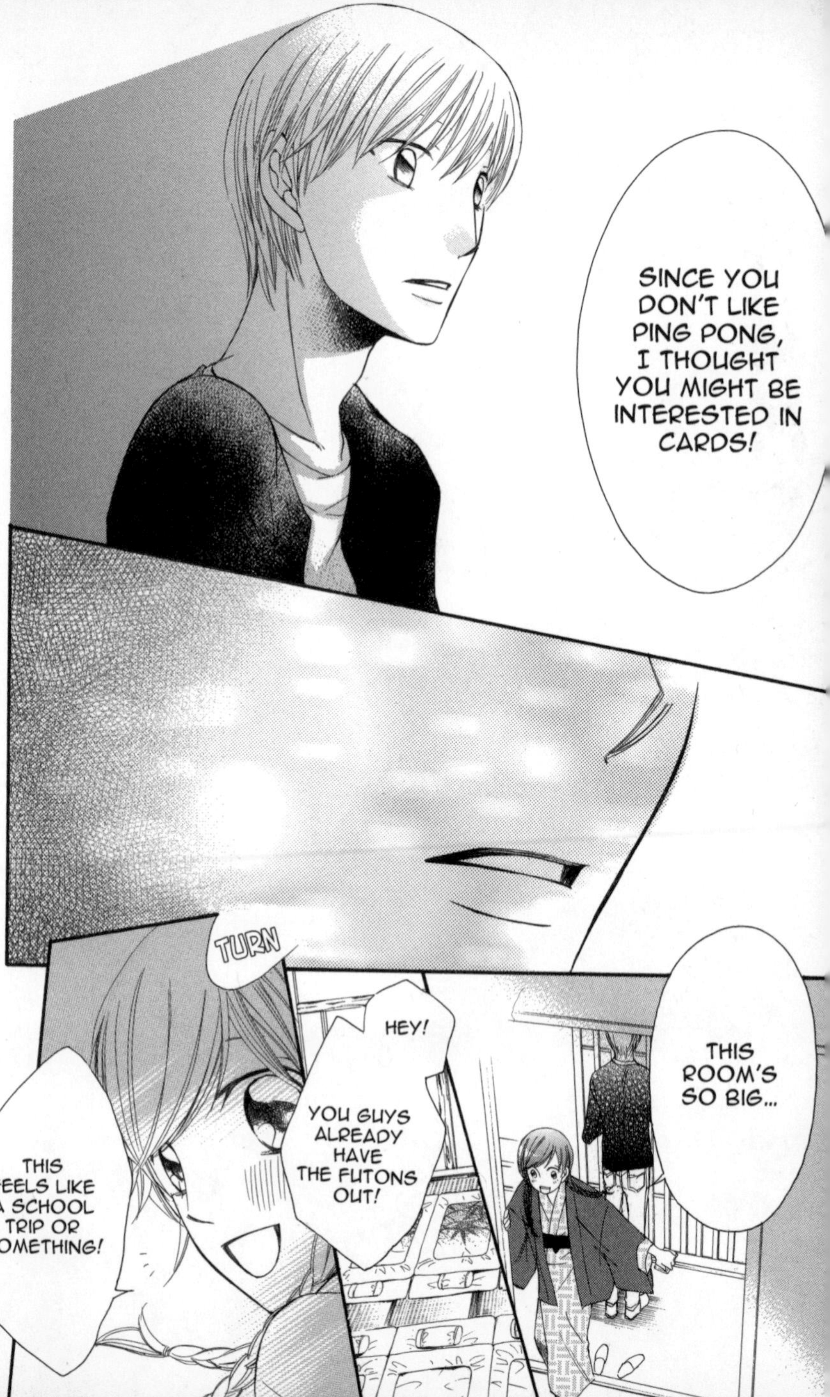
SINCE YOU DON'T LIKE PING PONG, I THOUGHT YOU MIGHT BE INTERESTED IN CARDS!
TURN
THIS ROOM'S SO BIG...
HEY!
YOU GUYS ALREADY HAVE THE FUTONS OUT!
THIS FEELS LIKE A SCHOOL TRIP OR SOMETHING!

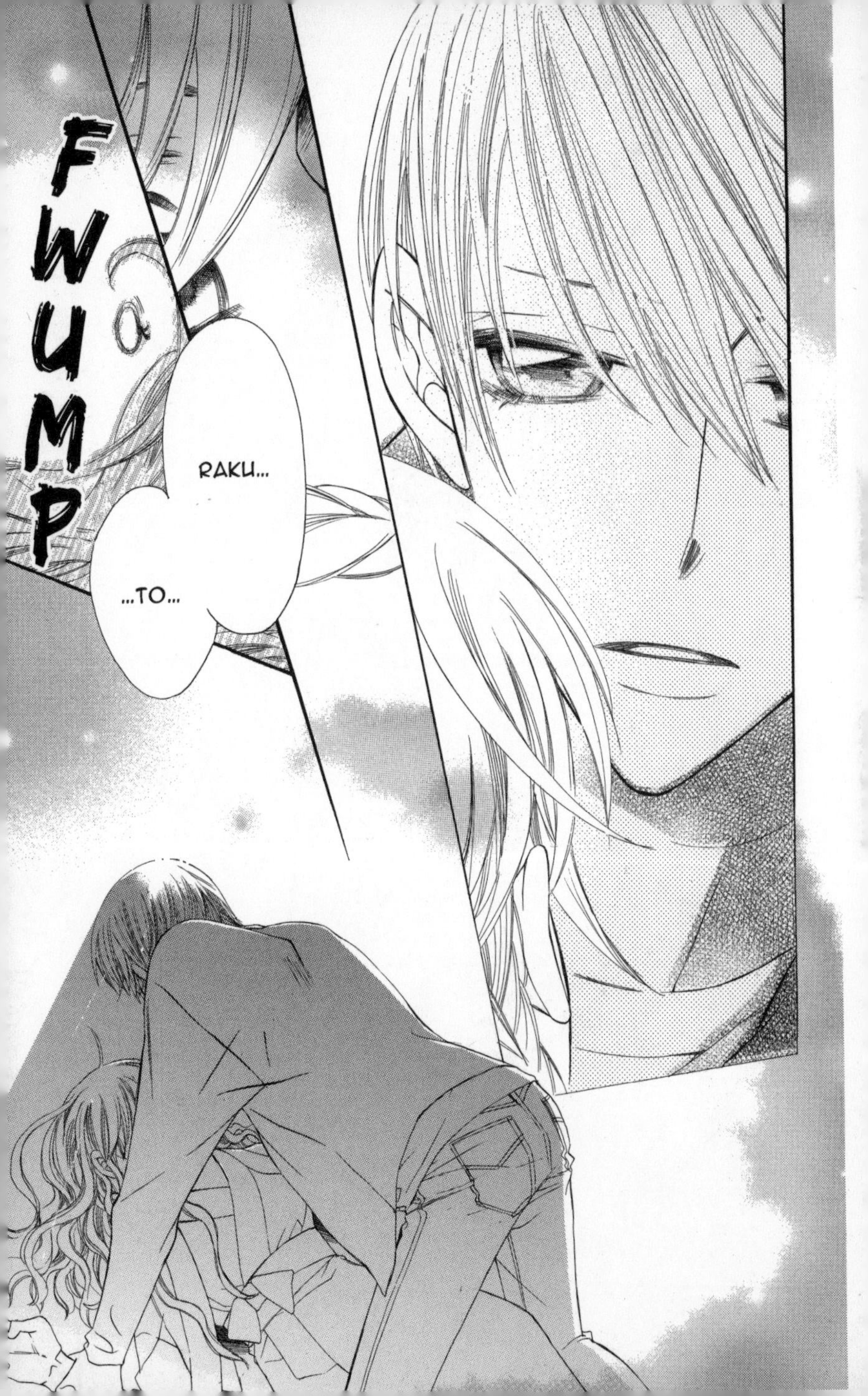
FWUMP
RAKU...
...TO...

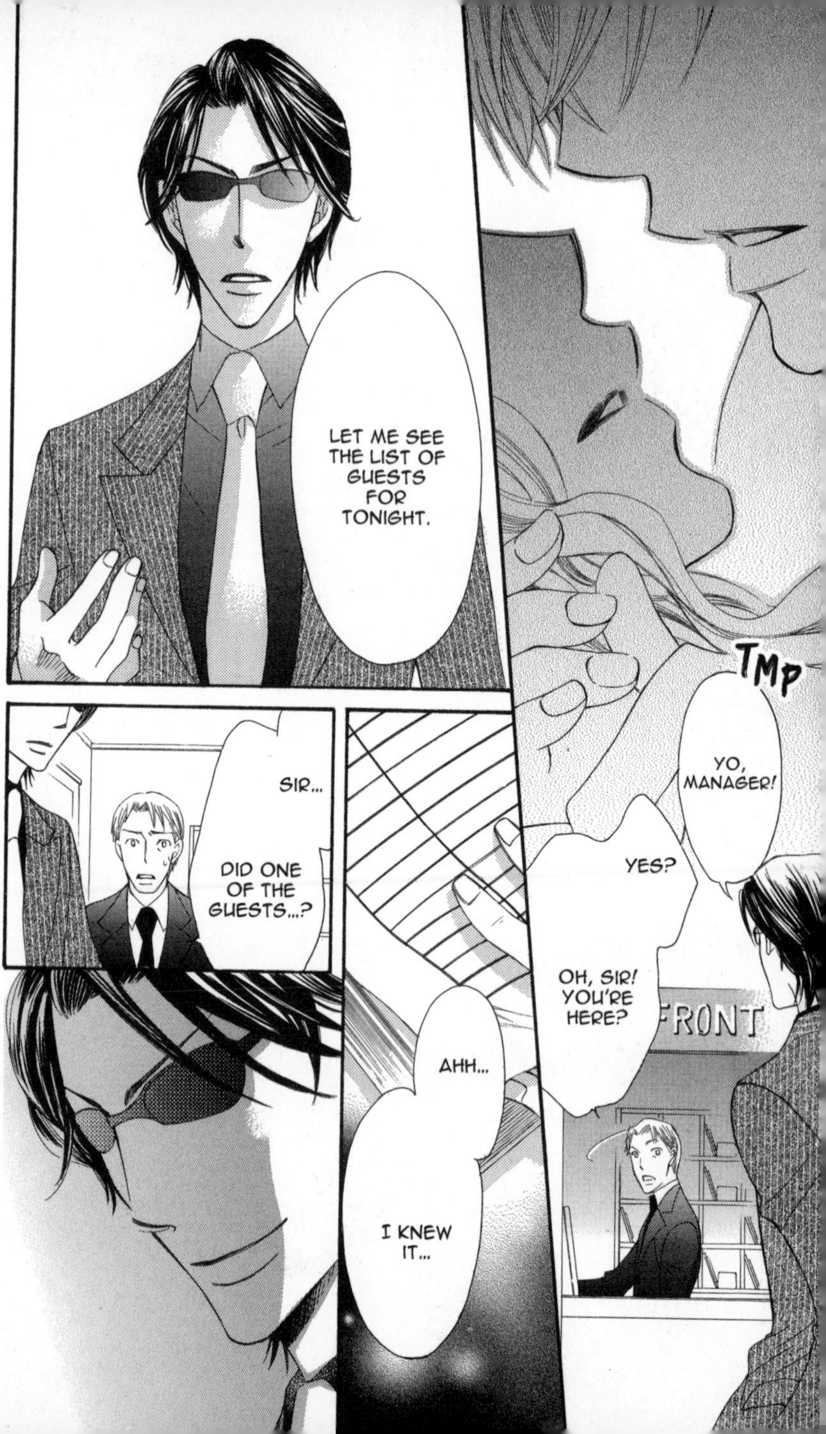
TMP
YO, MANAGER!
YES?
OH, SIR! YOU'RE HERE?
FRONT
LET ME SEE THE LIST OF GUESTS FOR TONIGHT.
SIR...
DID ONE OF THE GUESTS...?
AHH...
I KNEW IT...

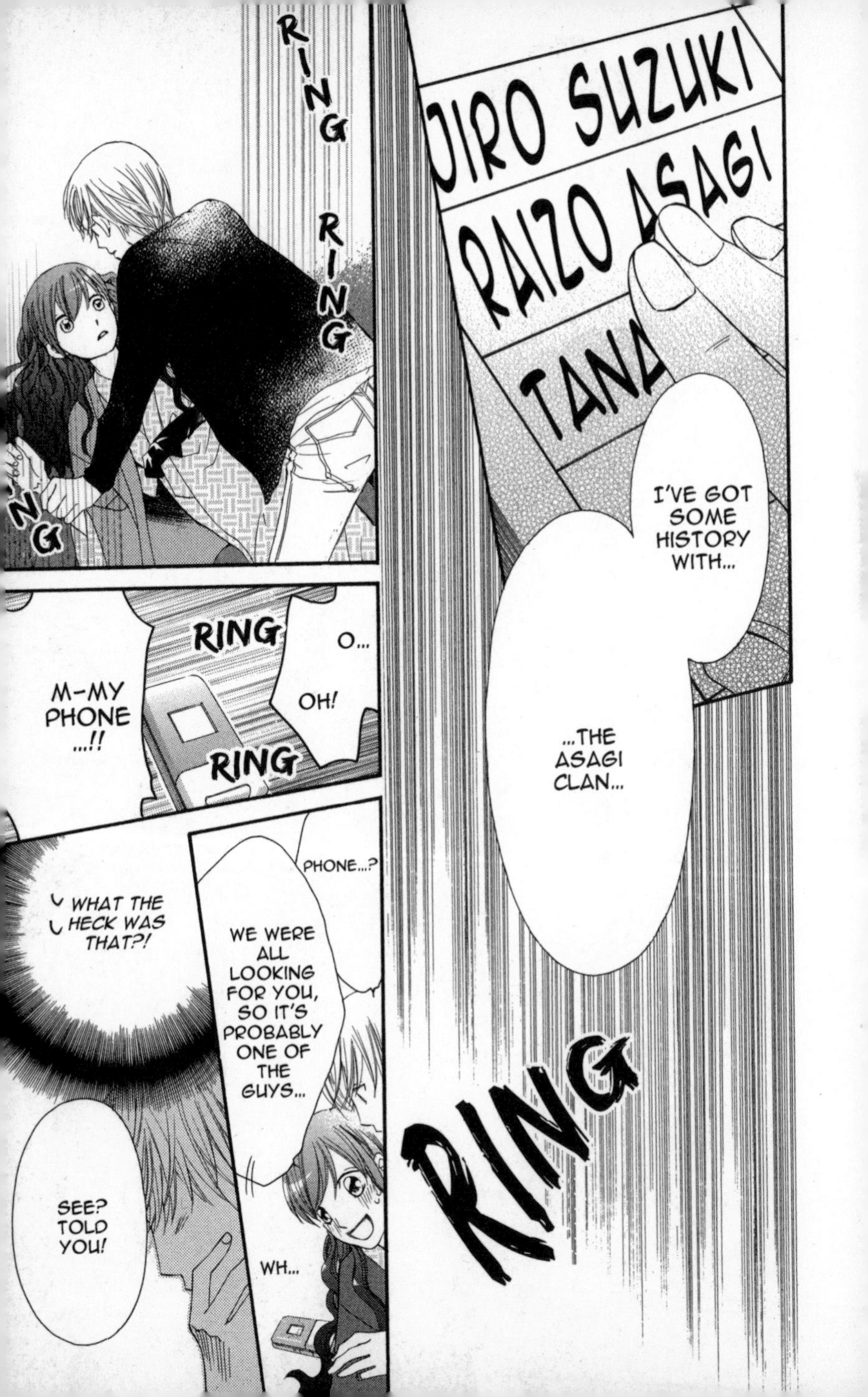
JIRO SUZUKI
RAIZO ASAGI
TANA
I'VE GOT SOME HISTORY WITH...
...THE ASAGI CLAN...
RING
RING
RING
RING
NG
O...
OH!
RING
RING
M-MY PHONE ...!!
PHONE...?
WE WERE ALL LOOKING FOR YOU, SO IT'S PROBABLY ONE OF THE GUYS...
WH...
WHAT THE HECK WAS THAT?!
SEE? TOLD YOU!

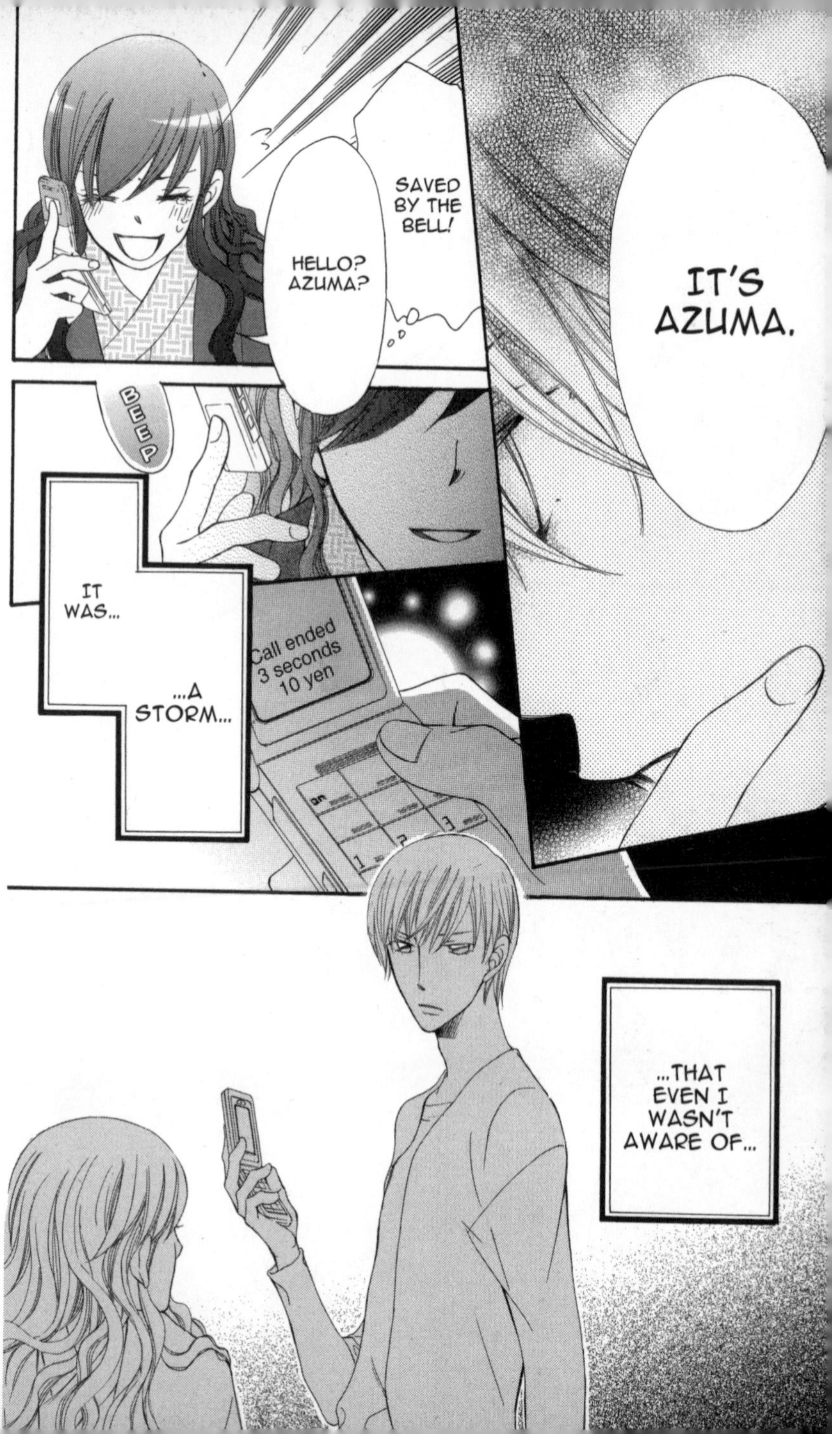
IT'S AZUMA.
SAVED BY THE BELL!
HELLO? AZUMA?
BEEP
IT WAS...
...A STORM...
Call ended
3 seconds
10 yen
...THAT EVEN I WASN'T AWARE OF...

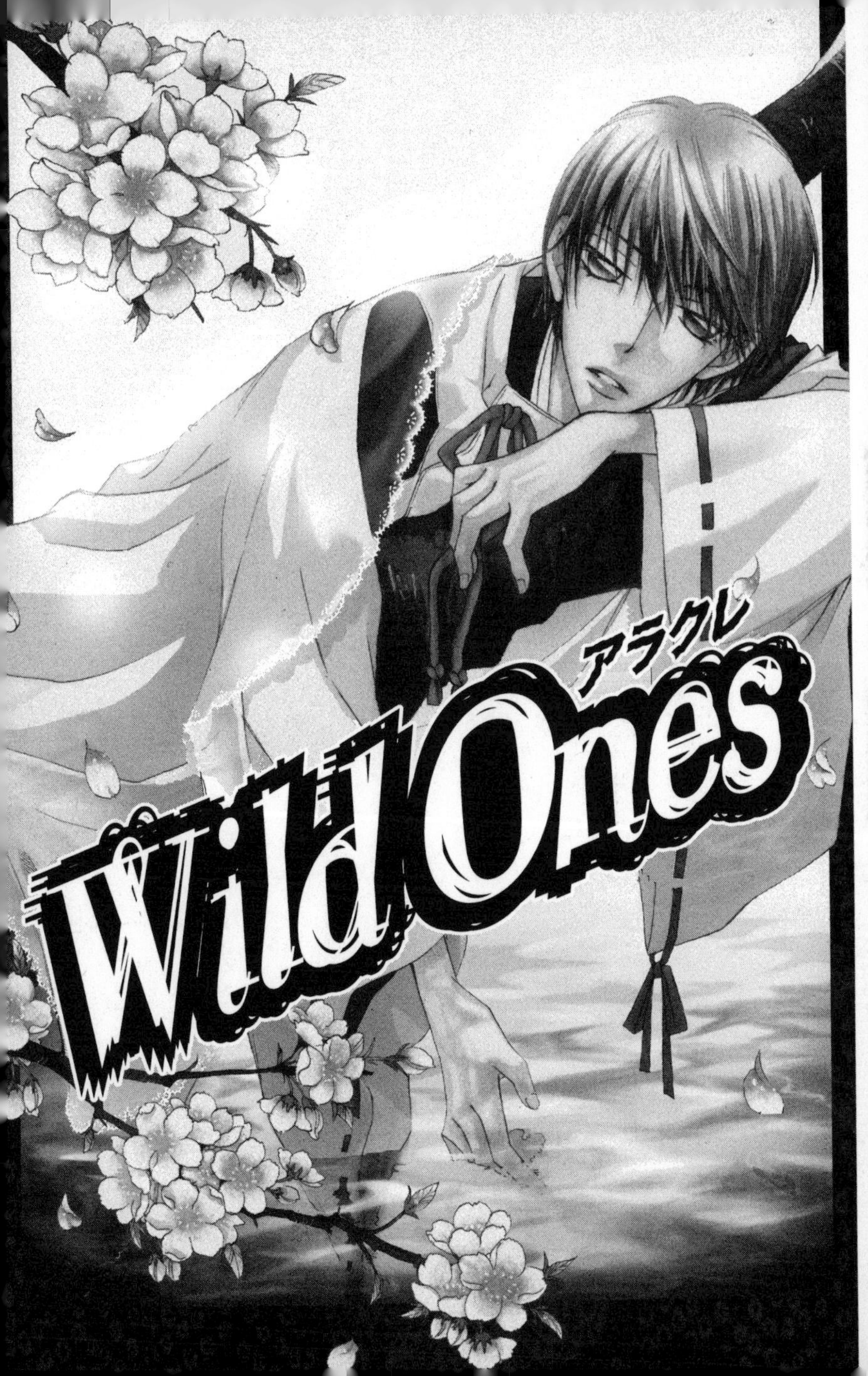
アラクレ
Wild Ones

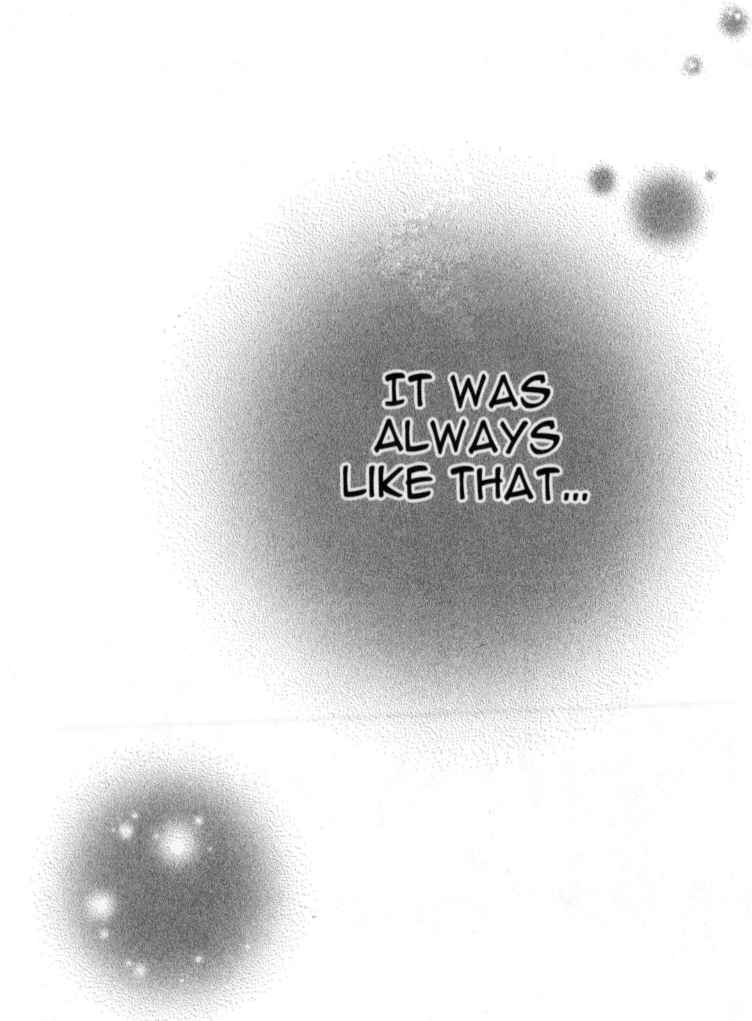
IT WAS ALWAYS LIKE THAT...

DON'T WISH FOR SOMETHING YOU CAN'T HAVE.

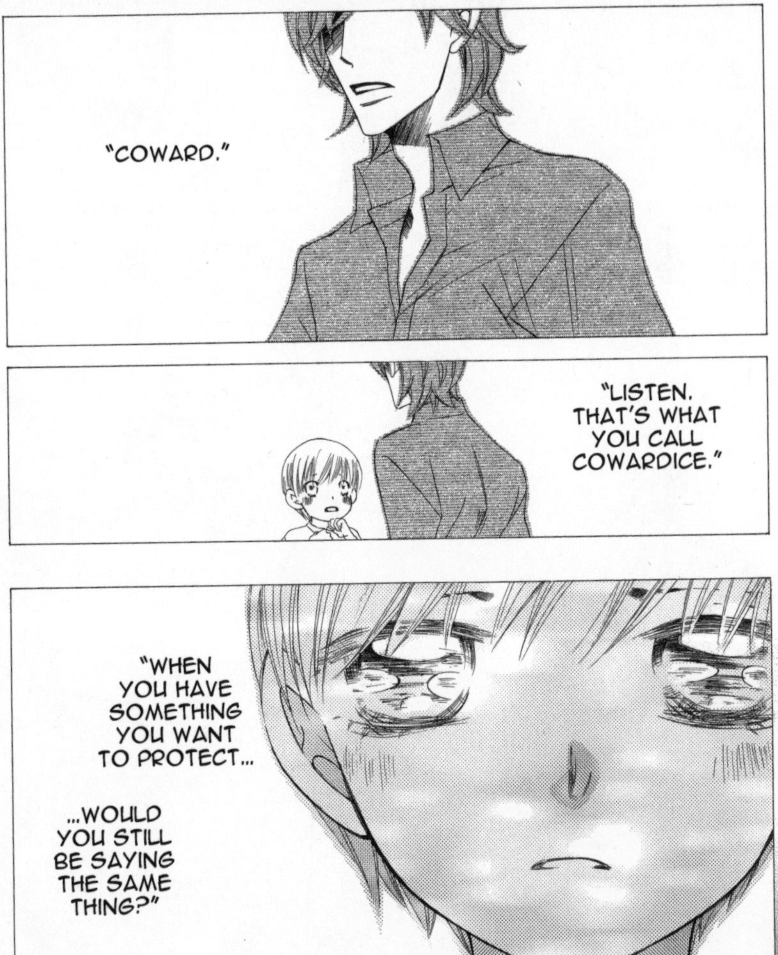

"COWARD."
"LISTEN. THAT'S WHAT YOU CALL COWARDICE."
"WHEN YOU HAVE SOMETHING YOU WANT TO PROTECT...
...WOULD YOU STILL BE SAYING THE SAME THING?"

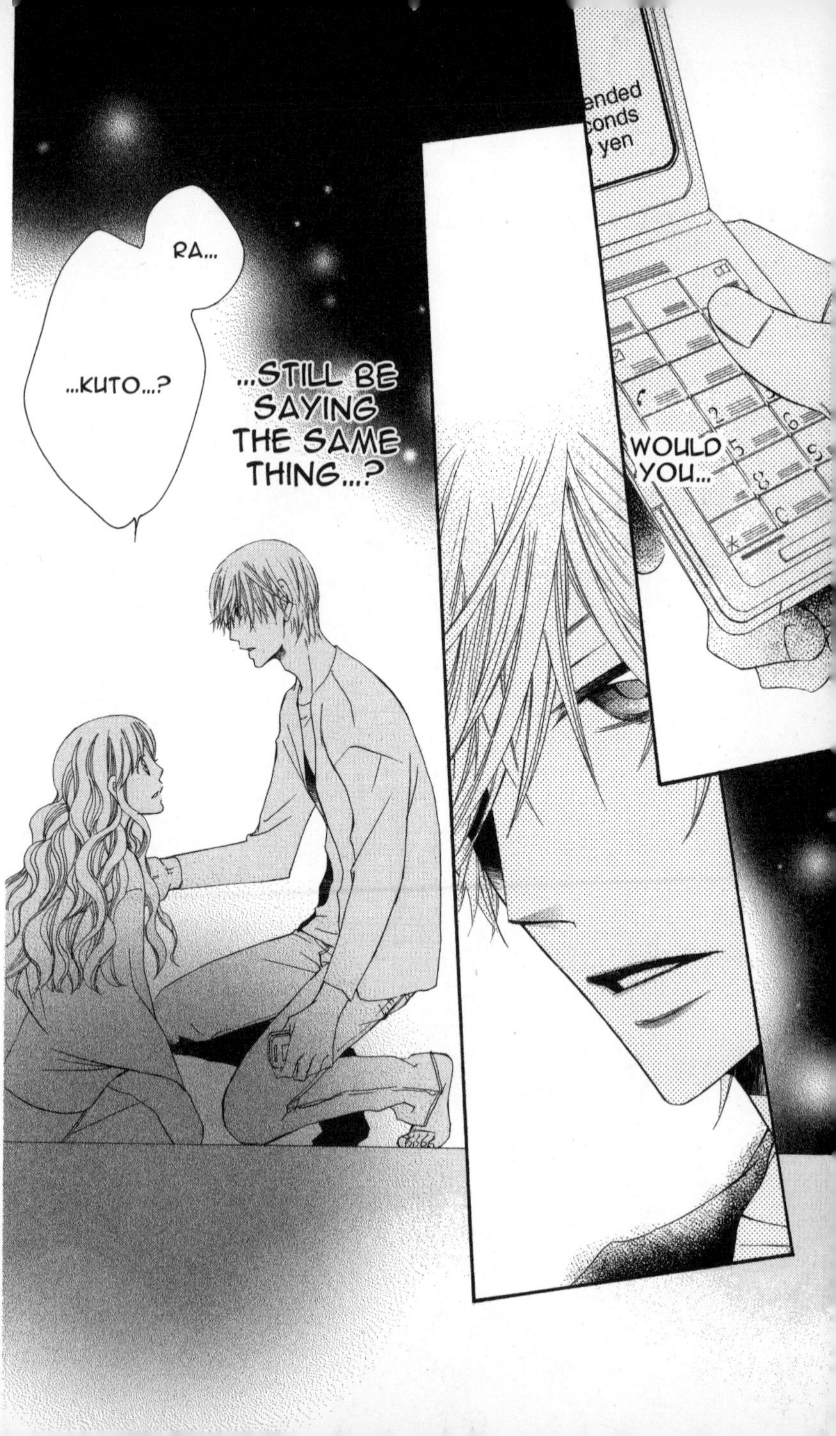
WOULD YOU...
...STILL BE SAYING THE SAME THING...?
RA...
...KUTO...?

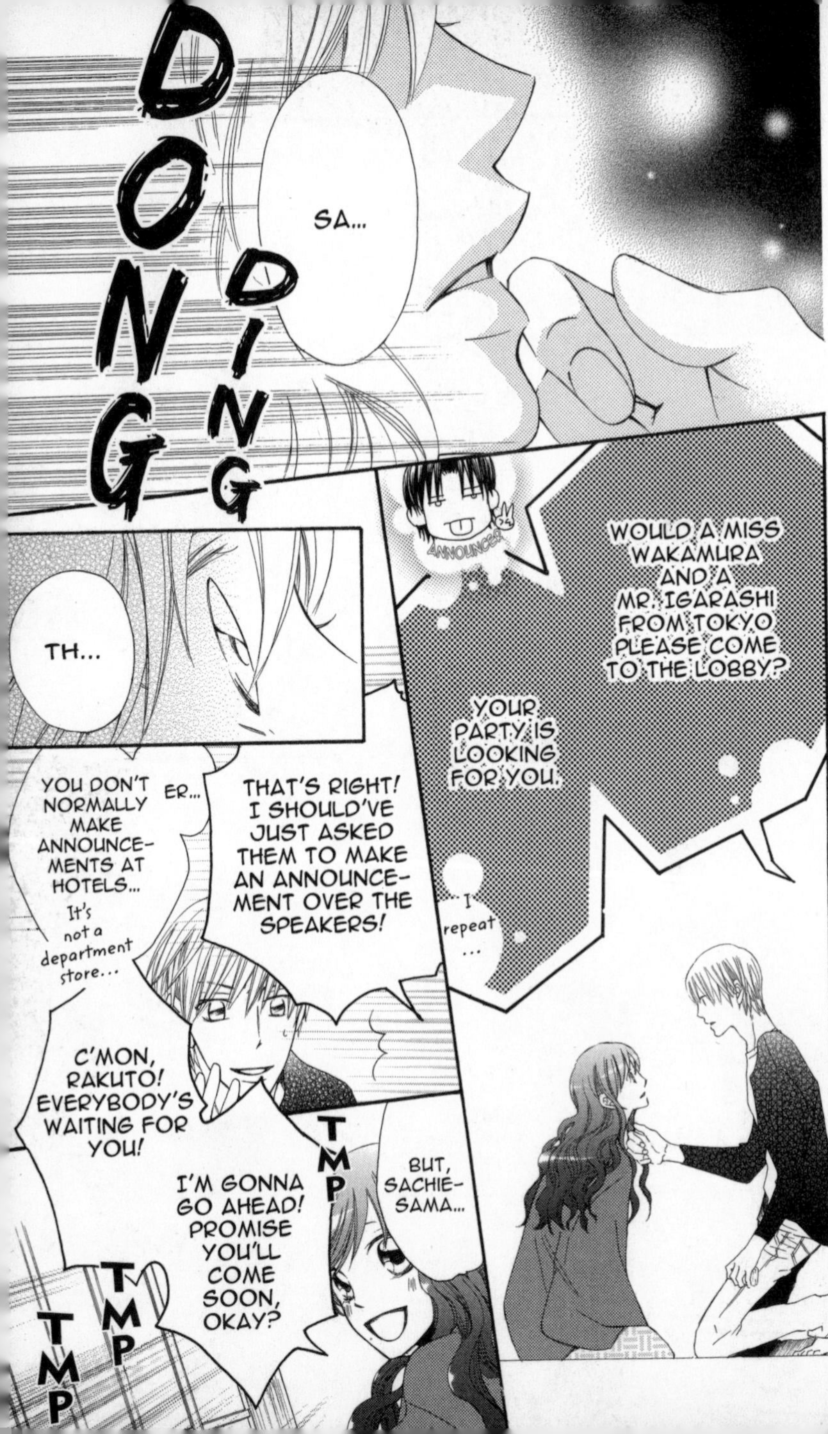
SA...
DING
DONG
ANNOUNCER
WOULD A MISS WAKAMURA AND A MR. IGARASHI FROM TOKYO PLEASE COME TO THE LOBBY?
YOUR PARTY IS LOOKING FOR YOU.
I repeat...
TH...
THAT'S RIGHT! I SHOULD'VE JUST ASKED THEM TO MAKE AN ANNOUNCEMENT OVER THE SPEAKERS!
ER...
YOU DON'T NORMALLY MAKE ANNOUNCEMENTS AT HOTELS...
It's not a department store...
C'MON, RAKUTO! EVERYBODY'S WAITING FOR YOU!
BUT, SACHIE-SAMA...
TMP
I'M GONNA GO AHEAD! PROMISE YOU'LL COME SOON, OKAY?
TMP
TMP

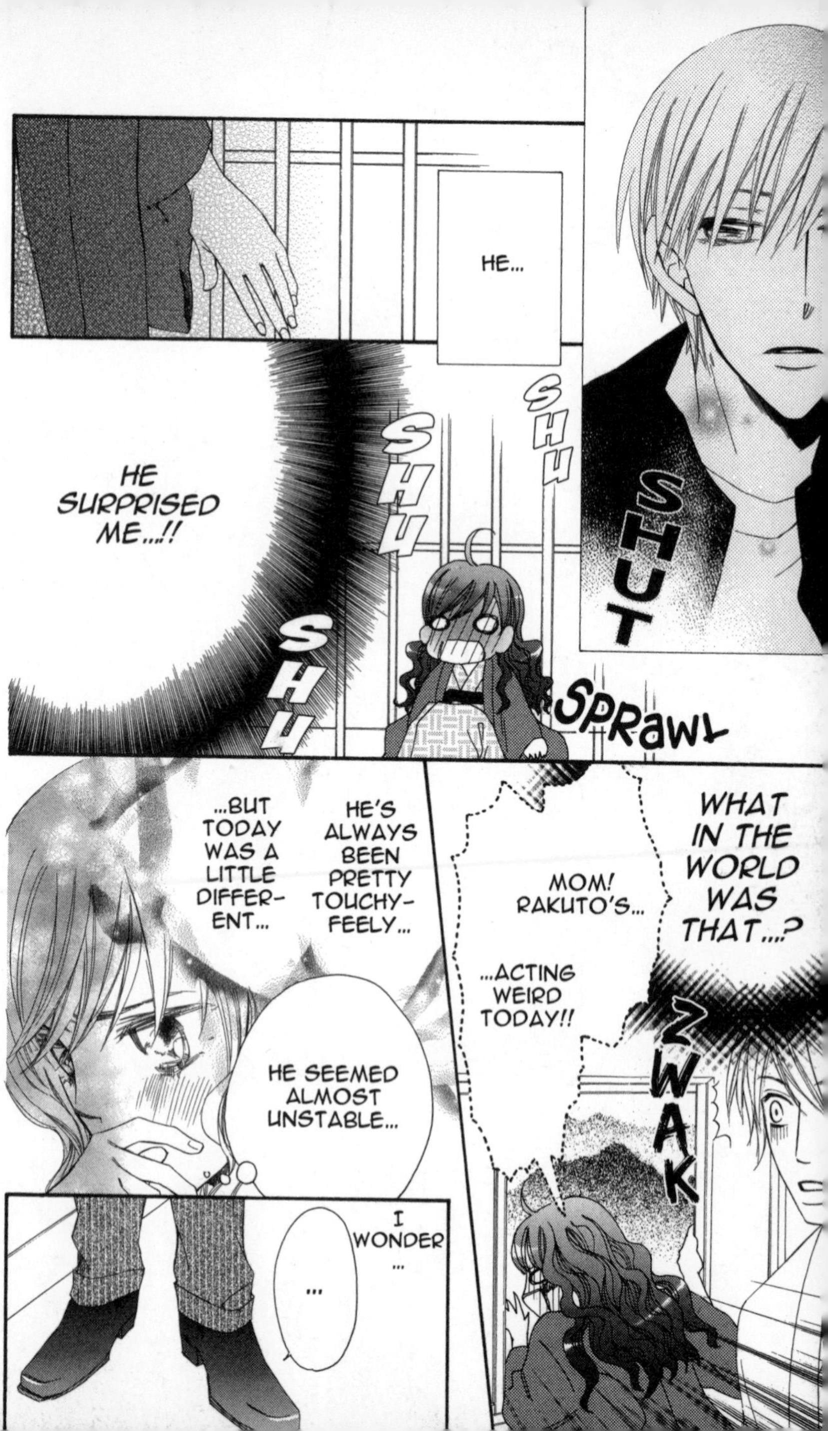

HE...
SHUT
SHU
SHU
SHU
SHU
HE SURPRISED ME...!!
SPRAWL
WHAT IN THE WORLD WAS THAT...?
MOM! RAKUTO'S...
...ACTING WEIRD TODAY!!
ZWAK
HE'S ALWAYS BEEN PRETTY TOUCHY-FEELY...
...BUT TODAY WAS A LITTLE DIFFER-ENT...
HE SEEMED ALMOST UNSTABLE...
I WONDER...
...

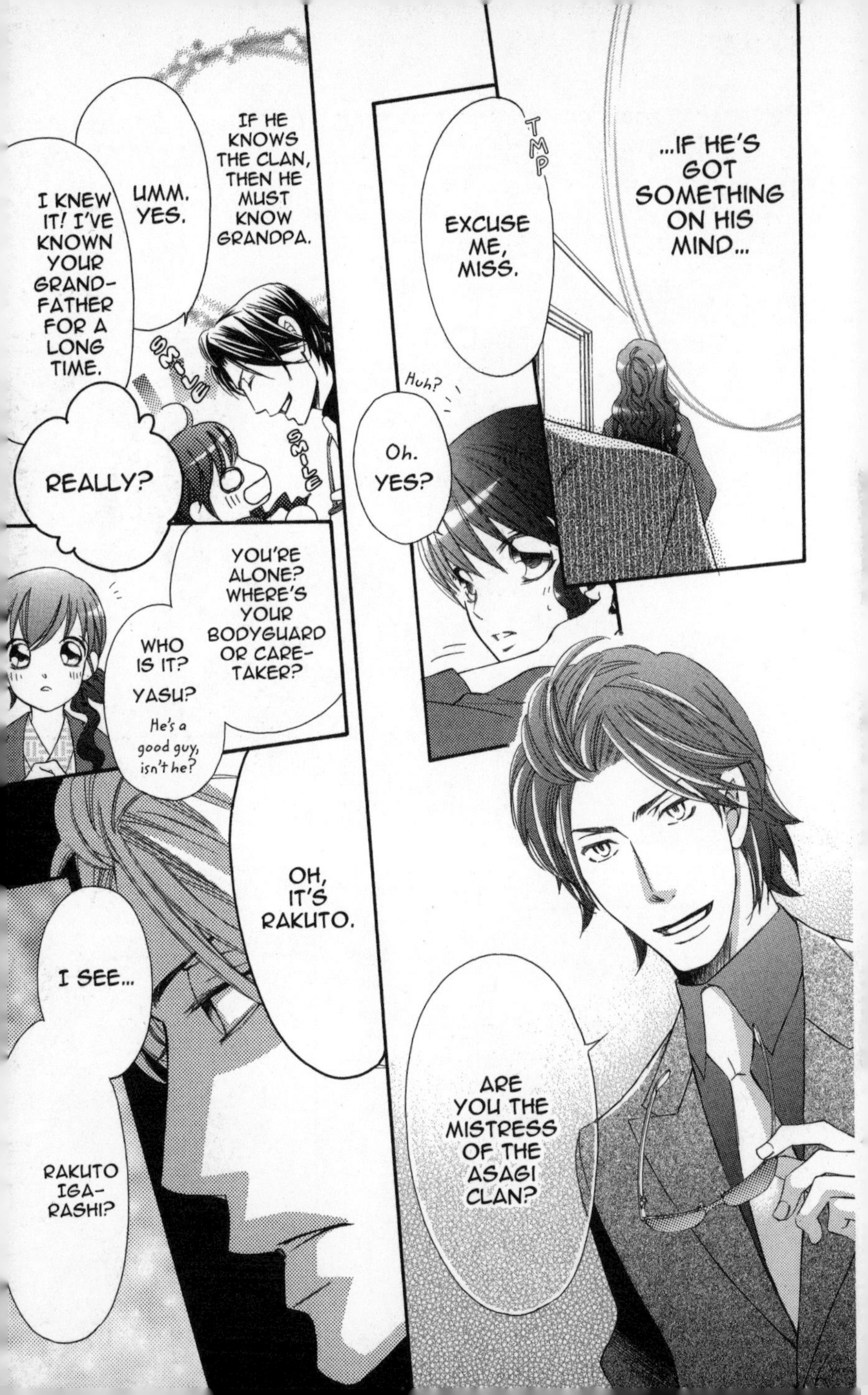

...IF HE'S GOT SOMETHING ON HIS MIND...
TMP
EXCUSE ME, MISS.
Huh?
Oh. YES?
ARE YOU THE MISTRESS OF THE ASAGI CLAN?
IF HE KNOWS THE CLAN, THEN HE MUST KNOW GRANDPA.
UMM. YES.
I KNEW IT! I'VE KNOWN YOUR GRANDFATHER FOR A LONG TIME.
SMILE
SMILE
REALLY?
YOU'RE ALONE? WHERE'S YOUR BODYGUARD OR CARETAKER?
WHO IS IT? YASU?
He's a good guy, isn't he?
OH, IT'S RAKUTO.
I SEE...
RAKUTO IGARASHI?

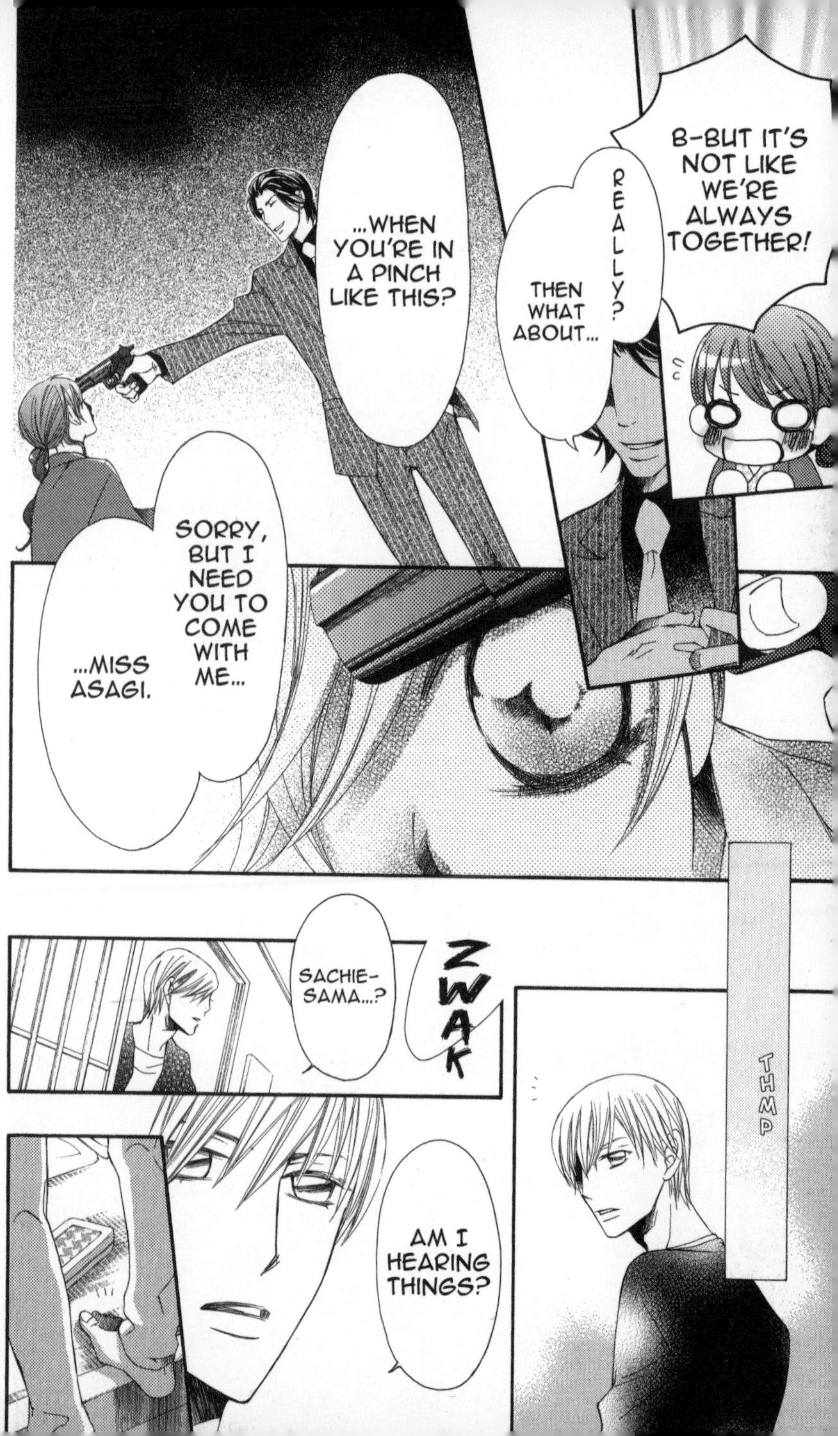
B-BUT IT'S NOT LIKE WE'RE ALWAYS TOGETHER!
REALLY?
THEN WHAT ABOUT...
...WHEN YOU'RE IN A PINCH LIKE THIS?
SORRY, BUT I NEED YOU TO COME WITH ME...
...MISS ASAGI.
THMP
SACHIE-SAMA...?
ZWAK
AM I HEARING THINGS?

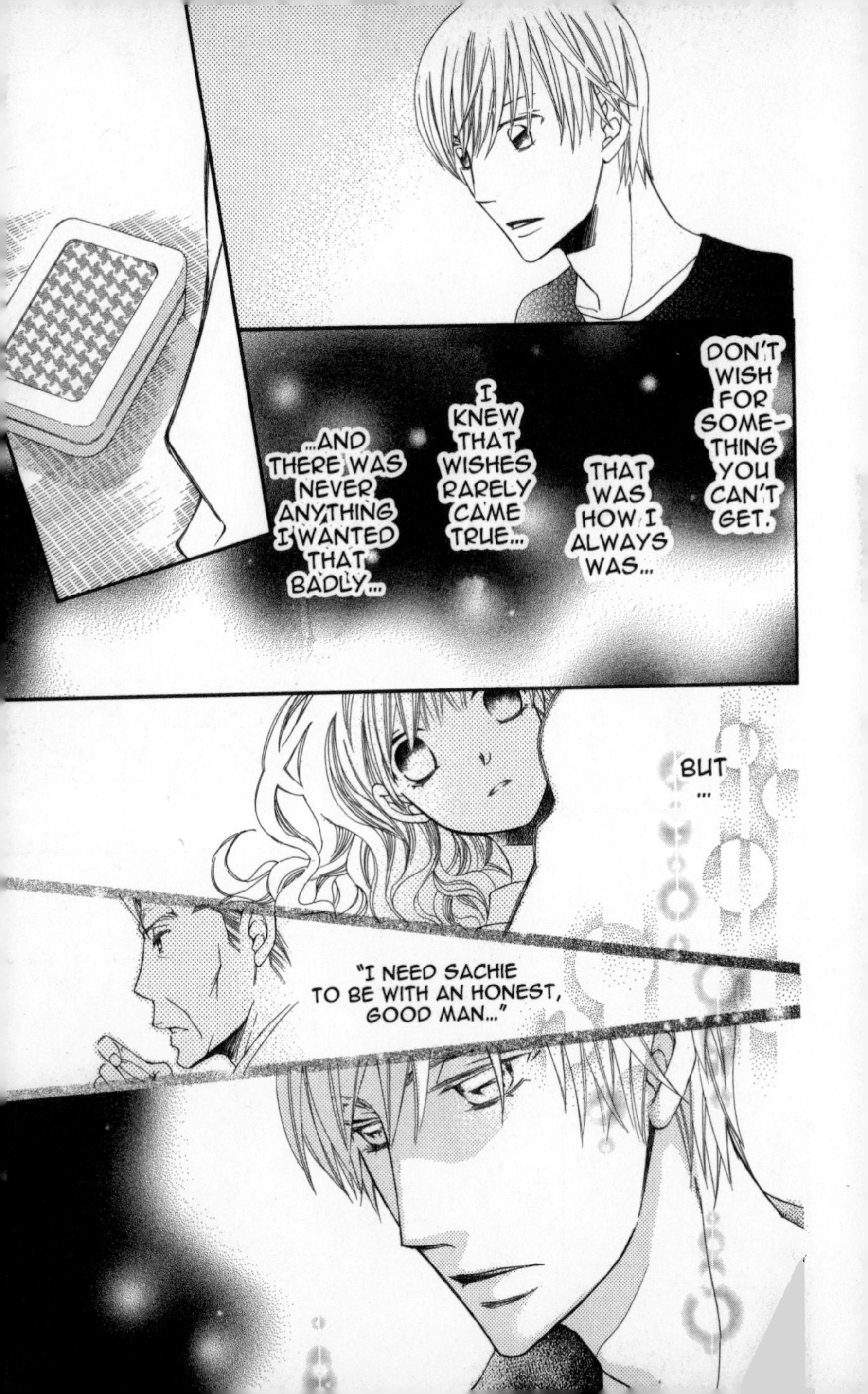
DON'T WISH FOR SOME-THING YOU CAN'T GET.
THAT WAS HOW I ALWAYS WAS...
I KNEW THAT WISHES RARELY CAME TRUE...
...AND THERE WAS NEVER ANYTHING I WANTED THAT BADLY...
BUT ...
"I NEED SACHIE TO BE WITH AN HONEST, GOOD MAN..."

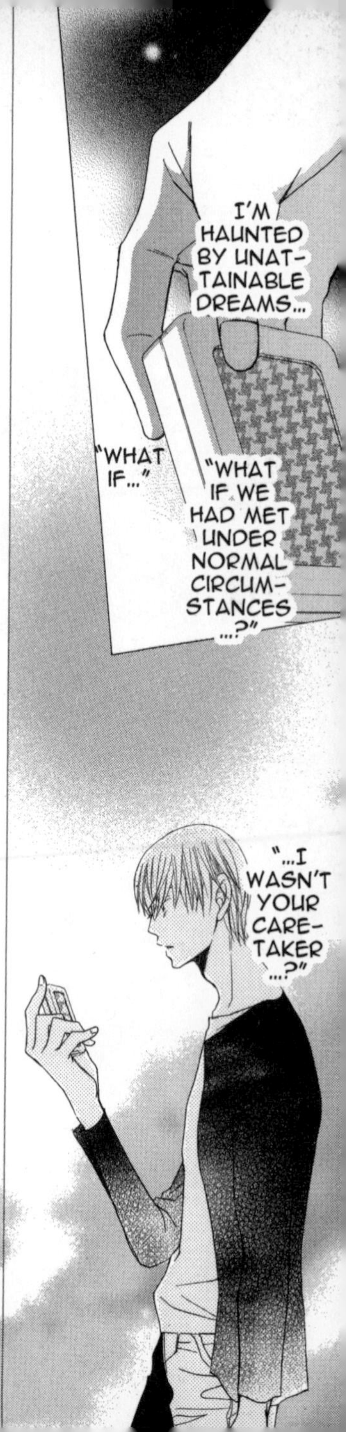
I'M HAUNTED BY UNAT-TAINABLE DREAMS...
"WHAT IF WE HAD MET UNDER NORMAL CIRCUM-STANCES ...?"
"WHAT IF..."
"...I WASN'T YOUR CARE-TAKER ...?"
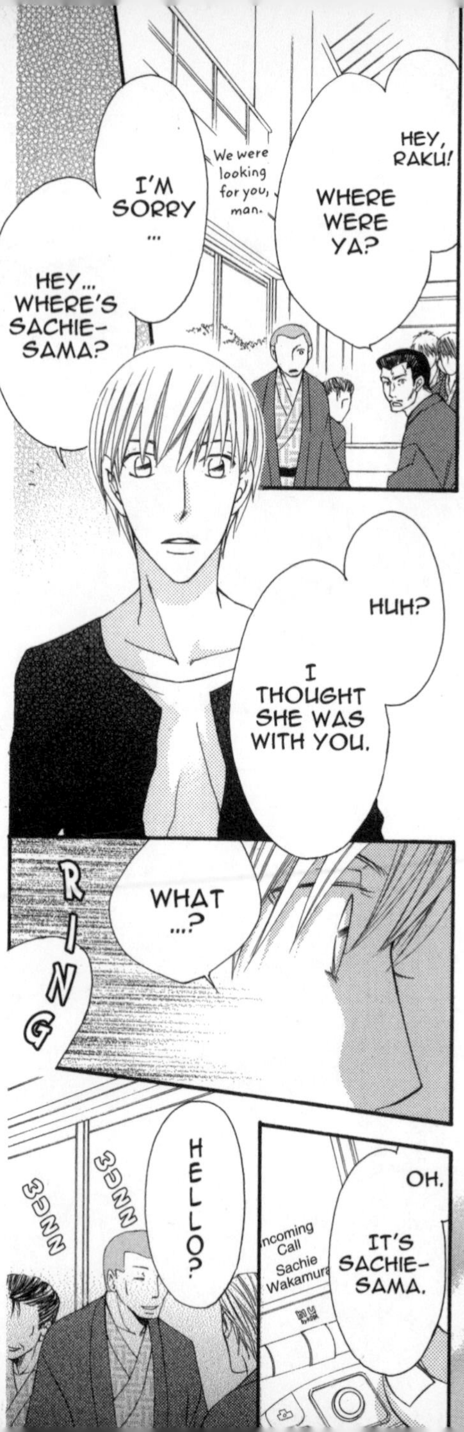
HEY, RAKU!
WHERE WERE YA?
We were looking for you, man.
I'M SORRY ...
HEY... WHERE'S SACHIE-SAMA?
HUH?
I THOUGHT SHE WAS WITH YOU.
WHAT ...?
RING
OH.
IT'S SACHIE-SAMA.
ncoming Call
Sachie Wakamura
HELLO?

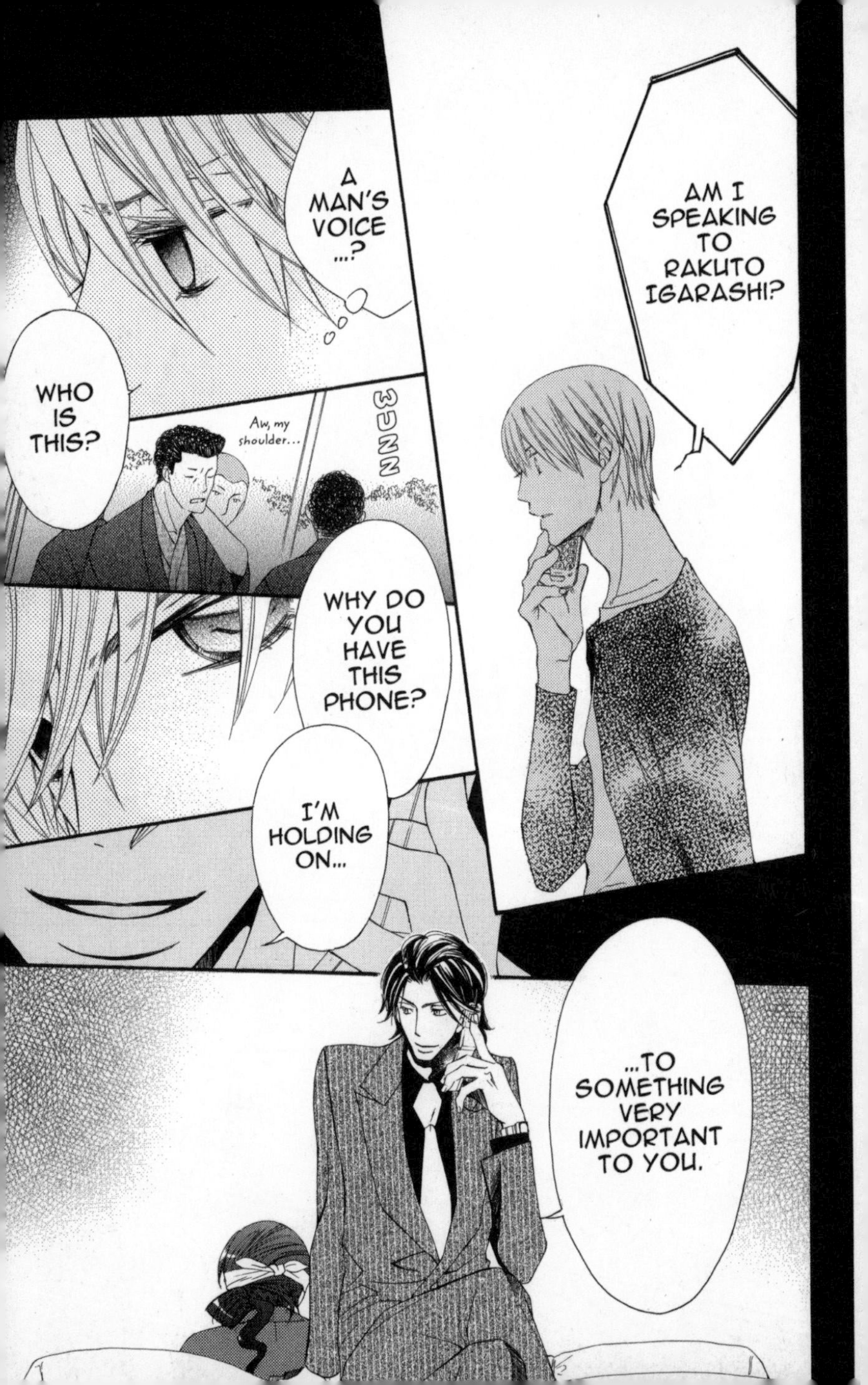
AM I SPEAKING TO RAKUTO IGARASHI?
A MAN'S VOICE ...?
WHO IS THIS?
BUZZ
Aw, my shoulder...
WHY DO YOU HAVE THIS PHONE?
I'M HOLDING ON...
...TO SOMETHING VERY IMPORTANT TO YOU.

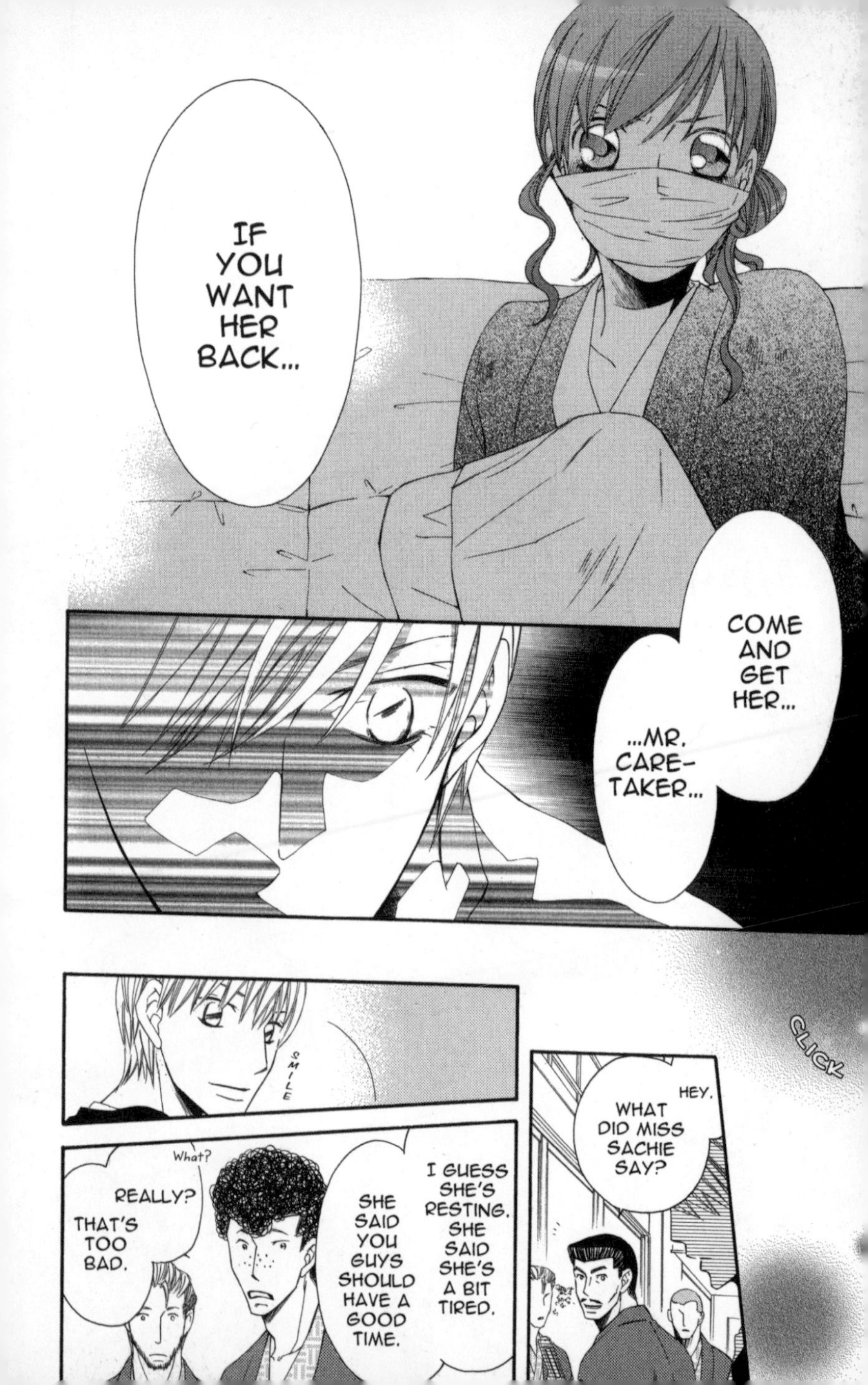
IF YOU WANT HER BACK...
COME AND GET HER...
...MR. CARETAKER...
CLICK
HEY.
WHAT DID MISS SACHIE SAY?
SMILE
I GUESS SHE'S RESTING. SHE SAID SHE'S A BIT TIRED.
SHE SAID YOU GUYS SHOULD HAVE A GOOD TIME.
What?
REALLY?
THAT'S TOO BAD.

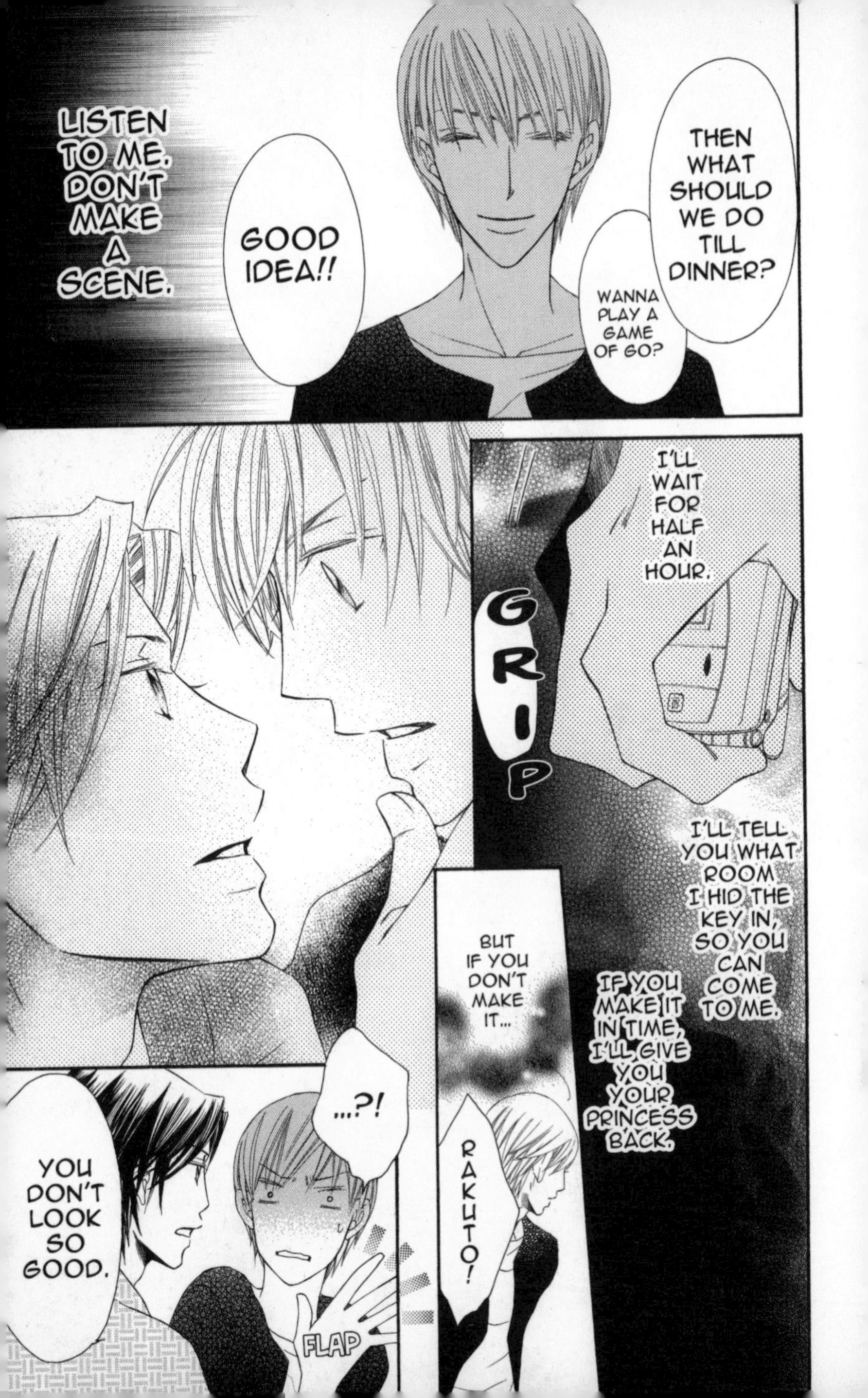
THEN WHAT SHOULD WE DO TILL DINNER?
WANNA PLAY A GAME OF GO?
GOOD IDEA!!
LISTEN TO ME. DON'T MAKE A SCENE.
I'LL WAIT FOR HALF AN HOUR.
GRIP
I'LL TELL YOU WHAT ROOM I HID THE KEY IN, SO YOU CAN COME TO ME.
IF YOU MAKE IT IN TIME, I'LL GIVE YOU YOUR PRINCESS BACK.
BUT IF YOU DON'T MAKE IT...
RAKUTO!
...?!
YOU DON'T LOOK SO GOOD.
FLAP

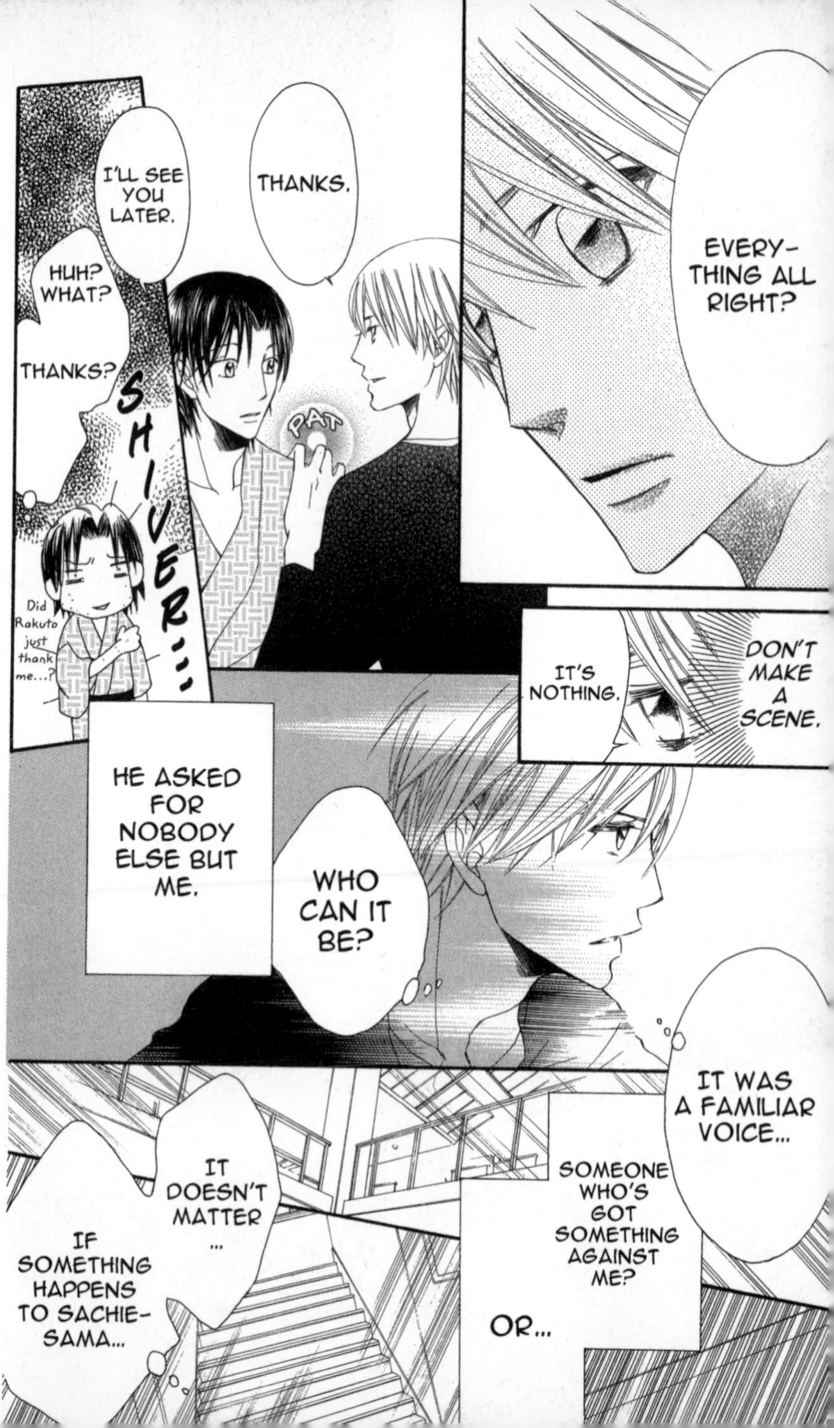
EVERY-THING ALL RIGHT?
THANKS.
PAT
I'LL SEE YOU LATER.
HUH? WHAT?
THANKS?
SHIVER...
Did Rakuto just thank me...?
DON'T MAKE A SCENE.
IT'S NOTHING.
WHO CAN IT BE?
HE ASKED FOR NOBODY ELSE BUT ME.
IT WAS A FAMILIAR VOICE...
SOMEONE WHO'S GOT SOMETHING AGAINST ME?
OR...
IT DOESN'T MATTER...
IF SOMETHING HAPPENS TO SACHIE-SAMA...

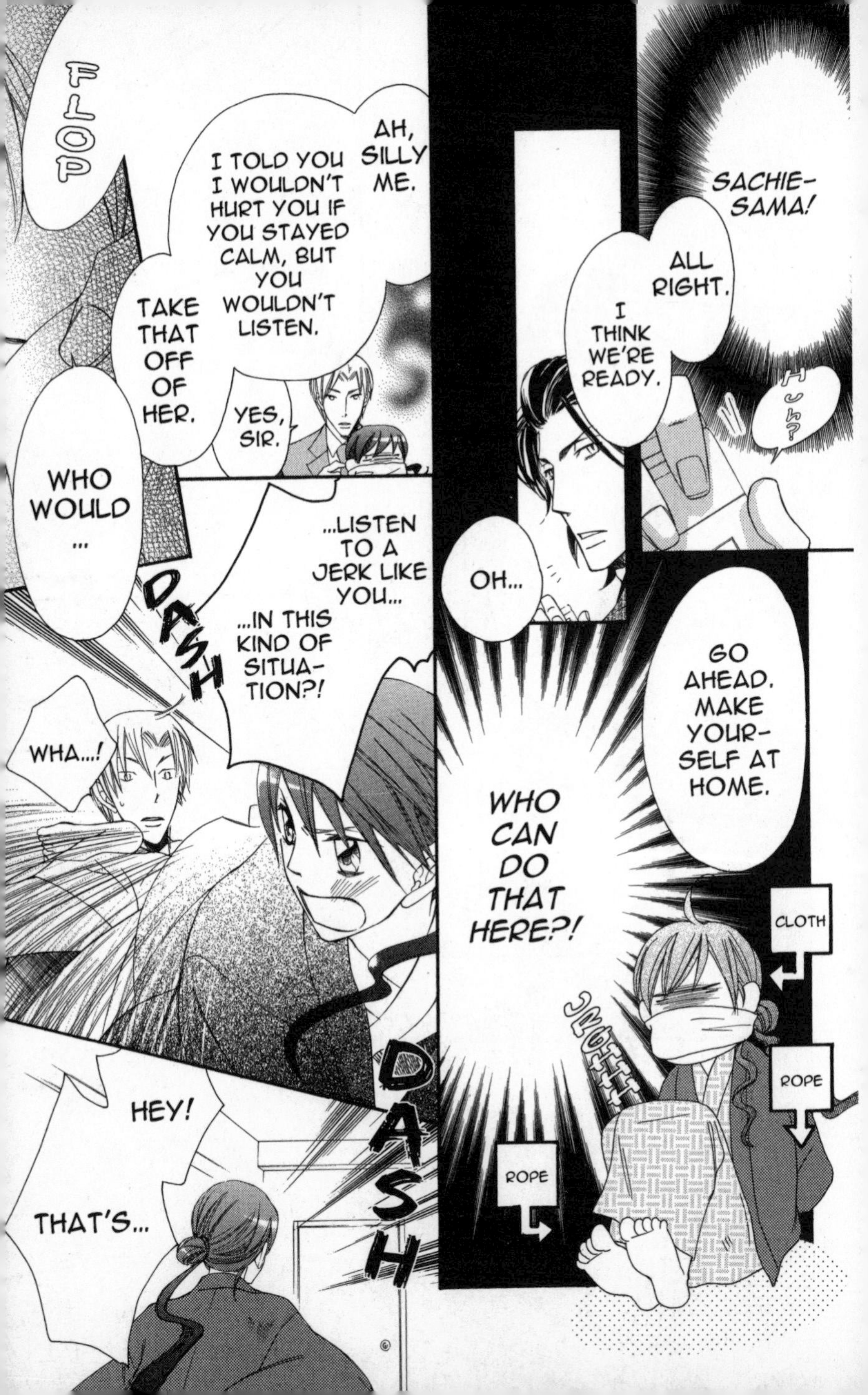
SACHIE-SAMA!
Huh?
ALL RIGHT.
I THINK WE'RE READY.
OH...
GO AHEAD. MAKE YOURSELF AT HOME.
WHO CAN DO THAT HERE?!
CLOTH
ROPE
ROPE
AH, SILLY ME.
I TOLD YOU I WOULDN'T HURT YOU IF YOU STAYED CALM, BUT YOU WOULDN'T LISTEN.
TAKE THAT OFF OF HER.
YES, SIR.
FLOP
WHO WOULD...
...LISTEN TO A JERK LIKE YOU...
...IN THIS KIND OF SITUATION?!
DASH
WHA...!
DASH
HEY!
THAT'S...

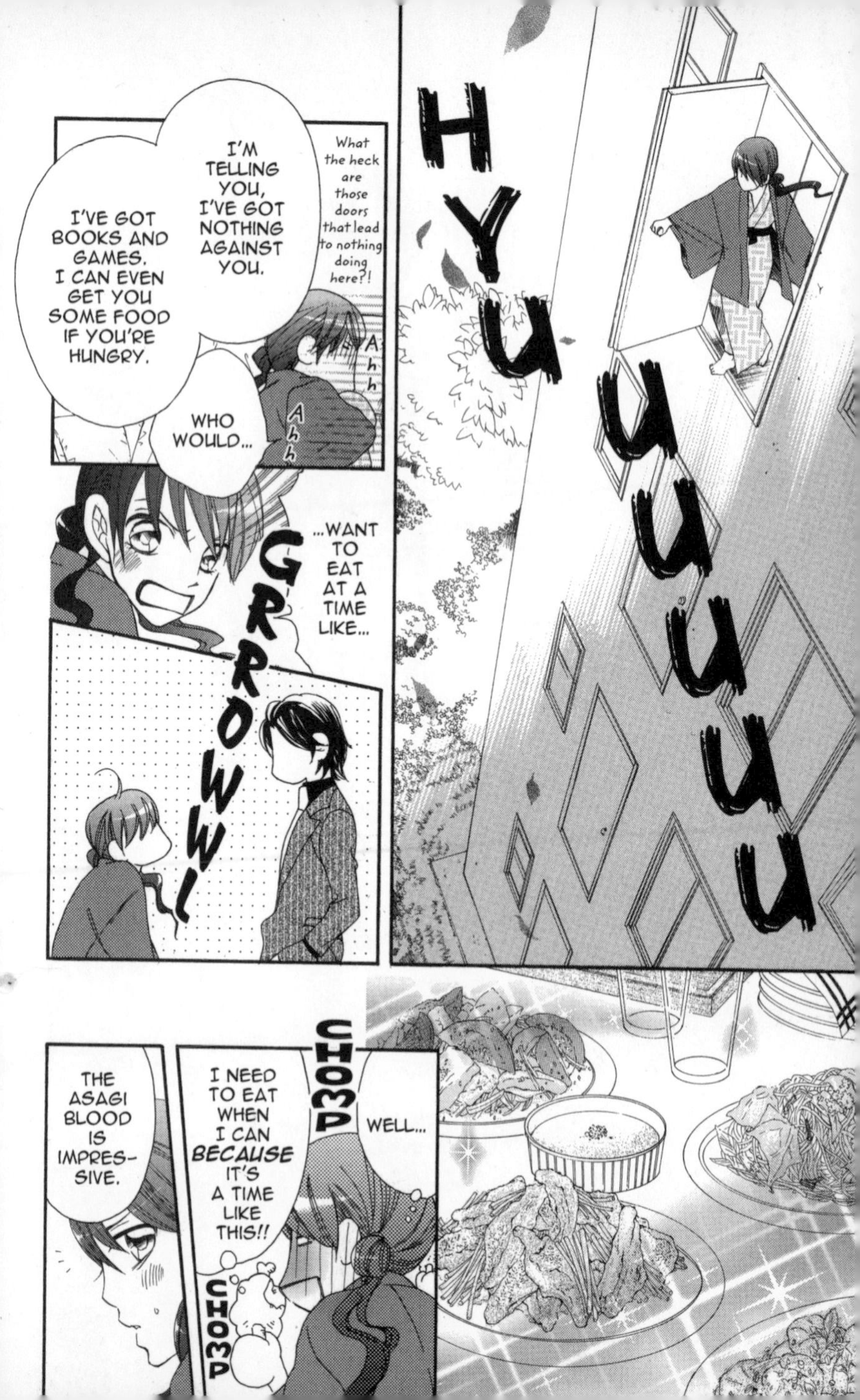
HYUUUUUUU
What the heck are those doors that lead to nothing doing here?!
I'M TELLING YOU, I'VE GOT NOTHING AGAINST YOU.
I'VE GOT BOOKS AND GAMES. I CAN EVEN GET YOU SOME FOOD IF YOU'RE HUNGRY.
Ahh
Ahh
WHO WOULD...
...WANT TO EAT AT A TIME LIKE...
GRROWWL
WELL...
CHOMP
I NEED TO EAT WHEN I CAN *BECAUSE* IT'S A TIME LIKE THIS!!
CHOMP
THE ASAGI BLOOD IS IMPRESSIVE.

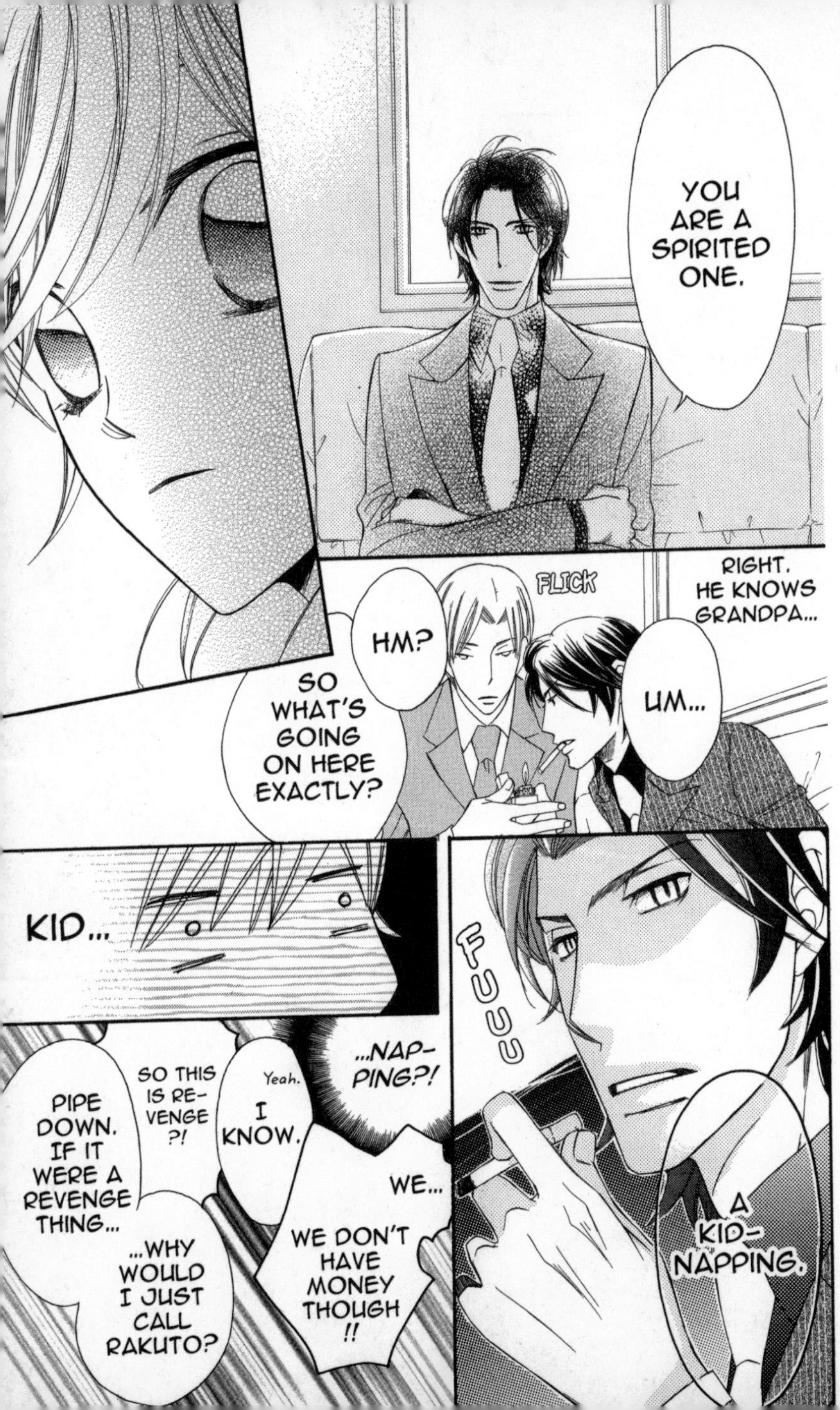
YOU ARE A SPIRITED ONE.
RIGHT. HE KNOWS GRANDPA...
UM...
FLICK
HM?
SO WHAT'S GOING ON HERE EXACTLY?
FUUUU
A KID-NAPPING.
KID...
...NAP-PING?!
Yeah.
I KNOW.
WE...
WE DON'T HAVE MONEY THOUGH!!
SO THIS IS RE-VENGE?!
PIPE DOWN. IF IT WERE A REVENGE THING...
...WHY WOULD I JUST CALL RAKUTO?

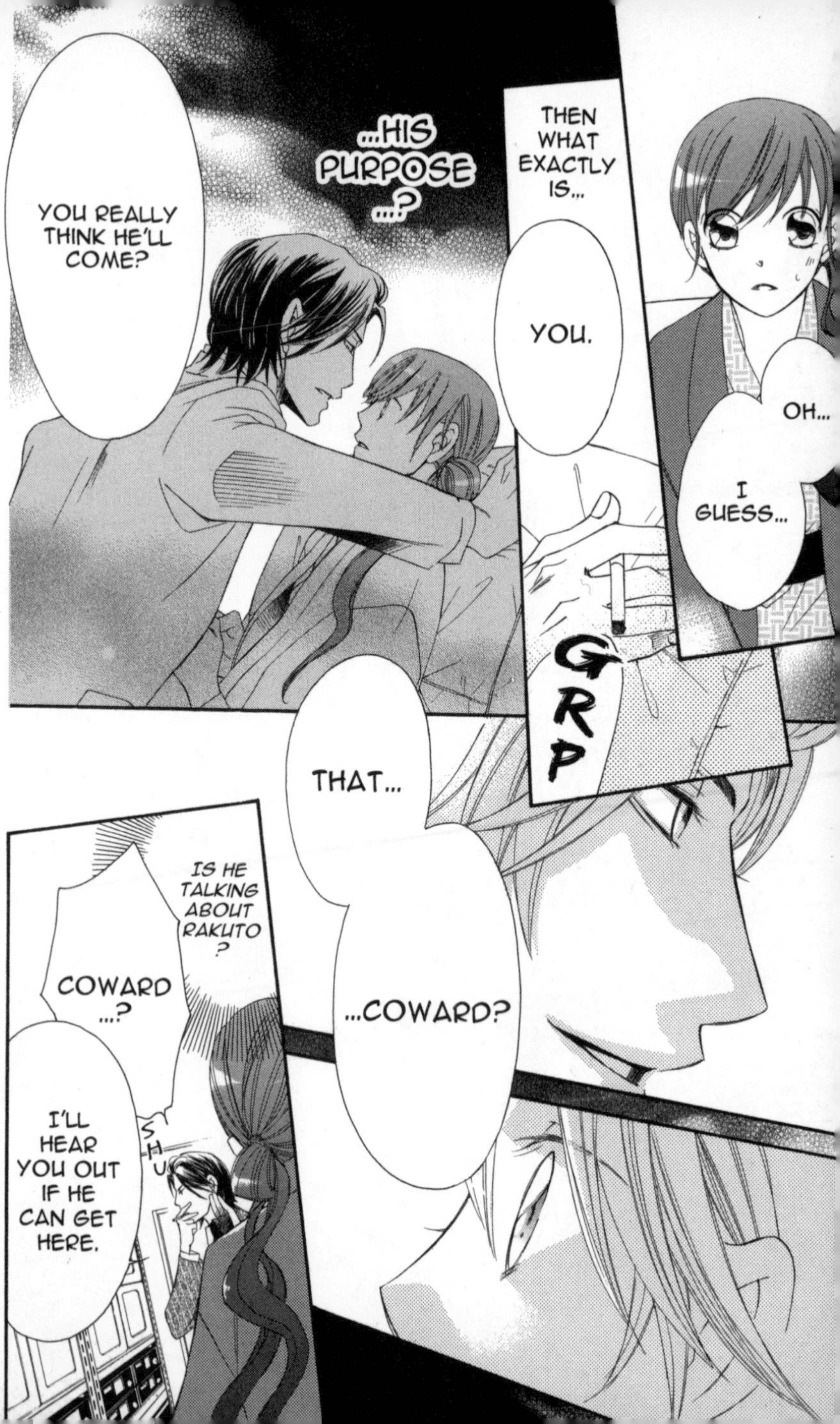
OH... I GUESS...
THEN WHAT EXACTLY IS...
...HIS PURPOSE ...?
YOU.
GRP
YOU REALLY THINK HE'LL COME?
THAT...
...COWARD?
IS HE TALKING ABOUT RAKUTO?
COWARD ...?
SHU
I'LL HEAR YOU OUT IF HE CAN GET HERE.

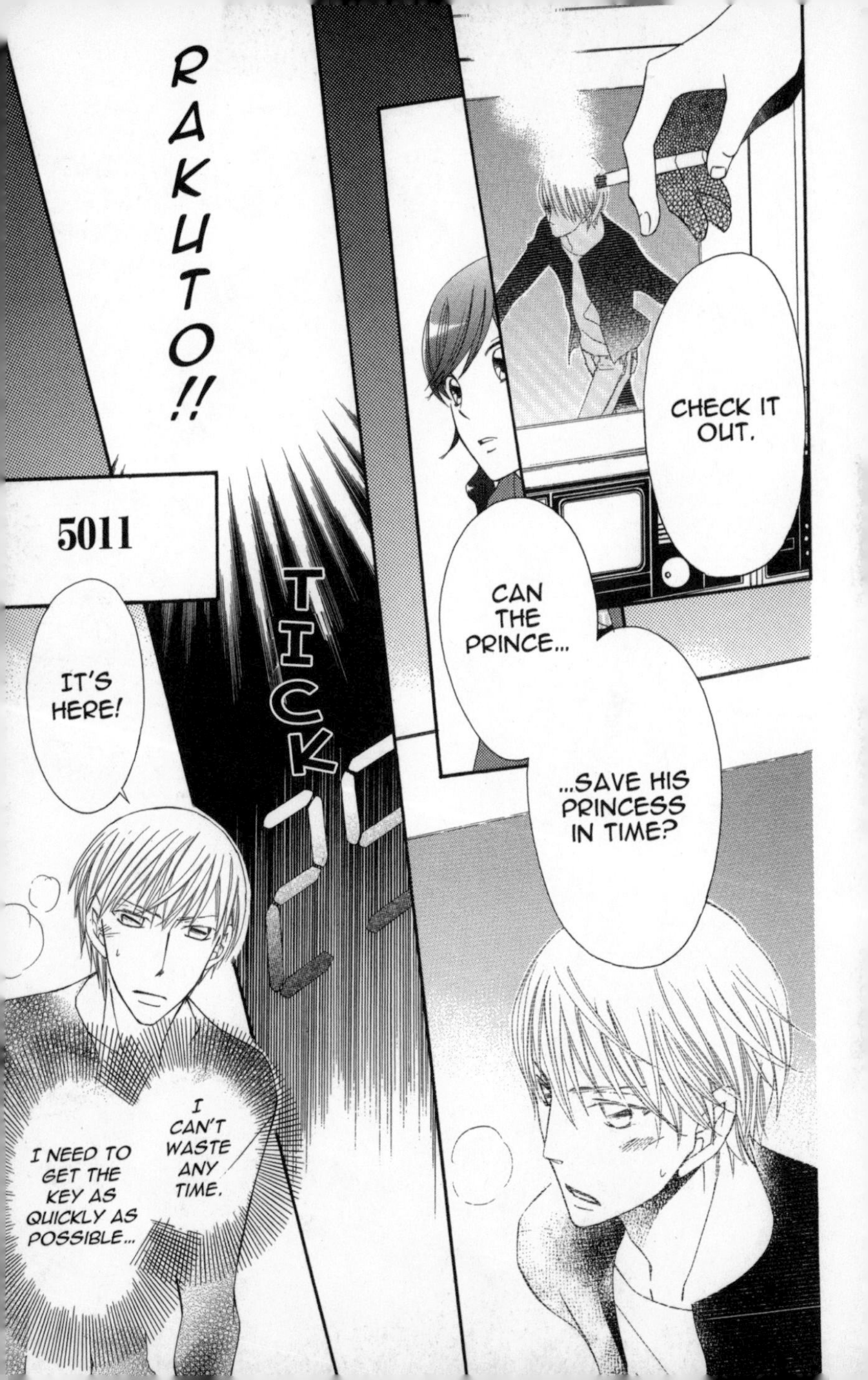
CHECK IT OUT.
CAN THE PRINCE...
...SAVE HIS PRINCESS IN TIME?
RAKUTO!!
5011
TICK
IT'S HERE!
I CAN'T WASTE ANY TIME.
I NEED TO GET THE KEY AS QUICKLY AS POSSIBLE...

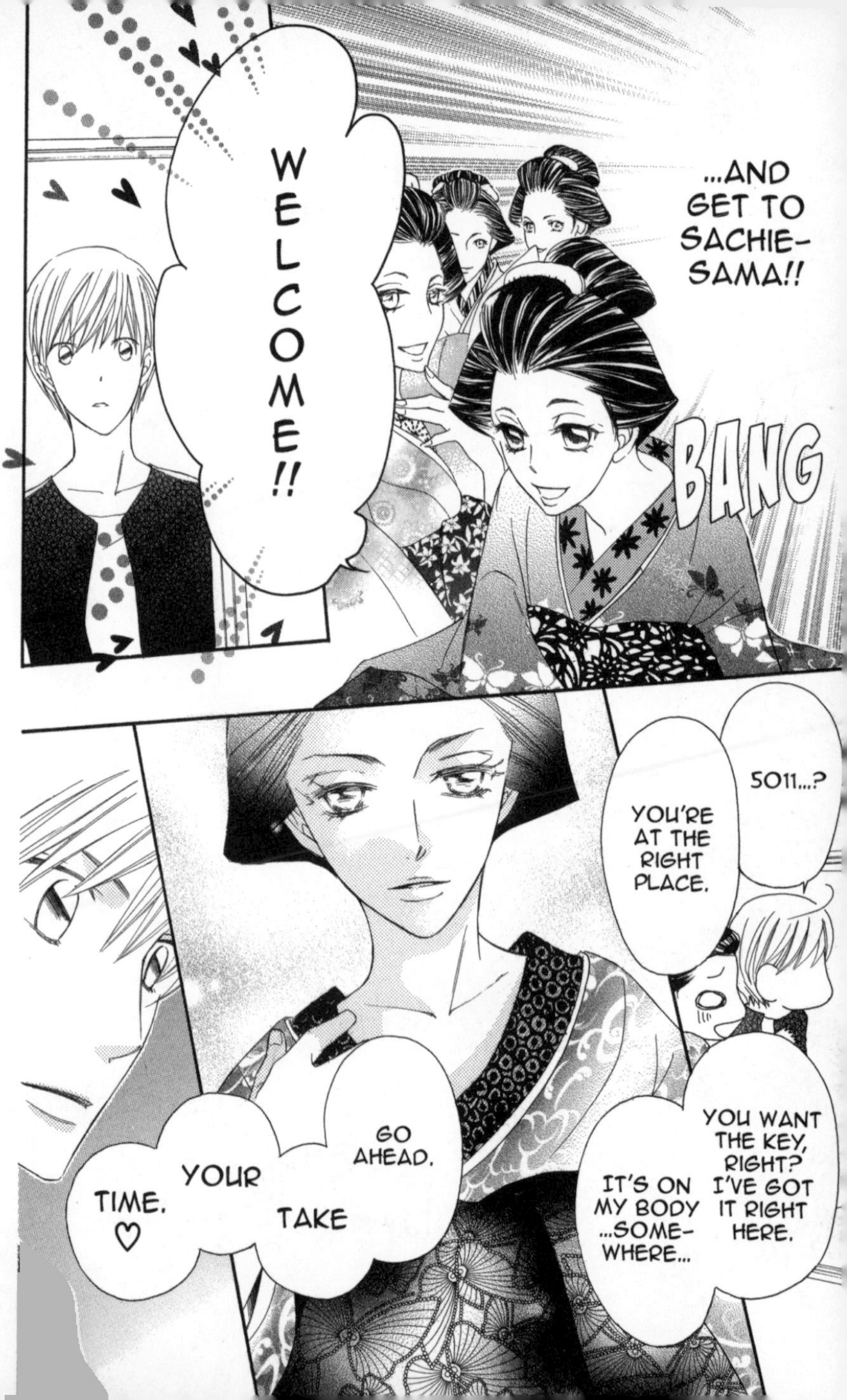
...AND GET TO SACHIE-SAMA!!
BANG
WELCOME!!
SOII...?
YOU'RE AT THE RIGHT PLACE.
YOU WANT THE KEY, RIGHT? I'VE GOT IT RIGHT HERE.
IT'S ON MY BODY ...SOME-WHERE...
GO AHEAD. TAKE YOUR TIME. ♡

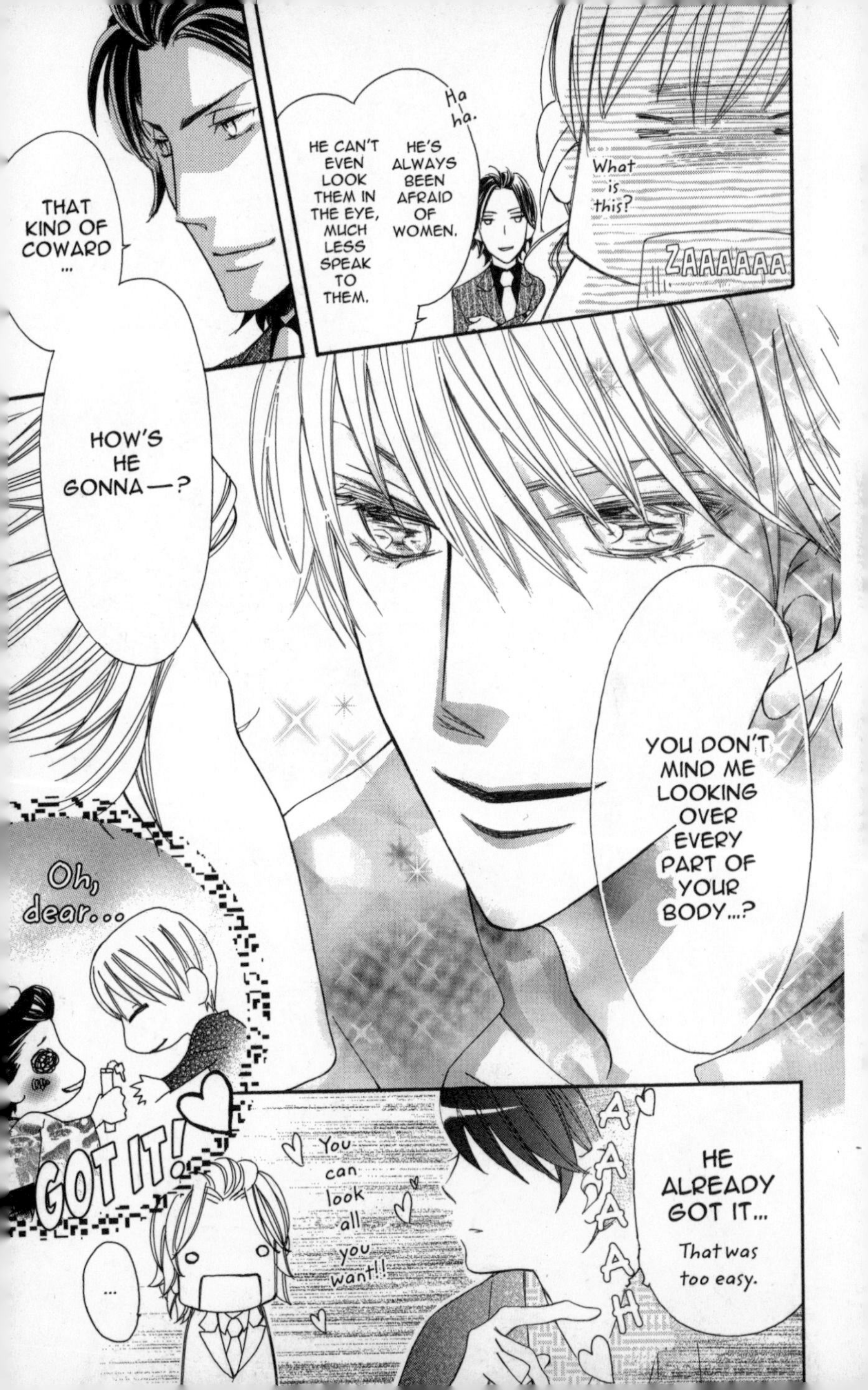
What is this?
ZAAAAAA
Ha ha.
HE'S ALWAYS BEEN AFRAID OF WOMEN.
HE CAN'T EVEN LOOK THEM IN THE EYE, MUCH LESS SPEAK TO THEM.
THAT KIND OF COWARD...
HOW'S HE GONNA—?
YOU DON'T MIND ME LOOKING OVER EVERY PART OF YOUR BODY...?
HE ALREADY GOT IT...
That was too easy.
AAAAAH
You can look all you want!!
...
Oh, dear...
GOT IT!

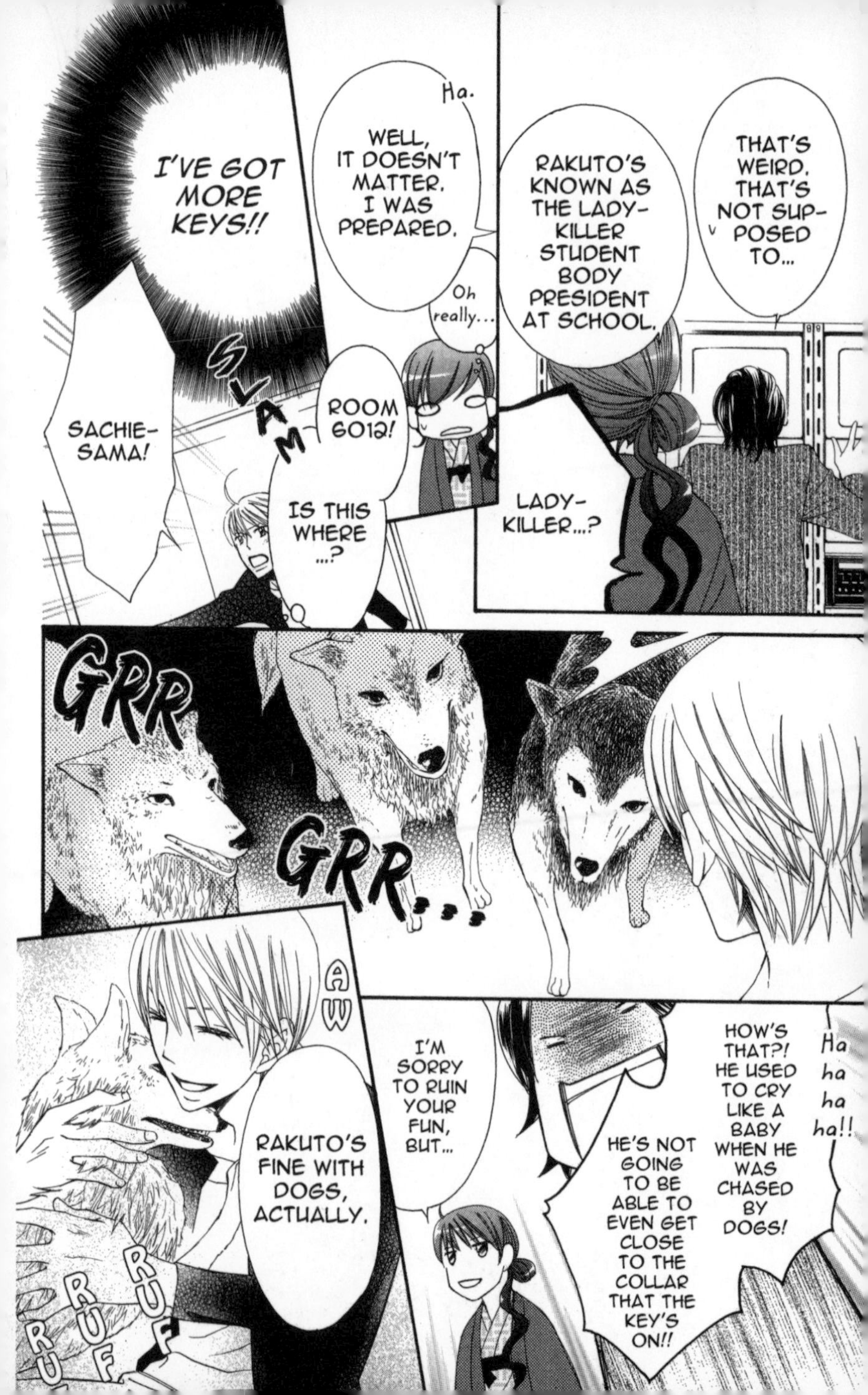
THAT'S WEIRD. THAT'S NOT SUPPOSED TO...
RAKUTO'S KNOWN AS THE LADY-KILLER STUDENT BODY PRESIDENT AT SCHOOL.
LADY-KILLER...?
Ha.
WELL, IT DOESN'T MATTER. I WAS PREPARED.
Oh really...
ROOM 6012!
IS THIS WHERE ...?
I'VE GOT MORE KEYS!!
SLAM
SACHIE-SAMA!
GRR
GRR...
Ha ha ha ha!!
HOW'S THAT?! HE USED TO CRY LIKE A BABY WHEN HE WAS CHASED BY DOGS!
HE'S NOT GOING TO BE ABLE TO EVEN GET CLOSE TO THE COLLAR THAT THE KEY'S ON!!
I'M SORRY TO RUIN YOUR FUN, BUT...
RAKUTO'S FINE WITH DOGS, ACTUALLY.
AW
RUF RUF RU

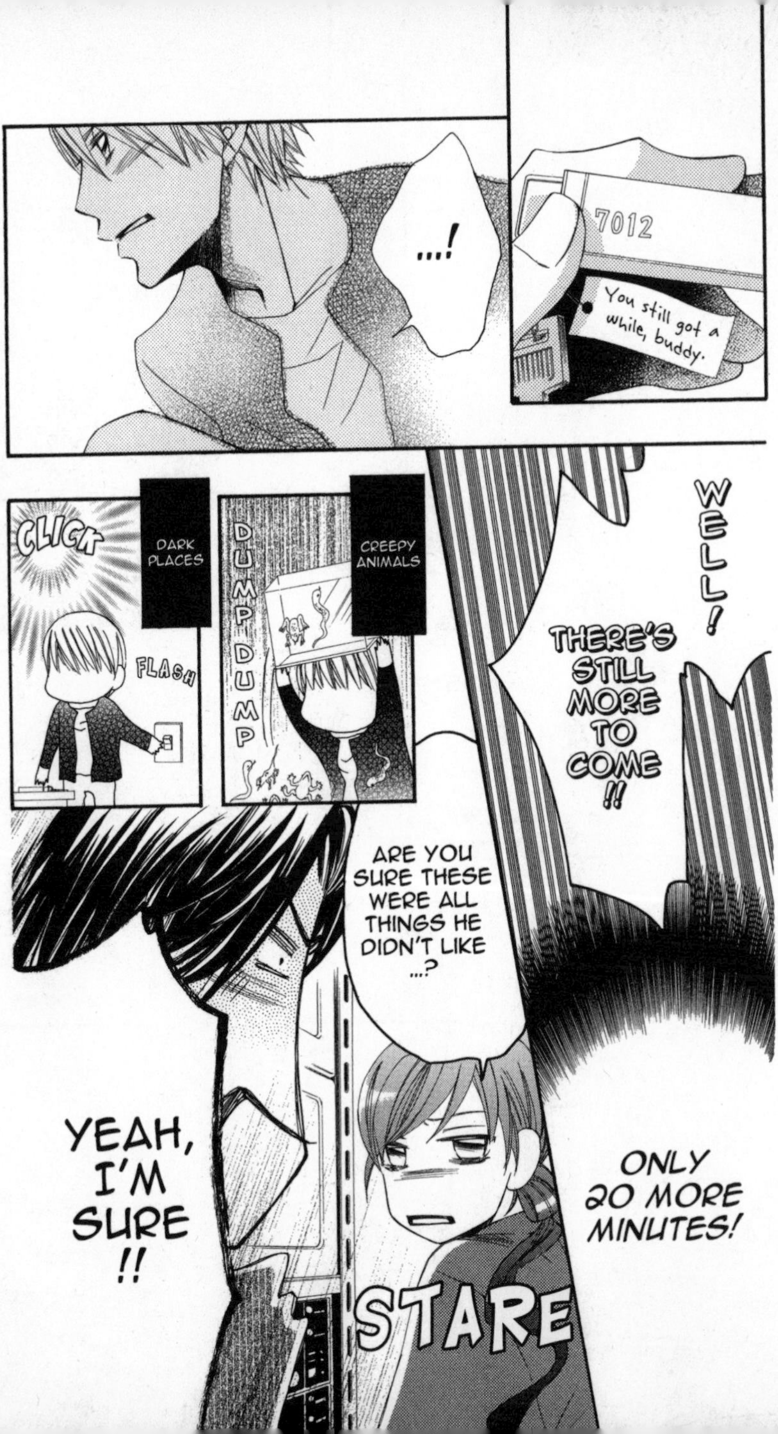

7012
You still got a while, buddy.
...!
WELL!
THERE'S STILL MORE TO COME!!
CREEPY ANIMALS
DUMP DUMP DUMP
DARK PLACES
CLICK
FLASH
ARE YOU SURE THESE WERE ALL THINGS HE DIDN'T LIKE ...?
ONLY 20 MORE MINUTES!
YEAH, I'M SURE!!
STARE

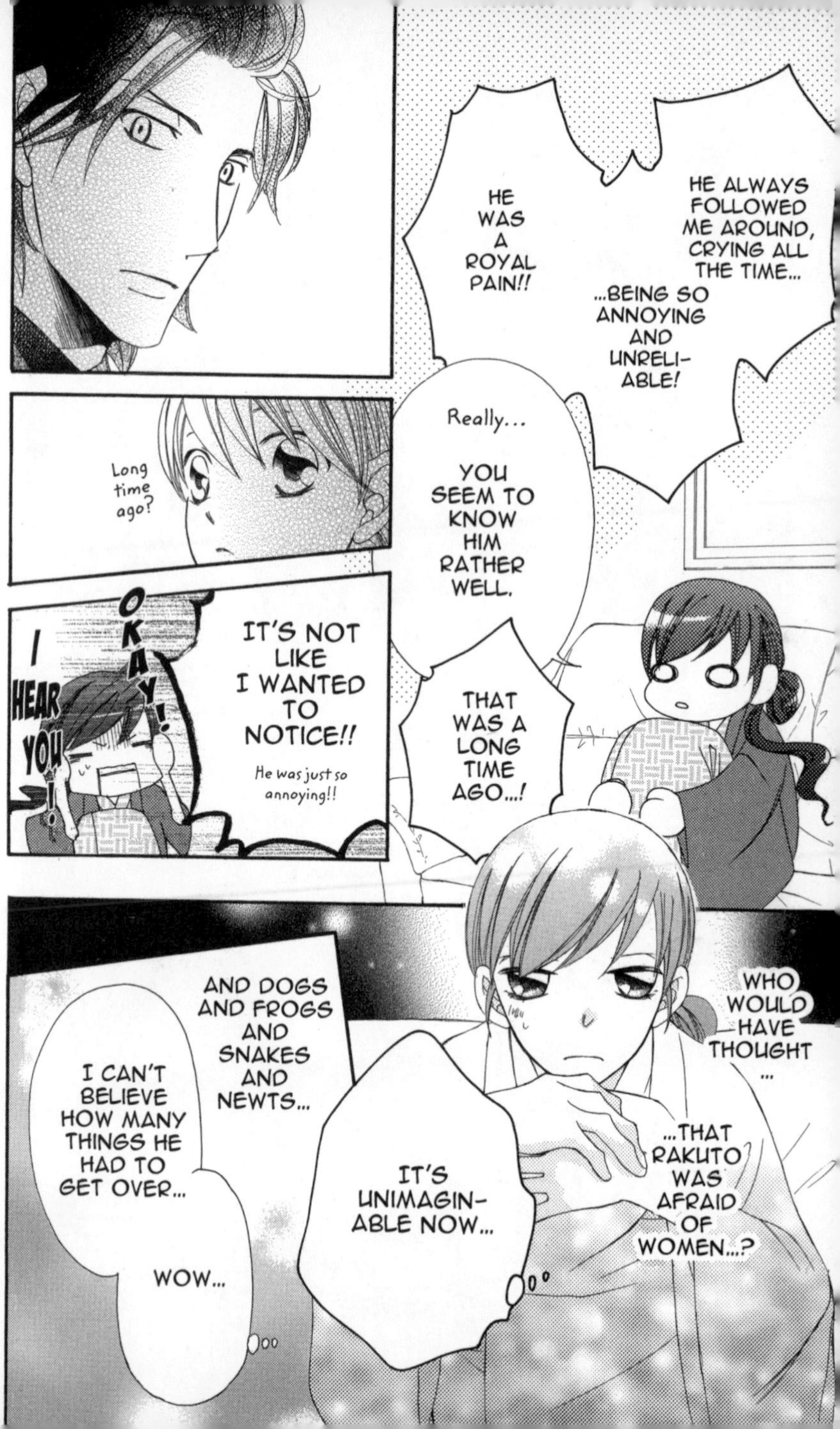
HE ALWAYS FOLLOWED ME AROUND, CRYING ALL THE TIME...
...BEING SO ANNOYING AND UNRELI-ABLE!
HE WAS A ROYAL PAIN!!
Really... YOU SEEM TO KNOW HIM RATHER WELL.
THAT WAS A LONG TIME AGO...!
Long time ago?
IT'S NOT LIKE I WANTED TO NOTICE!! He was just so annoying!!
OKAY! I HEAR YOU!
WHO WOULD HAVE THOUGHT...
...THAT RAKUTO WAS AFRAID OF WOMEN...?
IT'S UNIMAGIN-ABLE NOW...
AND DOGS AND FROGS AND SNAKES AND NEWTS...
I CAN'T BELIEVE HOW MANY THINGS HE HAD TO GET OVER...
WOW...

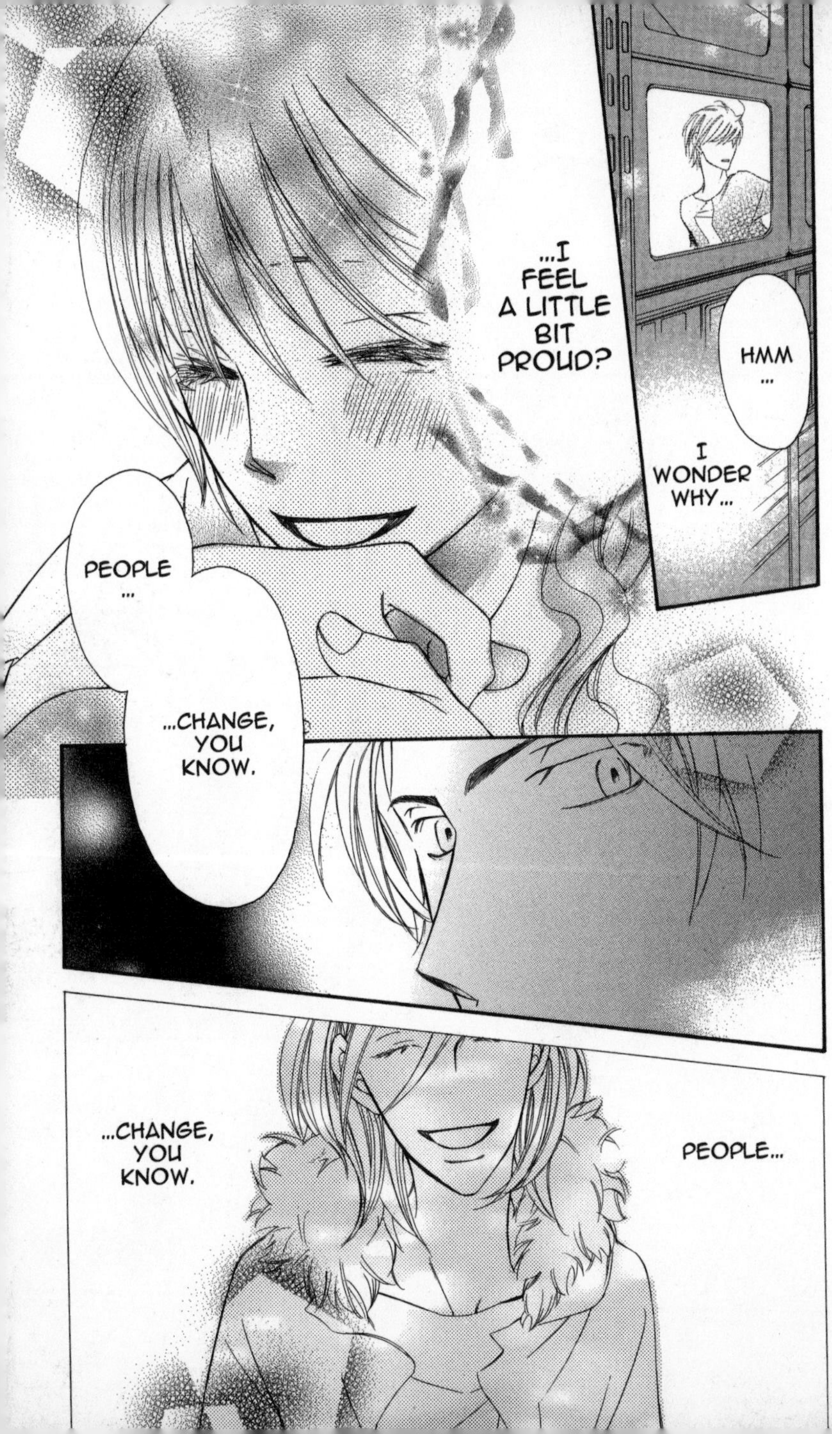
HMM...
I WONDER WHY...
...I FEEL A LITTLE BIT PROUD?
PEOPLE...
...CHANGE, YOU KNOW.
PEOPLE...
...CHANGE, YOU KNOW.

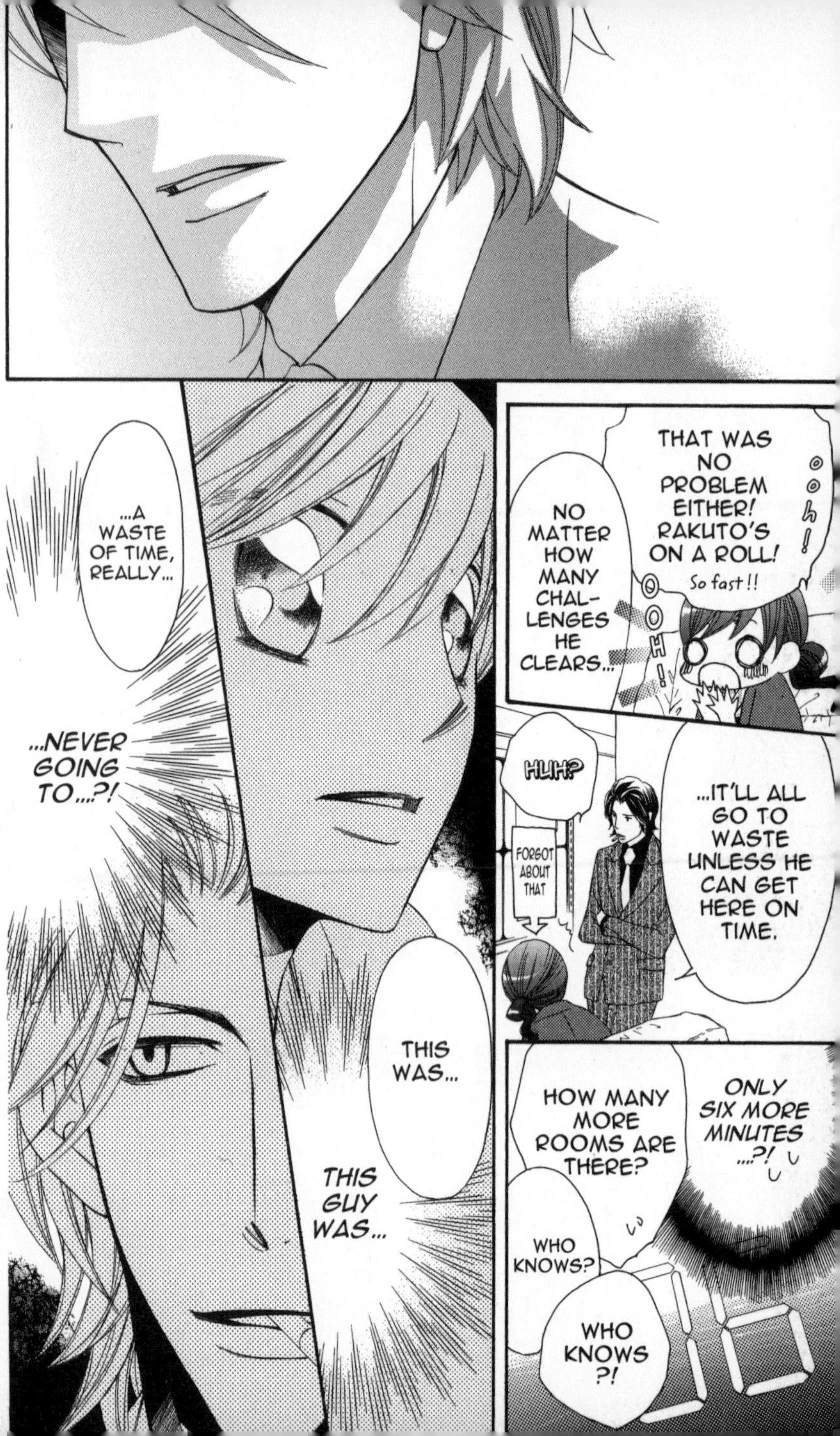
THAT WAS NO PROBLEM EITHER! RAKUTO'S ON A ROLL!
Oooh!
So fast!!
OOOH!
NO MATTER HOW MANY CHAL-LENGES HE CLEARS...
...IT'LL ALL GO TO WASTE UNLESS HE CAN GET HERE ON TIME.
HUH?
FORGOT ABOUT THAT
ONLY SIX MORE MINUTES...?!
HOW MANY MORE ROOMS ARE THERE?
WHO KNOWS?
WHO KNOWS?!
...A WASTE OF TIME, REALLY...
...NEVER GOING TO...?!
THIS WAS...
THIS GUY WAS...

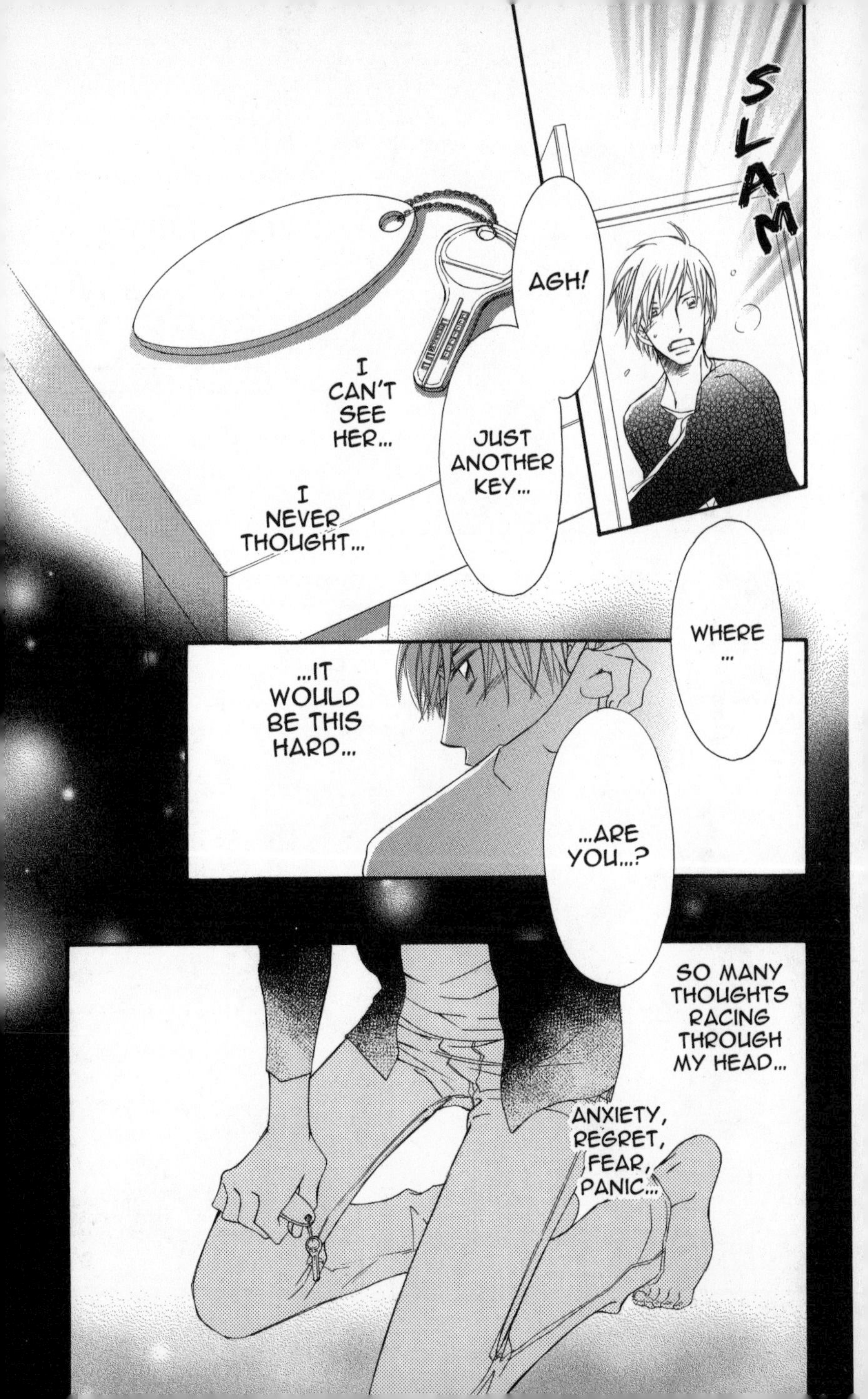
SLAM
AGH!
JUST ANOTHER KEY...
I CAN'T SEE HER...
I NEVER THOUGHT...
WHERE ...
...IT WOULD BE THIS HARD...
...ARE YOU...?
SO MANY THOUGHTS RACING THROUGH MY HEAD...
ANXIETY, REGRET, FEAR, PANIC...

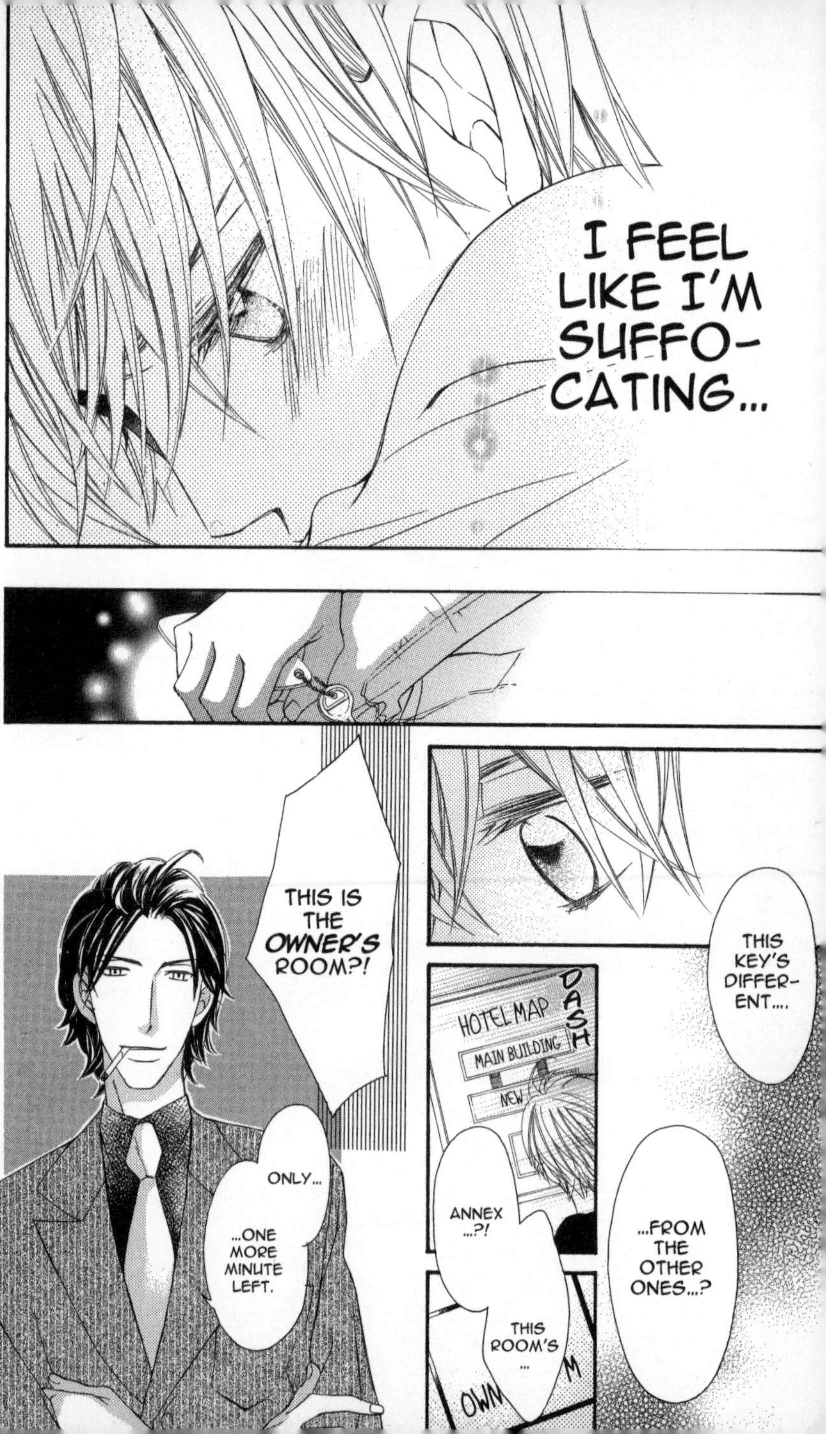
I FEEL LIKE I'M SUFFO-CATING...
THIS KEY'S DIFFER-ENT....
...FROM THE OTHER ONES...?
HOTEL MAP
MAIN BUILDING
NEW
DASH
ANNEX ...?!
THIS ROOM'S ...
OWN
M
THIS IS THE *OWNER'S* ROOM?!
ONLY...
...ONE MORE MINUTE LEFT.

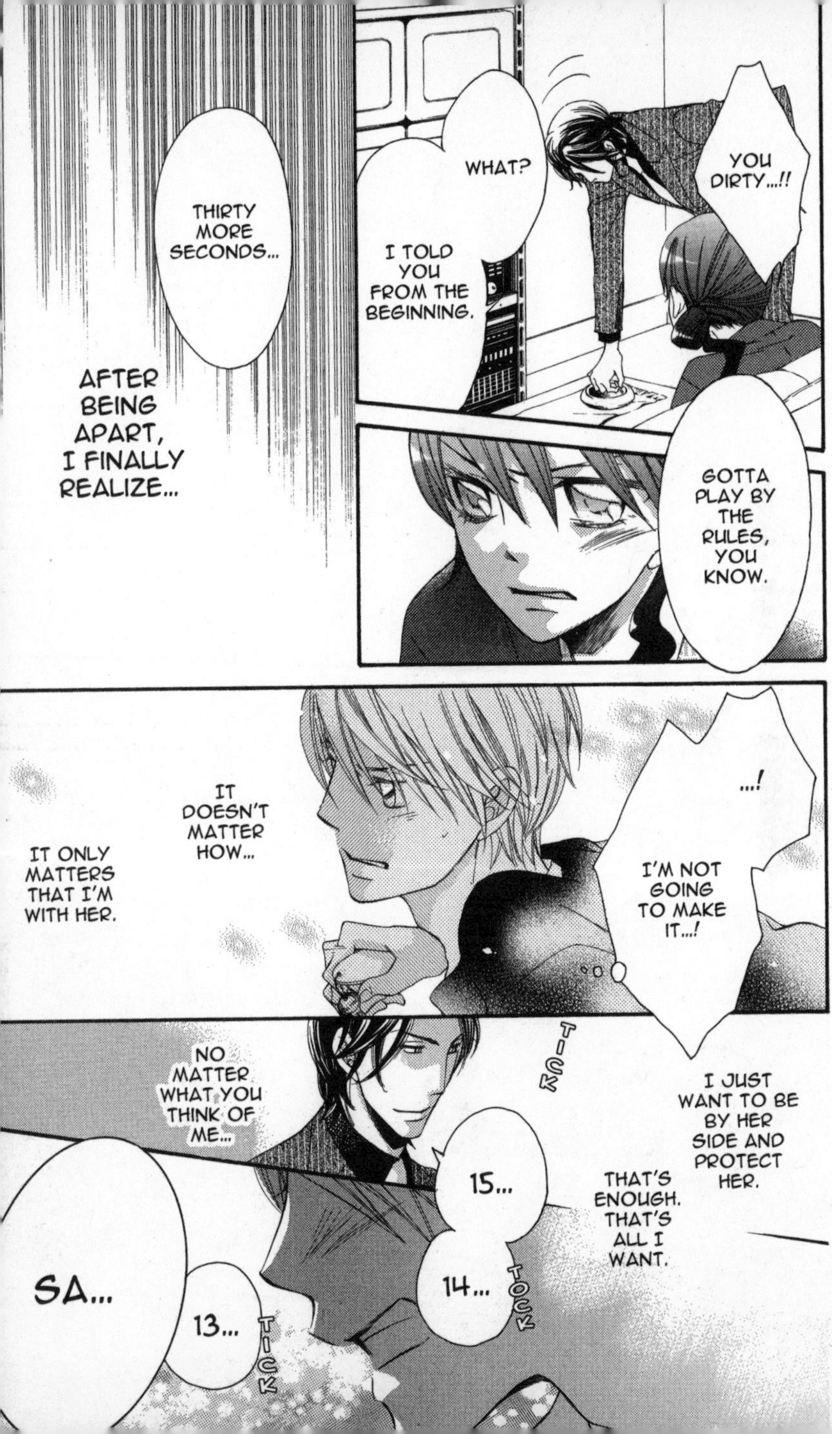
YOU DIRTY...!!
WHAT?
I TOLD YOU FROM THE BEGINNING.
GOTTA PLAY BY THE RULES, YOU KNOW.
THIRTY MORE SECONDS...
AFTER BEING APART, I FINALLY REALIZE...
...!
I'M NOT GOING TO MAKE IT...!
IT DOESN'T MATTER HOW...
IT ONLY MATTERS THAT I'M WITH HER.
TICK
I JUST WANT TO BE BY HER SIDE AND PROTECT HER.
NO MATTER WHAT YOU THINK OF ME...
THAT'S ENOUGH. THAT'S ALL I WANT.
15...
TOCK
14...
13...
TICK
SA...

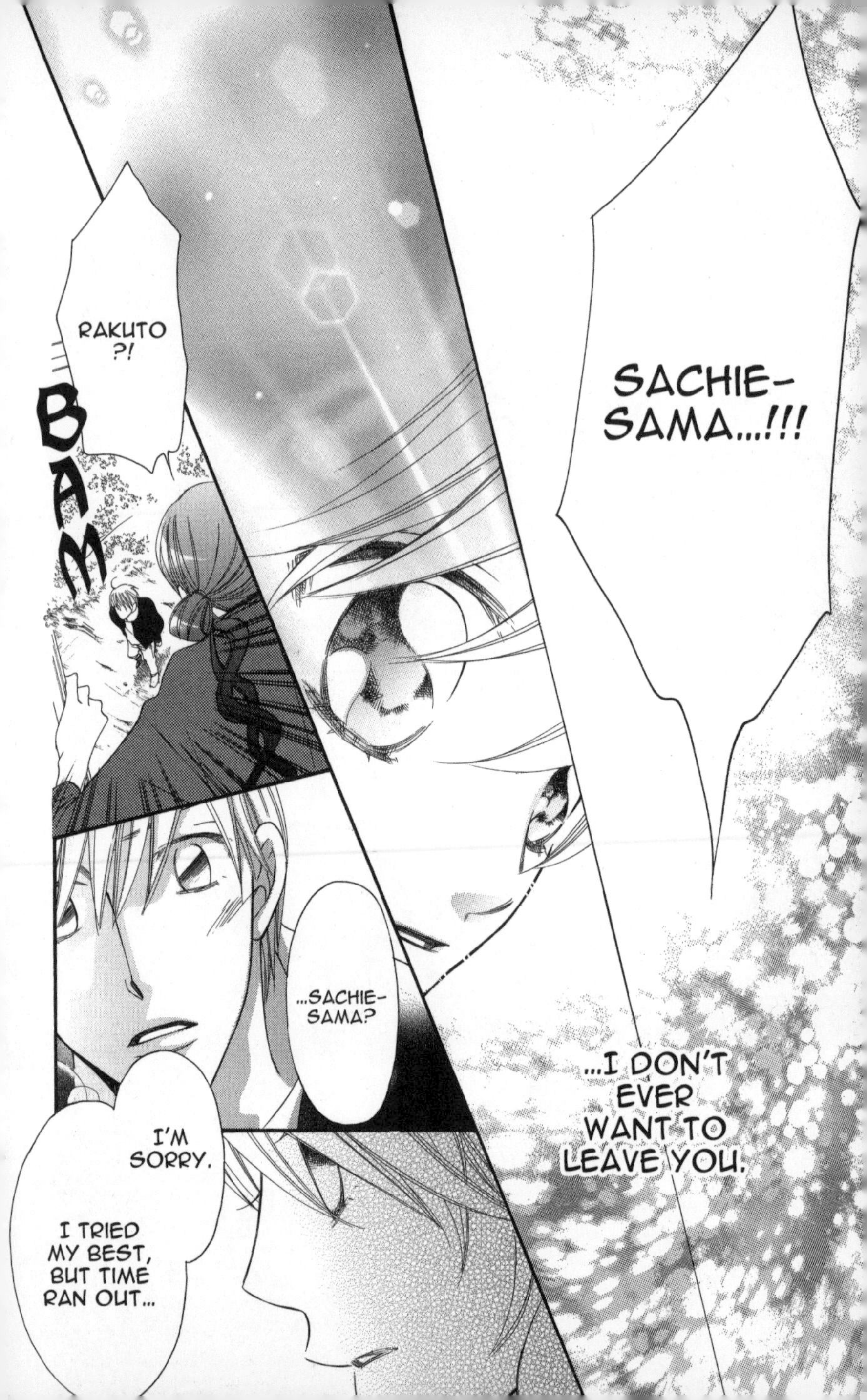
SACHIE-SAMA...!!!
RAKUTO ?!
BAM
...SACHIE-SAMA?
I'M SORRY.
I TRIED MY BEST, BUT TIME RAN OUT...
...I DON'T EVER WANT TO LEAVE YOU.

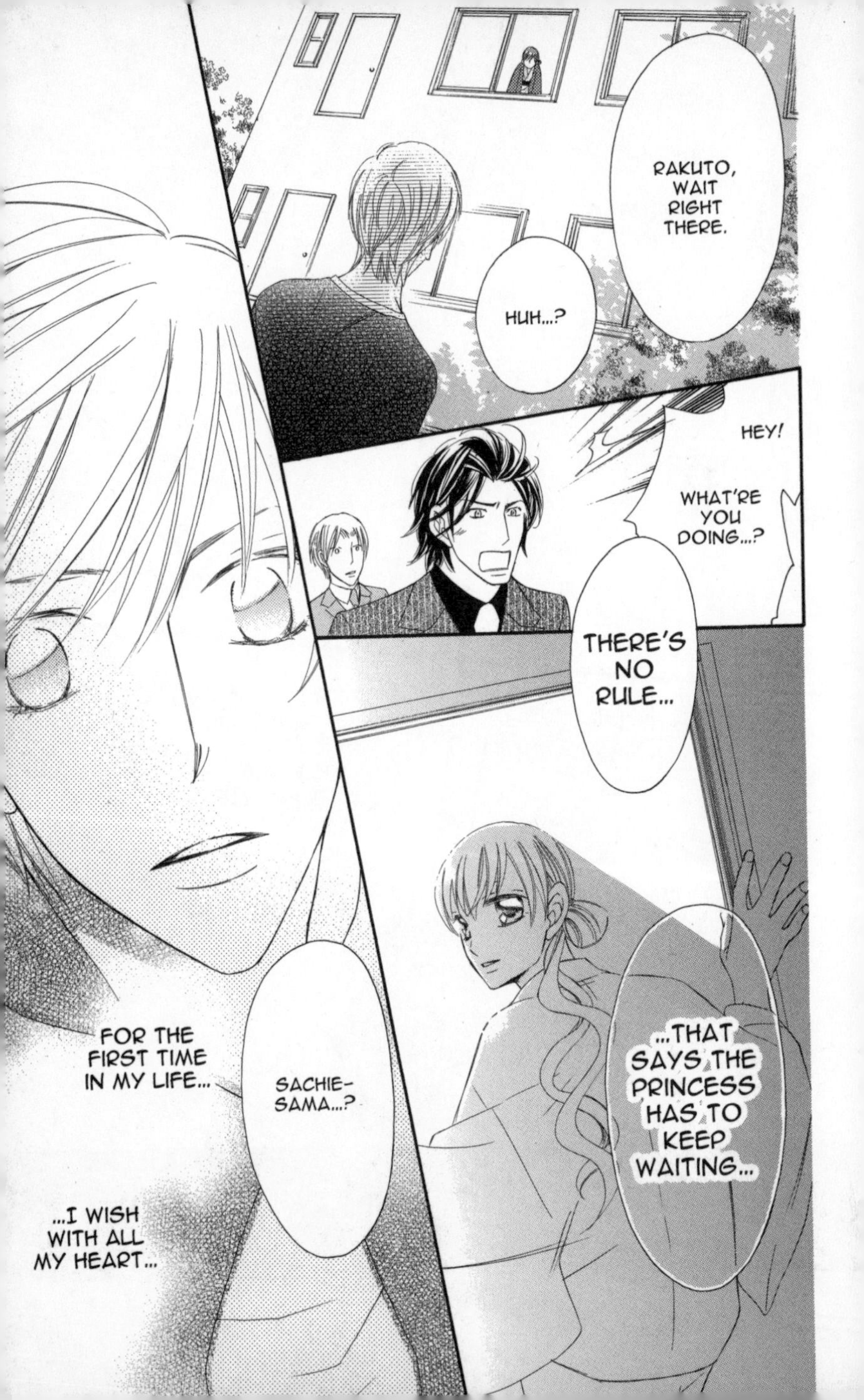
RAKUTO, WAIT RIGHT THERE.
HUH...?
HEY!
WHAT'RE YOU DOING...?
THERE'S NO RULE...
...THAT SAYS THE PRINCESS HAS TO KEEP WAITING...
SACHIE-SAMA...?
FOR THE FIRST TIME IN MY LIFE...
...I WISH WITH ALL MY HEART...

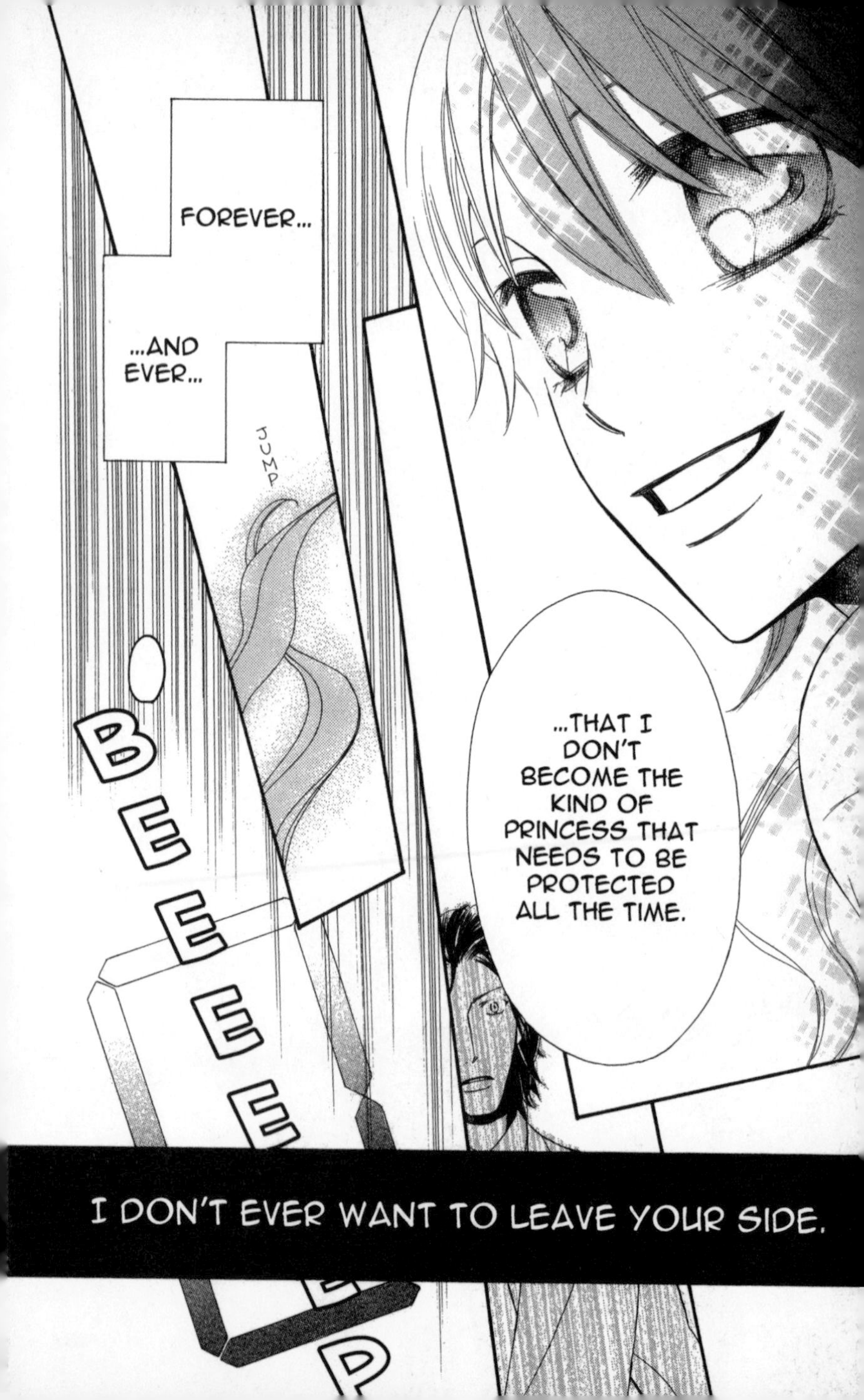
...THAT I DON'T BECOME THE KIND OF PRINCESS THAT NEEDS TO BE PROTECTED ALL THE TIME.
FOREVER...
...AND EVER...
JUMP
BEEEEEP
I DON'T EVER WANT TO LEAVE YOUR SIDE.

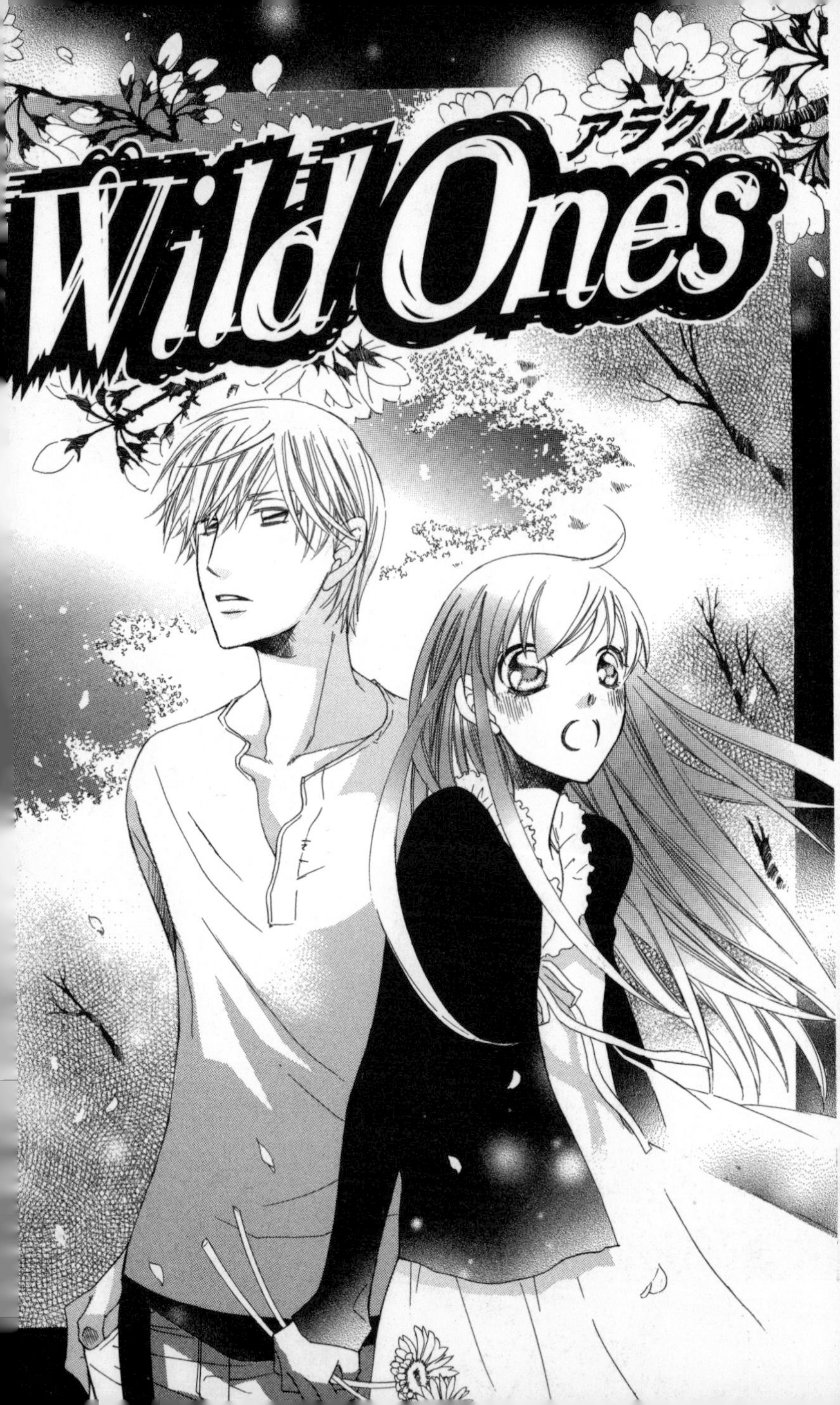
アラクレ
Wild Ones

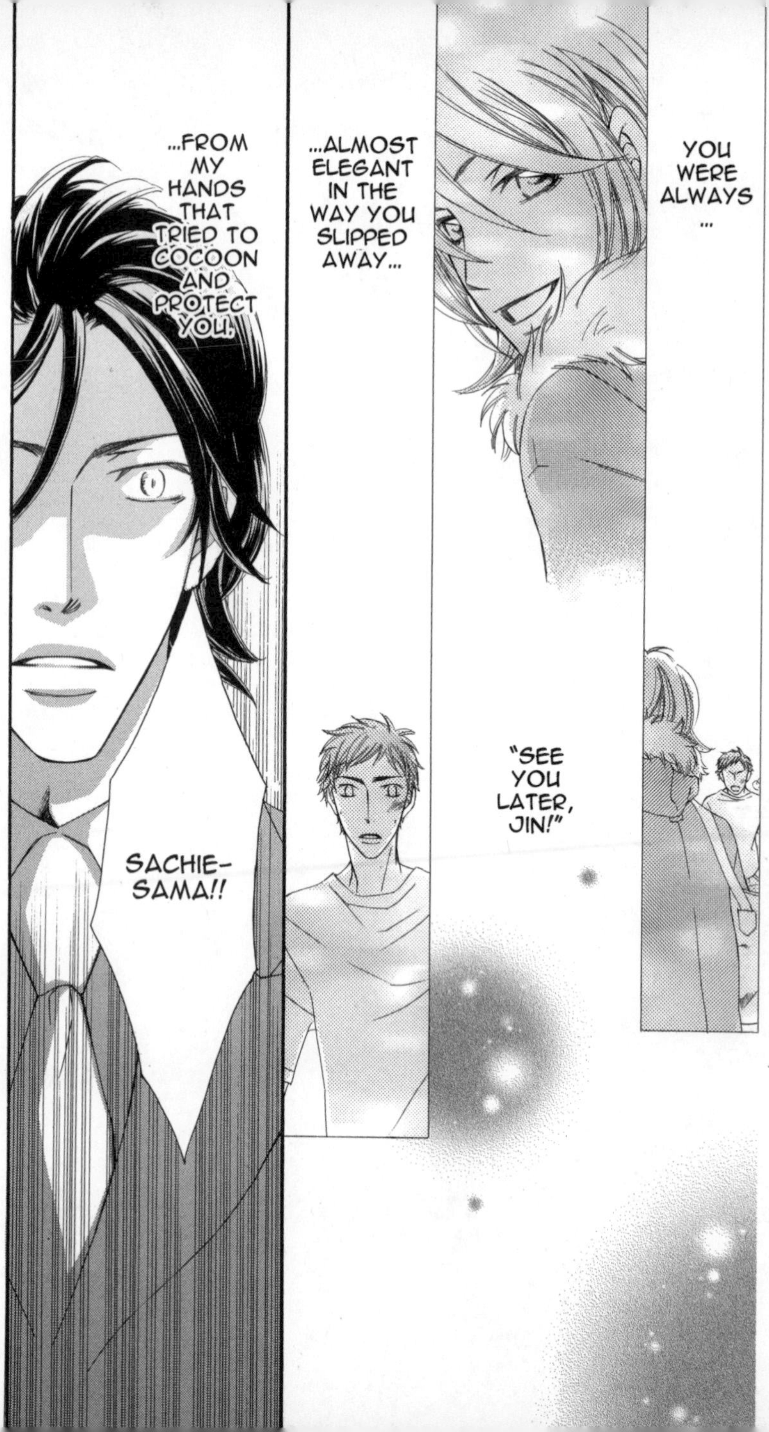
YOU WERE ALWAYS ...
"SEE YOU LATER, JIN!"
...ALMOST ELEGANT IN THE WAY YOU SLIPPED AWAY...
...FROM MY HANDS THAT TRIED TO COCOON AND PROTECT YOU.
SACHIE-SAMA!!

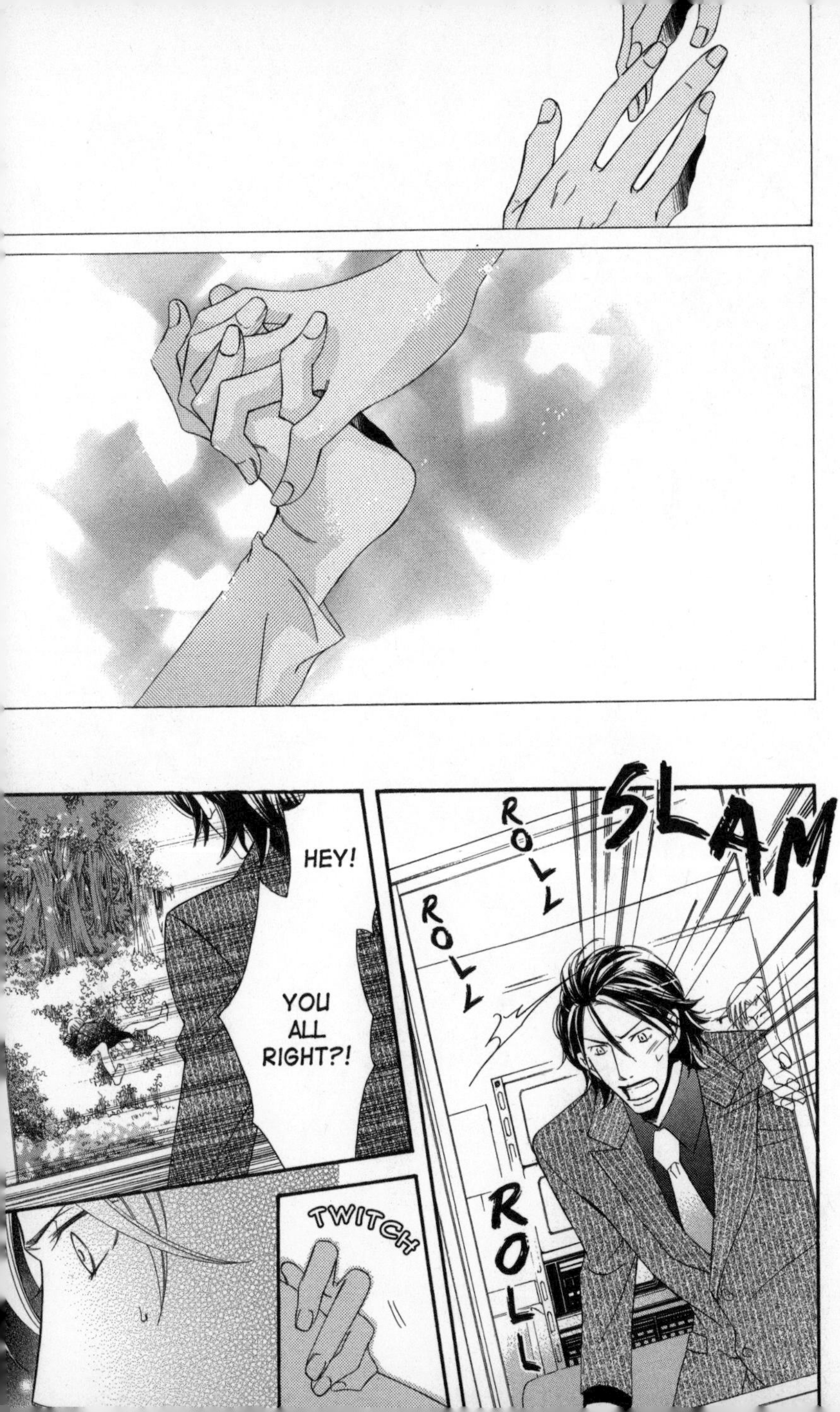
SLAM
ROLL
ROLL
ROLL
ROLL
ROLL
ROLL
HEY!
YOU ALL RIGHT?!
TWITCH

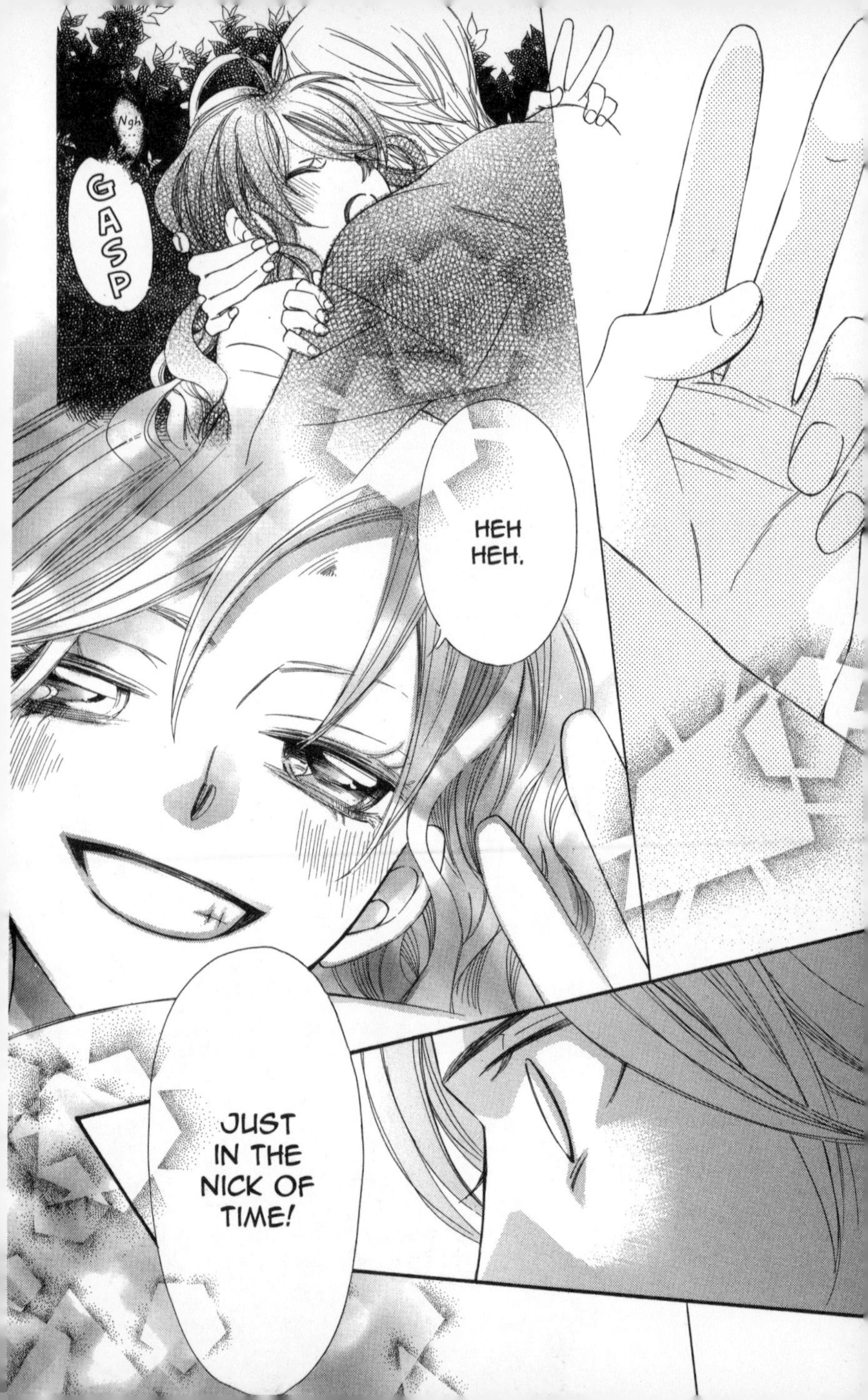
Ngh
GASP
HEH HEH.
JUST IN THE NICK OF TIME!

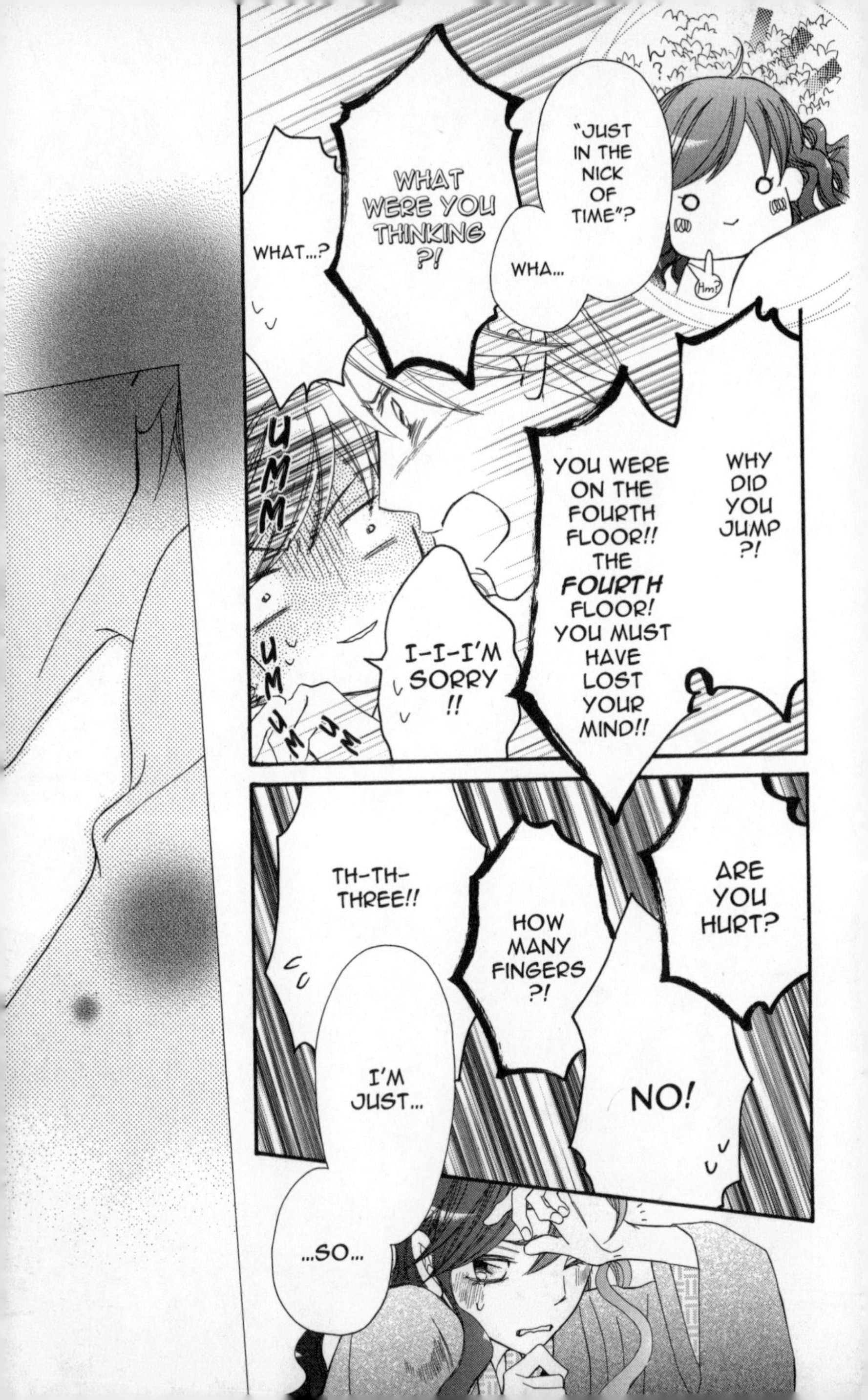
Hm?
"JUST IN THE NICK OF TIME"?
WHA...
WHAT WERE YOU THINKING?!
WHAT...?
WHY DID YOU JUMP?!
YOU WERE ON THE FOURTH FLOOR!! THE FOURTH FLOOR! YOU MUST HAVE LOST YOUR MIND!!
I-I-I'M SORRY!!
UMM
ARE YOU HURT?
NO!
HOW MANY FINGERS?!
TH-TH-THREE!!
I'M JUST...
...SO...

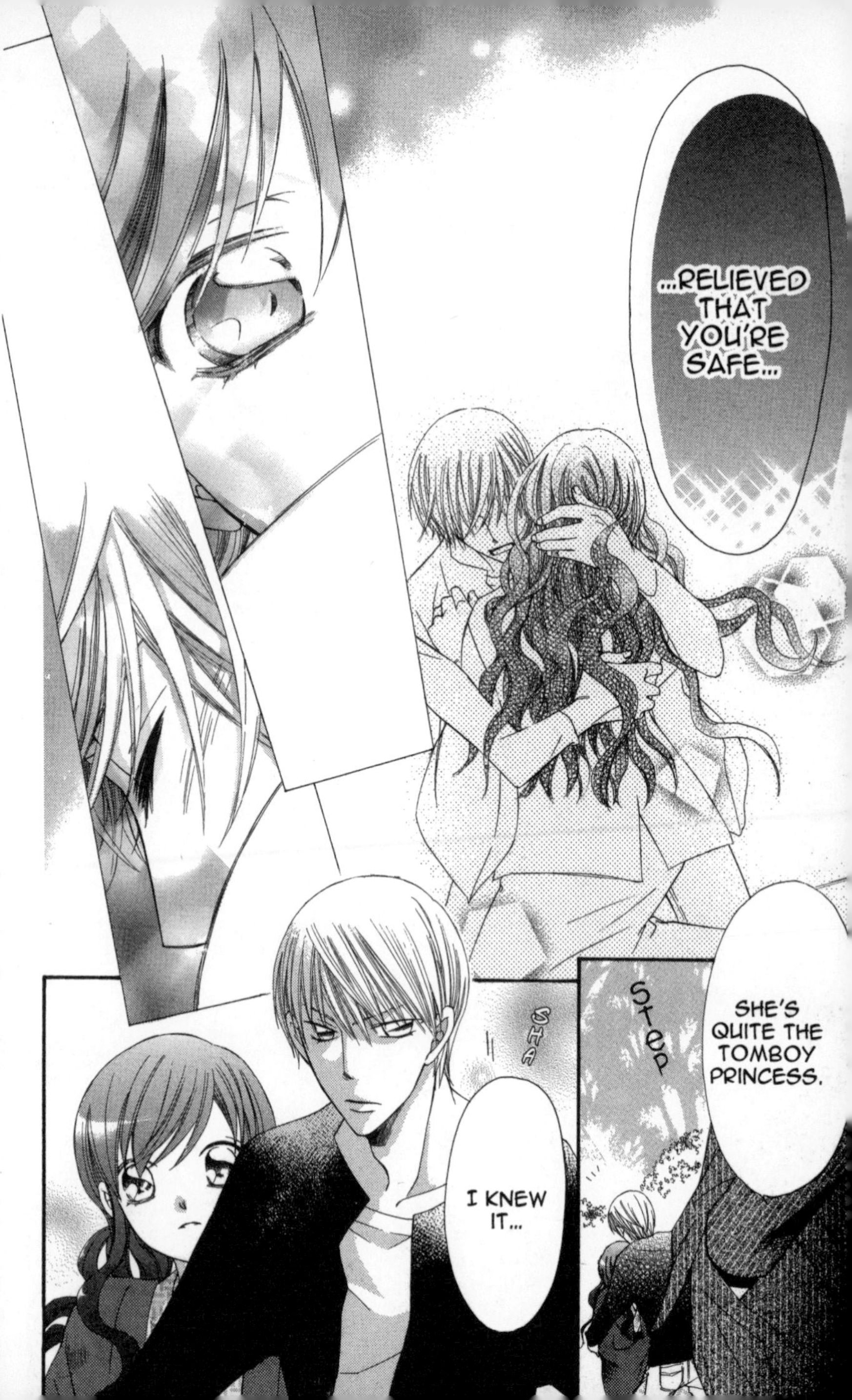
...RELIEVED THAT YOU'RE SAFE...
SHE'S QUITE THE TOMBOY PRINCESS.
STEP
SHA
I KNEW IT...

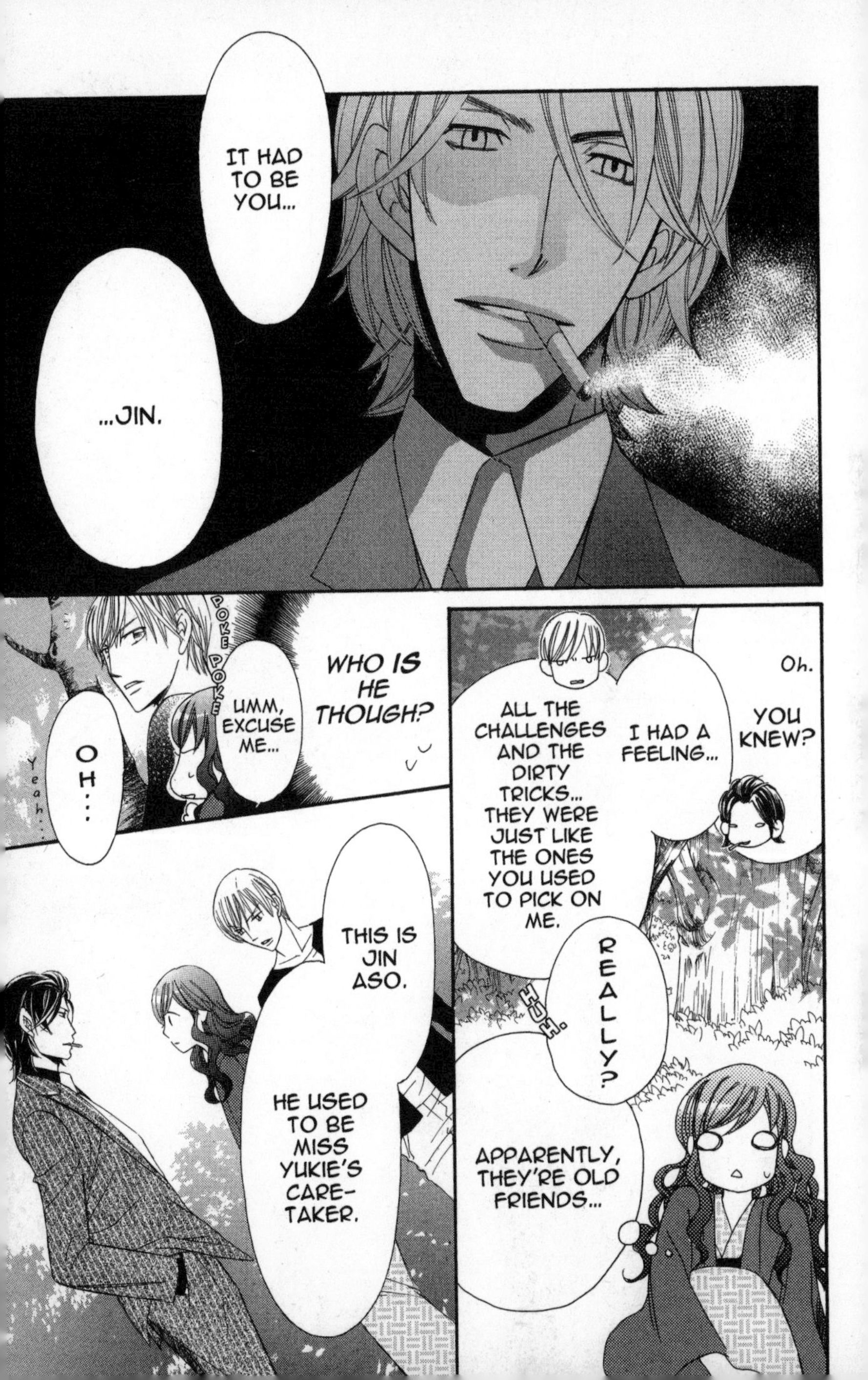
IT HAD TO BE YOU...
...JIN.
Oh.
YOU KNEW?
I HAD A FEELING...
ALL THE CHALLENGES AND THE DIRTY TRICKS... THEY WERE JUST LIKE THE ONES YOU USED TO PICK ON ME.
REALLY?
HUH.
APPARENTLY, THEY'RE OLD FRIENDS...
WHO IS HE THOUGH?
POKE POKE
UMM, EXCUSE ME...
OH...
Yeah...
THIS IS JIN ASO.
HE USED TO BE MISS YUKIE'S CARE-TAKER.

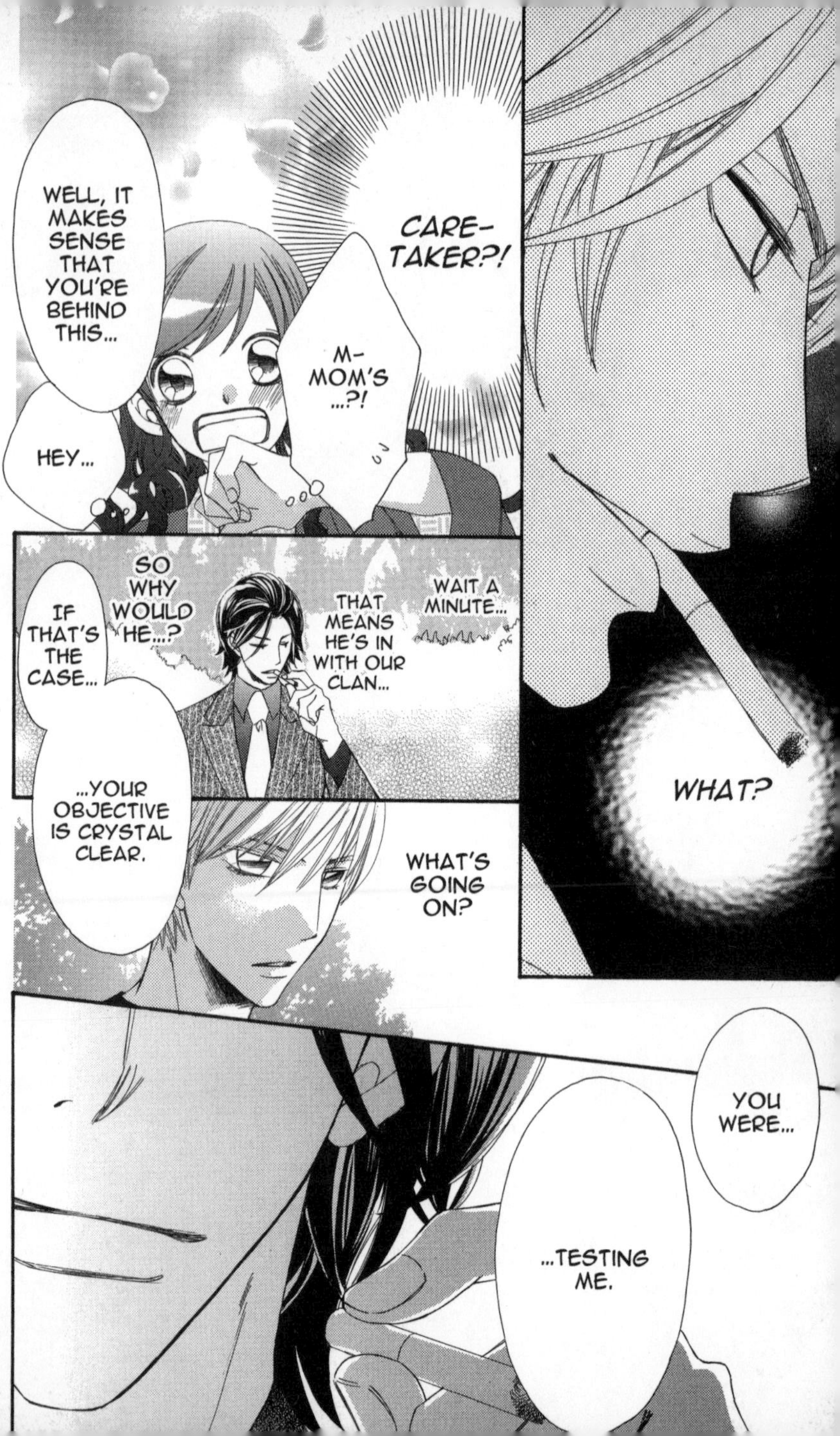
WHAT?
CARE-TAKER?!
M-MOM'S ...?!
WELL, IT MAKES SENSE THAT YOU'RE BEHIND THIS...
HEY...
WAIT A MINUTE...
THAT MEANS HE'S IN WITH OUR CLAN...
SO WHY WOULD HE...?
IF THAT'S THE CASE...
...YOUR OBJECTIVE IS CRYSTAL CLEAR.
WHAT'S GOING ON?
YOU WERE...
...TESTING ME.

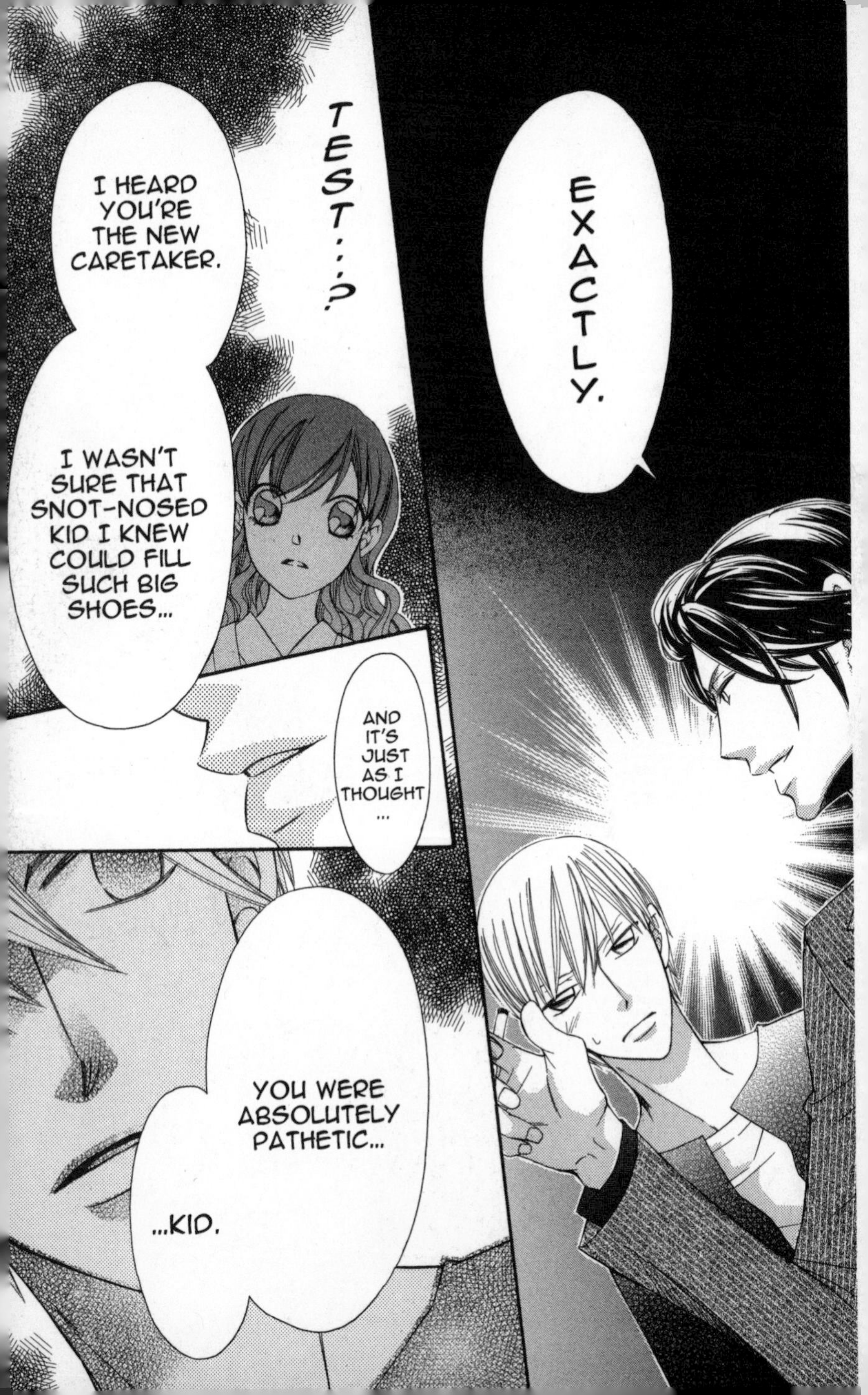
EXACTLY.
TEST...?
I HEARD YOU'RE THE NEW CARETAKER.
I WASN'T SURE THAT SNOT-NOSED KID I KNEW COULD FILL SUCH BIG SHOES...
AND IT'S JUST AS I THOUGHT...
YOU WERE ABSOLUTELY PATHETIC...
...KID.

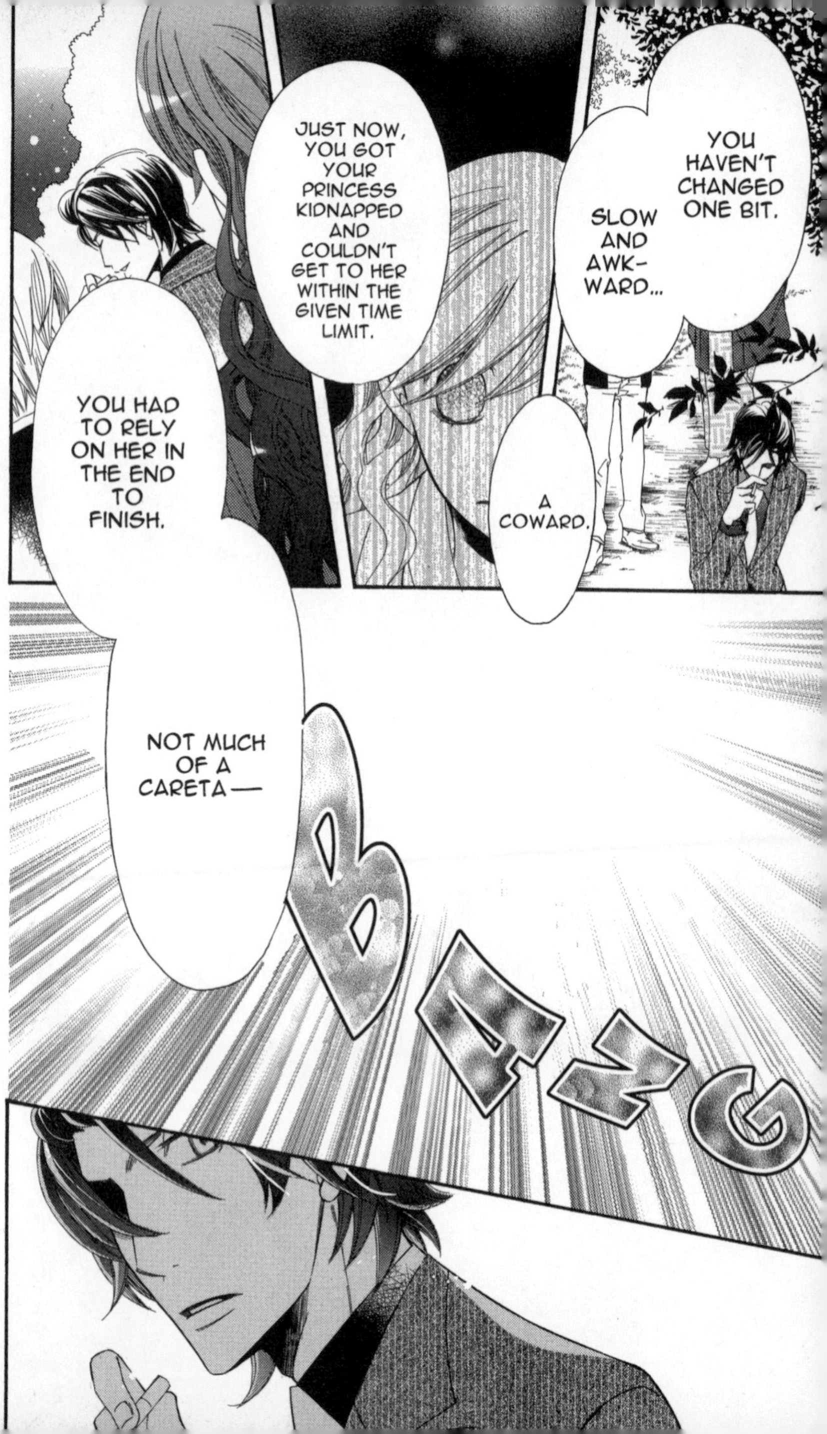
YOU HAVEN'T CHANGED ONE BIT.
SLOW AND AWK-WARD...
A COWARD.
JUST NOW, YOU GOT YOUR PRINCESS KIDNAPPED AND COULDN'T GET TO HER WITHIN THE GIVEN TIME LIMIT.
YOU HAD TO RELY ON HER IN THE END TO FINISH.
NOT MUCH OF A CARETA—
BANG

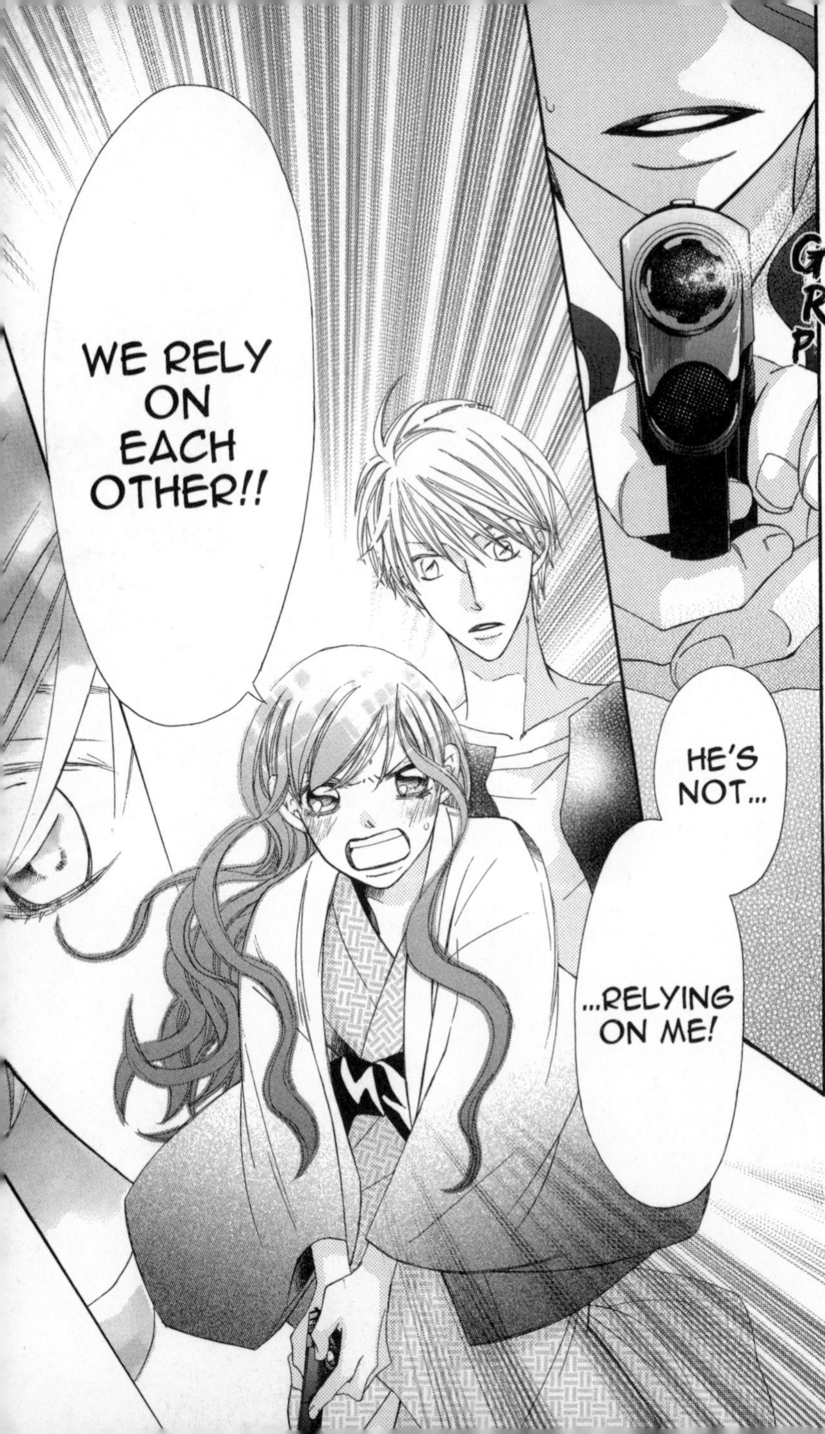
GRP
HE'S NOT...
...RELYING ON ME!
WE RELY ON EACH OTHER!!

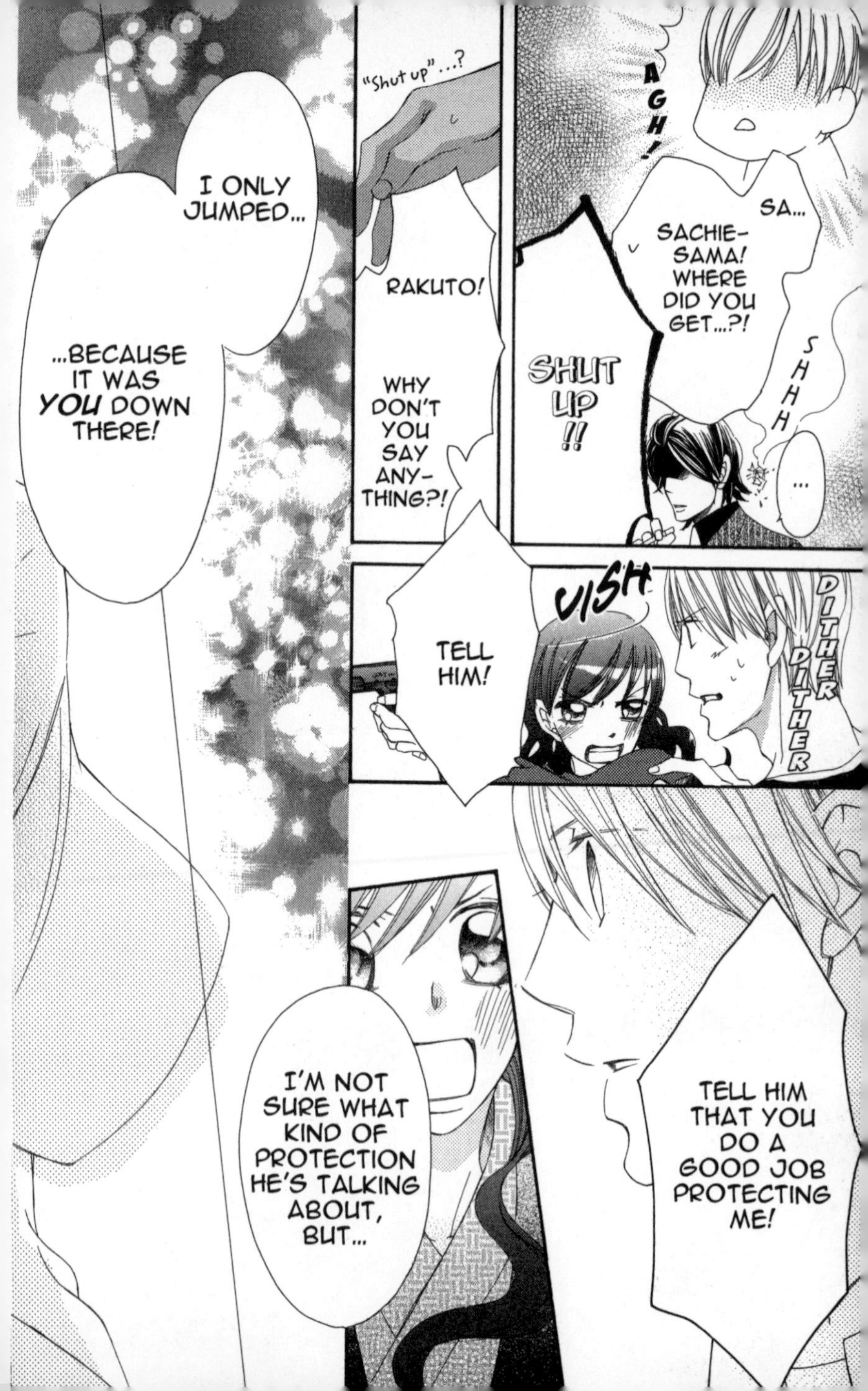
AGH!
SA...
SACHIE-SAMA! WHERE DID YOU GET...?!
SHHH
...
SHUT UP!!
"Shut up"...?
RAKUTO!
WHY DON'T YOU SAY ANYTHING?!
VISH
DITHER DITHER
TELL HIM!
TELL HIM THAT YOU DO A GOOD JOB PROTECTING ME!
I'M NOT SURE WHAT KIND OF PROTECTION HE'S TALKING ABOUT, BUT...
I ONLY JUMPED...
...BECAUSE IT WAS *YOU* DOWN THERE!

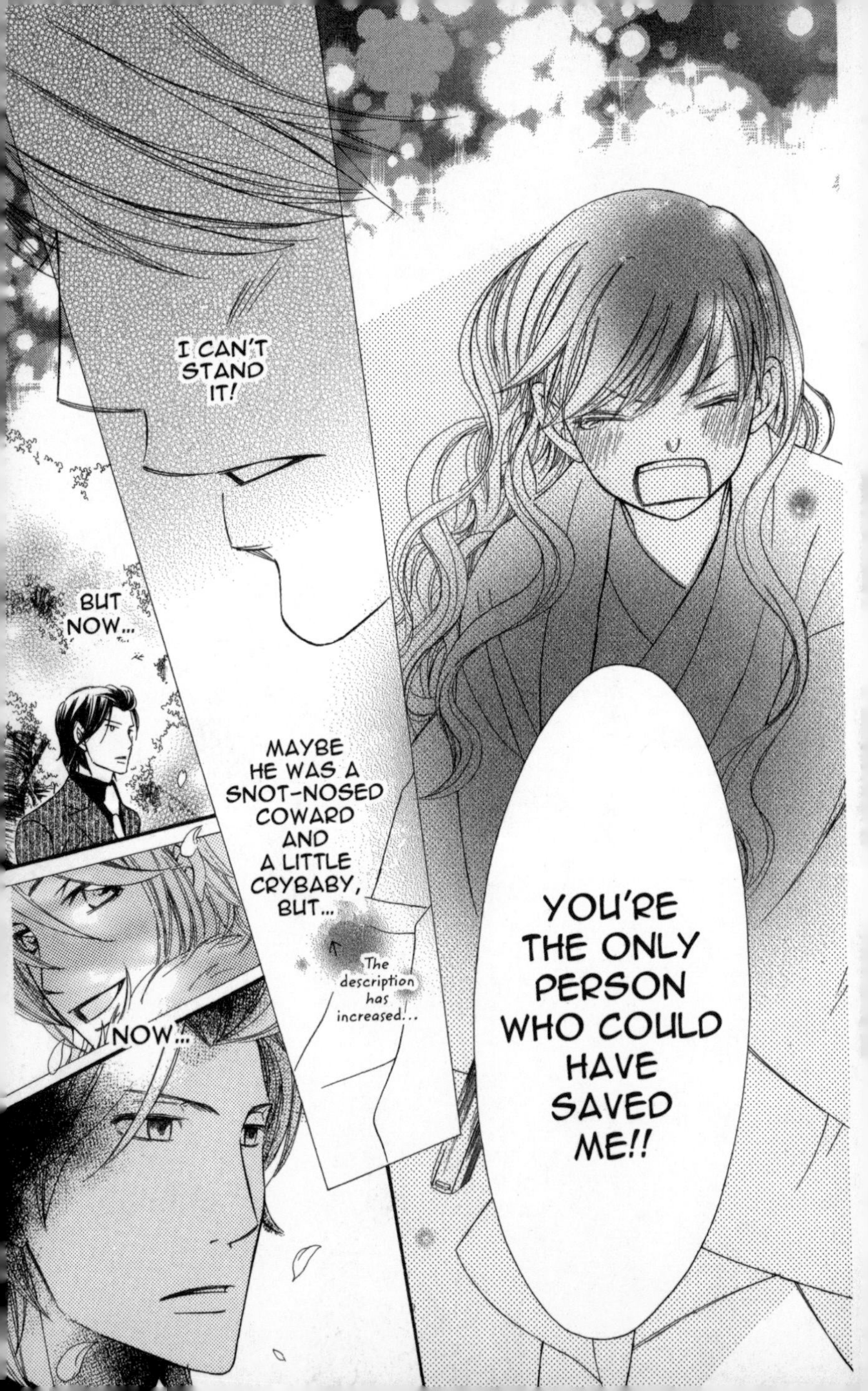
I CAN'T STAND IT!
MAYBE HE WAS A SNOT-NOSED COWARD AND A LITTLE CRYBABY, BUT...
The description has increased...
YOU'RE THE ONLY PERSON WHO COULD HAVE SAVED ME!!
BUT NOW...
NOW...

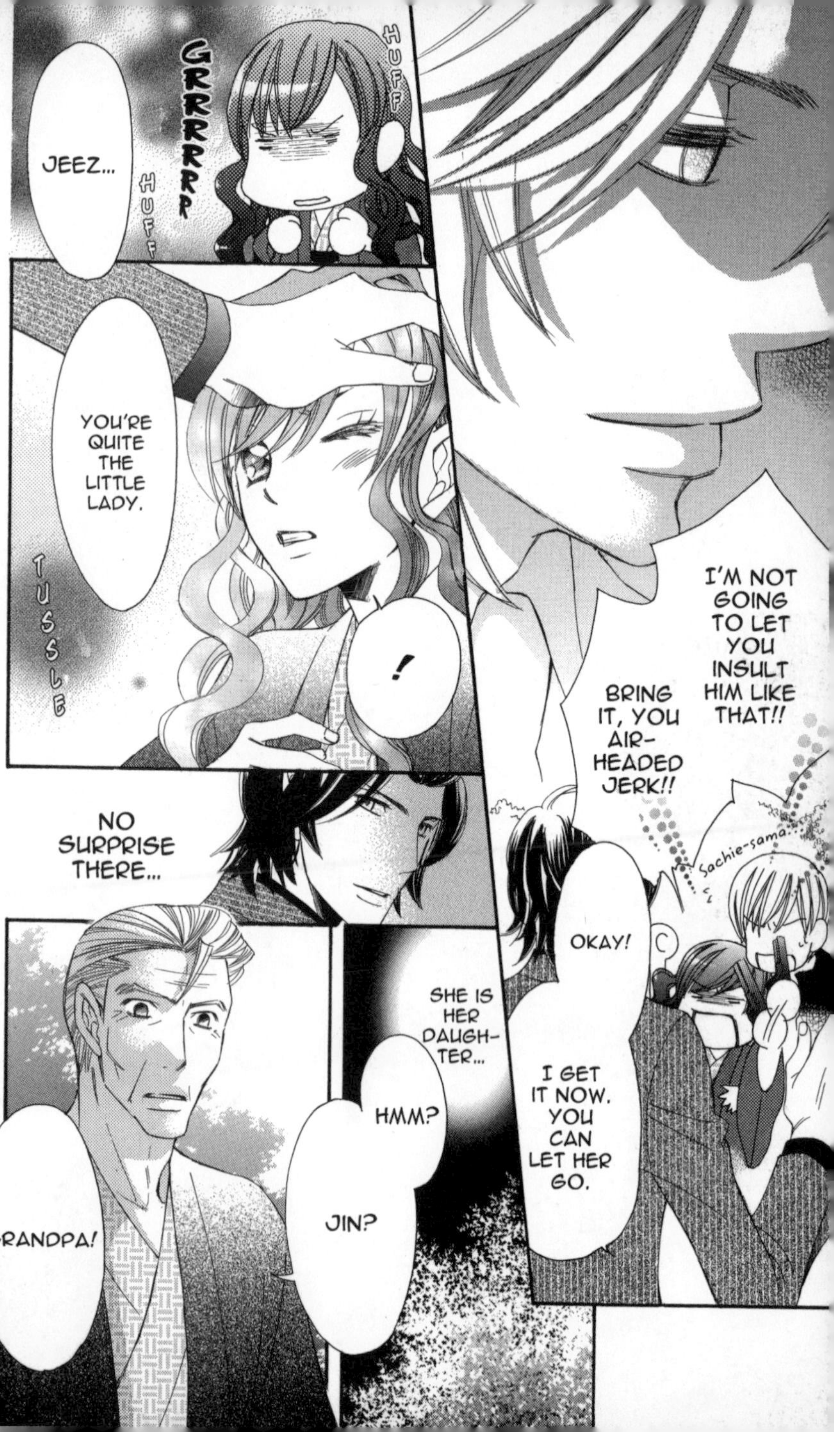
I'M NOT GOING TO LET YOU INSULT HIM LIKE THAT!!
BRING IT, YOU AIR-HEADED JERK!!
Sachie-sama...
OKAY!
I GET IT NOW. YOU CAN LET HER GO.
GRRRRRR
HUFF HUFF
JEEZ...
YOU'RE QUITE THE LITTLE LADY.
TUSSLE
!
NO SURPRISE THERE...
SHE IS HER DAUGHTER...
HMM?
JIN?
GRANDPA!

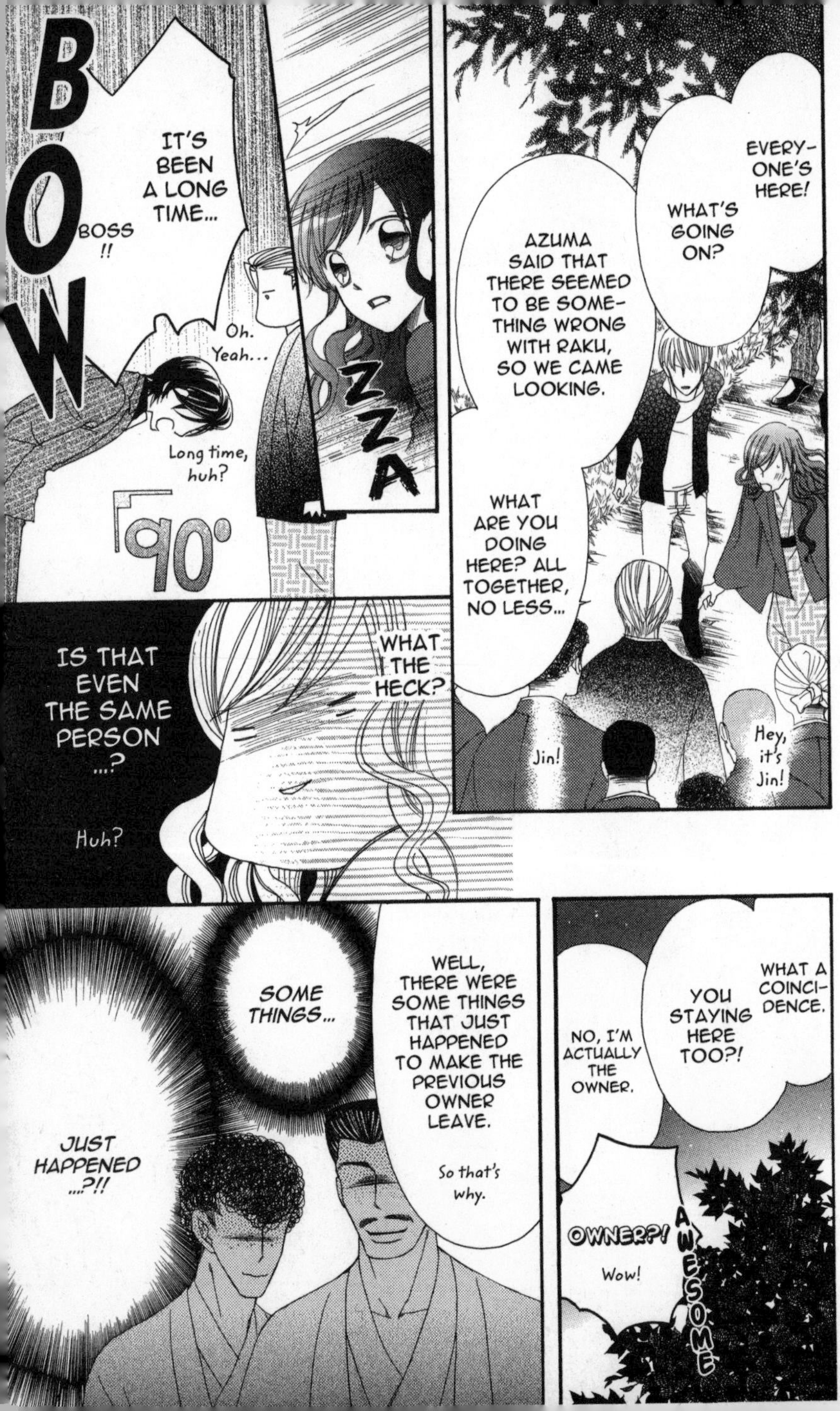
EVERY-ONE'S HERE!
WHAT'S GOING ON?
AZUMA SAID THAT THERE SEEMED TO BE SOME-THING WRONG WITH RAKU, SO WE CAME LOOKING.
WHAT ARE YOU DOING HERE? ALL TOGETHER, NO LESS...
Hey, it's Jin!
Jin!
ZZA
IT'S BEEN A LONG TIME... BOSS!!
BOW
Oh. Yeah...
Long time, huh?
90°
WHAT THE HECK?
IS THAT EVEN THE SAME PERSON ...?
Huh?
WHAT A COINCI-DENCE.
YOU STAYING HERE TOO?!
NO, I'M ACTUALLY THE OWNER.
OWNER?!
AWESOME
Wow!
WELL, THERE WERE SOME THINGS THAT JUST HAPPENED TO MAKE THE PREVIOUS OWNER LEAVE.
So that's why.
SOME THINGS...
JUST HAPPENED ...?!!

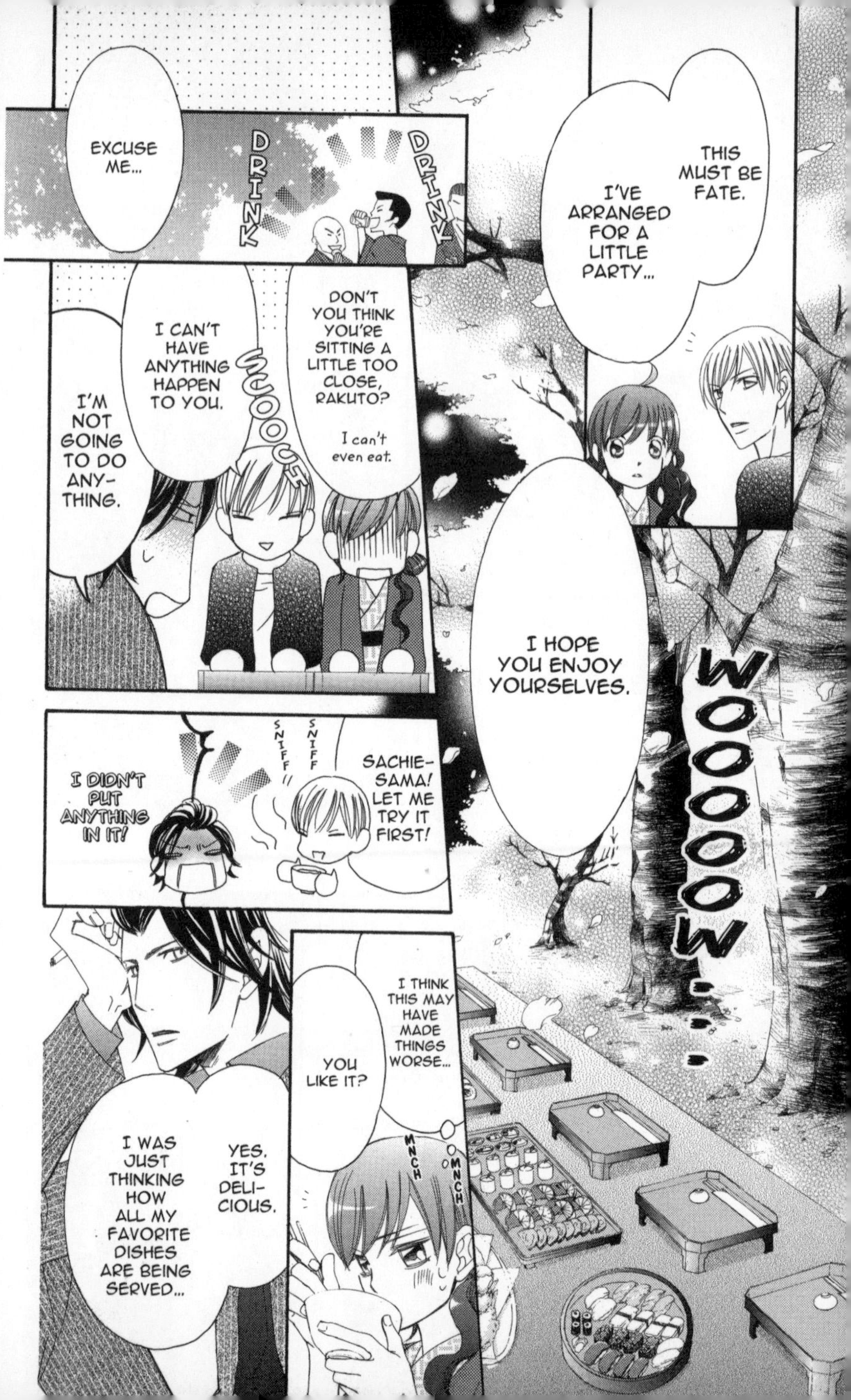
THIS MUST BE FATE.
I'VE ARRANGED FOR A LITTLE PARTY...
I HOPE YOU ENJOY YOURSELVES.
WOOOOOOW...
EXCUSE ME...
DRINK
DRINK
DON'T YOU THINK YOU'RE SITTING A LITTLE TOO CLOSE, RAKUTO?
I can't even eat.
I CAN'T HAVE ANYTHING HAPPEN TO YOU.
WOOOUCH
I'M NOT GOING TO DO ANY-THING.
SACHIE-SAMA! LET ME TRY IT FIRST!
SNIFF SNIFF
I DIDN'T PUT ANYTHING IN IT!
I THINK THIS MAY HAVE MADE THINGS WORSE...
YOU LIKE IT?
MNCH MNCH
YES. IT'S DELI-CIOUS.
I WAS JUST THINKING HOW ALL MY FAVORITE DISHES ARE BEING SERVED...

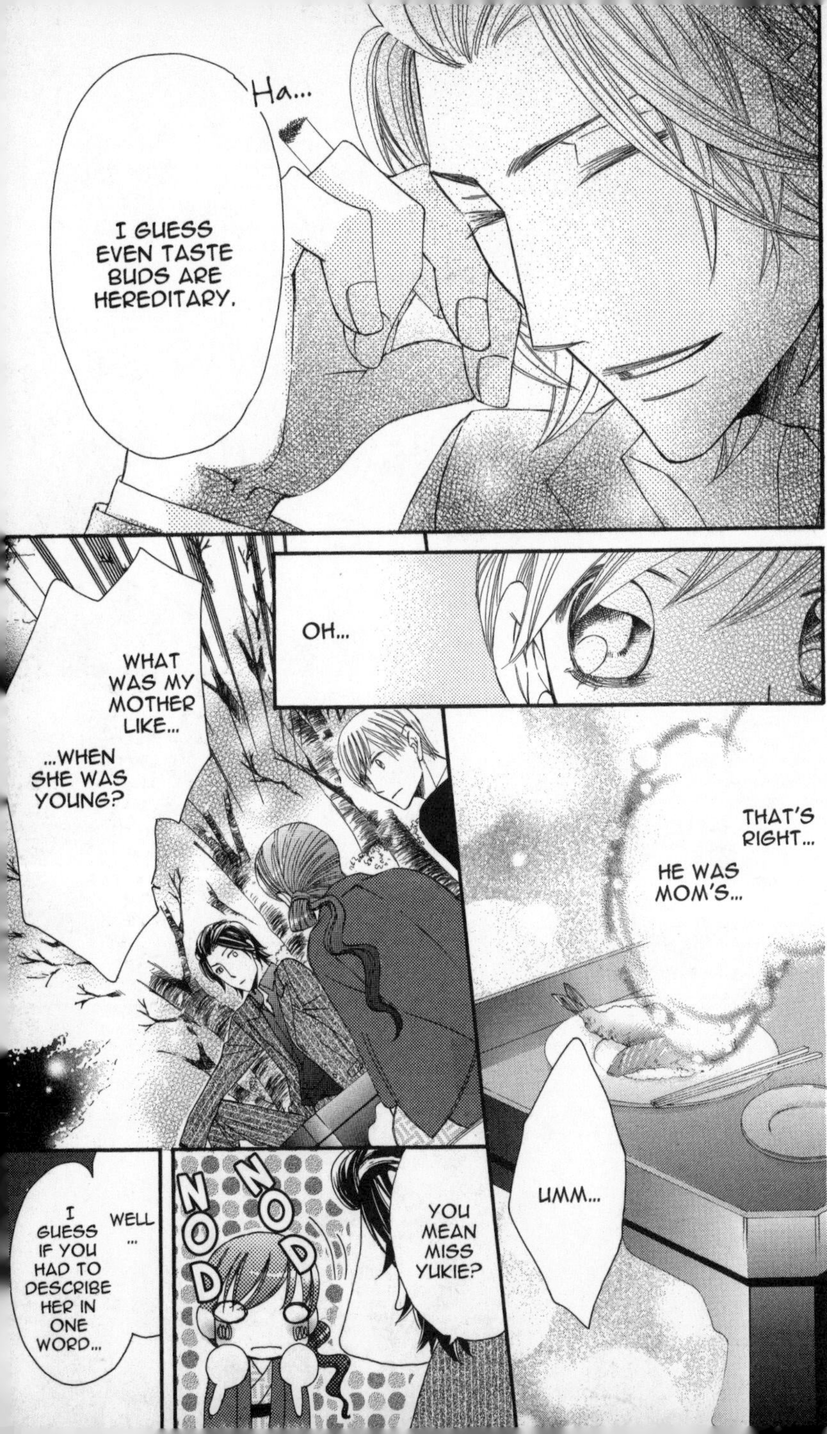
Ha...
I GUESS EVEN TASTE BUDS ARE HEREDITARY.
OH...
THAT'S RIGHT...
HE WAS MOM'S...
UMM...
WHAT WAS MY MOTHER LIKE...
...WHEN SHE WAS YOUNG?
YOU MEAN MISS YUKIE?
NOD NOD
WELL...
I GUESS IF YOU HAD TO DESCRIBE HER IN ONE WORD...

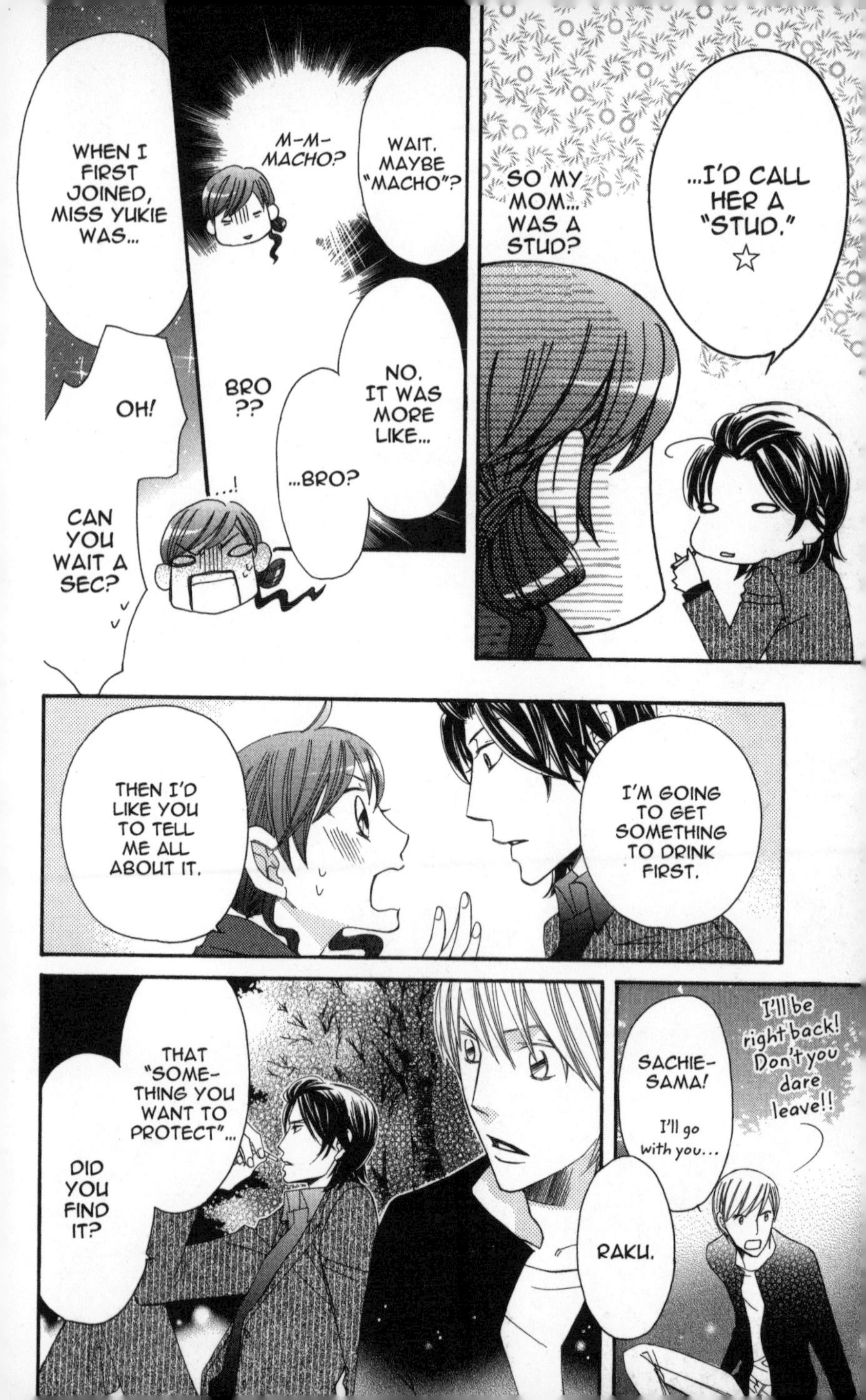
WHEN I FIRST JOINED, MISS YUKIE WAS...
...I'D CALL HER A "STUD." ☆
SO MY MOM... WAS A STUD?
WAIT. MAYBE "MACHO"?
M-M-MACHO?
NO. IT WAS MORE LIKE...
...BRO?
BRO ??
...!
OH!
CAN YOU WAIT A SEC?
I'M GOING TO GET SOMETHING TO DRINK FIRST.
THEN I'D LIKE YOU TO TELL ME ALL ABOUT IT.
I'll be right back! Don't you dare leave!!
SACHIE-SAMA!
I'll go with you...
RAKU.
THAT "SOMETHING YOU WANT TO PROTECT"...
DID YOU FIND IT?

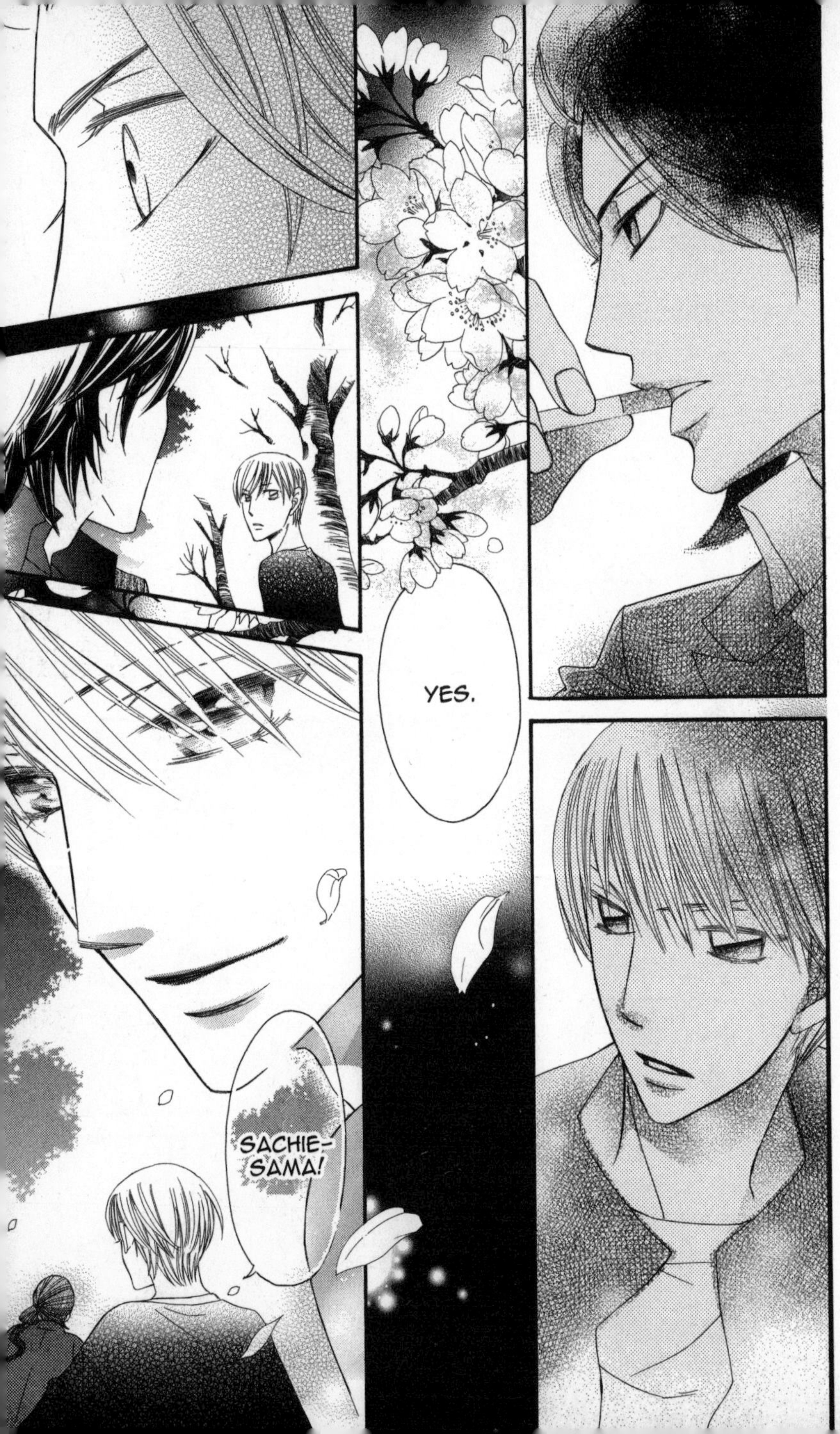
YES.
SACHIE-SAMA!

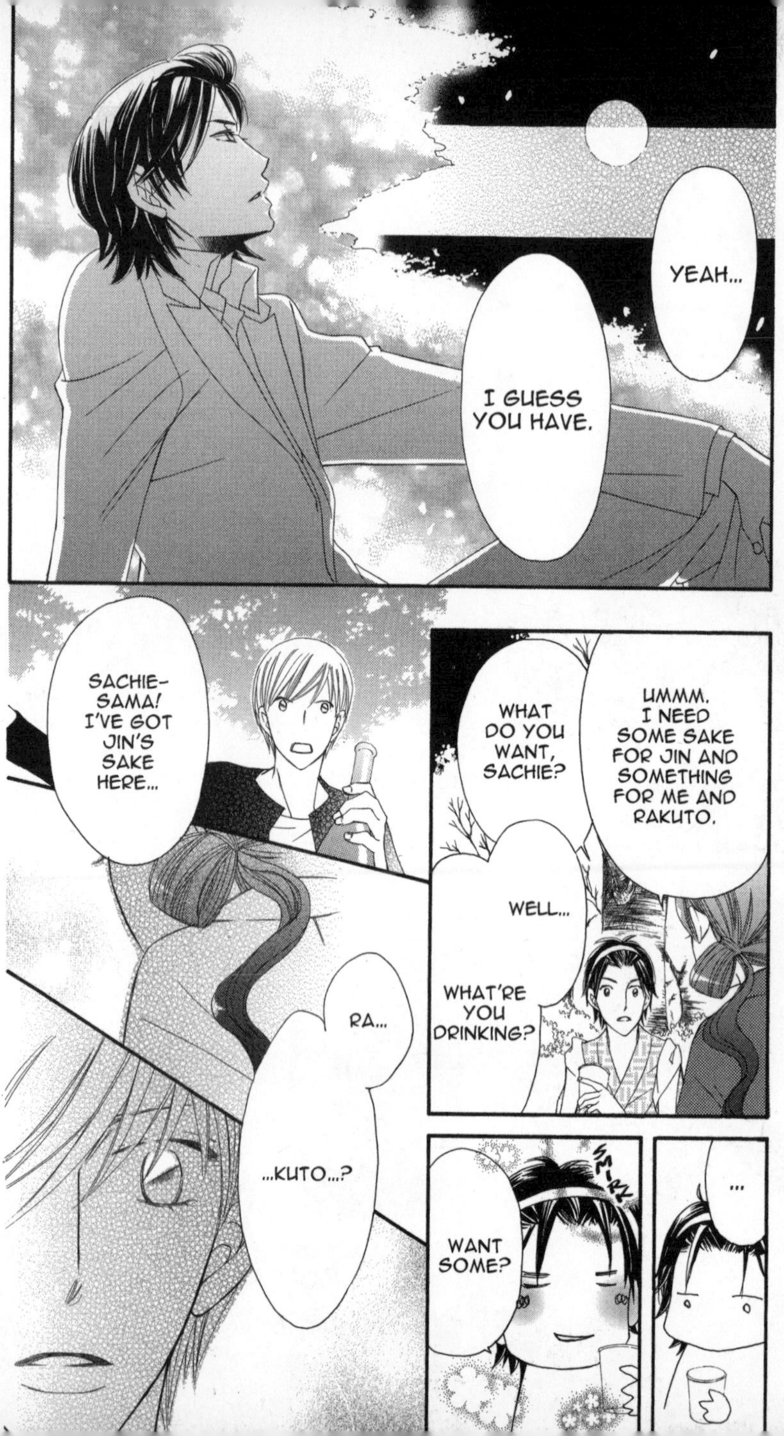
YEAH...
I GUESS YOU HAVE.
UMMM. I NEED SOME SAKE FOR JIN AND SOMETHING FOR ME AND RAKUTO.
WHAT DO YOU WANT, SACHIE?
WELL...
WHAT'RE YOU DRINKING?
...
SMIRK
WANT SOME?
SACHIE-SAMA! I'VE GOT JIN'S SAKE HERE...
RA...
...KUTO...?

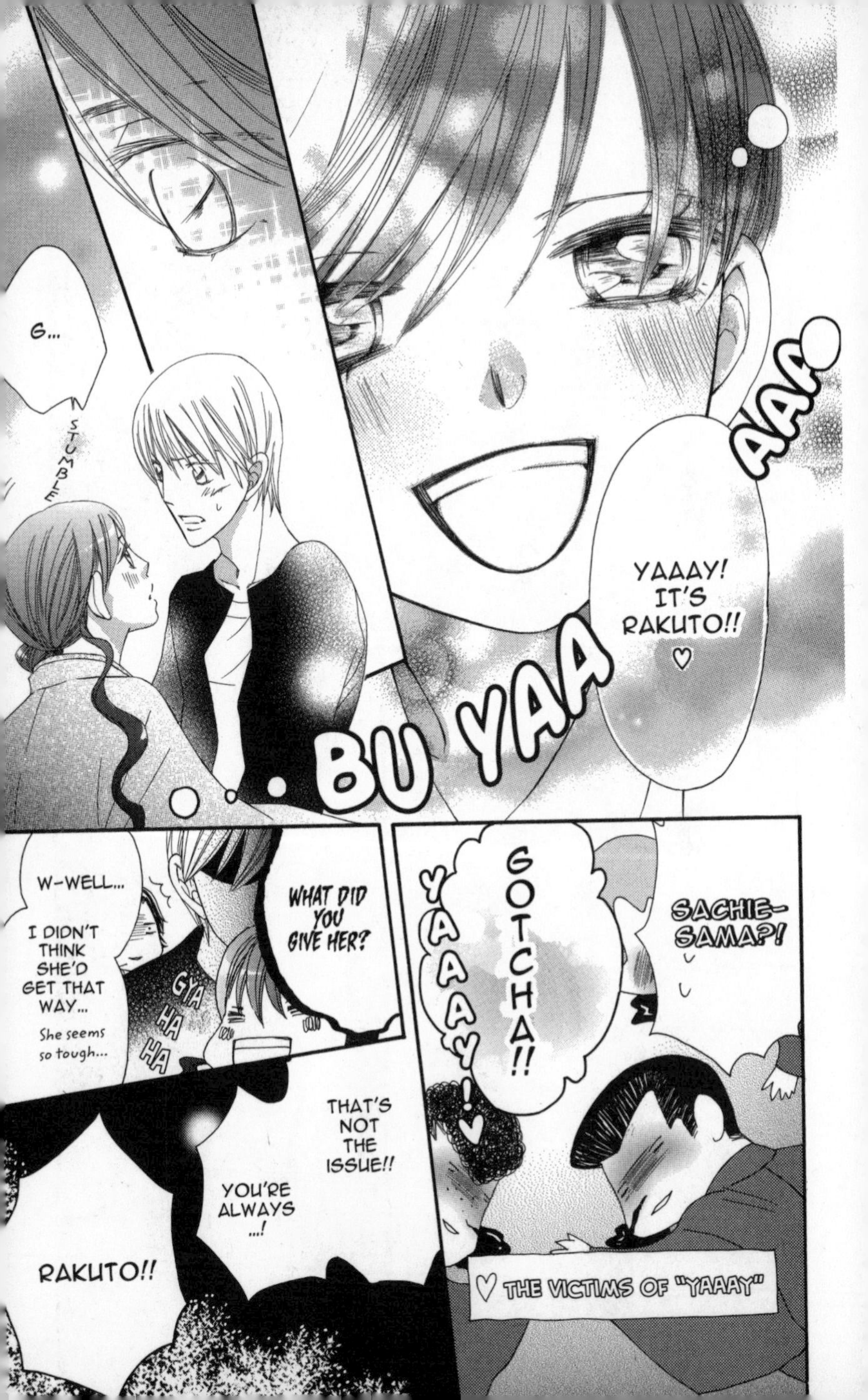
YAAAY! IT'S RAKUTO!! ♡
...BU YAA AAA
G...
STUMBLE
SACHIE-SAMA?!
GOTCHA!!
YAAAAY! ♡
♡ THE VICTIMS OF "YAAAY"
WHAT DID YOU GIVE HER?
W-WELL...
I DIDN'T THINK SHE'D GET THAT WAY...
She seems so tough...
GYA HA HA HA
THAT'S NOT THE ISSUE!!
YOU'RE ALWAYS ...!
RAKUTO!!

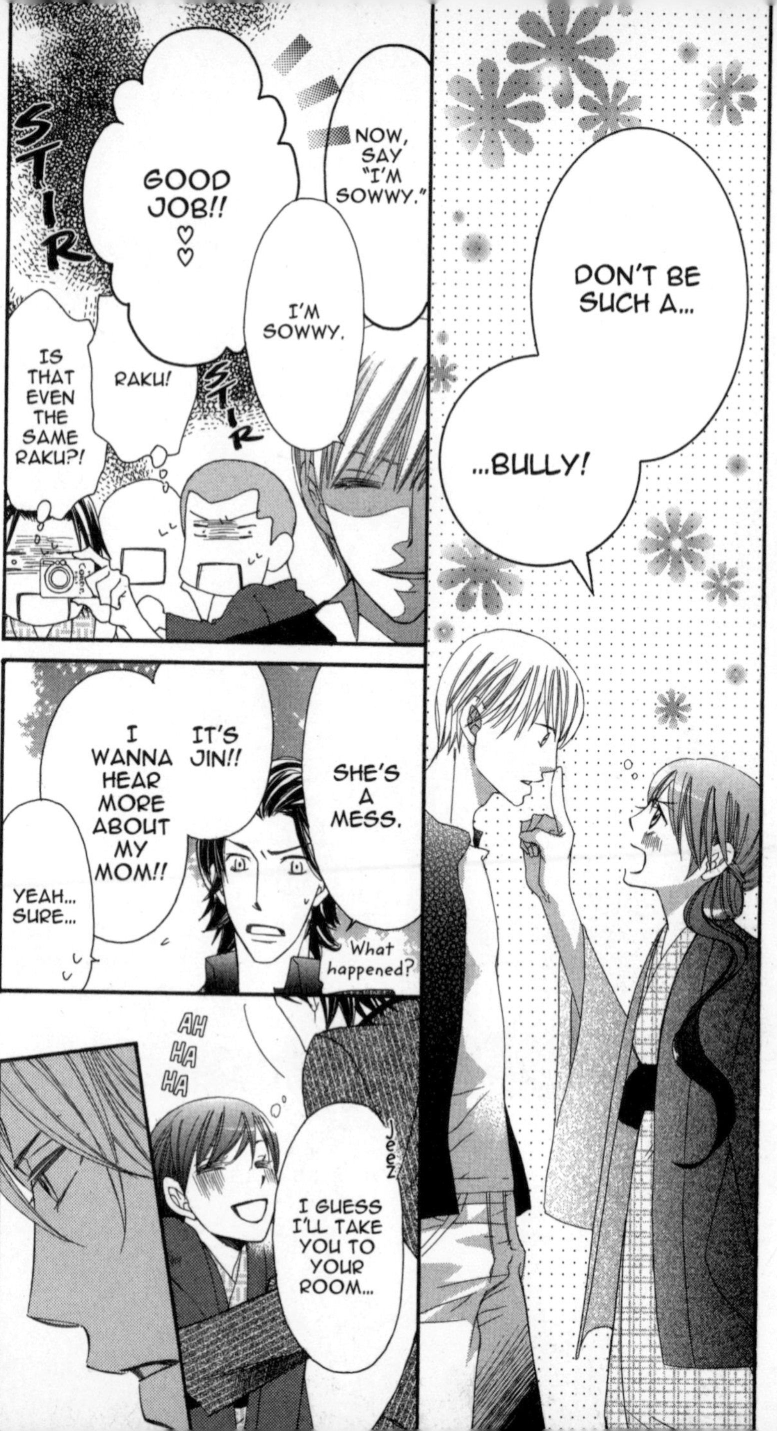
DON'T BE SUCH A...
...BULLY!
NOW, SAY "I'M SOWWY."
GOOD JOB!! ♡ ♡
STIR
I'M SOWWY.
STIR
RAKU!
IS THAT EVEN THE SAME RAKU?!
SHE'S A MESS.
IT'S JIN!!
I WANNA HEAR MORE ABOUT MY MOM!!
YEAH... SURE...
What happened?
AH HA HA HA
Jeez
I GUESS I'LL TAKE YOU TO YOUR ROOM...

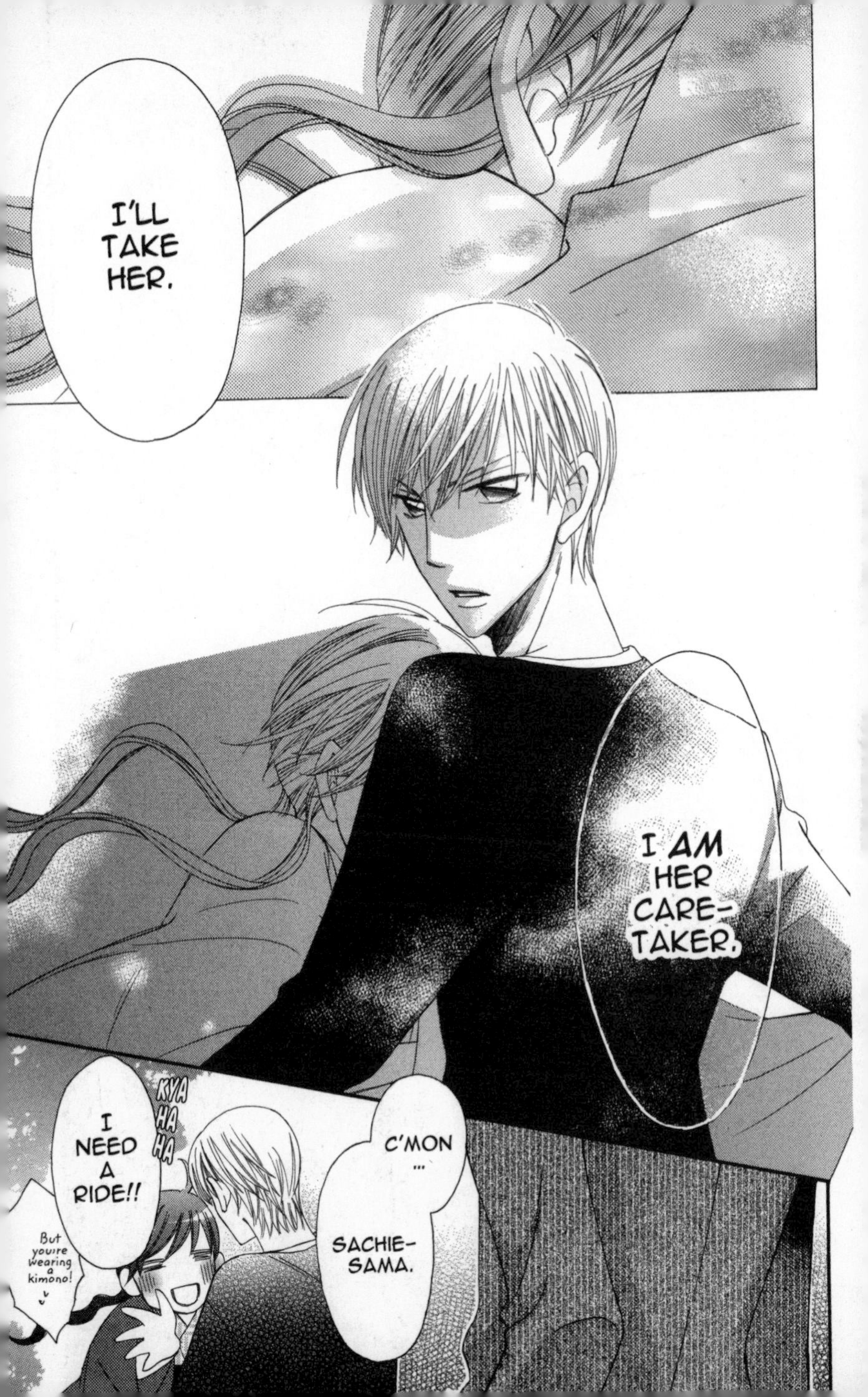
I'LL TAKE HER.
I AM HER CARE-TAKER.
C'MON ... SACHIE-SAMA.
KYA HA HA
I NEED A RIDE!!
But you're wearing a kimono!

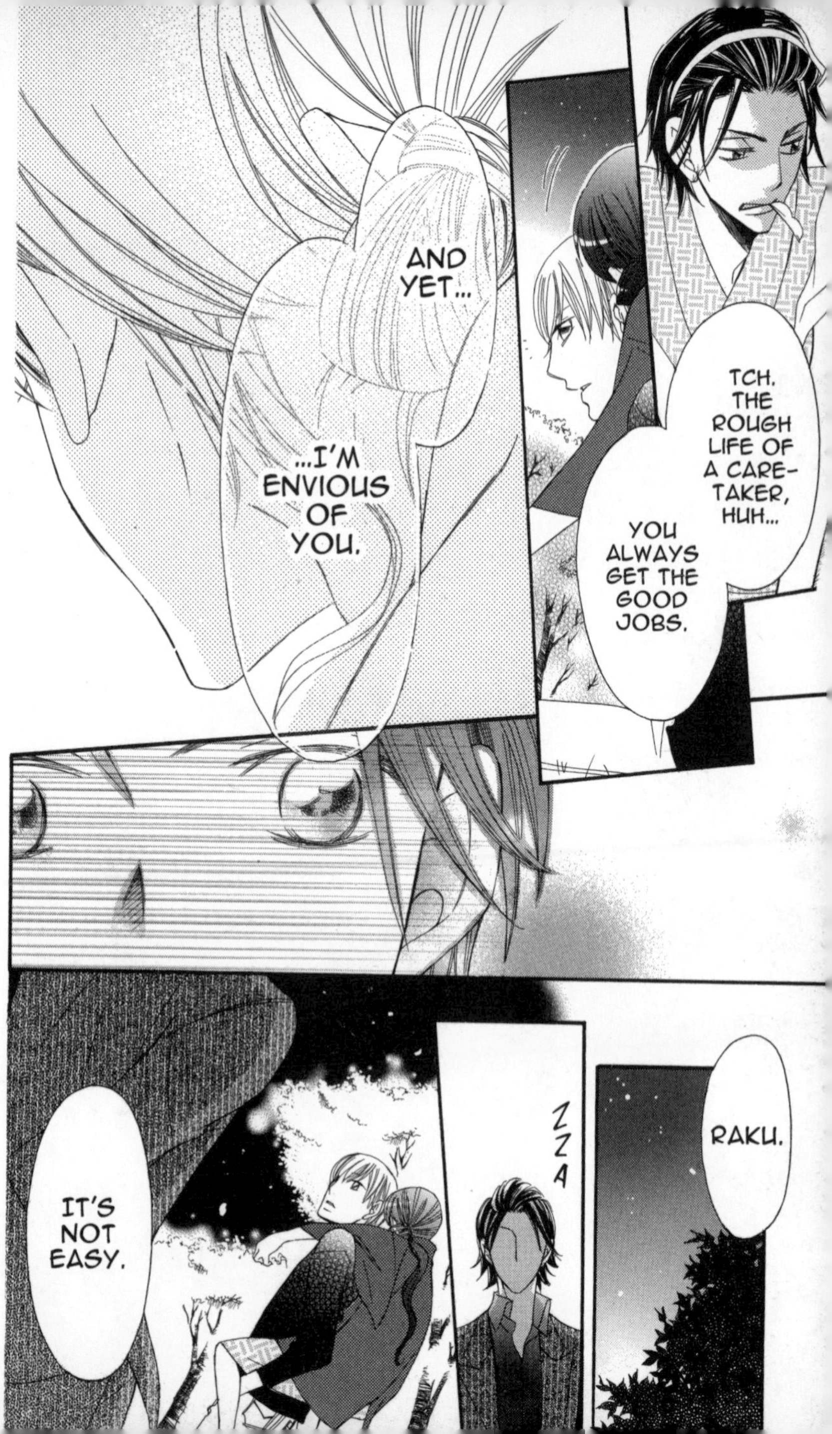
TCH. THE ROUGH LIFE OF A CARE-TAKER, HUH...
YOU ALWAYS GET THE GOOD JOBS.
AND YET...
...I'M ENVIOUS OF YOU.
RAKU.
ZZA
IT'S NOT EASY.

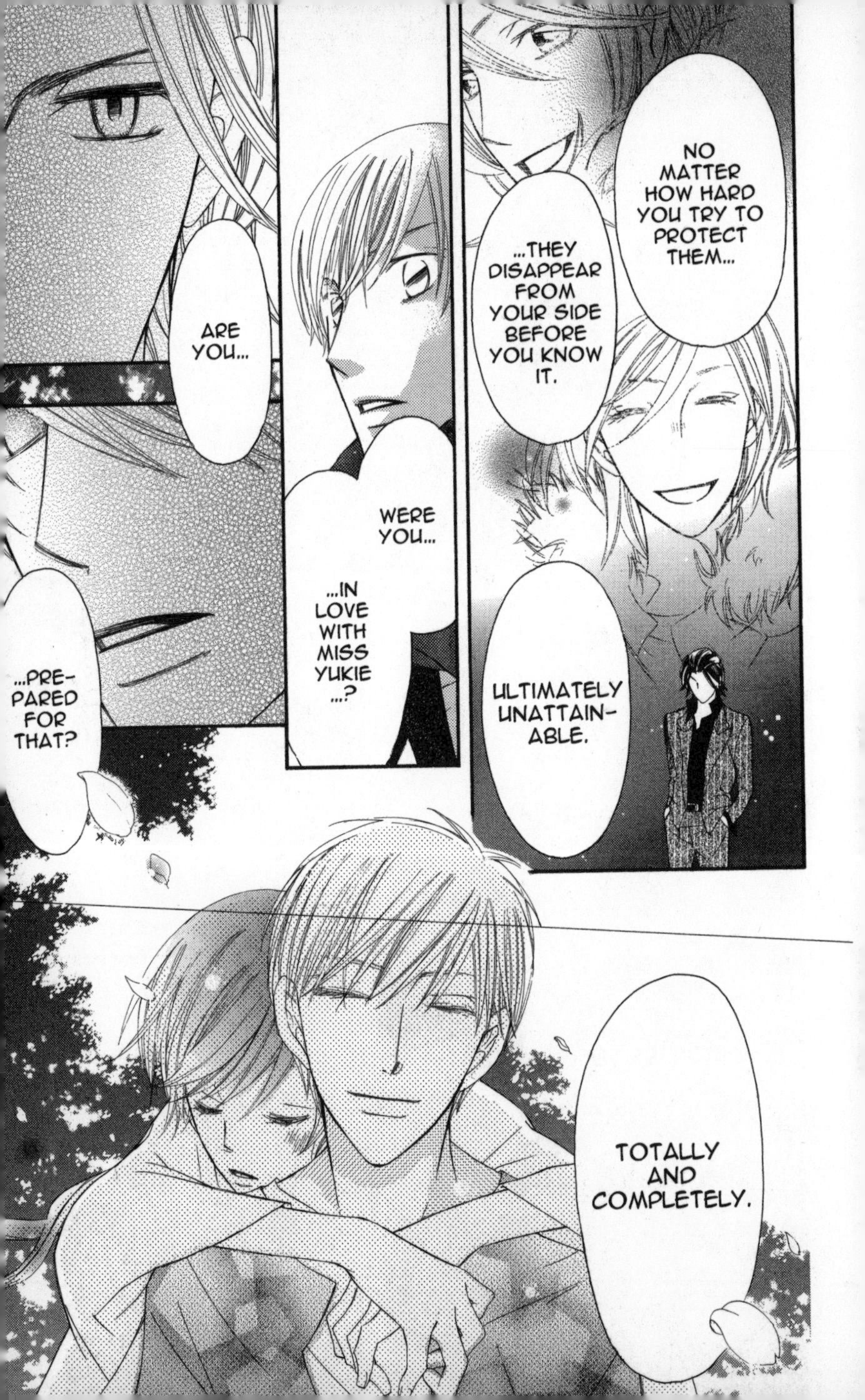
NO MATTER HOW HARD YOU TRY TO PROTECT THEM...
...THEY DISAPPEAR FROM YOUR SIDE BEFORE YOU KNOW IT.
ULTIMATELY UNATTAIN-ABLE.
WERE YOU...
...IN LOVE WITH MISS YUKIE ...?
ARE YOU...
...PRE-PARED FOR THAT?
TOTALLY AND COMPLETELY.

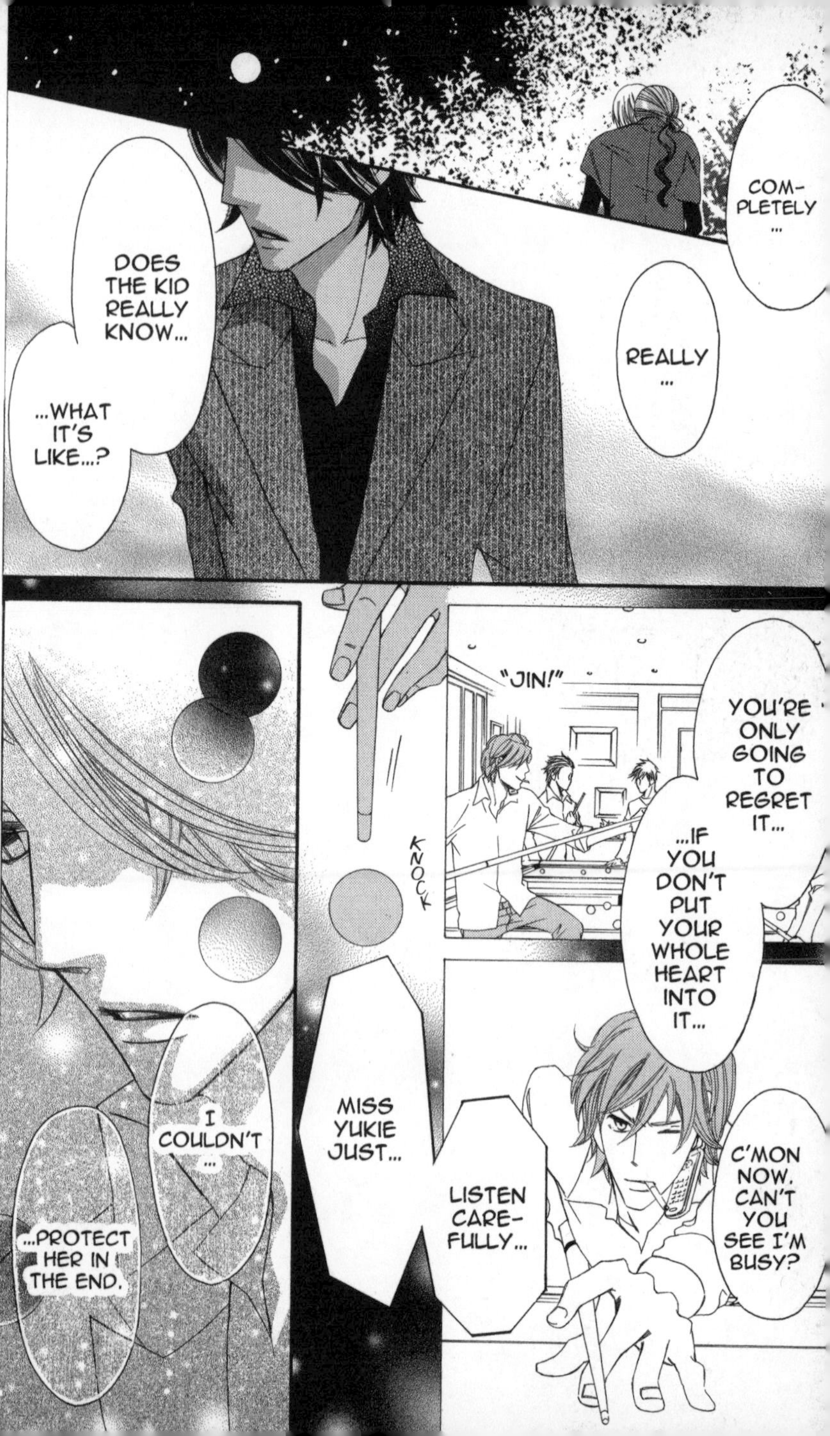
COM-PLETELY ...
REALLY ...
DOES THE KID REALLY KNOW...
...WHAT IT'S LIKE...?
YOU'RE ONLY GOING TO REGRET IT...
...IF YOU DON'T PUT YOUR WHOLE HEART INTO IT...
"JIN!"
C'MON NOW. CAN'T YOU SEE I'M BUSY?
LISTEN CARE-FULLY...
MISS YUKIE JUST...
KNOCK
I COULDN'T ...
...PROTECT HER IN THE END.

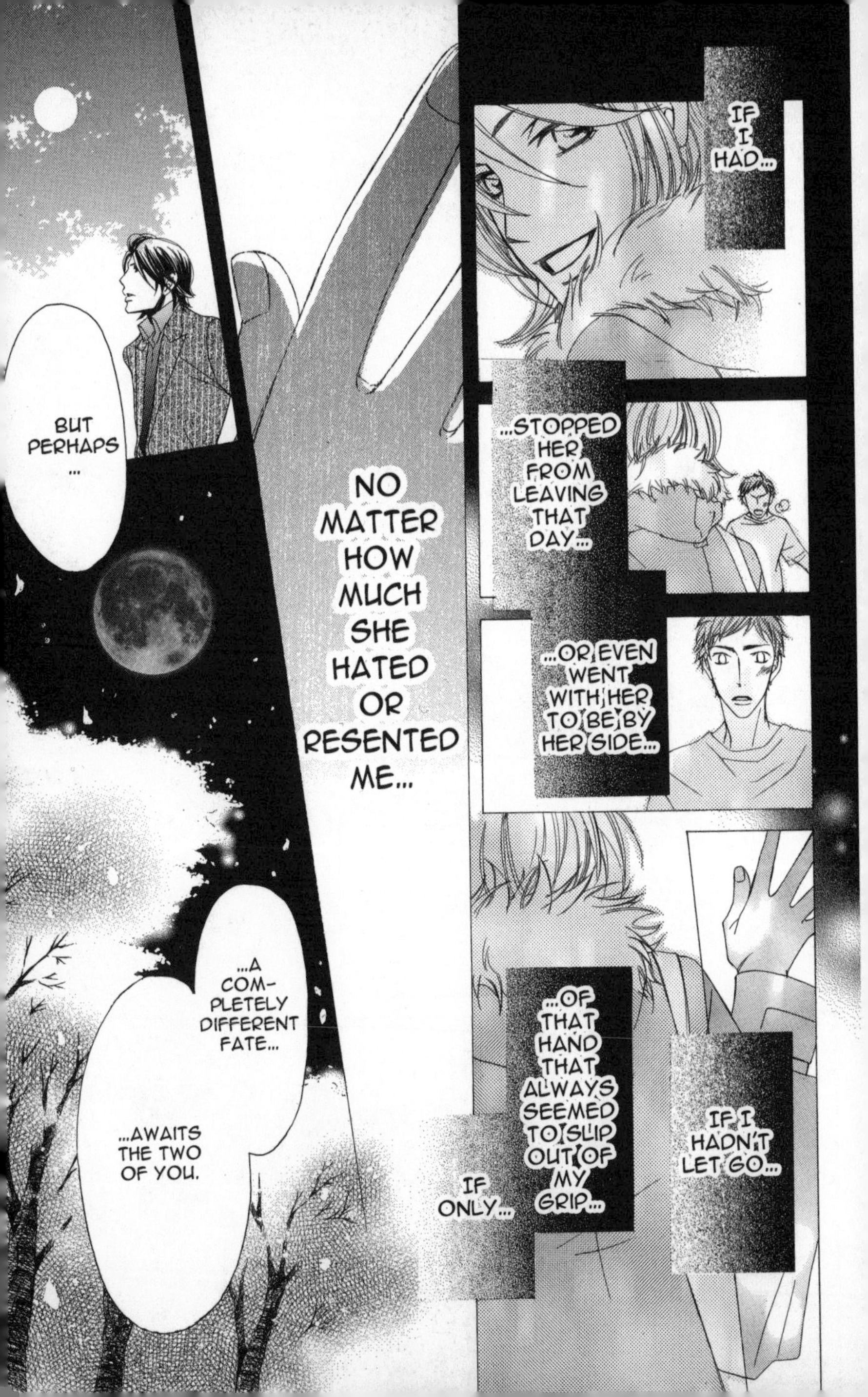
IF I HAD...
...STOPPED HER FROM LEAVING THAT DAY...
...OR EVEN WENT WITH HER TO BE BY HER SIDE...
IF I HADN'T LET GO...
...OF THAT HAND THAT ALWAYS SEEMED TO SLIP OUT OF MY GRIP...
IF ONLY...
NO MATTER HOW MUCH SHE HATED OR RESENTED ME...
BUT PERHAPS ...
...A COMPLETELY DIFFERENT FATE...
...AWAITS THE TWO OF YOU.

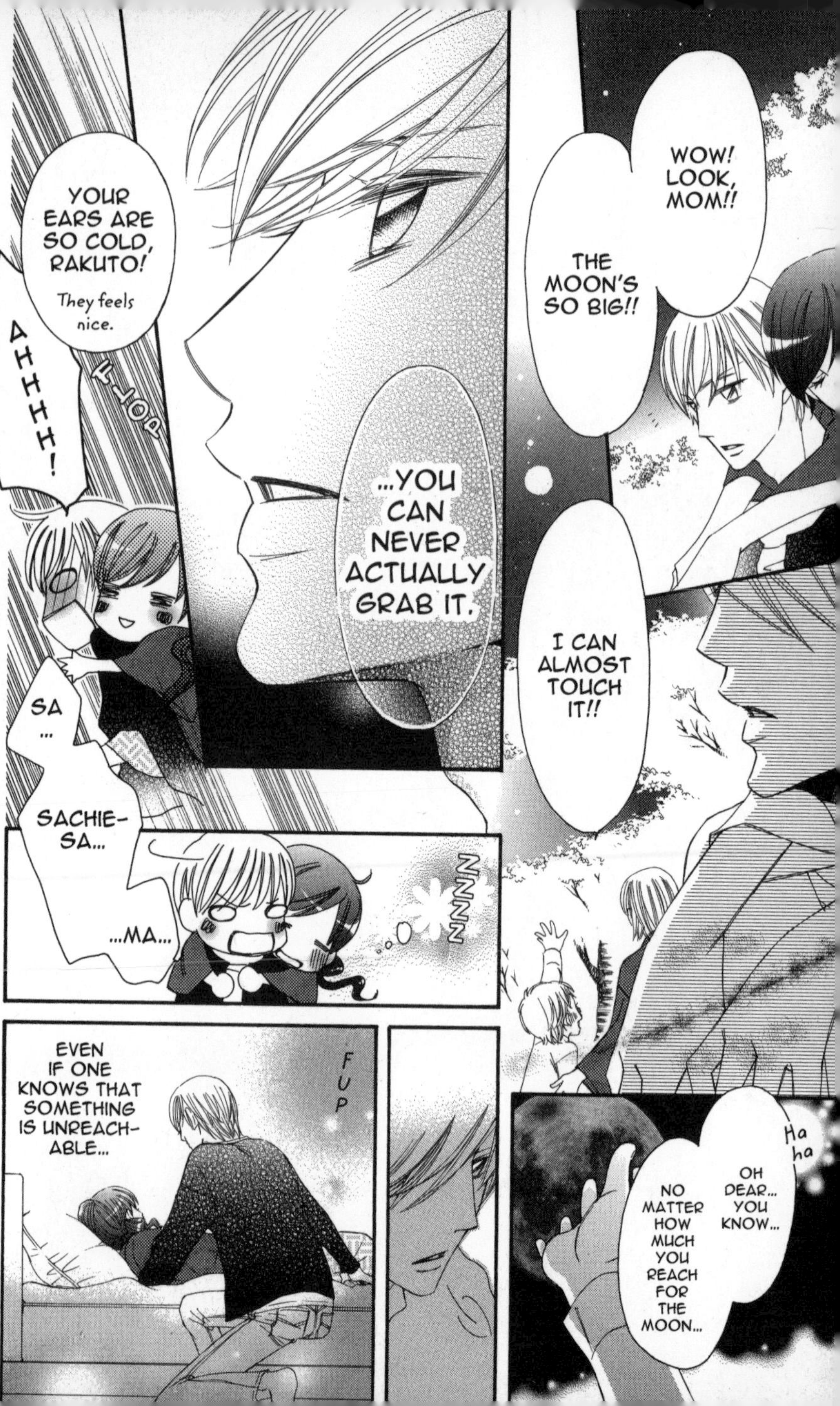
WOW! LOOK, MOM!!
THE MOON'S SO BIG!!
I CAN ALMOST TOUCH IT!!
...YOU CAN NEVER ACTUALLY GRAB IT.
YOUR EARS ARE SO COLD, RAKUTO!
They feels nice.
AHHHHH!
FLOP
SA...
SACHIE-SA...
...MA...
ZZZZ
Ha ha
OH DEAR... YOU KNOW...
NO MATTER HOW MUCH YOU REACH FOR THE MOON...
FUP
EVEN IF ONE KNOWS THAT SOMETHING IS UNREACHABLE...

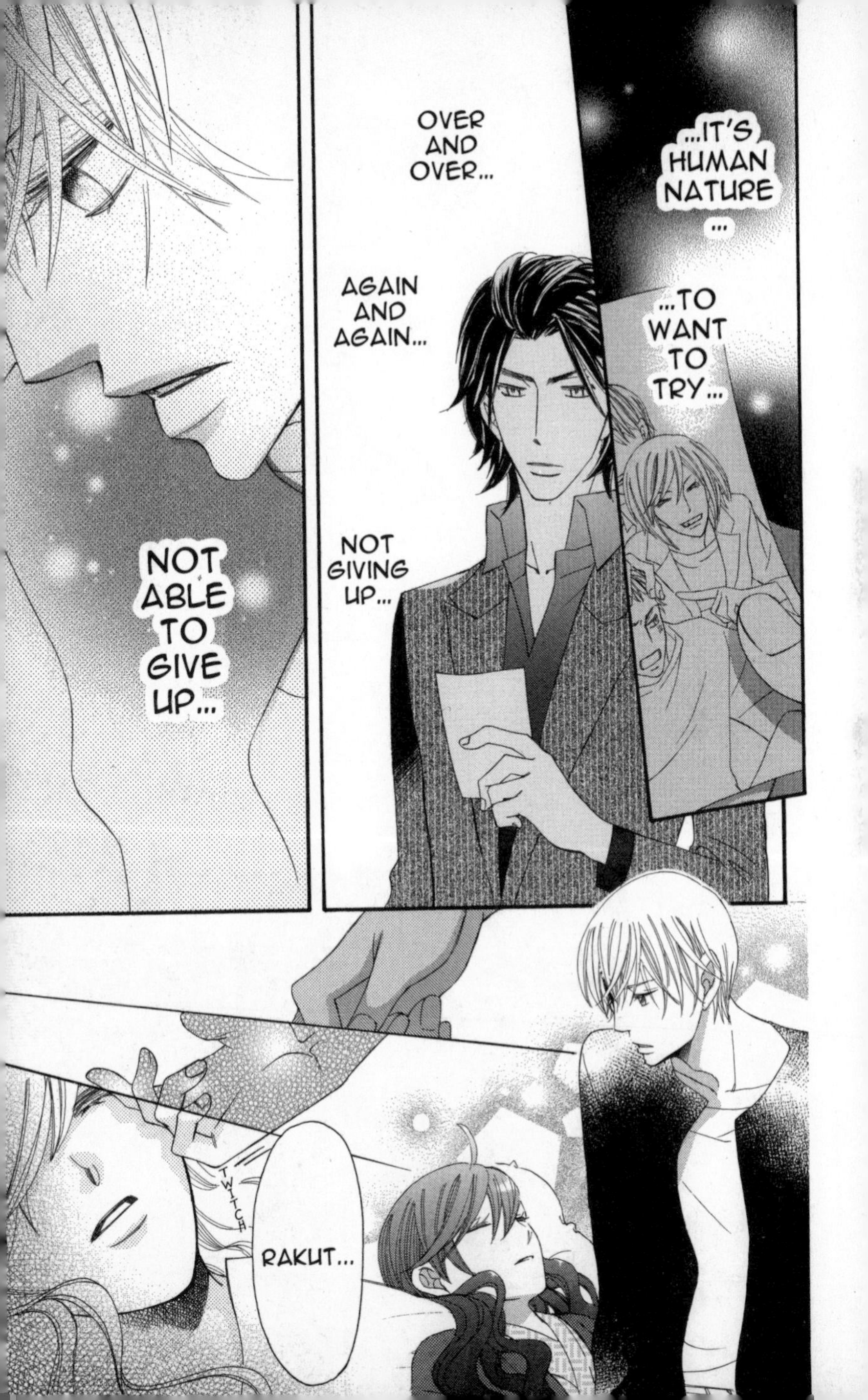
...IT'S HUMAN NATURE ...
...TO WANT TO TRY...
OVER AND OVER...
AGAIN AND AGAIN...
NOT GIVING UP...
NOT ABLE TO GIVE UP...
TWITCH
RAKUT...

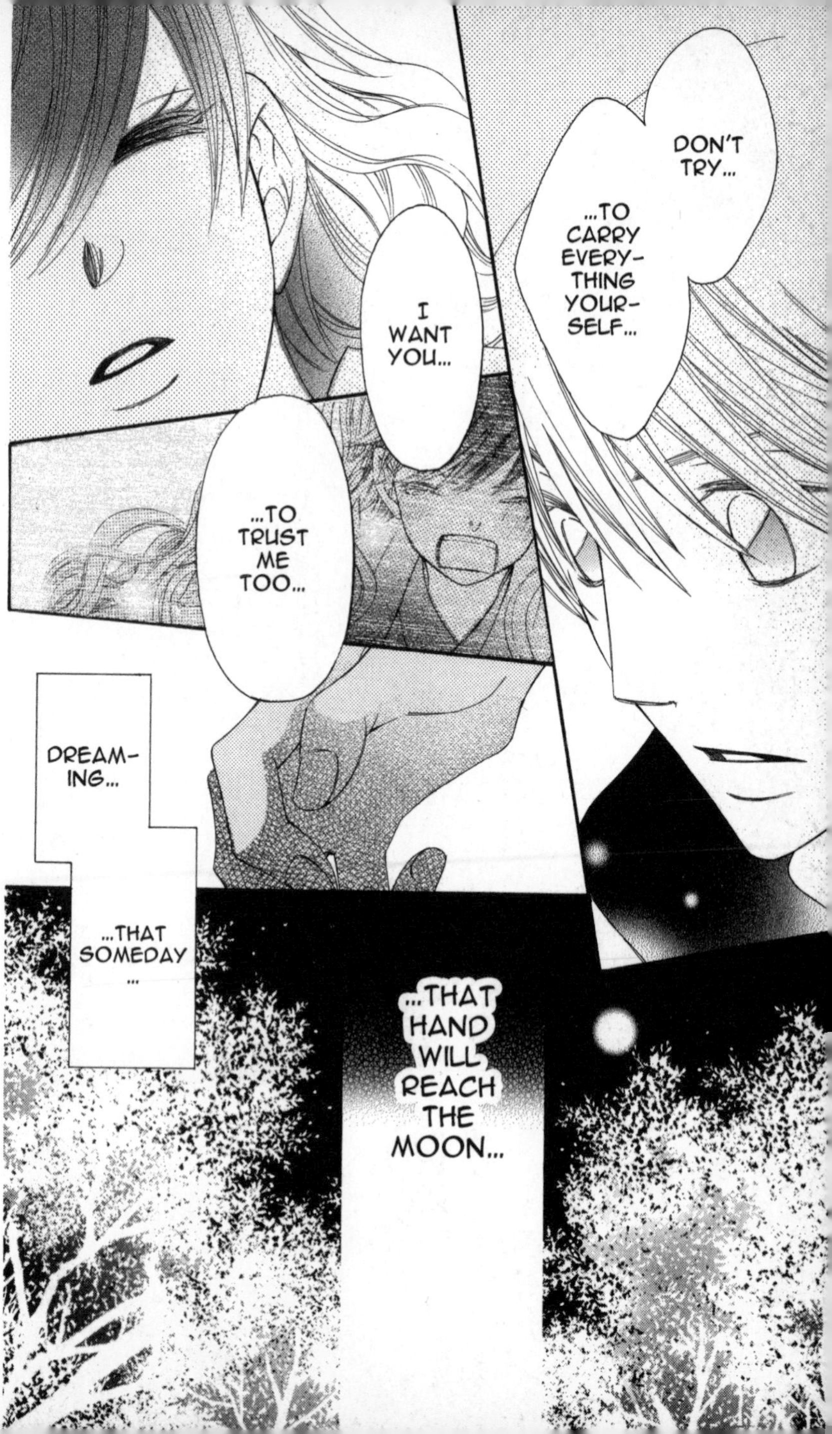
DON'T TRY...
...TO CARRY EVERY-THING YOUR-SELF...
I WANT YOU...
...TO TRUST ME TOO...
DREAMING...
...THAT SOMEDAY...
...THAT HAND WILL REACH THE MOON...

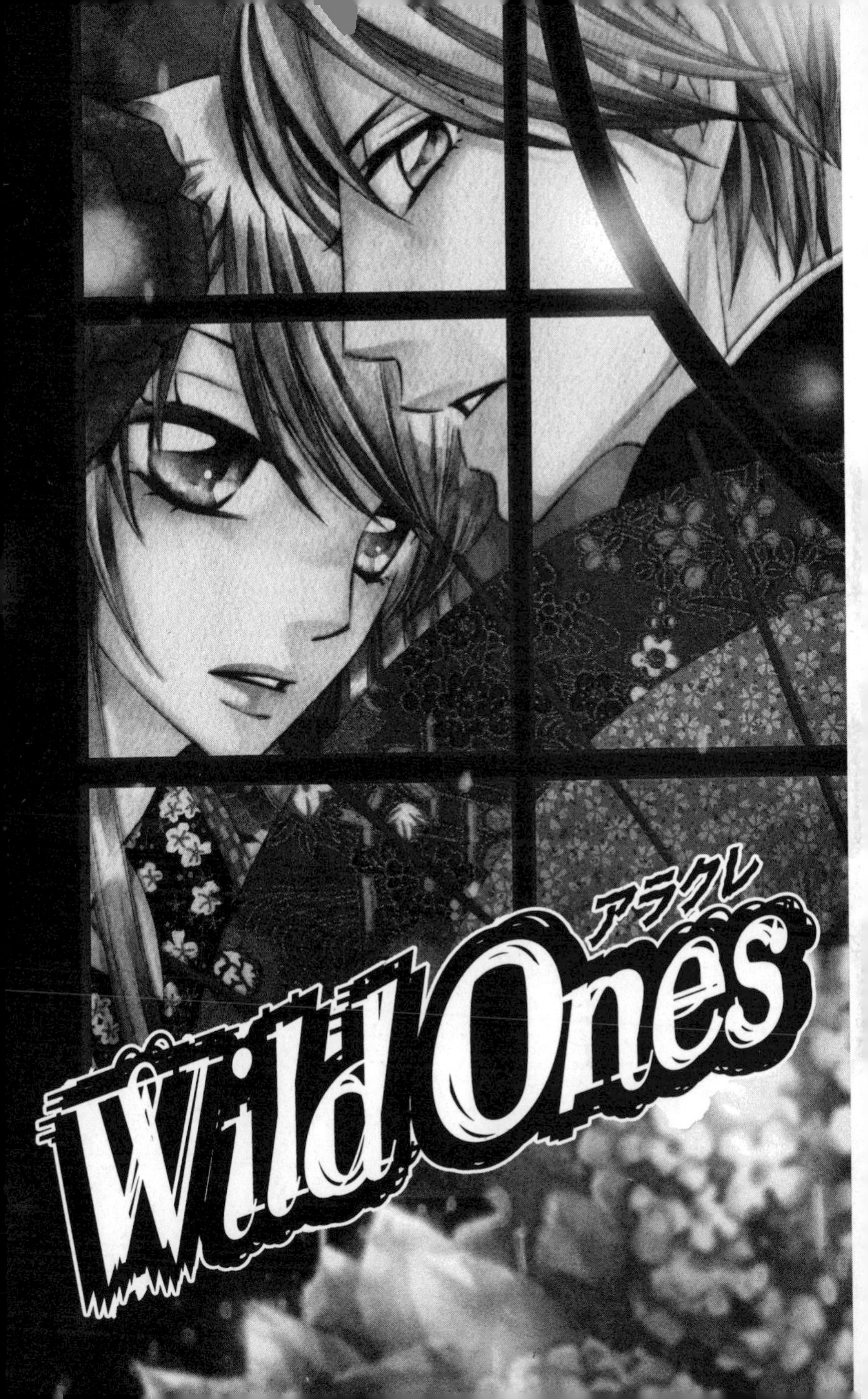
アラクレ
Wild Ones

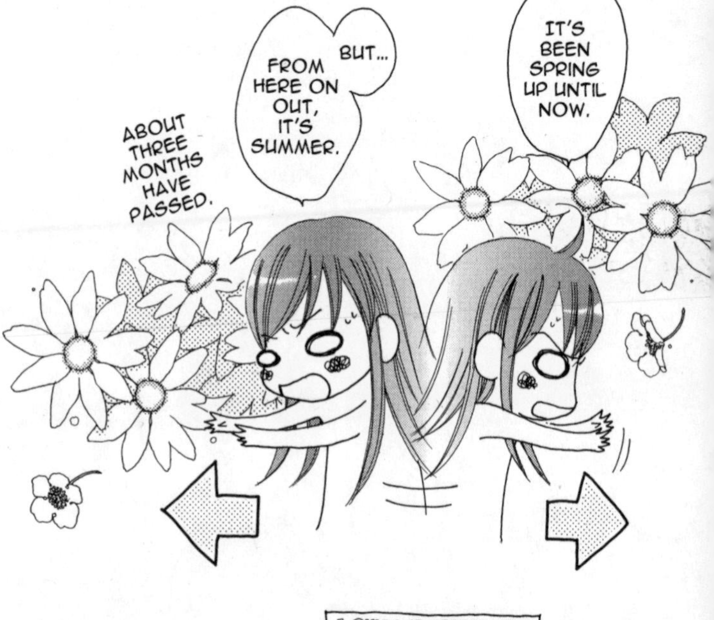
IT'S BEEN SPRING UP UNTIL NOW.
BUT... FROM HERE ON OUT, IT'S SUMMER.
ABOUT THREE MONTHS HAVE PASSED.

A QUICK ADMINISTRATIVE NOTE

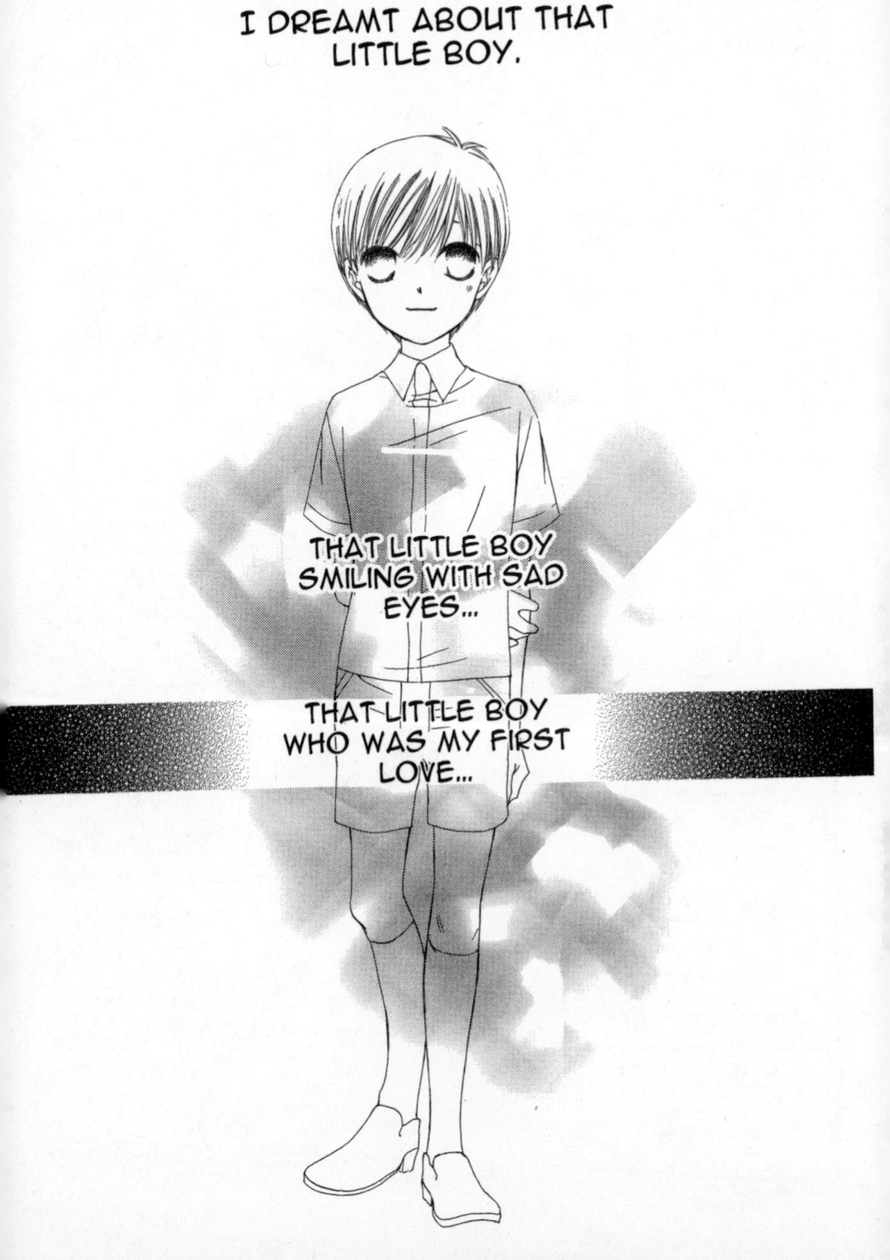
I DREAMT ABOUT THAT LITTLE BOY.
THAT LITTLE BOY SMILING WITH SAD EYES...
THAT LITTLE BOY WHO WAS MY FIRST LOVE...

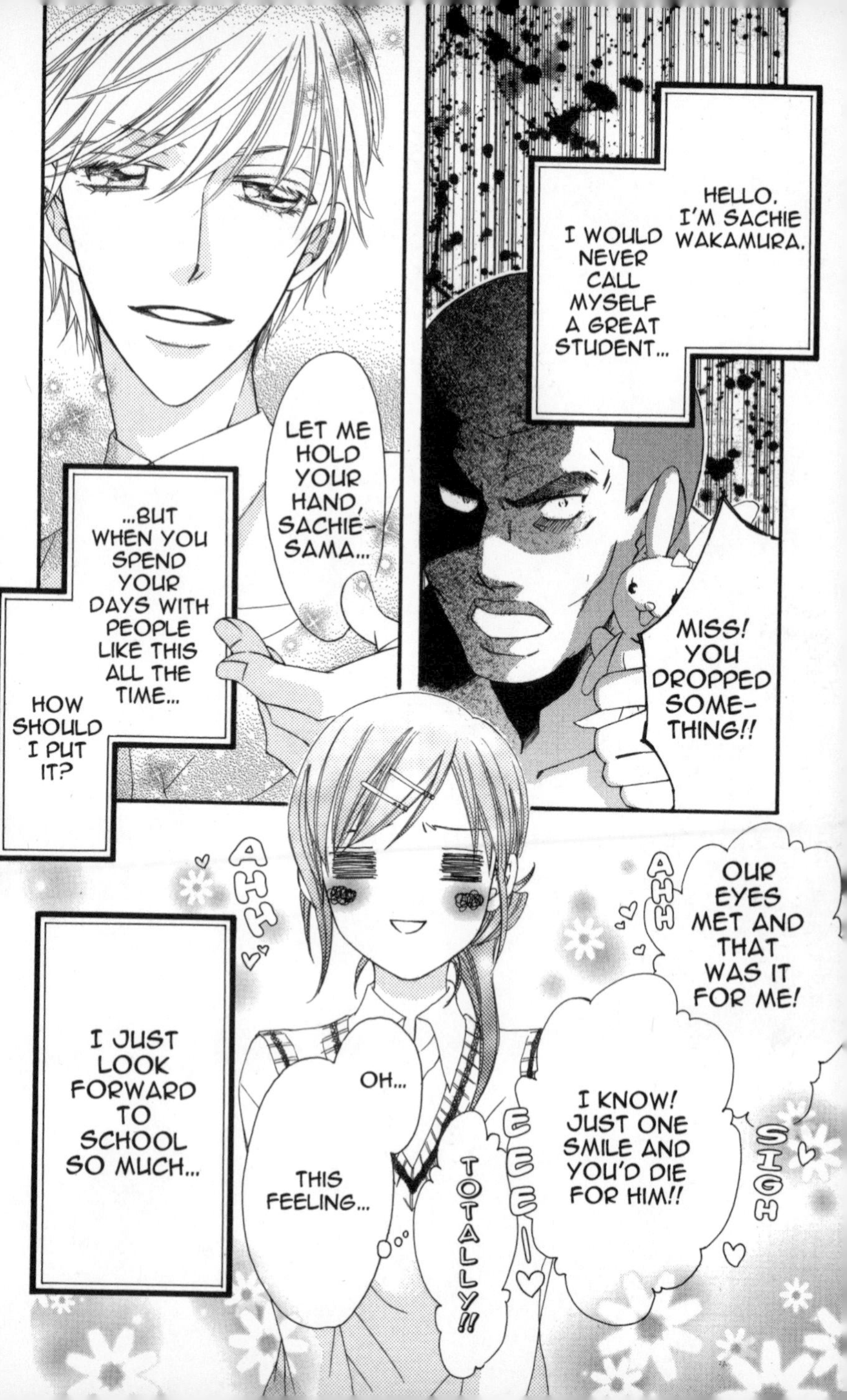
HELLO. I'M SACHIE WAKAMURA.
I WOULD NEVER CALL MYSELF A GREAT STUDENT...
MISS! YOU DROPPED SOME-THING!!
LET ME HOLD YOUR HAND, SACHIE-SAMA...
...BUT WHEN YOU SPEND YOUR DAYS WITH PEOPLE LIKE THIS ALL THE TIME...
HOW SHOULD I PUT IT?
AHH
OUR EYES MET AND THAT WAS IT FOR ME!
SIGH
I KNOW! JUST ONE SMILE AND YOU'D DIE FOR HIM!!
EEEI
TOTALLY!!
OH...
THIS FEELING...
AHH
I JUST LOOK FORWARD TO SCHOOL SO MUCH...

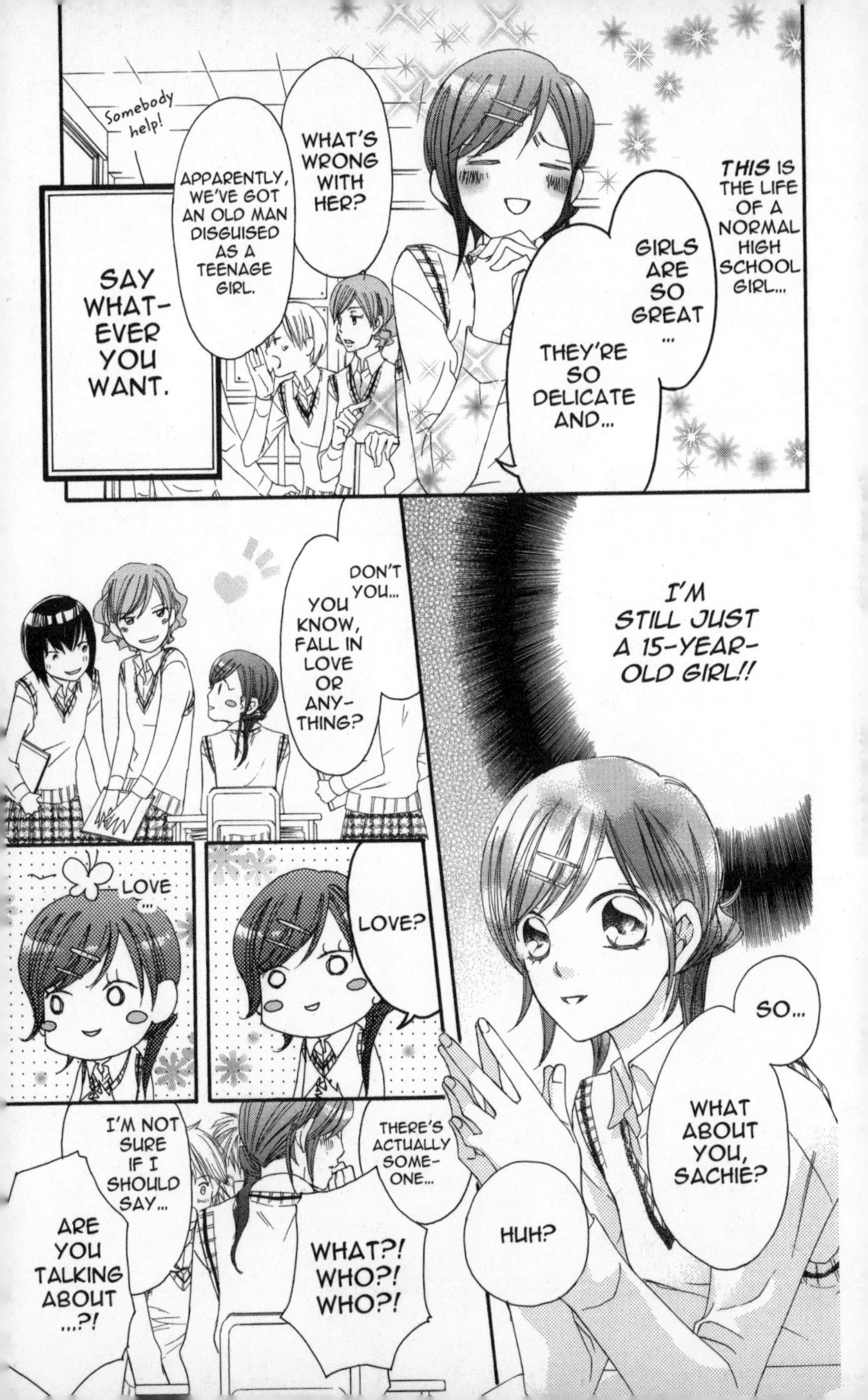
THIS IS THE LIFE OF A NORMAL HIGH SCHOOL GIRL...
GIRLS ARE SO GREAT ...
THEY'RE SO DELICATE AND...
WHAT'S WRONG WITH HER?
APPARENTLY, WE'VE GOT AN OLD MAN DISGUISED AS A TEENAGE GIRL.
Somebody help!
SAY WHAT-EVER YOU WANT.
I'M STILL JUST A 15-YEAR-OLD GIRL!!
SO...
WHAT ABOUT YOU, SACHIE?
HUH?
DON'T YOU... YOU KNOW, FALL IN LOVE OR ANYTHING?
LOVE?
LOVE ...
THERE'S ACTUALLY SOME-ONE...
WHAT?! WHO?! WHO?!
I'M NOT SURE IF I SHOULD SAY...
ARE YOU TALKING ABOUT ...?!

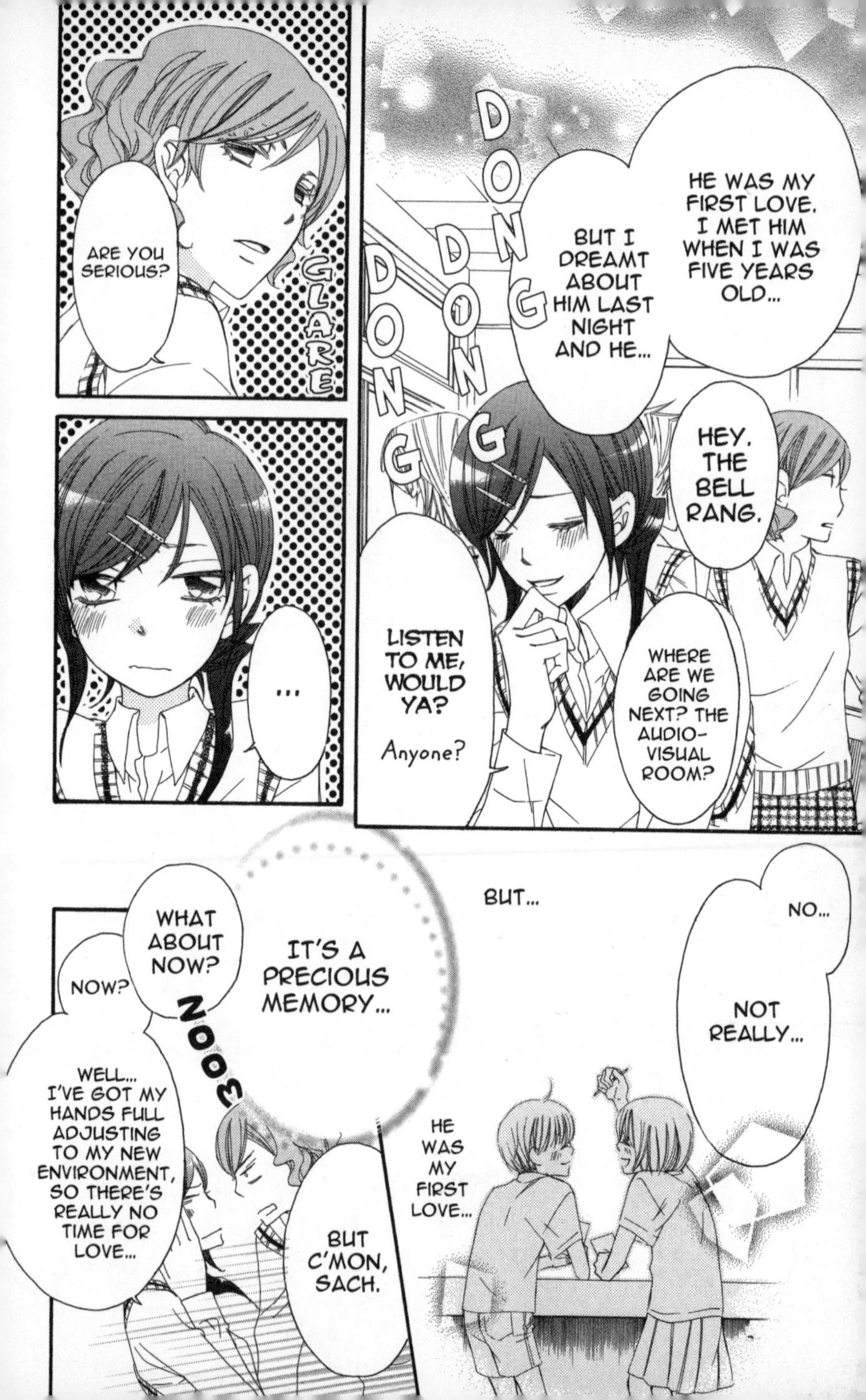
HE WAS MY FIRST LOVE. I MET HIM WHEN I WAS FIVE YEARS OLD...
BUT I DREAMT ABOUT HIM LAST NIGHT AND HE...
DONG
DONG
DONG
HEY. THE BELL RANG.
WHERE ARE WE GOING NEXT? THE AUDIO-VISUAL ROOM?
LISTEN TO ME, WOULD YA?
Anyone?
GLARE
ARE YOU SERIOUS?
...
NO...
BUT...
NOT REALLY...
HE WAS MY FIRST LOVE...
IT'S A PRECIOUS MEMORY...
WHAT ABOUT NOW?
NOW?
ZOOM
BUT C'MON, SACH.
WELL... I'VE GOT MY HANDS FULL ADJUSTING TO MY NEW ENVIRONMENT, SO THERE'S REALLY NO TIME FOR LOVE...

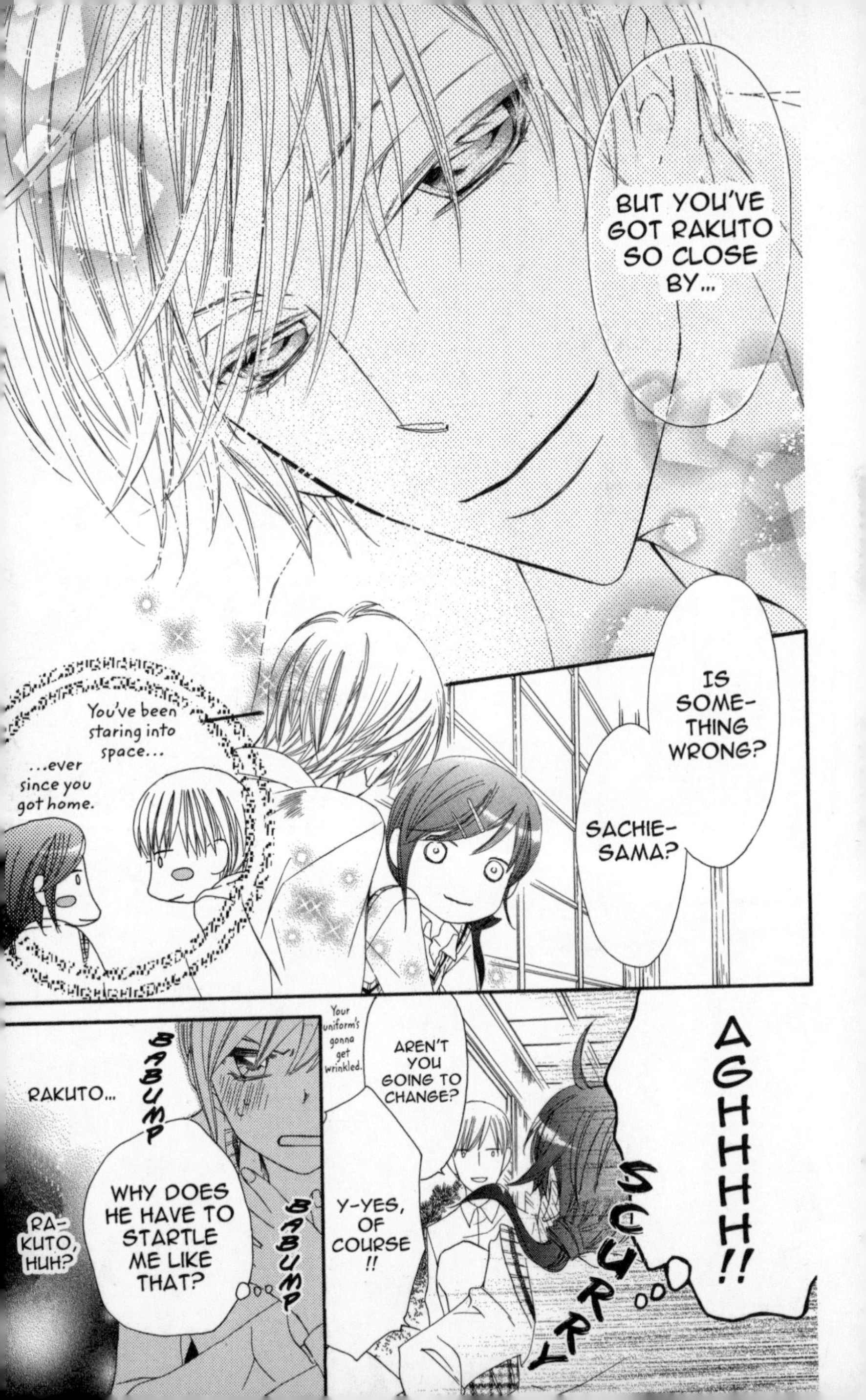
BUT YOU'VE GOT RAKUTO SO CLOSE BY...
IS SOME-THING WRONG?
SACHIE-SAMA?
You've been staring into space...
...ever since you got home.
AGHHHH!!
SCURRY
Your uniform's gonna get wrinkled.
AREN'T YOU GOING TO CHANGE?
Y-YES, OF COURSE!!
BABUMP
RAKUTO...
BABUMP
WHY DOES HE HAVE TO STARTLE ME LIKE THAT?
BABUMP
RA-KUTO, HUH?

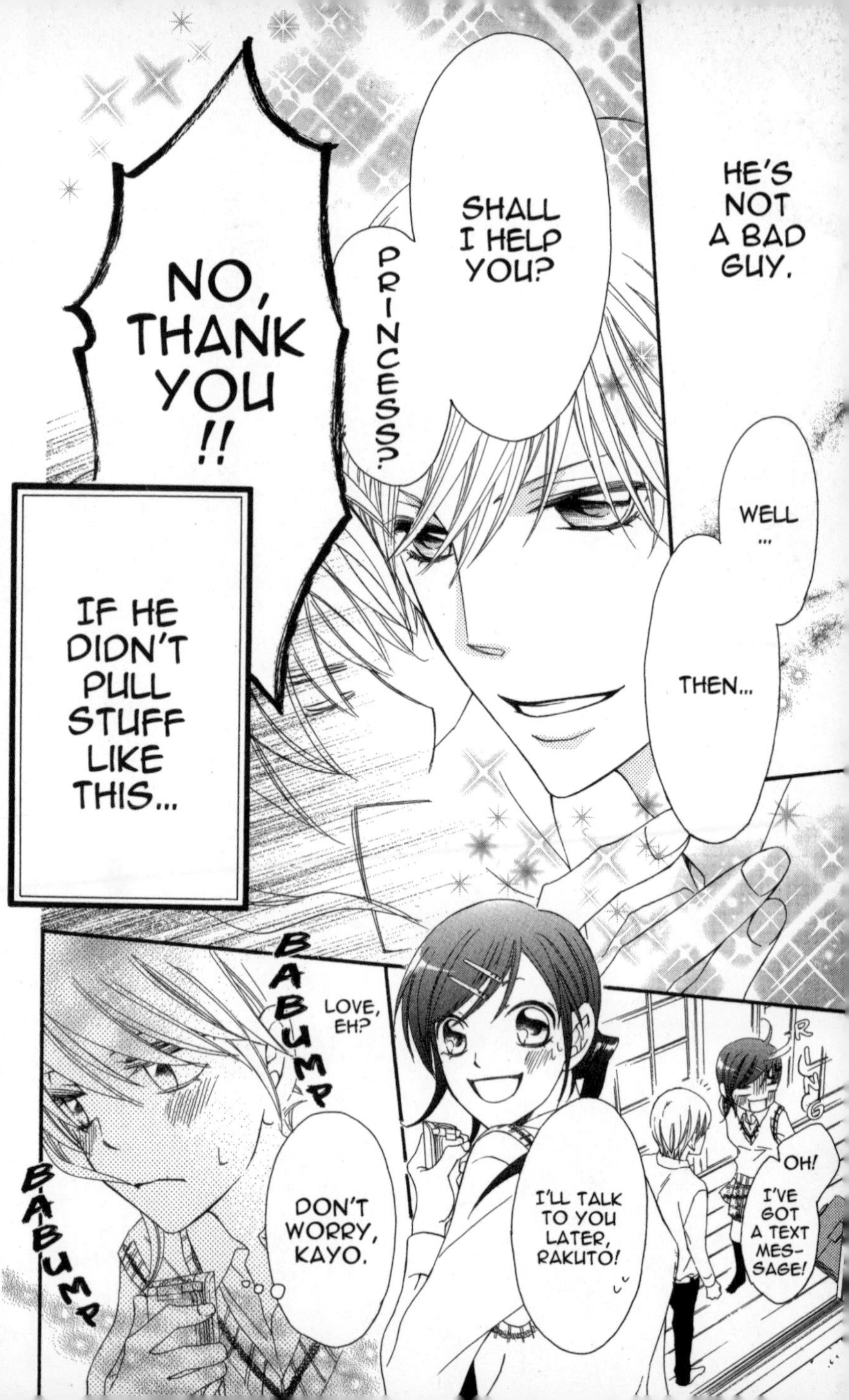
HE'S NOT A BAD GUY.
WELL...
THEN...
SHALL I HELP YOU?
PRINCESS?
NO, THANK YOU!!
IF HE DIDN'T PULL STUFF LIKE THIS...
RING
OH!
I'VE GOT A TEXT MES-SAGE!
I'LL TALK TO YOU LATER, RAKUTO!
LOVE, EH?
BABUMP
DON'T WORRY, KAYO.
BABUMP

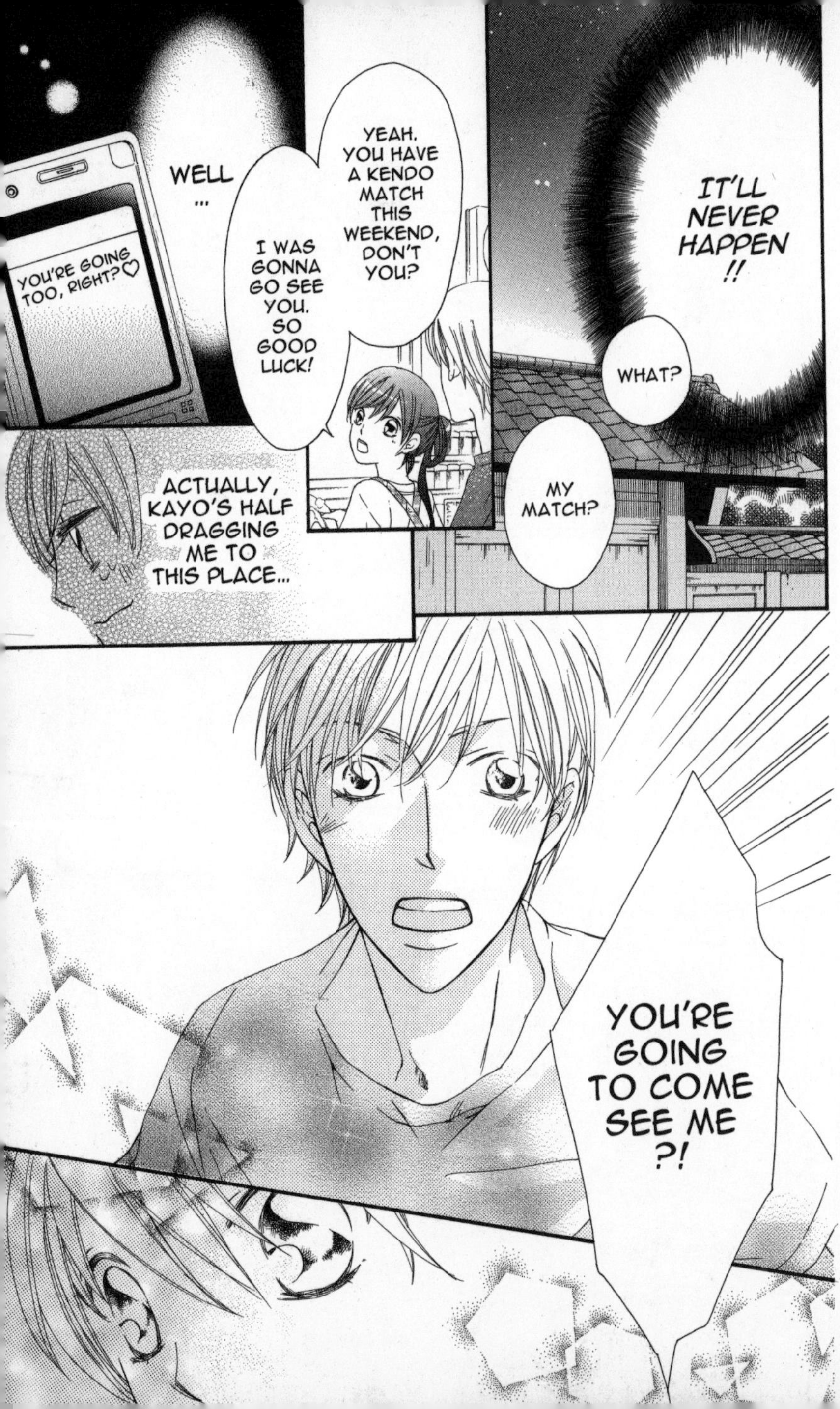

IT'LL NEVER HAPPEN !!
WHAT?
MY MATCH?
YEAH. YOU HAVE A KENDO MATCH THIS WEEKEND, DON'T YOU?
I WAS GONNA GO SEE YOU. SO GOOD LUCK!
YOU'RE GOING TOO, RIGHT?♡
WELL ...
ACTUALLY, KAYO'S HALF DRAGGING ME TO THIS PLACE...
YOU'RE GOING TO COME SEE ME ?!

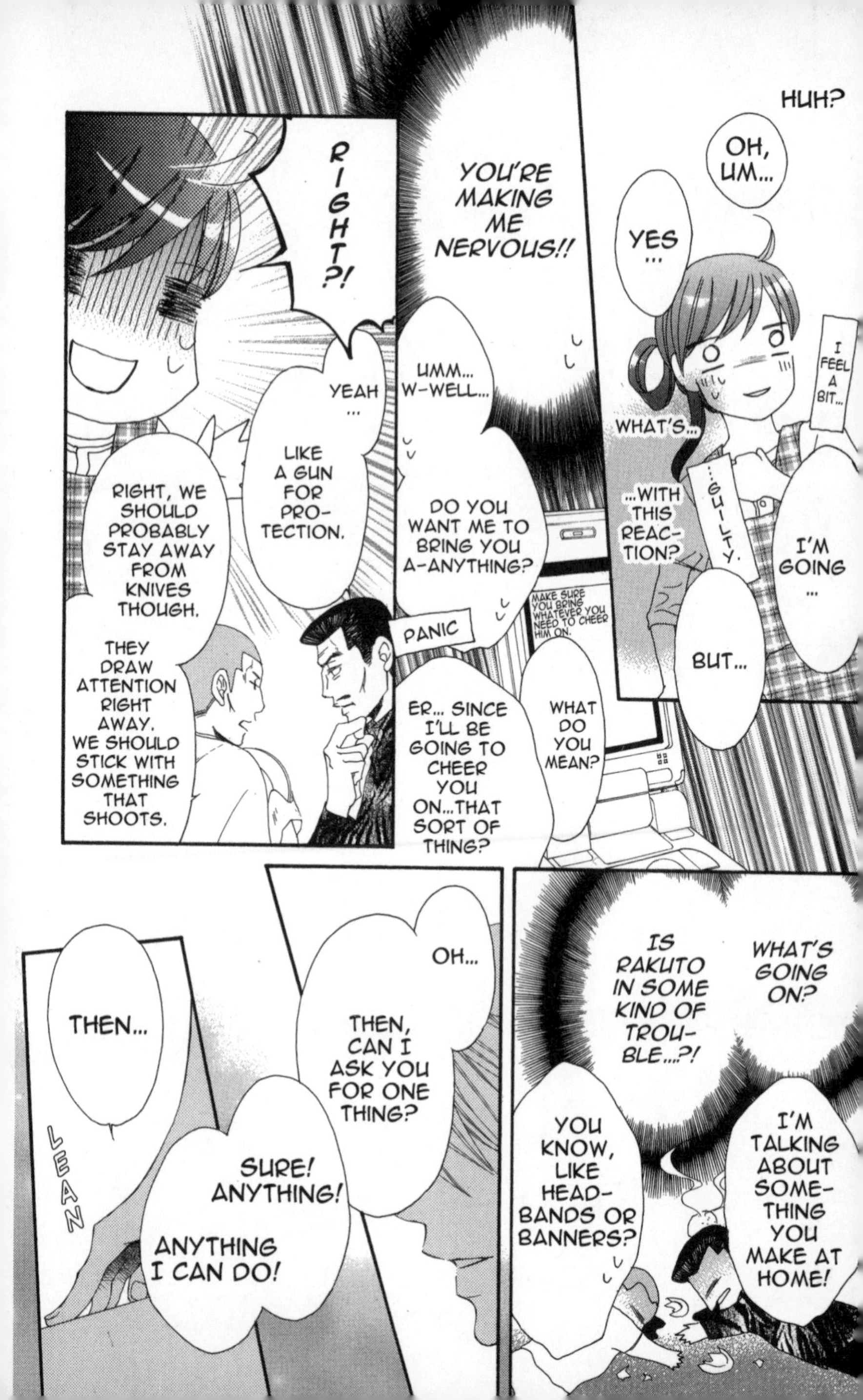
HUH?
OH, UM...
YES...
I FEEL A BIT...
...GUILTY.
WHAT'S...
...WITH THIS REAC-TION?
I'M GOING...
BUT...
YOU'RE MAKING ME NERVOUS!!
UMM... W-WELL...
DO YOU WANT ME TO BRING YOU A-ANYTHING?
PANIC
MAKE SURE YOU BRING WHATEVER YOU NEED TO CHEER HIM ON.
WHAT DO YOU MEAN?
ER... SINCE I'LL BE GOING TO CHEER YOU ON...THAT SORT OF THING?
RIGHT?!
YEAH...
LIKE A GUN FOR PRO-TECTION.
RIGHT, WE SHOULD PROBABLY STAY AWAY FROM KNIVES THOUGH.
THEY DRAW ATTENTION RIGHT AWAY. WE SHOULD STICK WITH SOMETHING THAT SHOOTS.
WHAT'S GOING ON?
IS RAKUTO IN SOME KIND OF TROU-BLE...?!
I'M TALKING ABOUT SOME-THING YOU MAKE AT HOME!
YOU KNOW, LIKE HEAD-BANDS OR BANNERS?
OH...
THEN, CAN I ASK YOU FOR ONE THING?
SURE! ANYTHING!
ANYTHING I CAN DO!
THEN...
LEAN

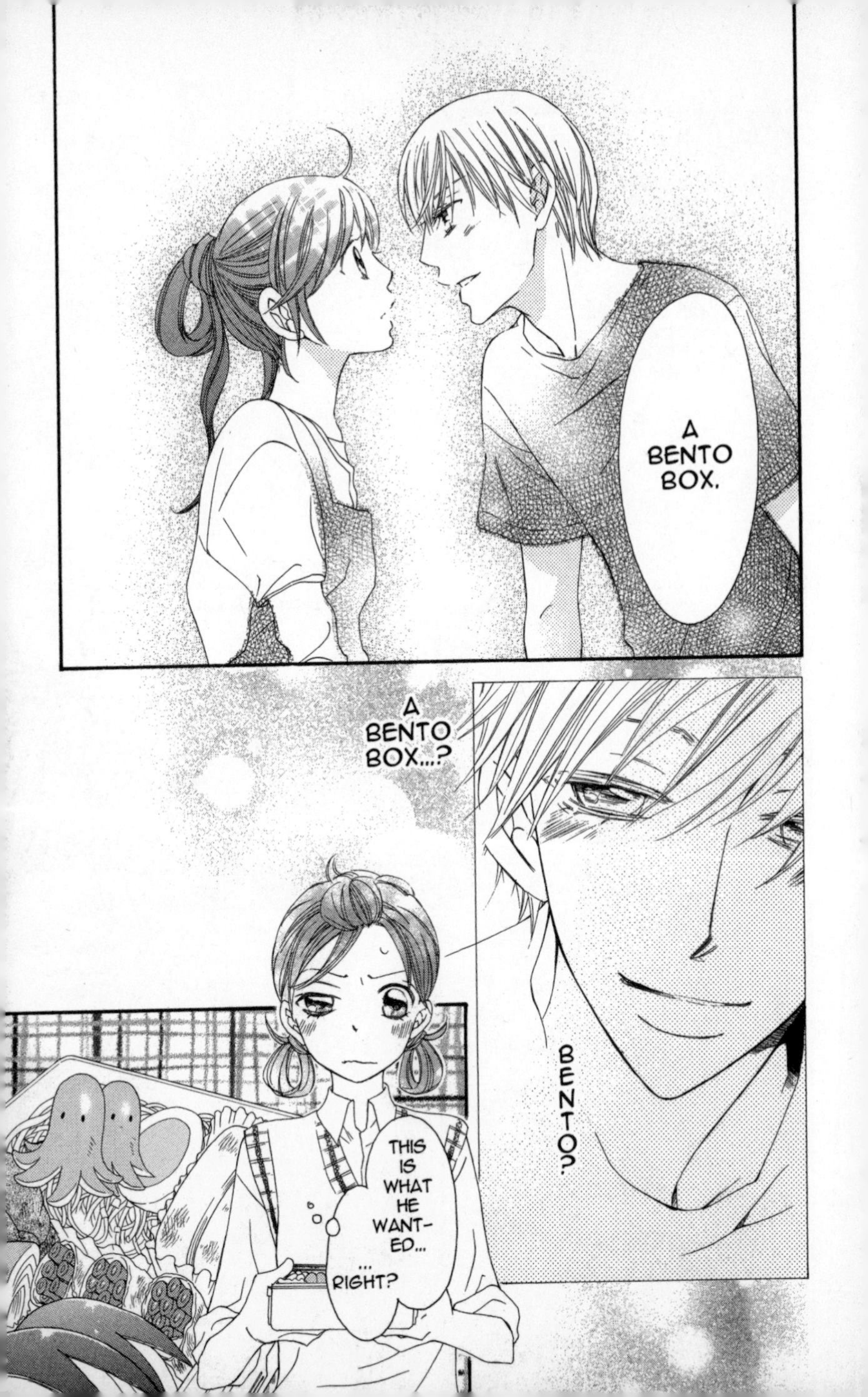
A BENTO BOX.
A BENTO BOX...?
BENTO?
THIS IS WHAT HE WANTED... ...RIGHT?

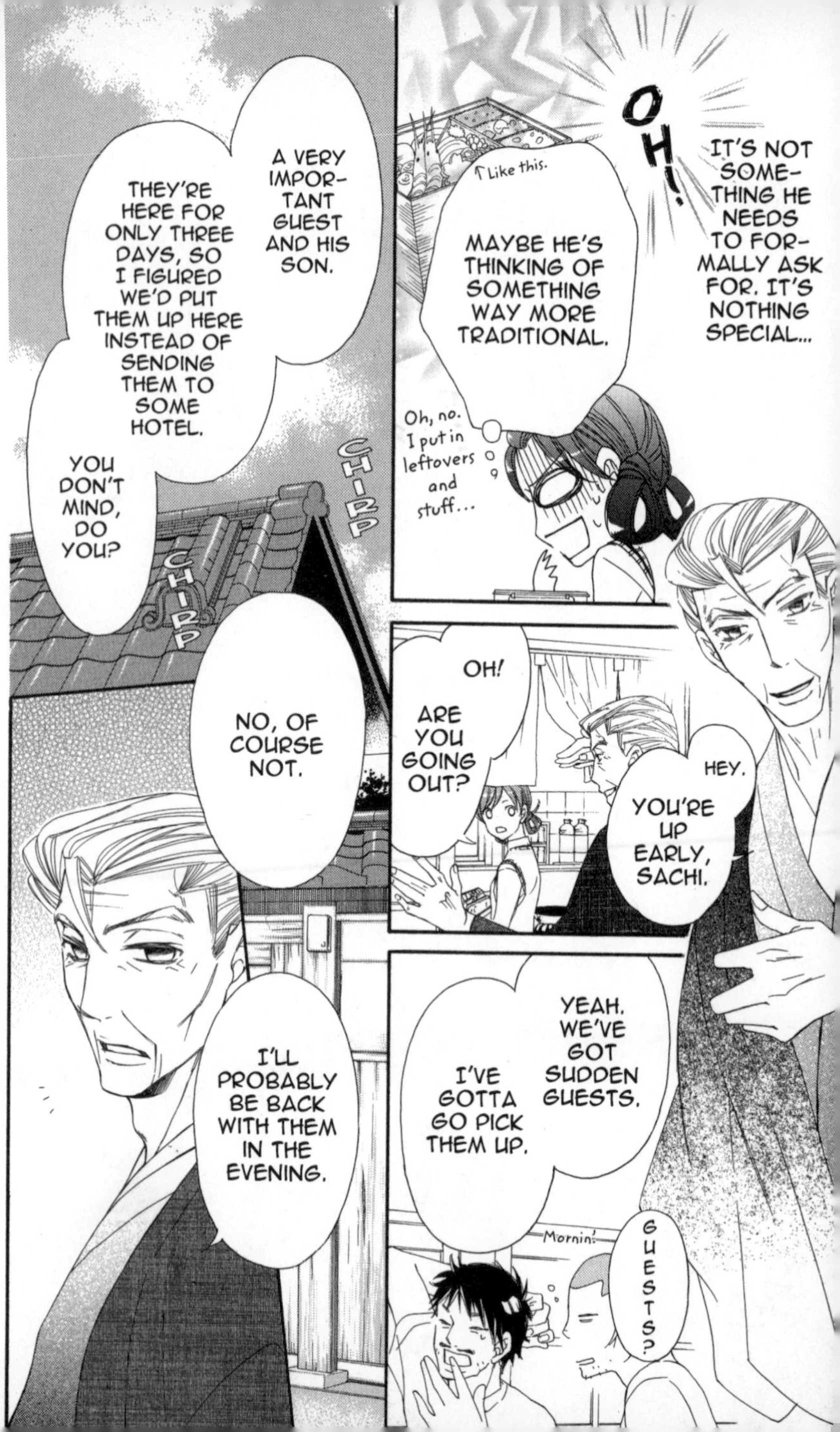
OH!
IT'S NOT SOMETHING HE NEEDS TO FORMALLY ASK FOR. IT'S NOTHING SPECIAL...
MAYBE HE'S THINKING OF SOMETHING WAY MORE TRADITIONAL.
↑Like this.
Oh, no. I put in leftovers and stuff...
HEY. YOU'RE UP EARLY, SACHI.
OH! ARE YOU GOING OUT?
YEAH. WE'VE GOT SUDDEN GUESTS.
I'VE GOTTA GO PICK THEM UP.
GUESTS?
Mornin'.
A VERY IMPORTANT GUEST AND HIS SON.
THEY'RE HERE FOR ONLY THREE DAYS, SO I FIGURED WE'D PUT THEM UP HERE INSTEAD OF SENDING THEM TO SOME HOTEL.
YOU DON'T MIND, DO YOU?
CHIRP
CHIRP
NO, OF COURSE NOT.
I'LL PROBABLY BE BACK WITH THEM IN THE EVENING.

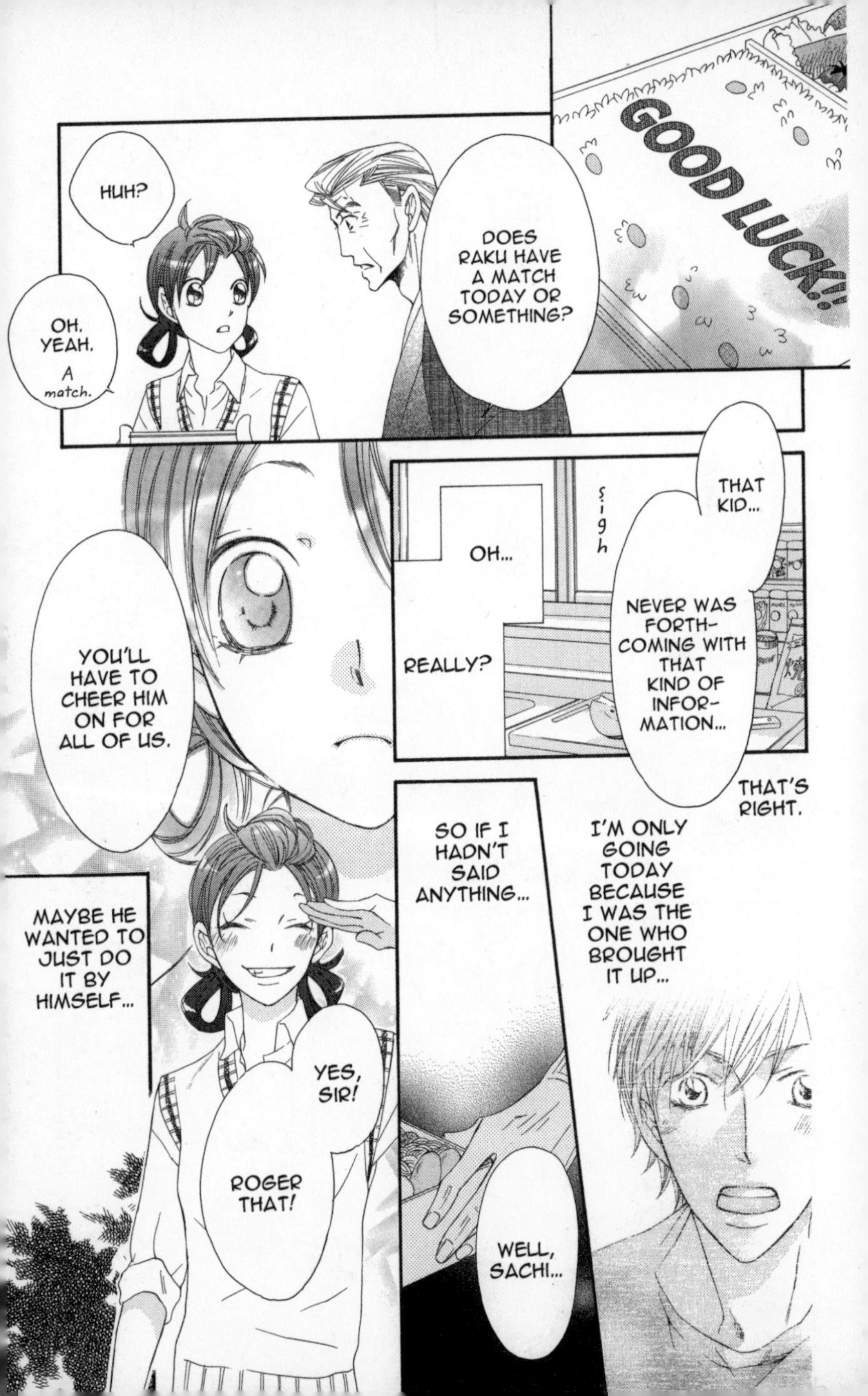
GOOD LUCK!!
DOES RAKU HAVE A MATCH TODAY OR SOMETHING?
HUH?
OH. YEAH.
A match.
THAT KID...
NEVER WAS FORTH-COMING WITH THAT KIND OF INFOR-MATION...
sigh
OH...
REALLY?
YOU'LL HAVE TO CHEER HIM ON FOR ALL OF US.
THAT'S RIGHT.
I'M ONLY GOING TODAY BECAUSE I WAS THE ONE WHO BROUGHT IT UP...
SO IF I HADN'T SAID ANYTHING...
WELL, SACHI...
MAYBE HE WANTED TO JUST DO IT BY HIMSELF...
YES, SIR!
ROGER THAT!

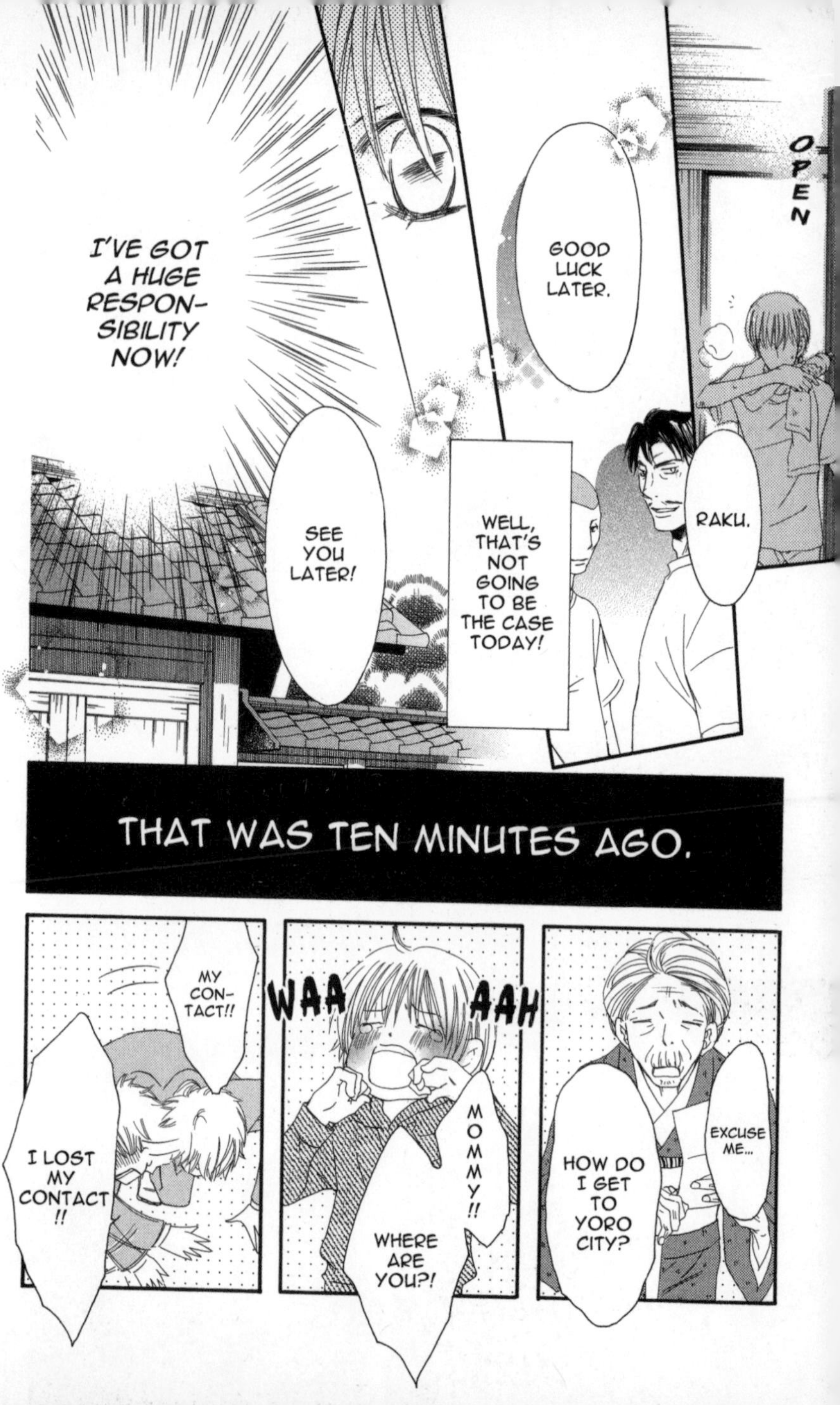

OPEN
RAKU.
GOOD LUCK LATER.
WELL, THAT'S NOT GOING TO BE THE CASE TODAY!
SEE YOU LATER!
I'VE GOT A HUGE RESPONSIBILITY NOW!
THAT WAS TEN MINUTES AGO.
EXCUSE ME...
HOW DO I GET TO YORO CITY?
WAA AAH
MOMMY!!
WHERE ARE YOU?!
MY CONTACT!!
I LOST MY CONTACT!!

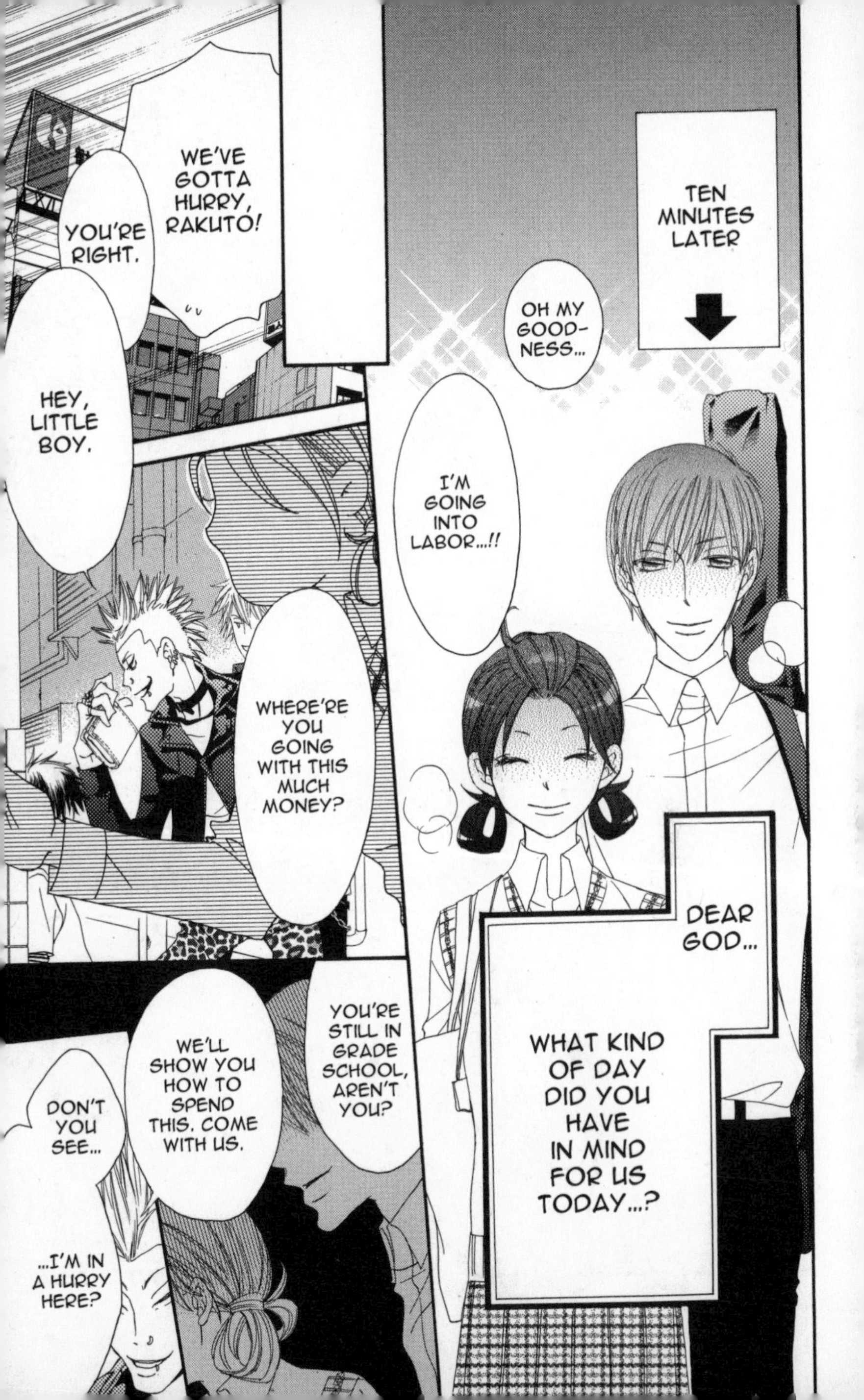
TEN MINUTES LATER
OH MY GOODNESS...
I'M GOING INTO LABOR...!!
DEAR GOD...
WHAT KIND OF DAY DID YOU HAVE IN MIND FOR US TODAY...?
WE'VE GOTTA HURRY, RAKUTO!
YOU'RE RIGHT.
HEY, LITTLE BOY.
WHERE'RE YOU GOING WITH THIS MUCH MONEY?
YOU'RE STILL IN GRADE SCHOOL, AREN'T YOU?
WE'LL SHOW YOU HOW TO SPEND THIS. COME WITH US.
DON'T YOU SEE...
...I'M IN A HURRY HERE?

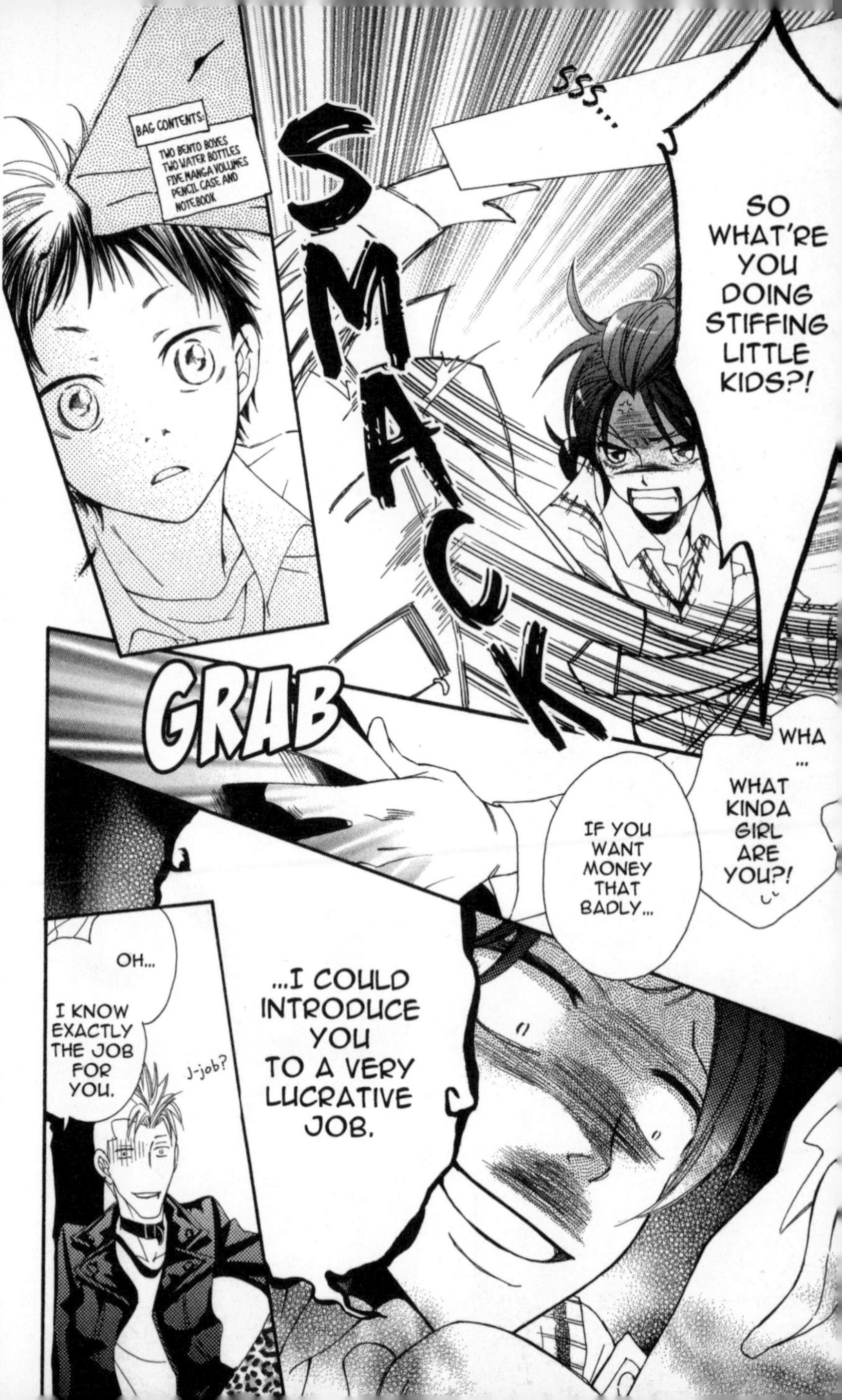
SSS...
SO WHAT'RE YOU DOING STIFFING LITTLE KIDS?!
SMACK
BAG CONTENTS:
TWO BENTO BOXES
TWO WATER BOTTLES
FIVE MANGA VOLUMES
PENCIL CASE AND NOTEBOOK
WHA... WHAT KINDA GIRL ARE YOU?!
GRAB
IF YOU WANT MONEY THAT BADLY...
...I COULD INTRODUCE YOU TO A VERY LUCRATIVE JOB.
OH...
I KNOW EXACTLY THE JOB FOR YOU.
J-job?

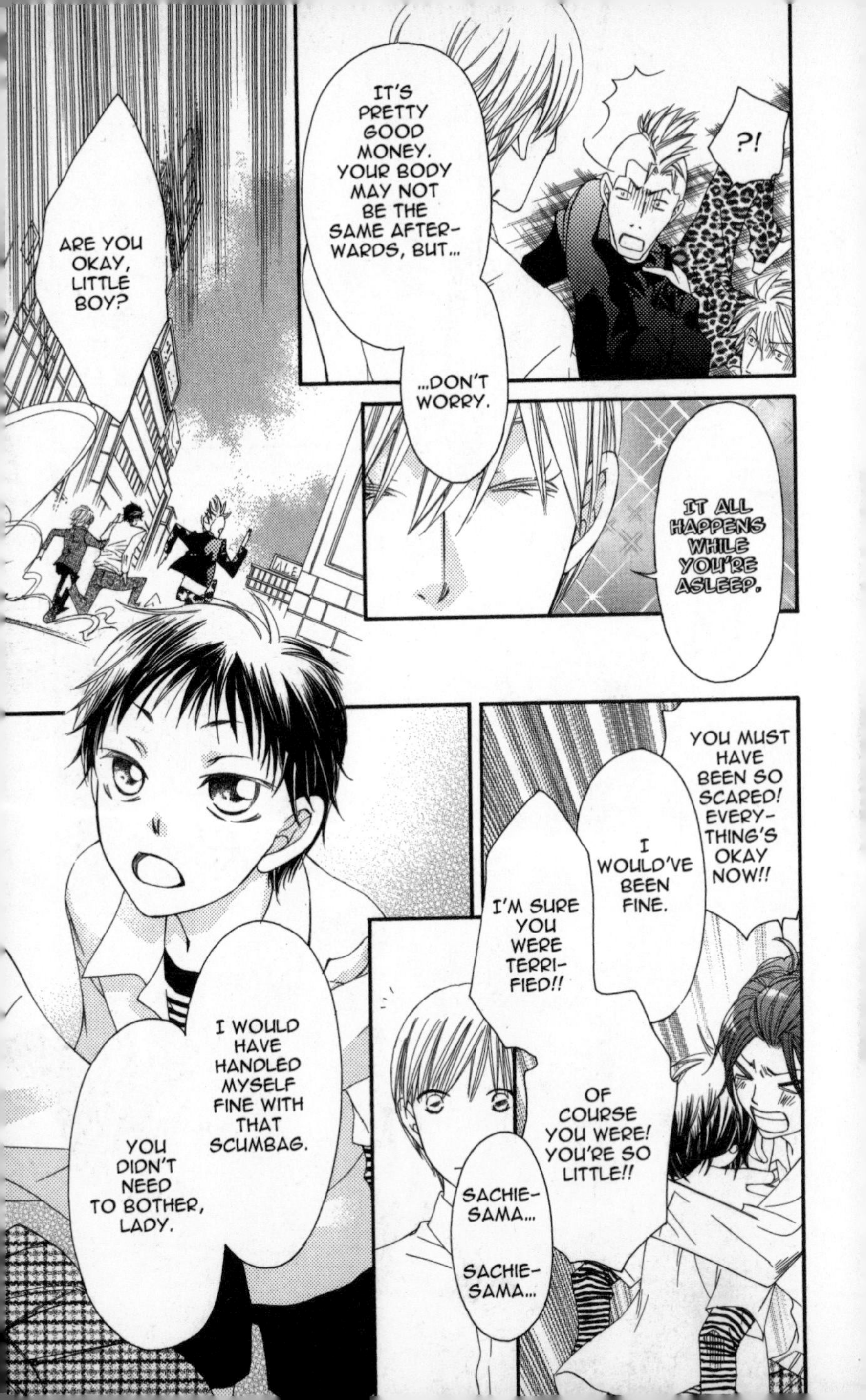
?!
IT'S PRETTY GOOD MONEY. YOUR BODY MAY NOT BE THE SAME AFTER-WARDS, BUT...
...DON'T WORRY.
IT ALL HAPPENS WHILE YOU'RE ASLEEP.
ARE YOU OKAY, LITTLE BOY?
YOU MUST HAVE BEEN SO SCARED! EVERY-THING'S OKAY NOW!!
I WOULD'VE BEEN FINE.
I'M SURE YOU WERE TERRI-FIED!!
OF COURSE YOU WERE! YOU'RE SO LITTLE!!
SACHIE-SAMA...
SACHIE-SAMA...
I WOULD HAVE HANDLED MYSELF FINE WITH THAT SCUMBAG.
YOU DIDN'T NEED TO BOTHER, LADY.

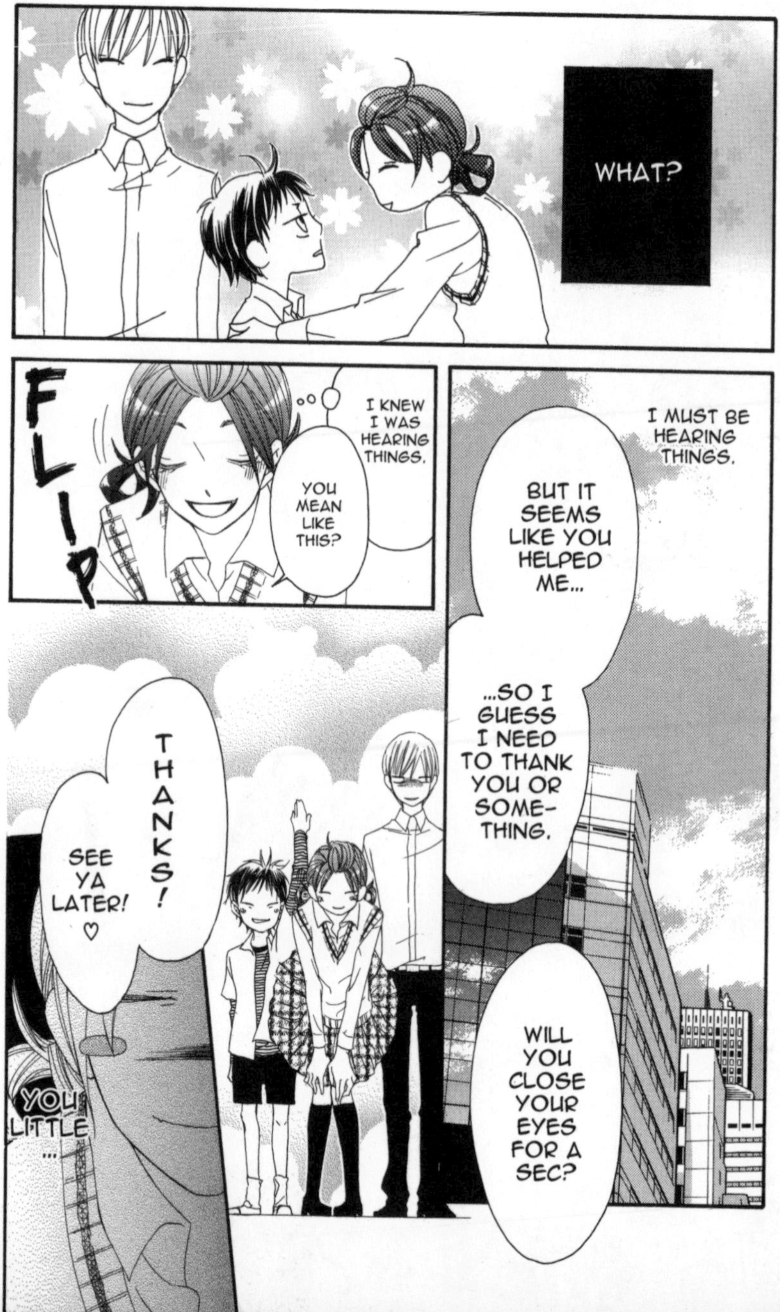
WHAT?
I MUST BE HEARING THINGS.
BUT IT SEEMS LIKE YOU HELPED ME...
...SO I GUESS I NEED TO THANK YOU OR SOME-THING.
WILL YOU CLOSE YOUR EYES FOR A SEC?
I KNEW I WAS HEARING THINGS.
YOU MEAN LIKE THIS?
FLIP
THANKS!
SEE YA LATER! ♡
YOU LITTLE ...

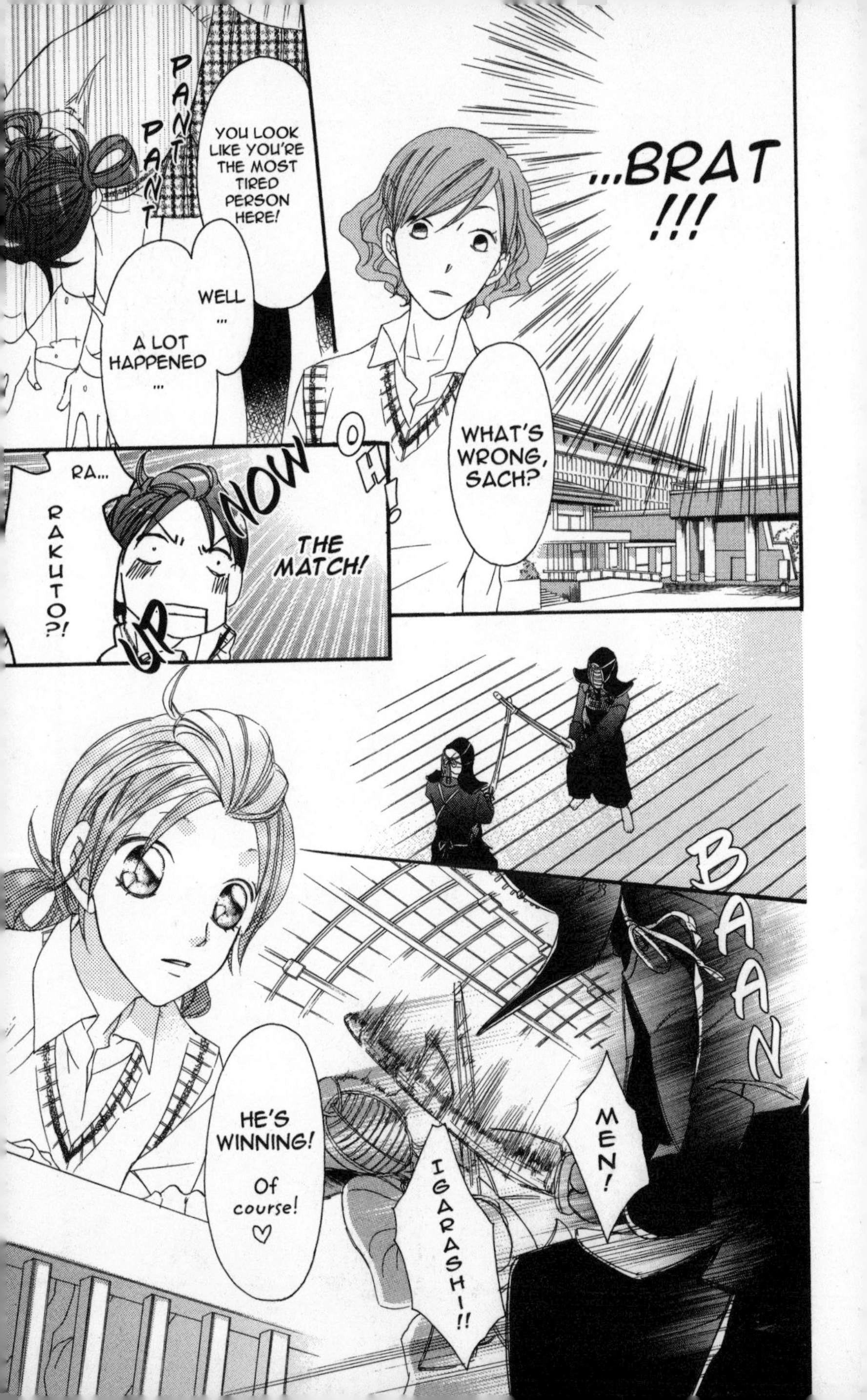
...BRAT!!!
WHAT'S WRONG, SACH?
YOU LOOK LIKE YOU'RE THE MOST TIRED PERSON HERE!
PANT PANT
WELL... A LOT HAPPENED...
OH!
NOW UP
THE MATCH!
RA...
RAKUTO?!
BAAN
MEN!
IGARASHI!!
HE'S WINNING!
Of course! ♥

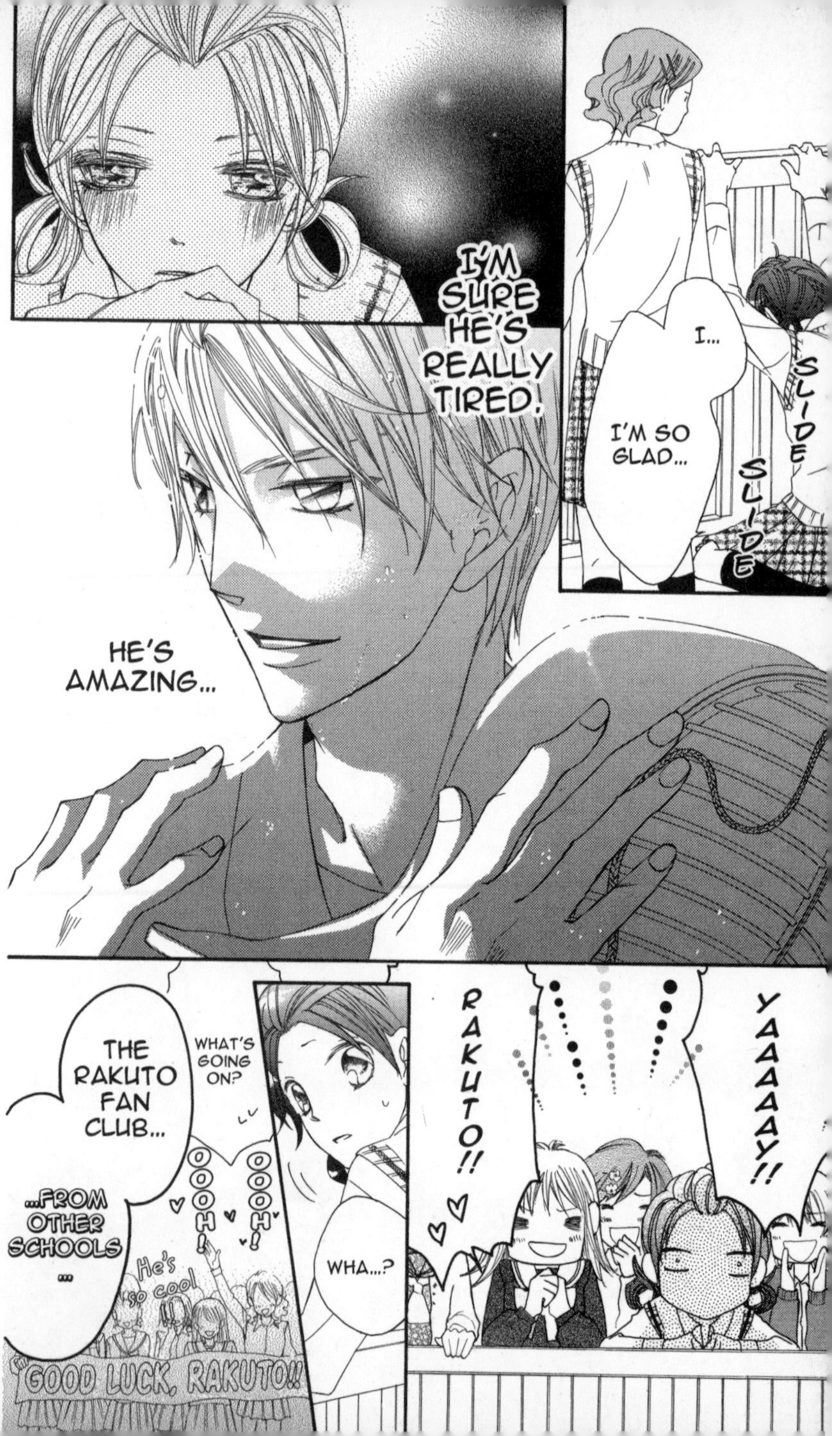
I...
I'M SO GLAD...
SLIDE
SLIDE
I'M SURE HE'S REALLY TIRED.
HE'S AMAZING...
YAAAAAY!!
RAKUTO!!
WHAT'S GOING ON?
WHA...?
THE RAKUTO FAN CLUB...
OOOOH!
OOOOH!
...FROM OTHER SCHOOLS...
He's so cool!!
"GOOD LUCK, RAKUTO!!"

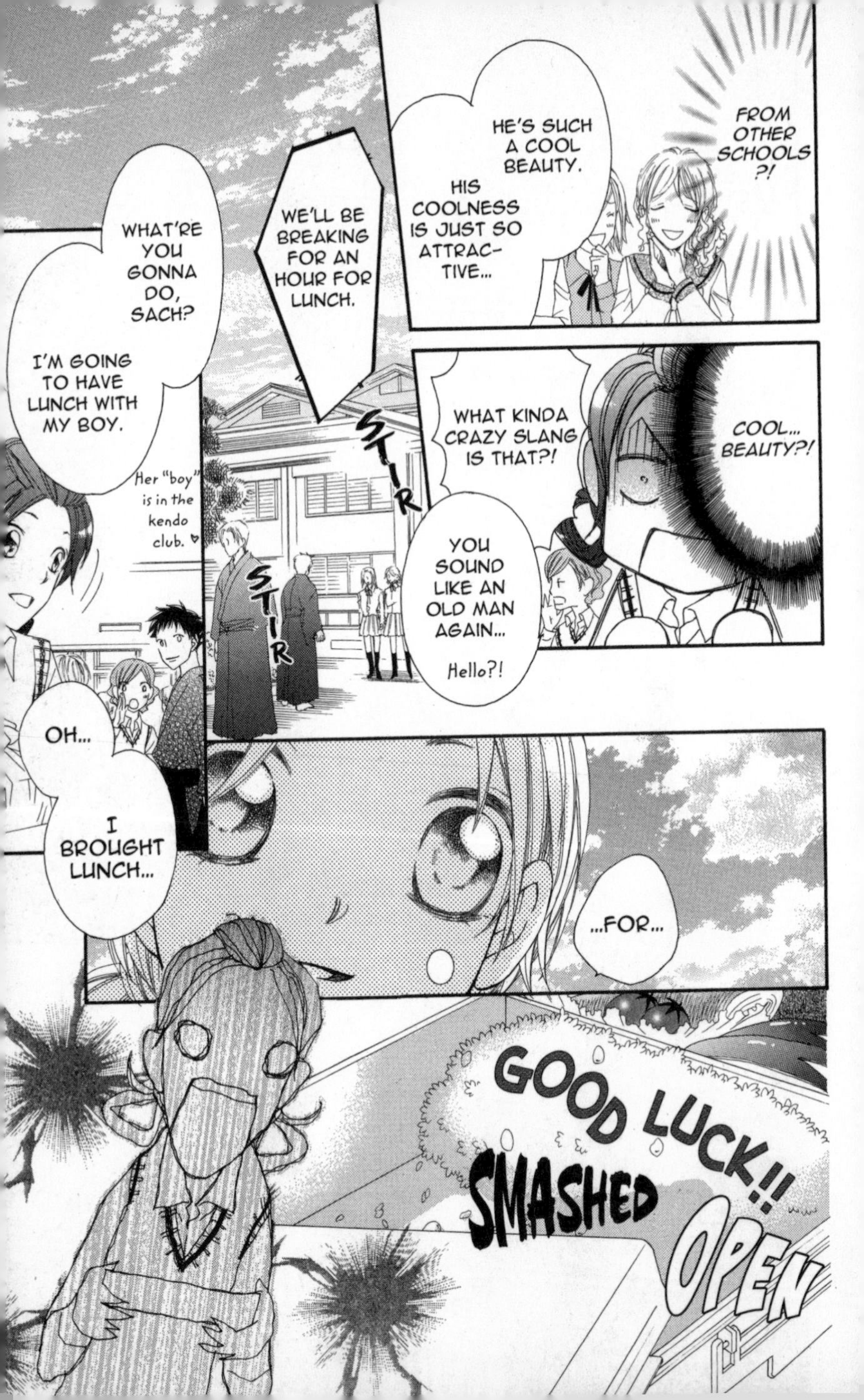
FROM OTHER SCHOOLS?!
HE'S SUCH A COOL BEAUTY.
HIS COOLNESS IS JUST SO ATTRAC-TIVE...
COOL... BEAUTY?!
WHAT KINDA CRAZY SLANG IS THAT?!
YOU SOUND LIKE AN OLD MAN AGAIN...
Hello?!
WE'LL BE BREAKING FOR AN HOUR FOR LUNCH.
STIR
STIR
WHAT'RE YOU GONNA DO, SACH?
I'M GOING TO HAVE LUNCH WITH MY BOY.
Her "boy" is in the kendo club. ♥
OH...
I BROUGHT LUNCH...
...FOR...
GOOD LUCK!!
SMASHED
OPEN

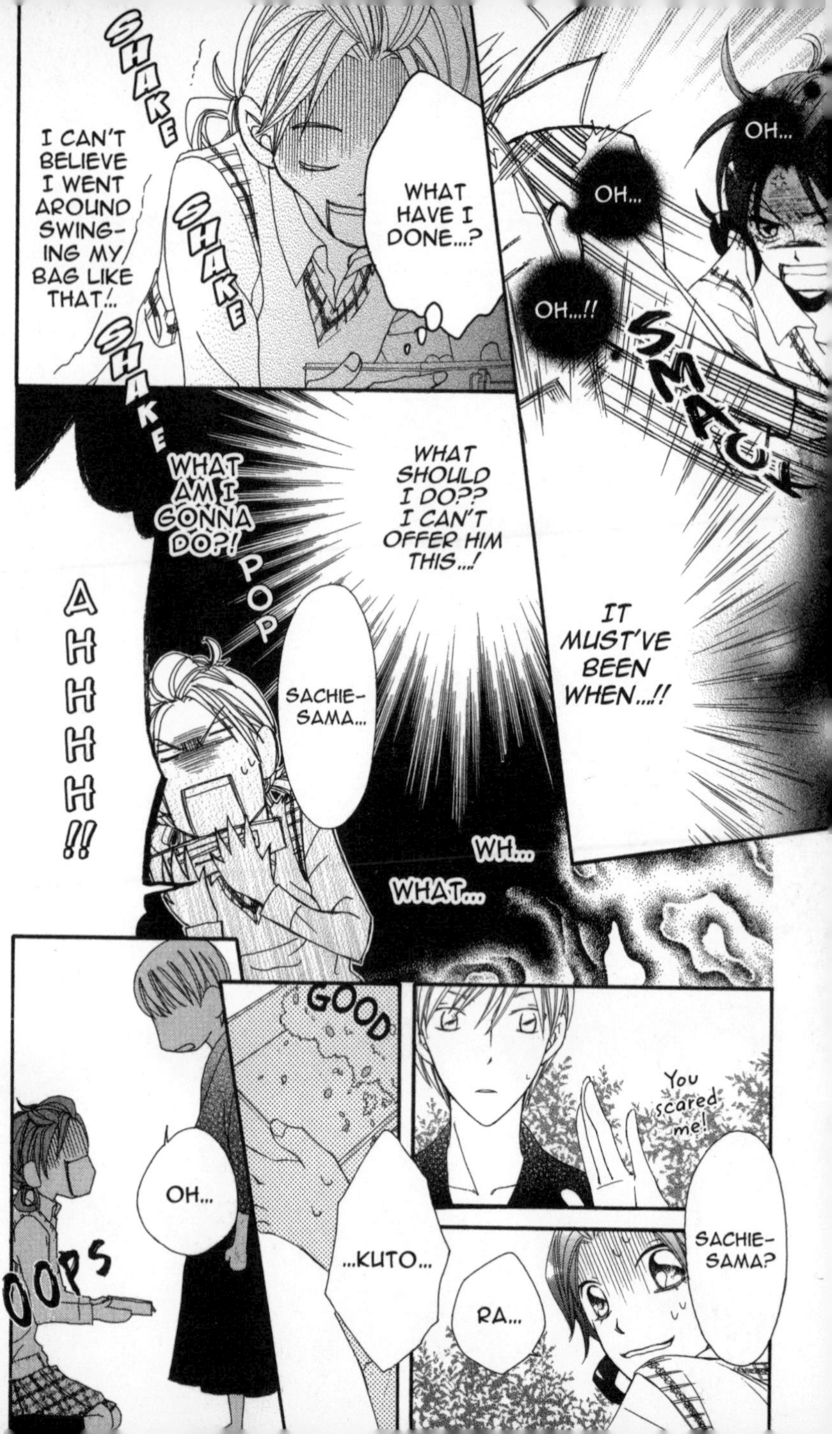

OH...
OH...
OH...!!
SMACK
IT MUST'VE BEEN WHEN...!!
WHAT HAVE I DONE...?
SHAKE
SHAKE
I CAN'T BELIEVE I WENT AROUND SWINGING MY BAG LIKE THAT!...
SHAKE
WHAT SHOULD I DO?? I CAN'T OFFER HIM THIS...!
WHAT AM I GONNA DO?!
POP
SACHIE-SAMA...
AHHHHHH!!
WH...
WHAT...
You scared me!
SACHIE-SAMA?
RA...
...KUTO...
GOOD
OH...
OOPS

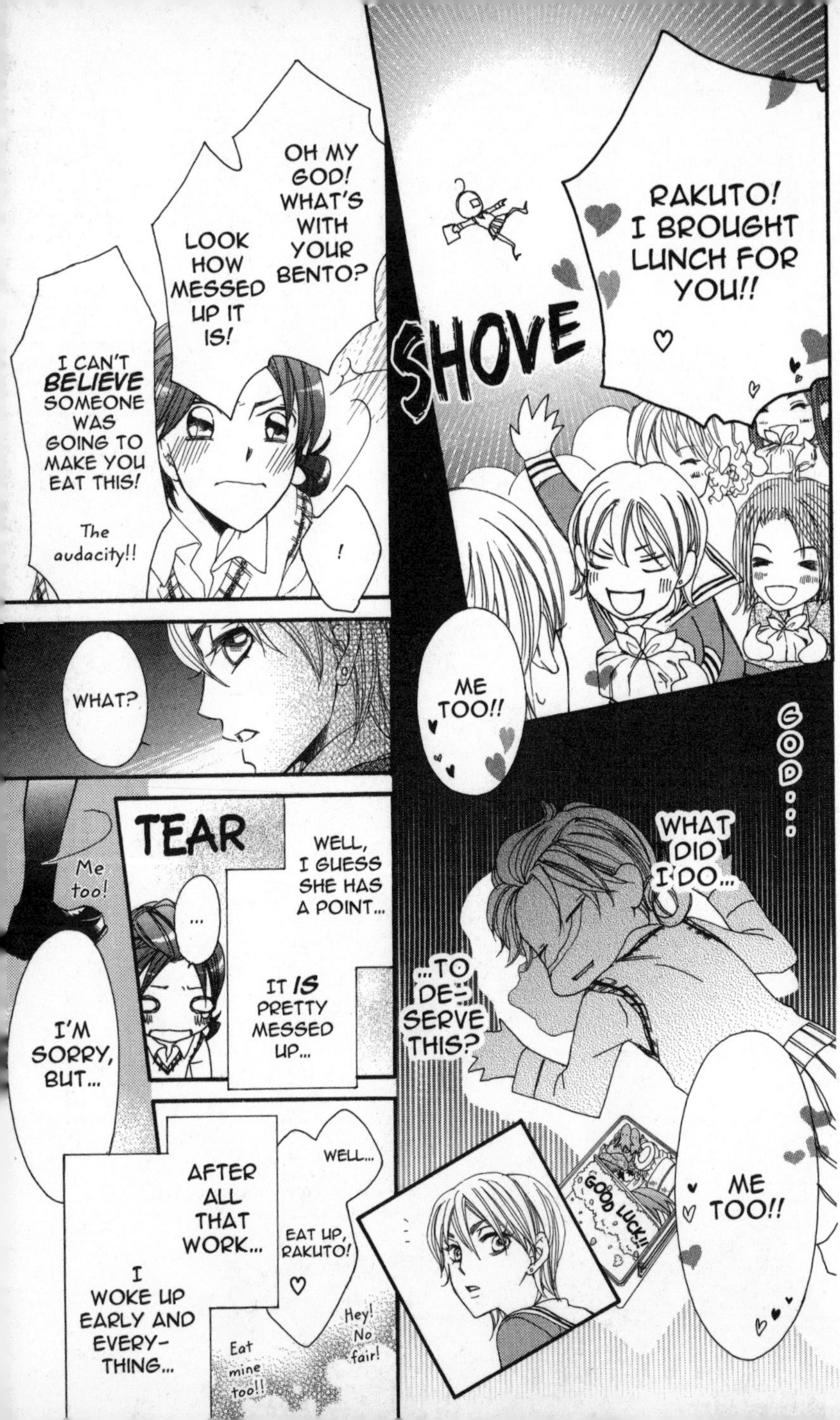
RAKUTO! I BROUGHT LUNCH FOR YOU!!
SHOVE
ME TOO!!
GOD...
WHAT DID I DO...
...TO DE-SERVE THIS?
ME TOO!!
GOOD LUCK!!
OH MY GOD! WHAT'S WITH YOUR BENTO?
LOOK HOW MESSED UP IT IS!
I CAN'T **BELIEVE** SOMEONE WAS GOING TO MAKE YOU EAT THIS!
The audacity!!
!
WHAT?
TEAR
WELL, I GUESS SHE HAS A POINT...
IT ***IS*** PRETTY MESSED UP...
...
Me too!
I'M SORRY, BUT...
WELL...
EAT UP, RAKUTO!
Hey! No fair!
Eat mine too!!
AFTER ALL THAT WORK...
I WOKE UP EARLY AND EVERY-THING...

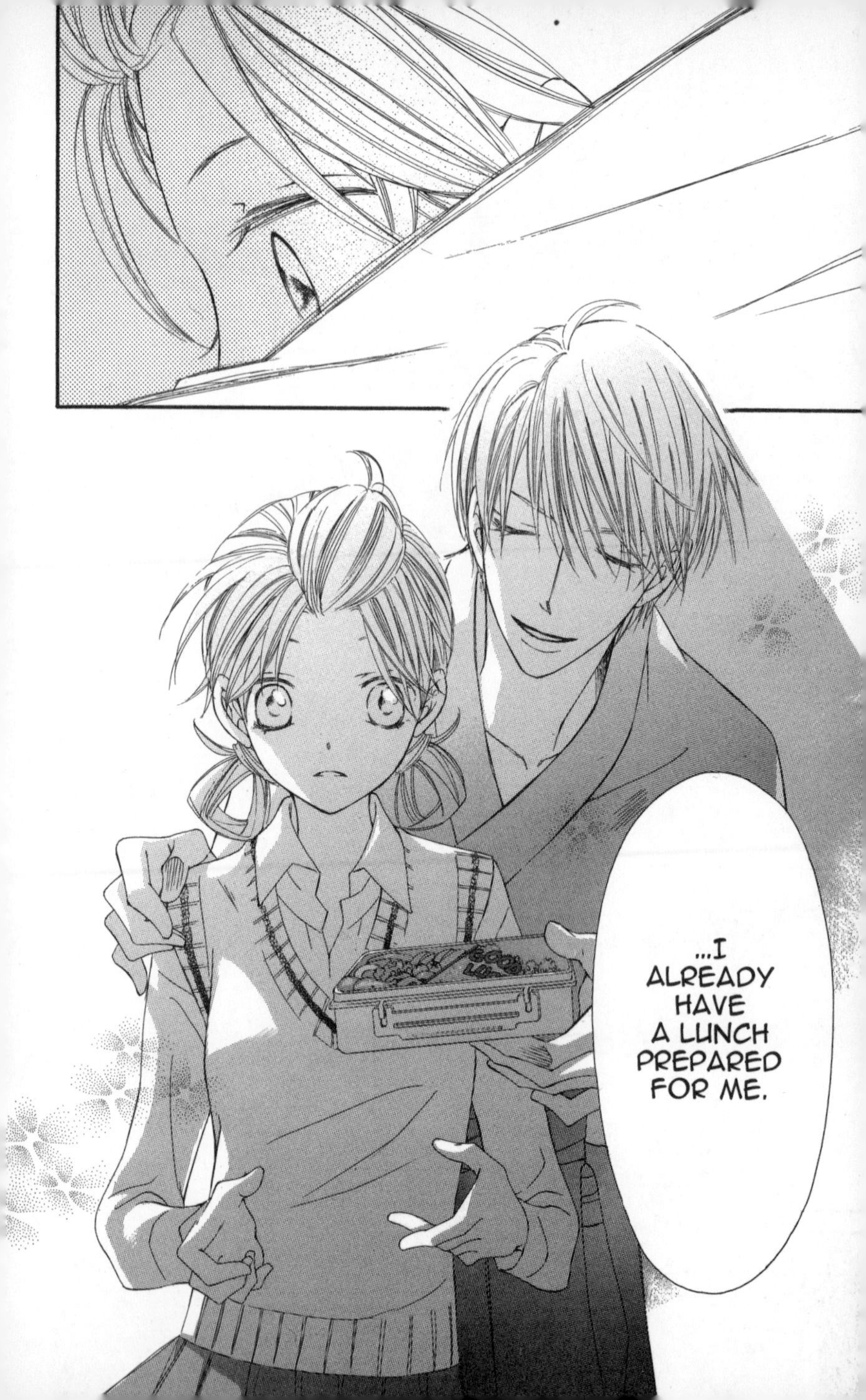
...I ALREADY HAVE A LUNCH PREPARED FOR ME.

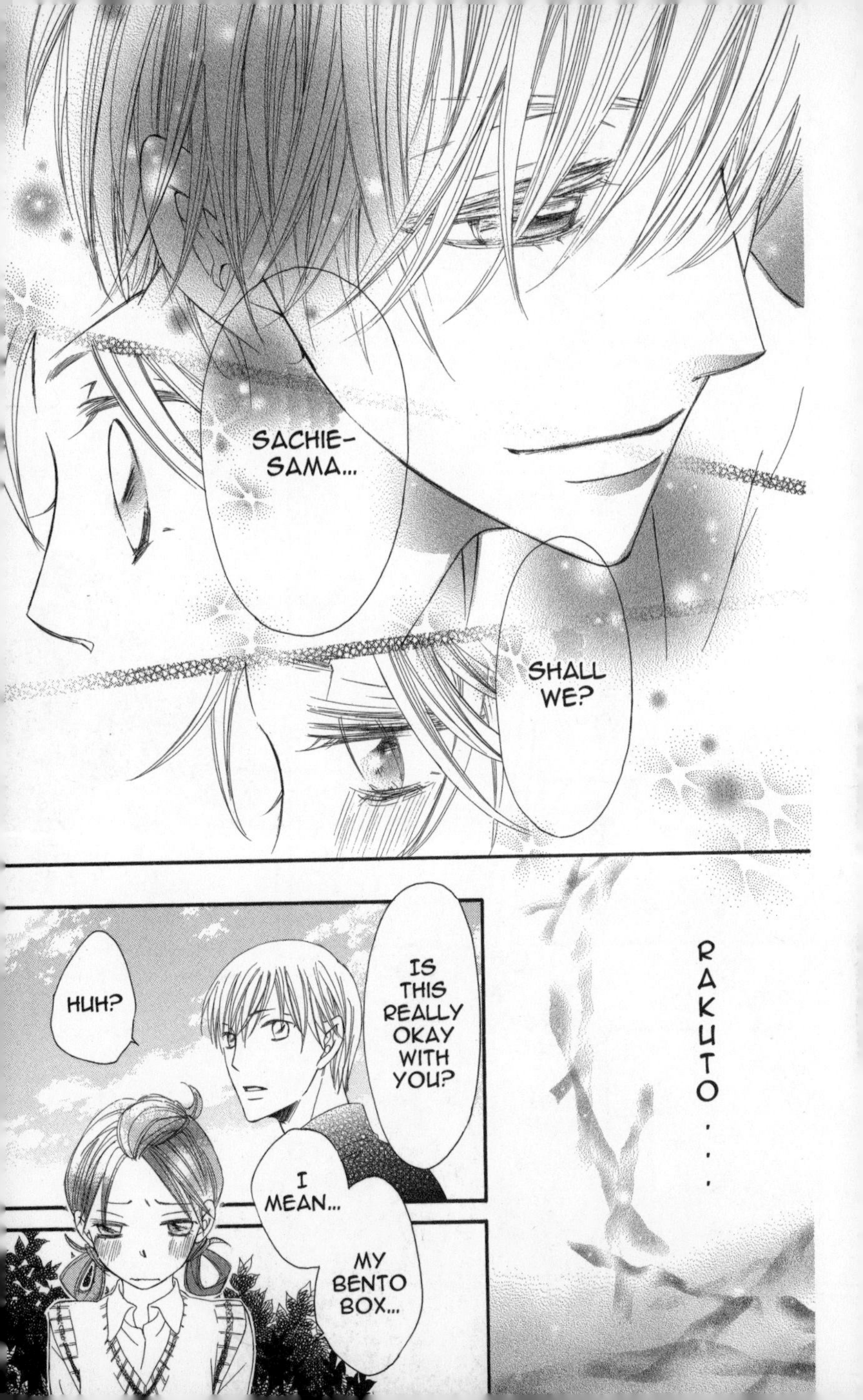
SACHIE-SAMA...
SHALL WE?
RAKUTO...
IS THIS REALLY OKAY WITH YOU?
HUH?
I MEAN...
MY BENTO BOX...

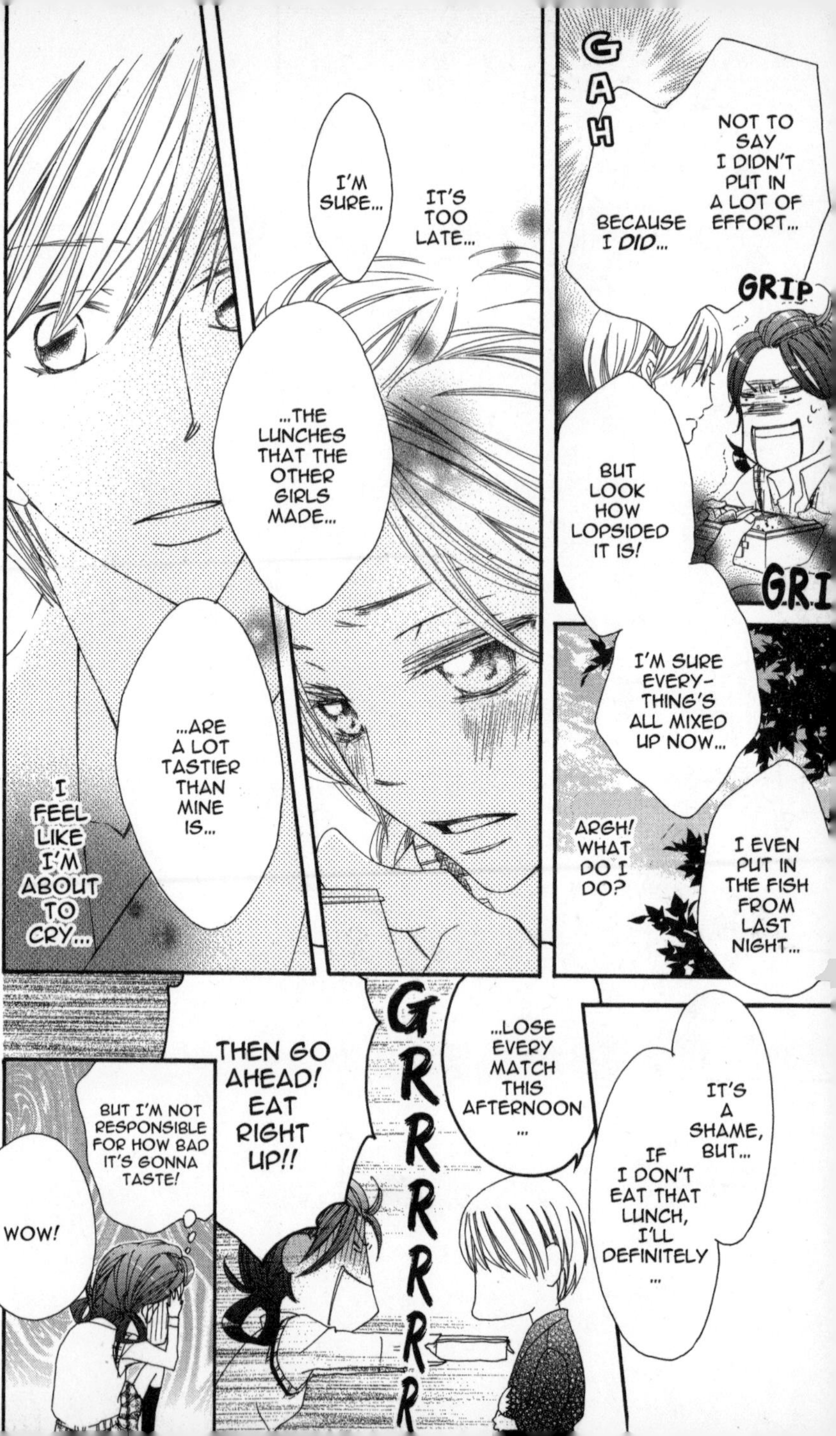
GAH
NOT TO SAY I DIDN'T PUT IN A LOT OF EFFORT...
BECAUSE I *DID*...
GRIP
BUT LOOK HOW LOPSIDED IT IS!
GRI
I'M SURE EVERY-THING'S ALL MIXED UP NOW...
I EVEN PUT IN THE FISH FROM LAST NIGHT...
ARGH! WHAT DO I DO?
I'M SURE...
IT'S TOO LATE...
...THE LUNCHES THAT THE OTHER GIRLS MADE...
...ARE A LOT TASTIER THAN MINE IS...
I FEEL LIKE I'M ABOUT TO CRY...
IT'S A SHAME, BUT...
IF I DON'T EAT THAT LUNCH, I'LL DEFINITELY...
...LOSE EVERY MATCH THIS AFTERNOON...
GRRRRRR
THEN GO AHEAD! EAT RIGHT UP!!
BUT I'M NOT RESPONSIBLE FOR HOW BAD IT'S GONNA TASTE!
WOW!

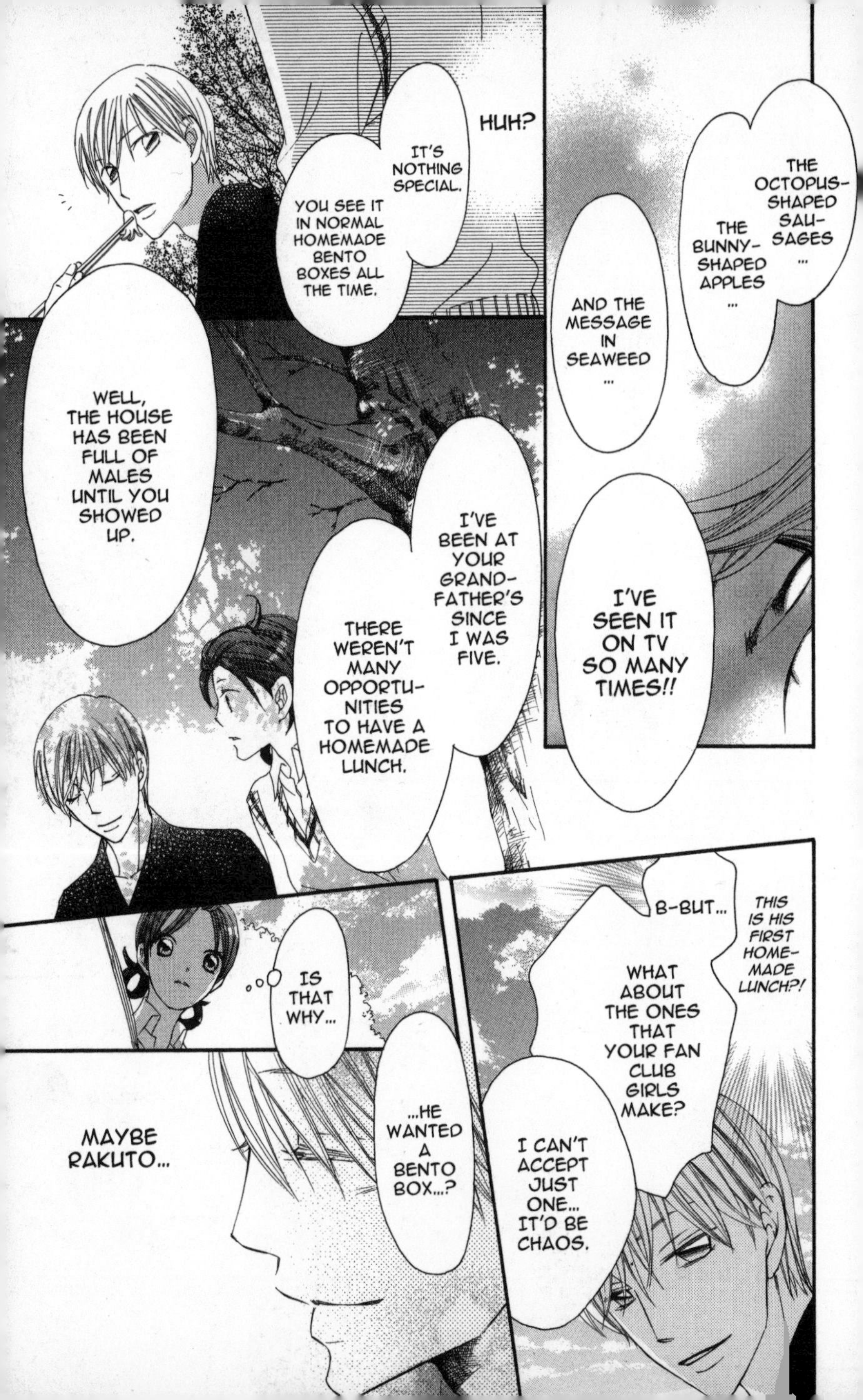
THE OCTOPUS-SHAPED SAUSAGES...
THE BUNNY-SHAPED APPLES...
AND THE MESSAGE IN SEAWEED...
I'VE SEEN IT ON TV SO MANY TIMES!!
HUH?
IT'S NOTHING SPECIAL.
YOU SEE IT IN NORMAL HOMEMADE BENTO BOXES ALL THE TIME.
I'VE BEEN AT YOUR GRANDFATHER'S SINCE I WAS FIVE.
THERE WEREN'T MANY OPPORTUNITIES TO HAVE A HOMEMADE LUNCH.
WELL, THE HOUSE HAS BEEN FULL OF MALES UNTIL YOU SHOWED UP.
B-BUT...
THIS IS HIS FIRST HOMEMADE LUNCH?!
WHAT ABOUT THE ONES THAT YOUR FAN CLUB GIRLS MAKE?
I CAN'T ACCEPT JUST ONE... IT'D BE CHAOS.
IS THAT WHY...
...HE WANTED A BENTO BOX...?
MAYBE RAKUTO...

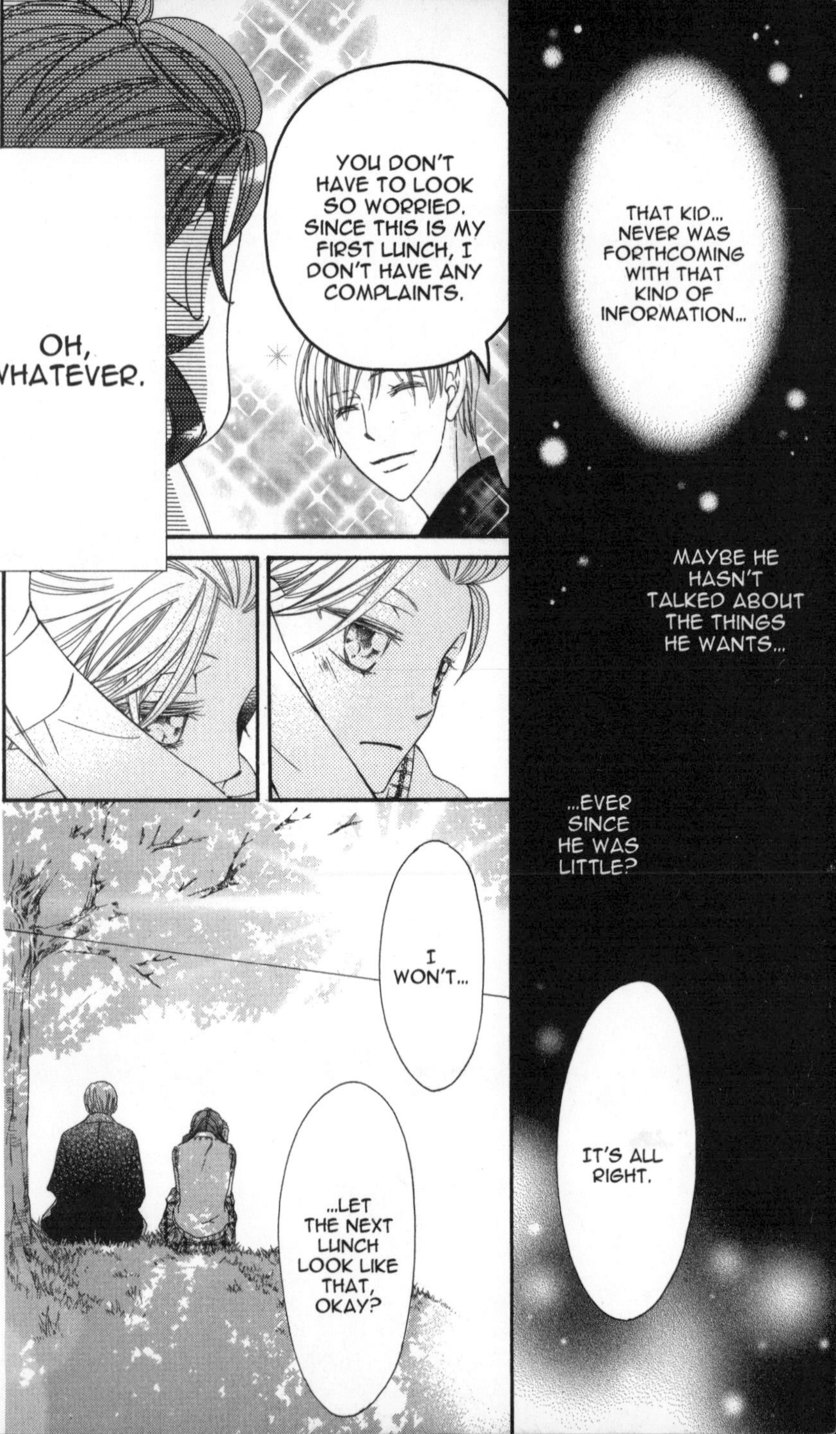
THAT KID... NEVER WAS FORTHCOMING WITH THAT KIND OF INFORMATION...
MAYBE HE HASN'T TALKED ABOUT THE THINGS HE WANTS...
...EVER SINCE HE WAS LITTLE?
IT'S ALL RIGHT.
YOU DON'T HAVE TO LOOK SO WORRIED. SINCE THIS IS MY FIRST LUNCH, I DON'T HAVE ANY COMPLAINTS.
OH, WHATEVER.
I WON'T...
...LET THE NEXT LUNCH LOOK LIKE THAT, OKAY?

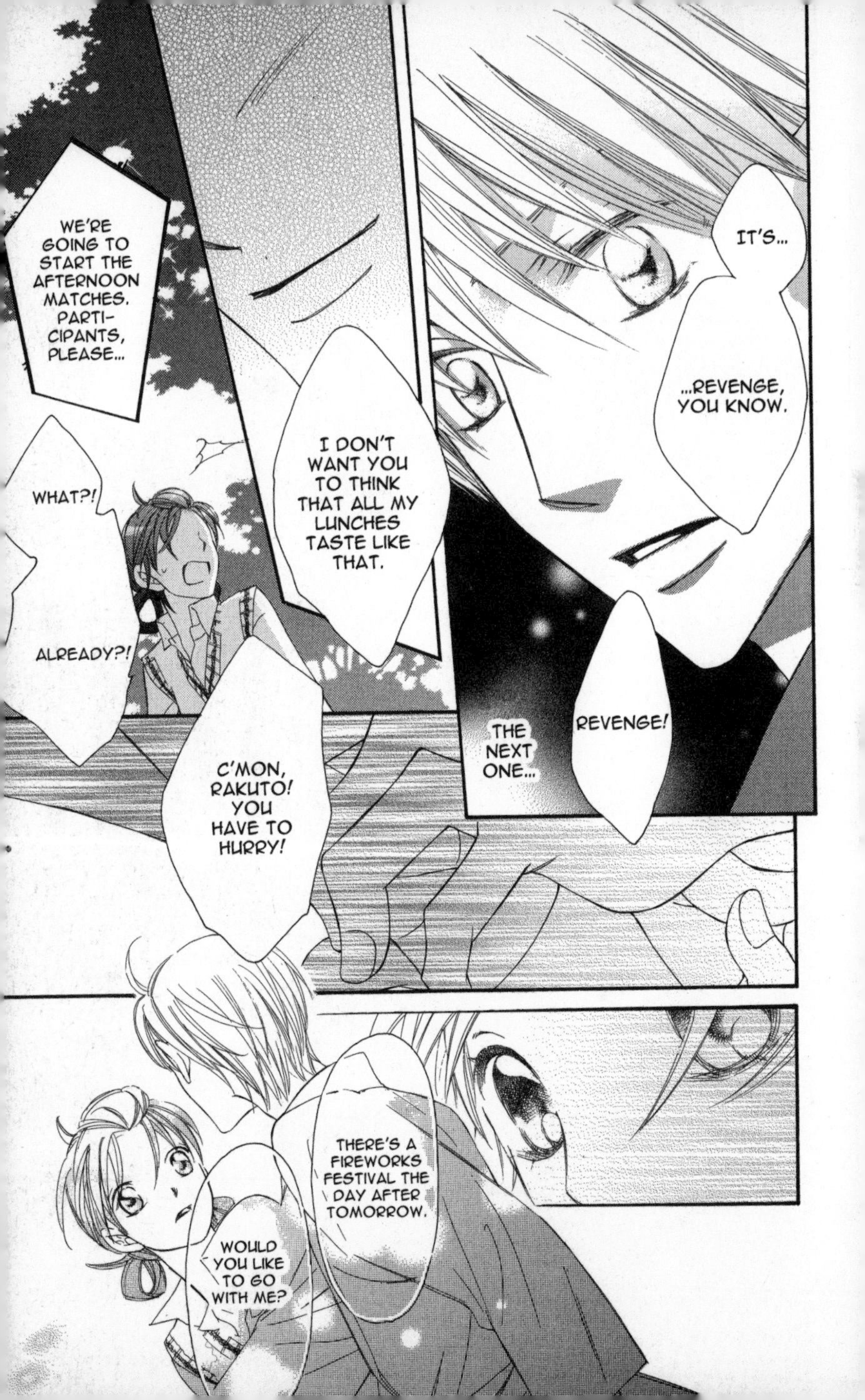
IT'S...
...REVENGE, YOU KNOW.
REVENGE!
THE NEXT ONE...
I DON'T WANT YOU TO THINK THAT ALL MY LUNCHES TASTE LIKE THAT.
WE'RE GOING TO START THE AFTERNOON MATCHES. PARTI-CIPANTS, PLEASE...
WHAT?!
ALREADY?!
C'MON, RAKUTO! YOU HAVE TO HURRY!
THERE'S A FIREWORKS FESTIVAL THE DAY AFTER TOMORROW.
WOULD YOU LIKE TO GO WITH ME?

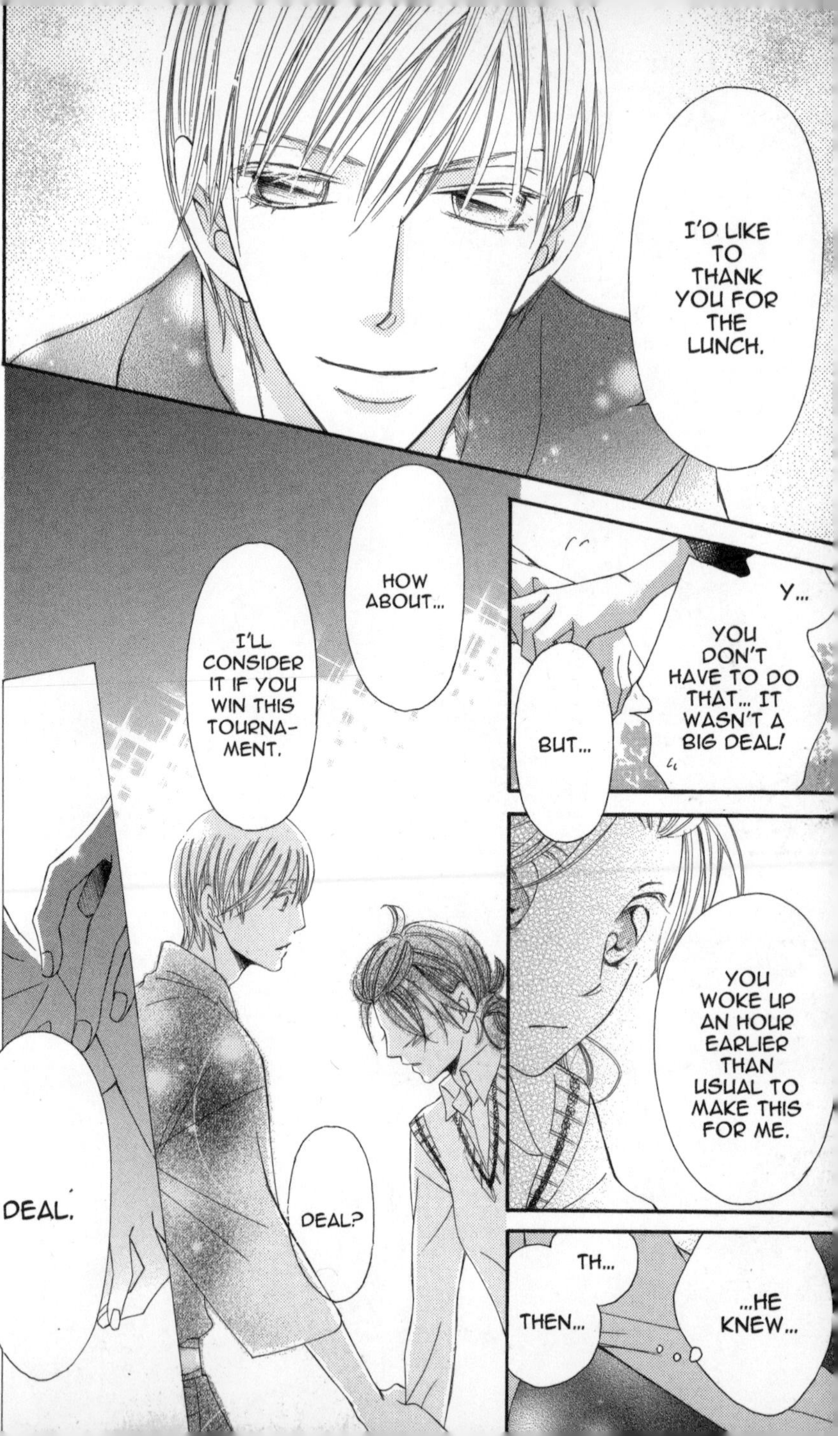
I'D LIKE TO THANK YOU FOR THE LUNCH.
Y...
YOU DON'T HAVE TO DO THAT... IT WASN'T A BIG DEAL!
BUT...
YOU WOKE UP AN HOUR EARLIER THAN USUAL TO MAKE THIS FOR ME.
...HE KNEW...
TH... THEN...
HOW ABOUT...
I'LL CONSIDER IT IF YOU WIN THIS TOURNA-MENT.
DEAL?
DEAL.

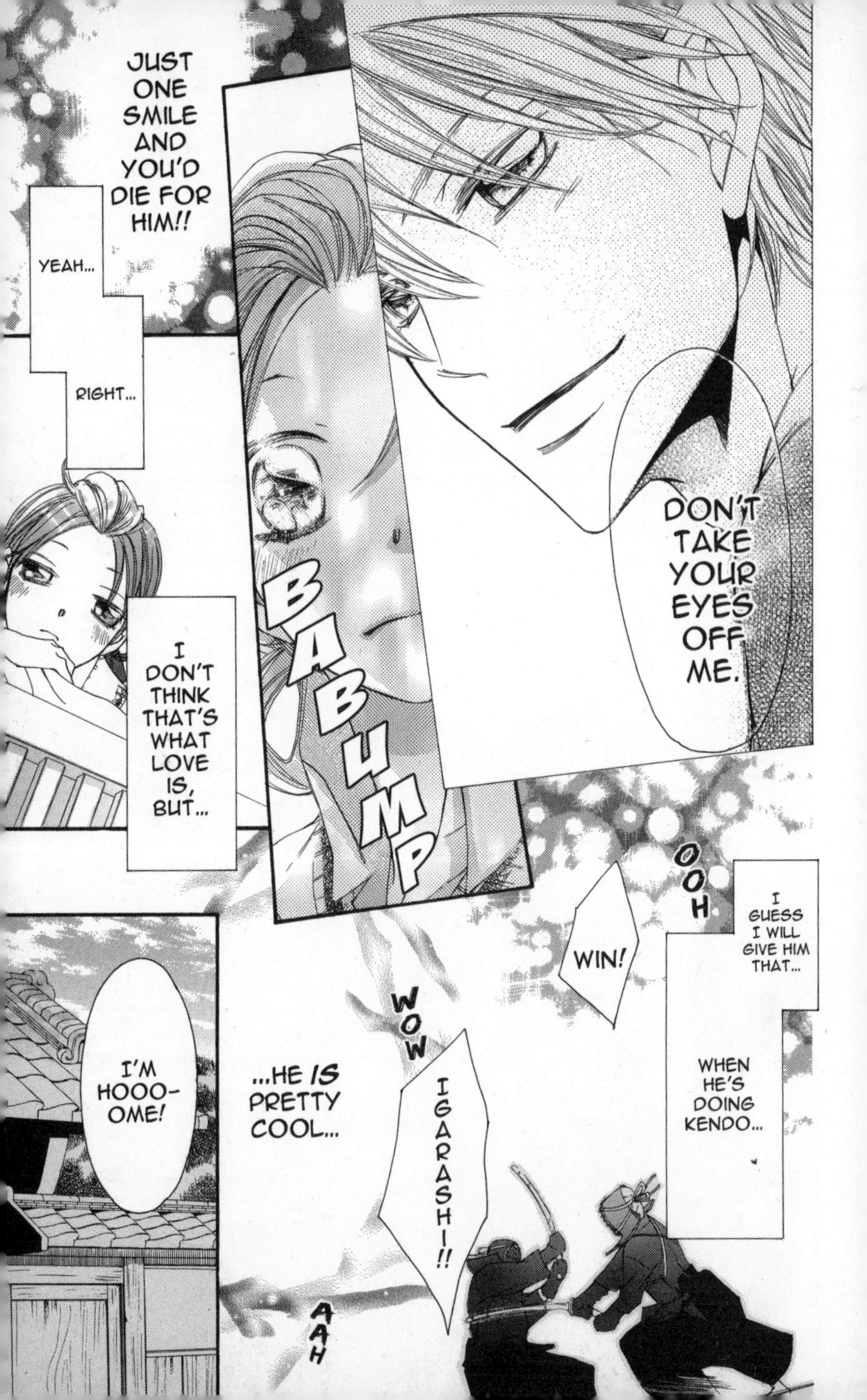
DON'T TAKE YOUR EYES OFF ME.
BABUMP
JUST ONE SMILE AND YOU'D DIE FOR HIM!!
YEAH...
RIGHT...
I DON'T THINK THAT'S WHAT LOVE IS, BUT...
I GUESS I WILL GIVE HIM THAT...
WHEN HE'S DOING KENDO...
OOOH
WIN!
IGARASHI!!
WOW
...HE *IS* PRETTY COOL...
AAH
I'M HOOOO-OME!

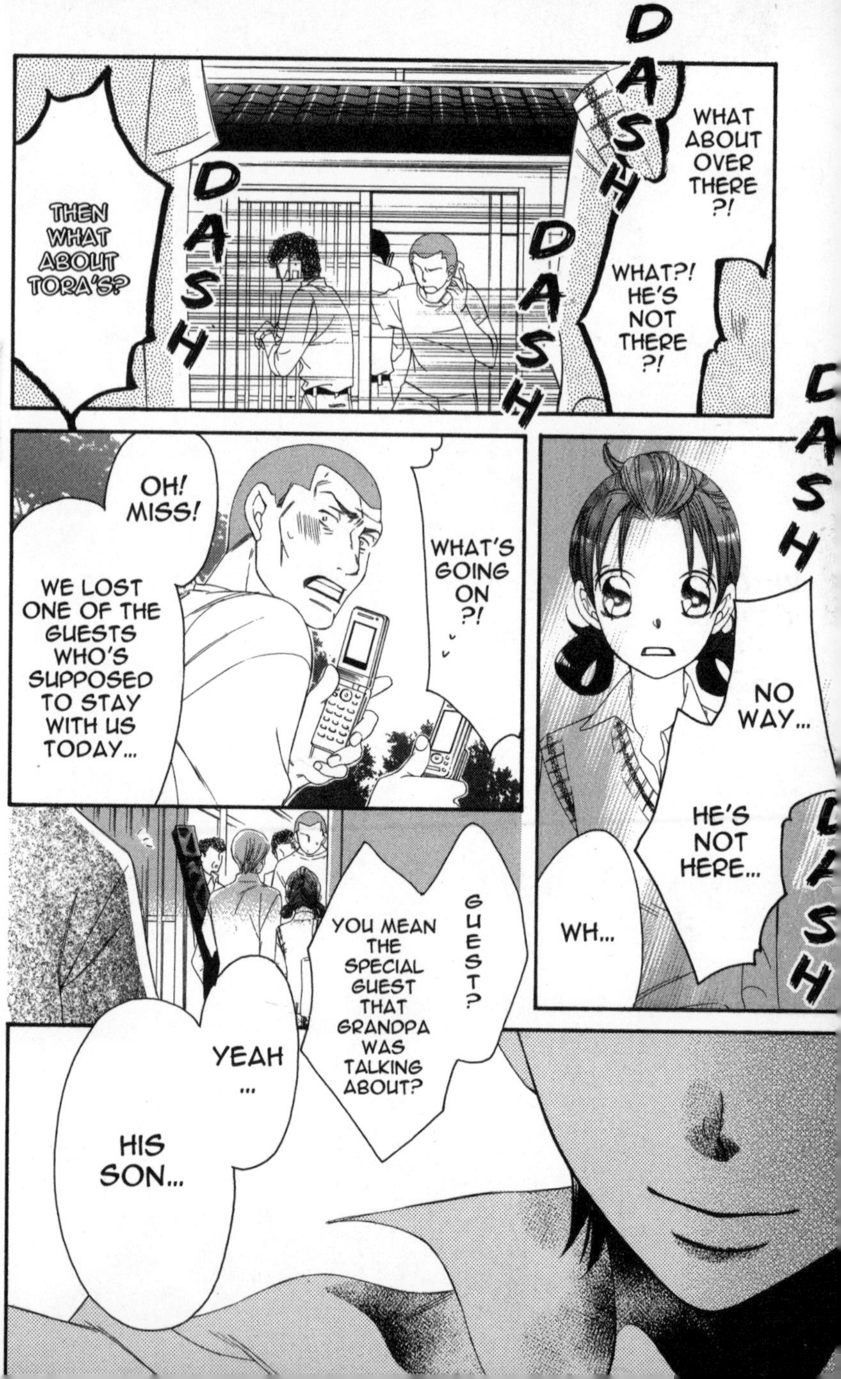
DASH
WHAT ABOUT OVER THERE?!
DASH
WHAT?! HE'S NOT THERE?!
DASH
THEN WHAT ABOUT TORA'S?
DASH
DASH
NO WAY...
HE'S NOT HERE...
WH...
DASH
WHAT'S GOING ON?!
OH! MISS!
WE LOST ONE OF THE GUESTS WHO'S SUPPOSED TO STAY WITH US TODAY...
GUEST?
YOU MEAN THE SPECIAL GUEST THAT GRANDPA WAS TALKING ABOUT?
YEAH...
HIS SON...

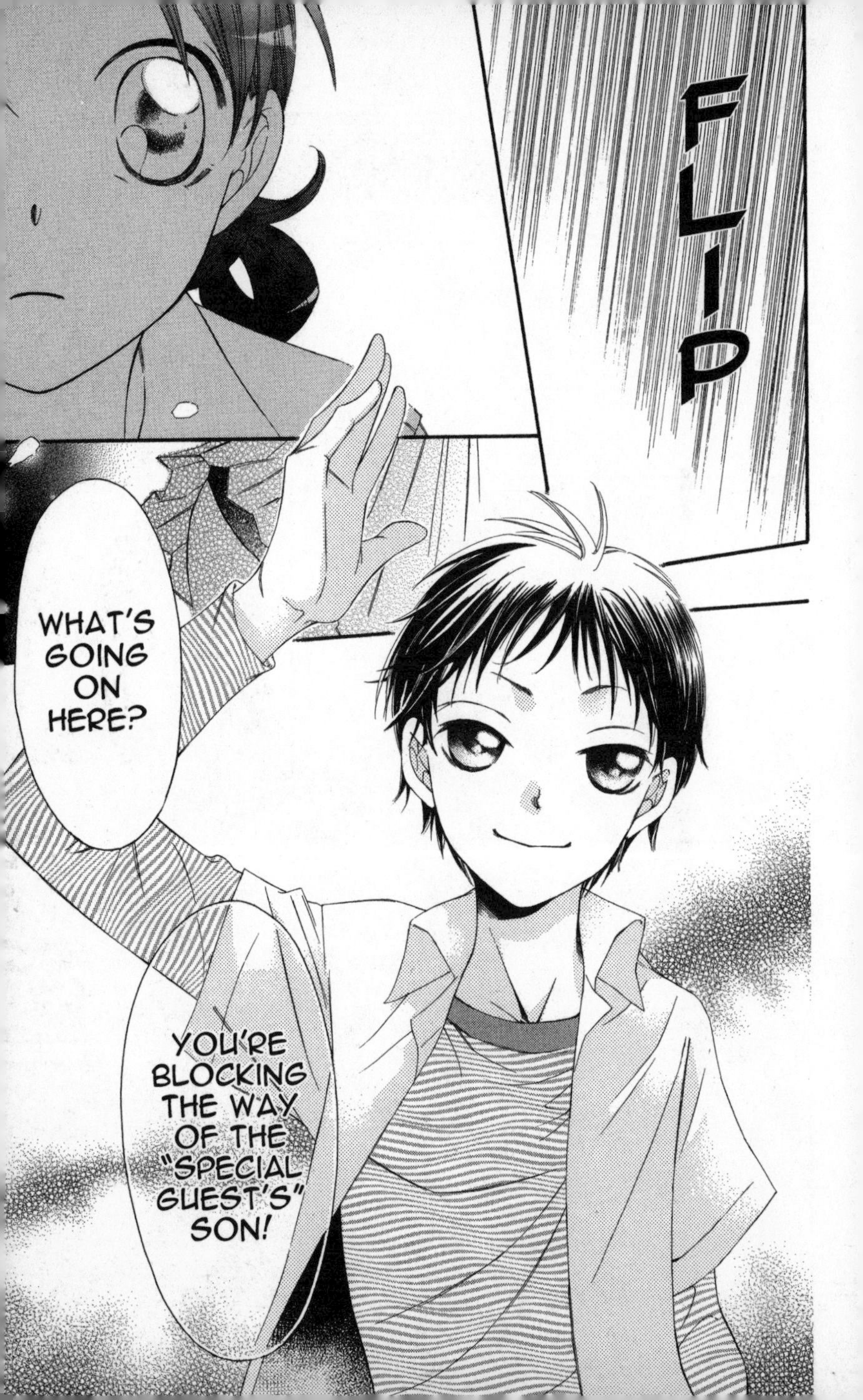
FLIP
YOU'RE BLOCKING THE WAY OF THE "SPECIAL GUEST'S" SON!
WHAT'S GOING ON HERE?

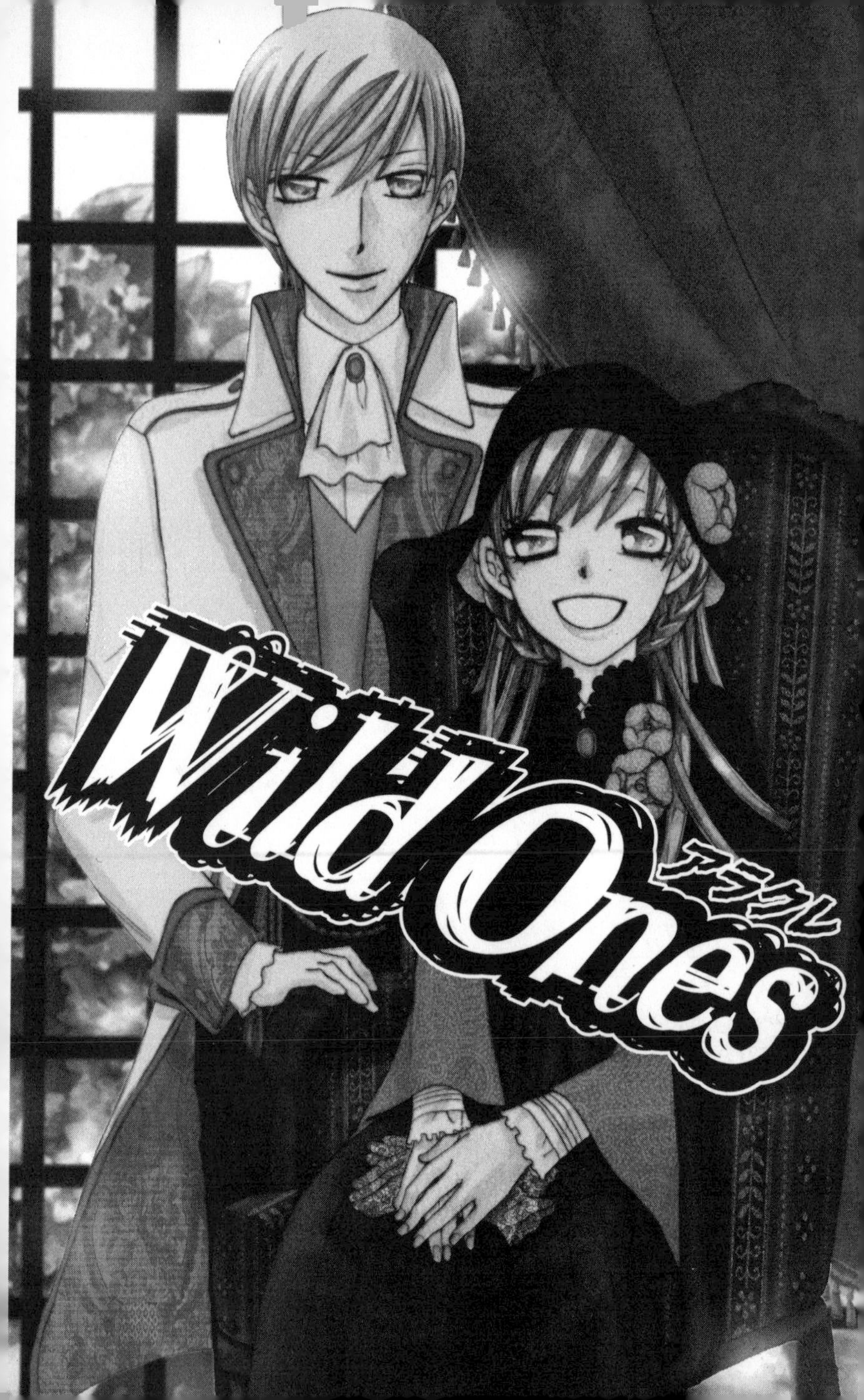
Wild Ones
アラクレ

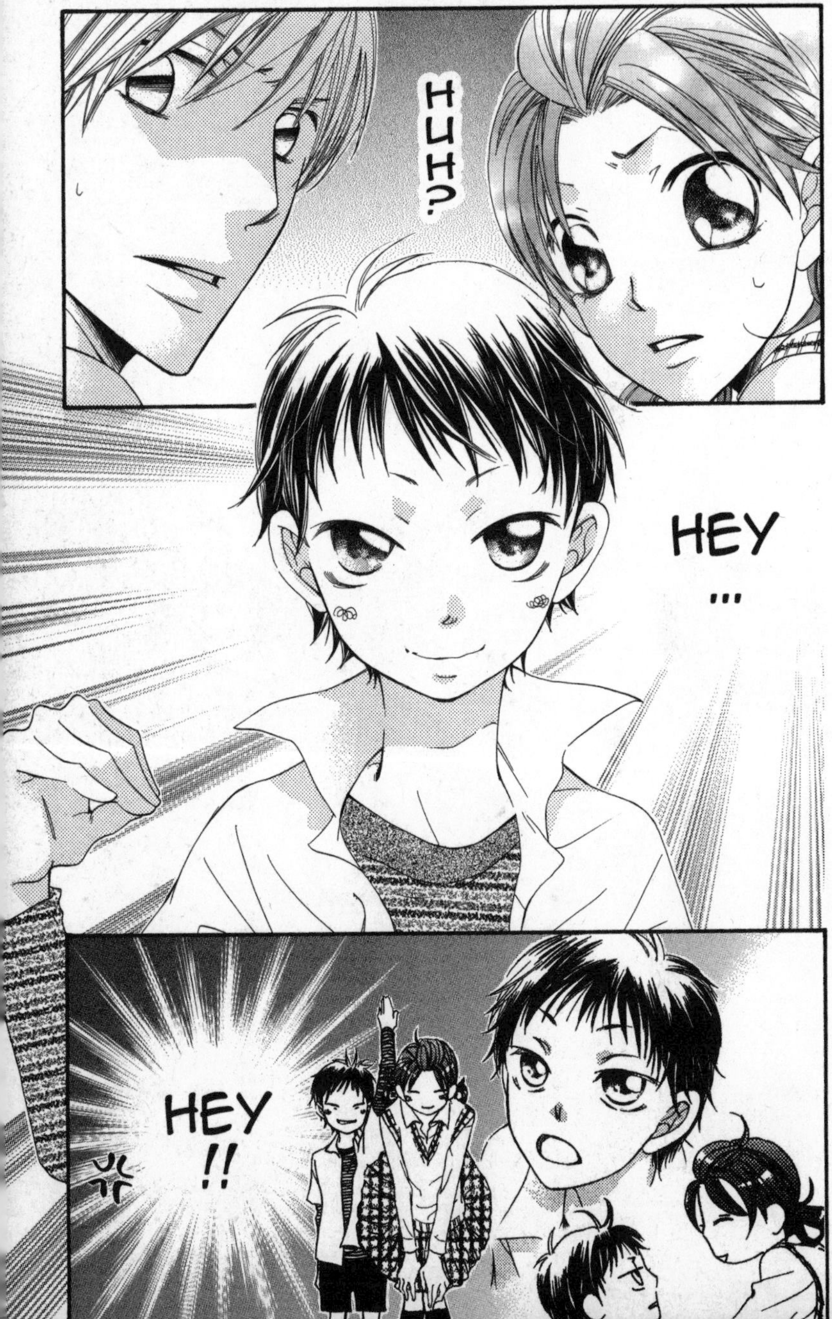
HUH?
HEY ...
HEY !!

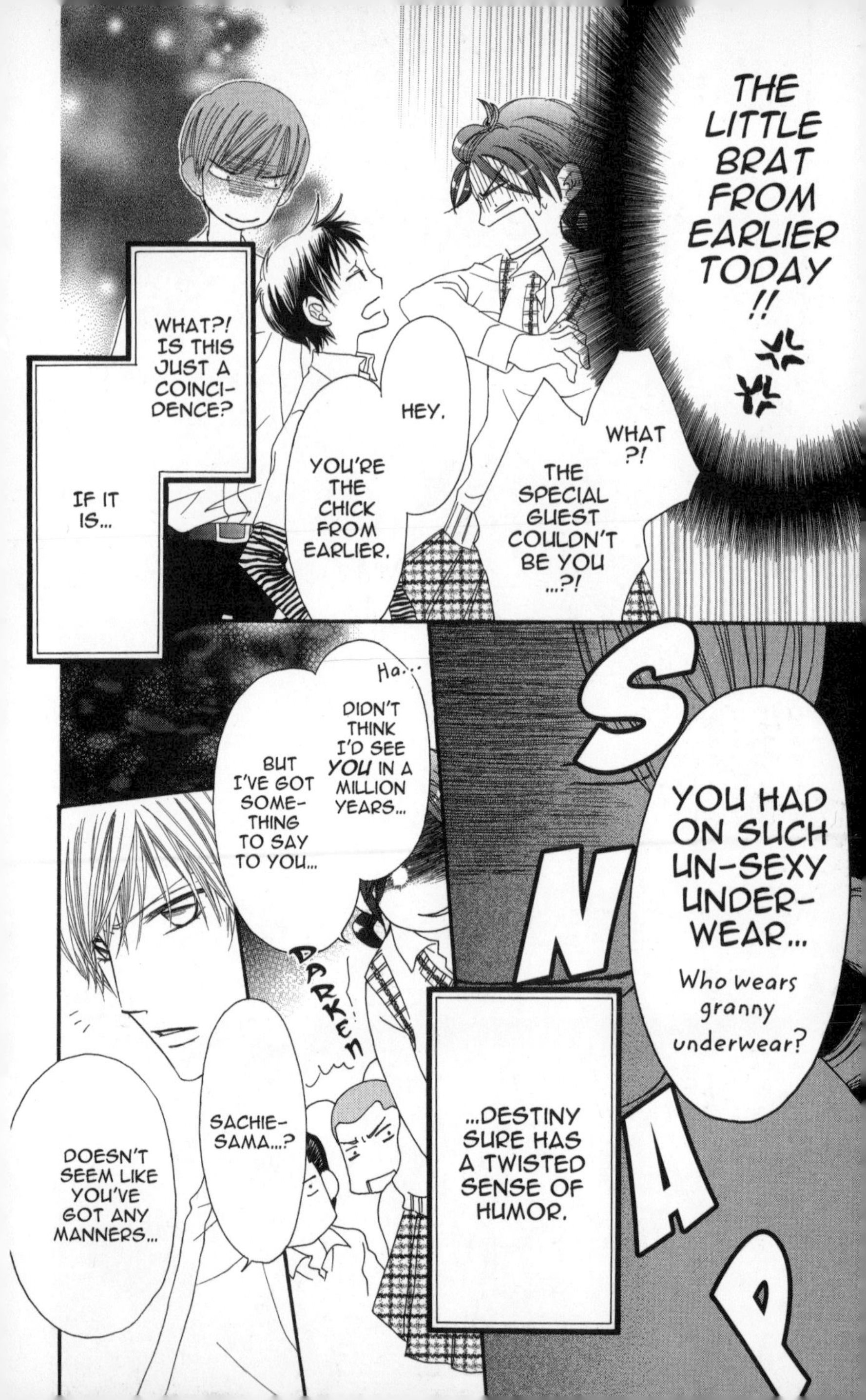
THE LITTLE BRAT FROM EARLIER TODAY!!
WHAT?!
THE SPECIAL GUEST COULDN'T BE YOU...?!
HEY.
YOU'RE THE CHICK FROM EARLIER.
WHAT?! IS THIS JUST A COINCIDENCE?
IF IT IS...
SNAP
YOU HAD ON SUCH UN-SEXY UNDERWEAR...
Who wears granny underwear?
...DESTINY SURE HAS A TWISTED SENSE OF HUMOR.
Ha...
DIDN'T THINK I'D SEE YOU IN A MILLION YEARS...
BUT I'VE GOT SOMETHING TO SAY TO YOU...
DARKEN
SACHIE-SAMA...?
DOESN'T SEEM LIKE YOU'VE GOT ANY MANNERS...

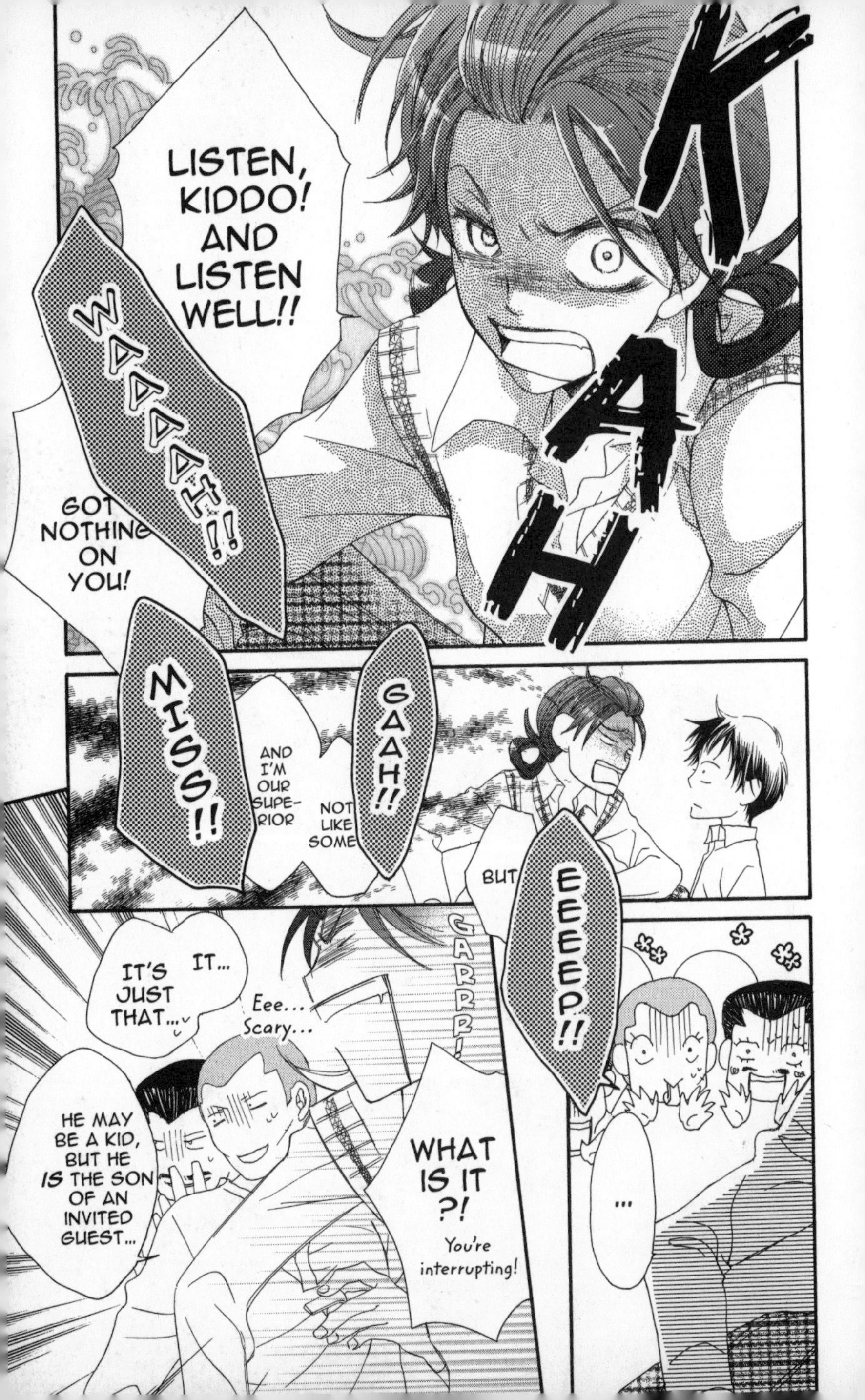
KAH
LISTEN, KIDDO! AND LISTEN WELL!!
WAAAAH!!
GOT NOTHING ON YOU!
BUT
NOT LIKE SOME
GAAH!!
AND I'M OUR SUPE-RIOR
MISS!!
EEEEP!!
...
GARRR!
WHAT IS IT ?!
You're interrupting!
Eee... Scary...
IT...
IT'S JUST THAT...
HE MAY BE A KID, BUT HE *IS* THE SON OF AN INVITED GUEST...

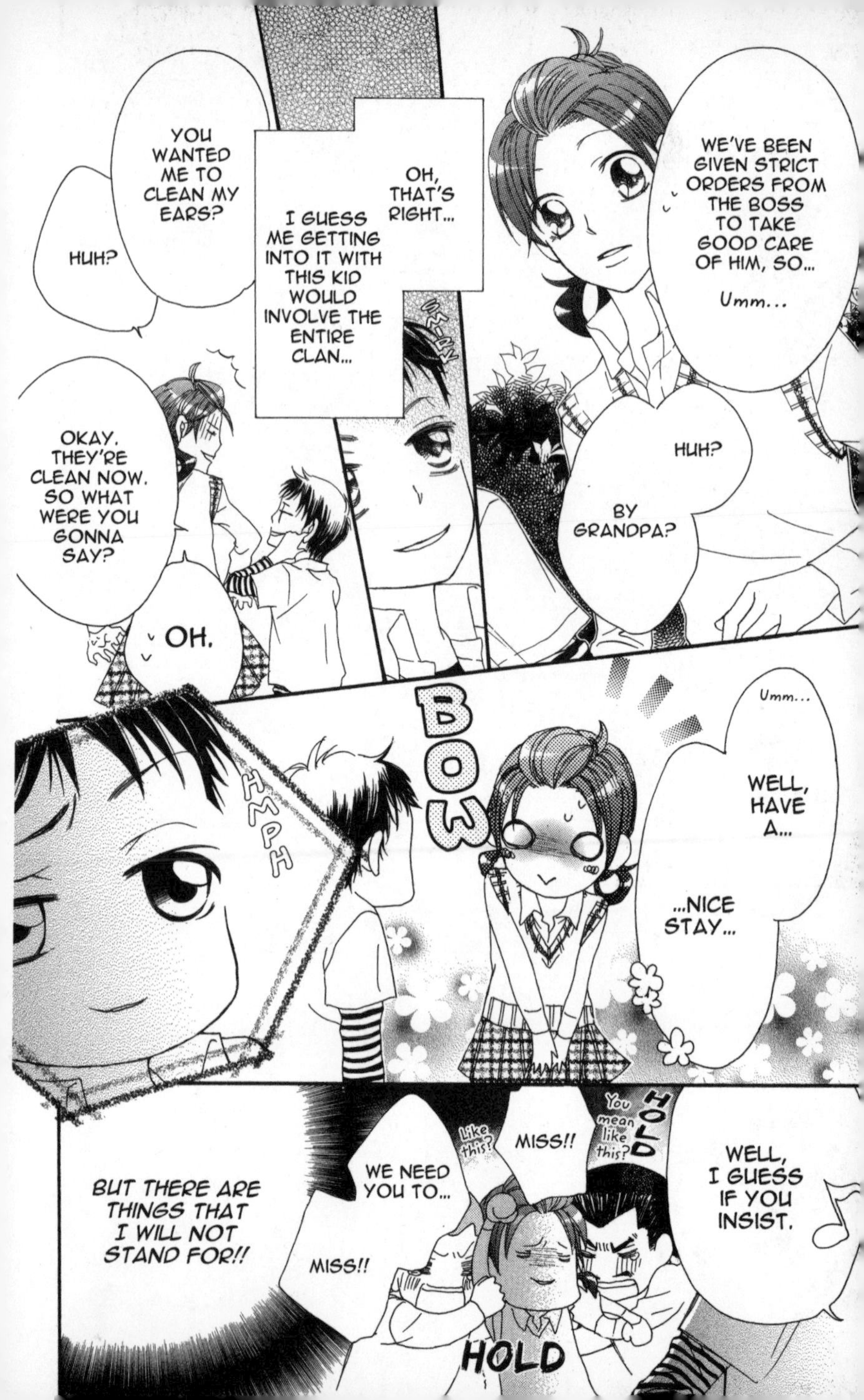
WE'VE BEEN GIVEN STRICT ORDERS FROM THE BOSS TO TAKE GOOD CARE OF HIM, SO... Umm...
HUH?
BY GRANDPA?
OH, THAT'S RIGHT...
I GUESS ME GETTING INTO IT WITH THIS KID WOULD INVOLVE THE ENTIRE CLAN...
SMIRK
YOU WANTED ME TO CLEAN MY EARS?
HUH?
OKAY. THEY'RE CLEAN NOW. SO WHAT WERE YOU GONNA SAY?
OH.
Umm...
WELL, HAVE A...
...NICE STAY...
BOW
HMPH
WELL, I GUESS IF YOU INSIST.
HOLD
You mean like this?
MISS!!
Like this?
WE NEED YOU TO...
MISS!!
HOLD
BUT THERE ARE THINGS THAT I WILL NOT STAND FOR!!

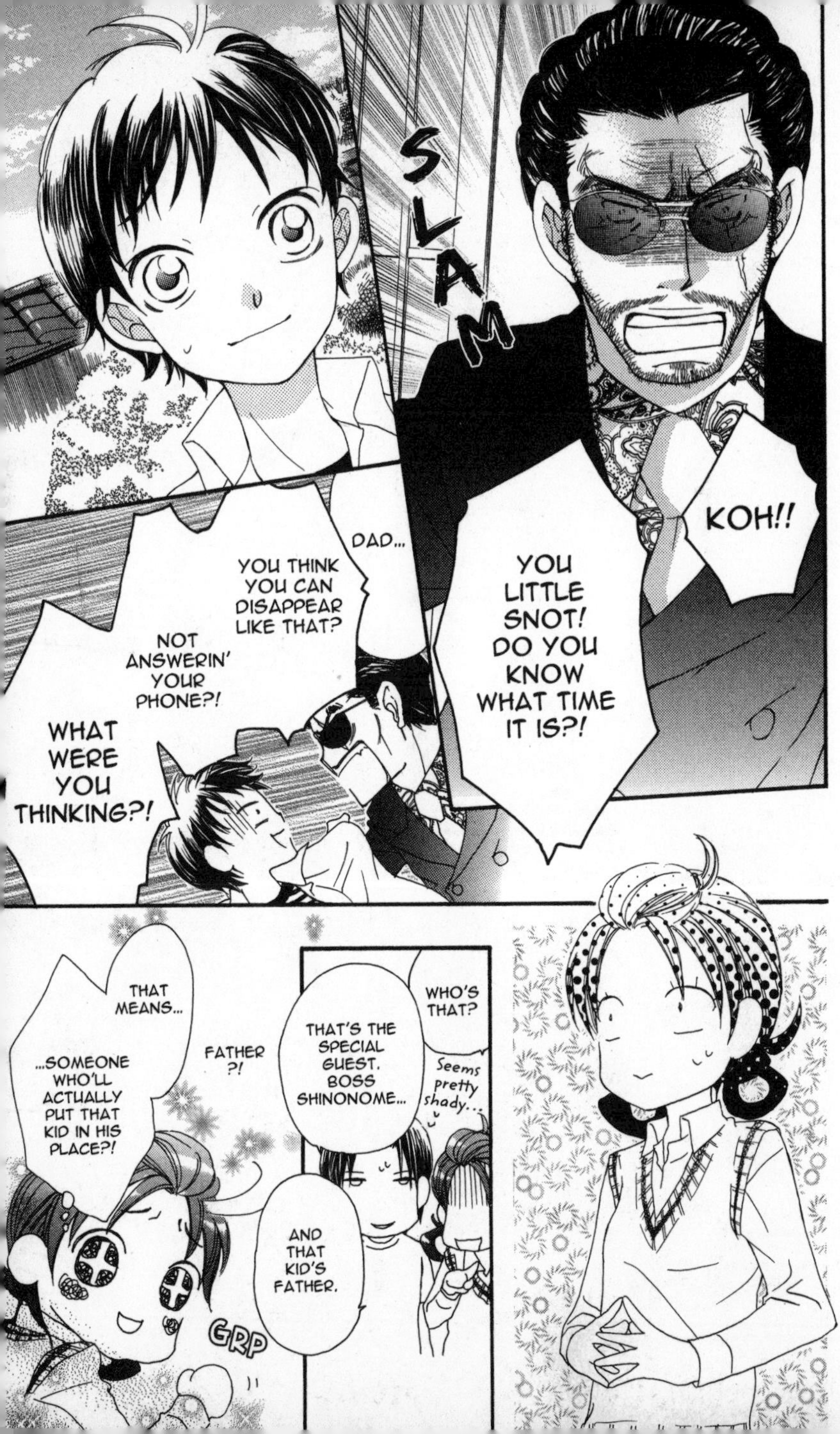
SLAM
KOH!!
YOU LITTLE SNOT! DO YOU KNOW WHAT TIME IT IS?!
DAD...
YOU THINK YOU CAN DISAPPEAR LIKE THAT?
NOT ANSWERIN' YOUR PHONE?!
WHAT WERE YOU THINKING?!
WHO'S THAT?
THAT'S THE SPECIAL GUEST. BOSS SHINONOME...
Seems pretty shady...
AND THAT KID'S FATHER.
FATHER?!
THAT MEANS...
...SOMEONE WHO'LL ACTUALLY PUT THAT KID IN HIS PLACE?!
GRP

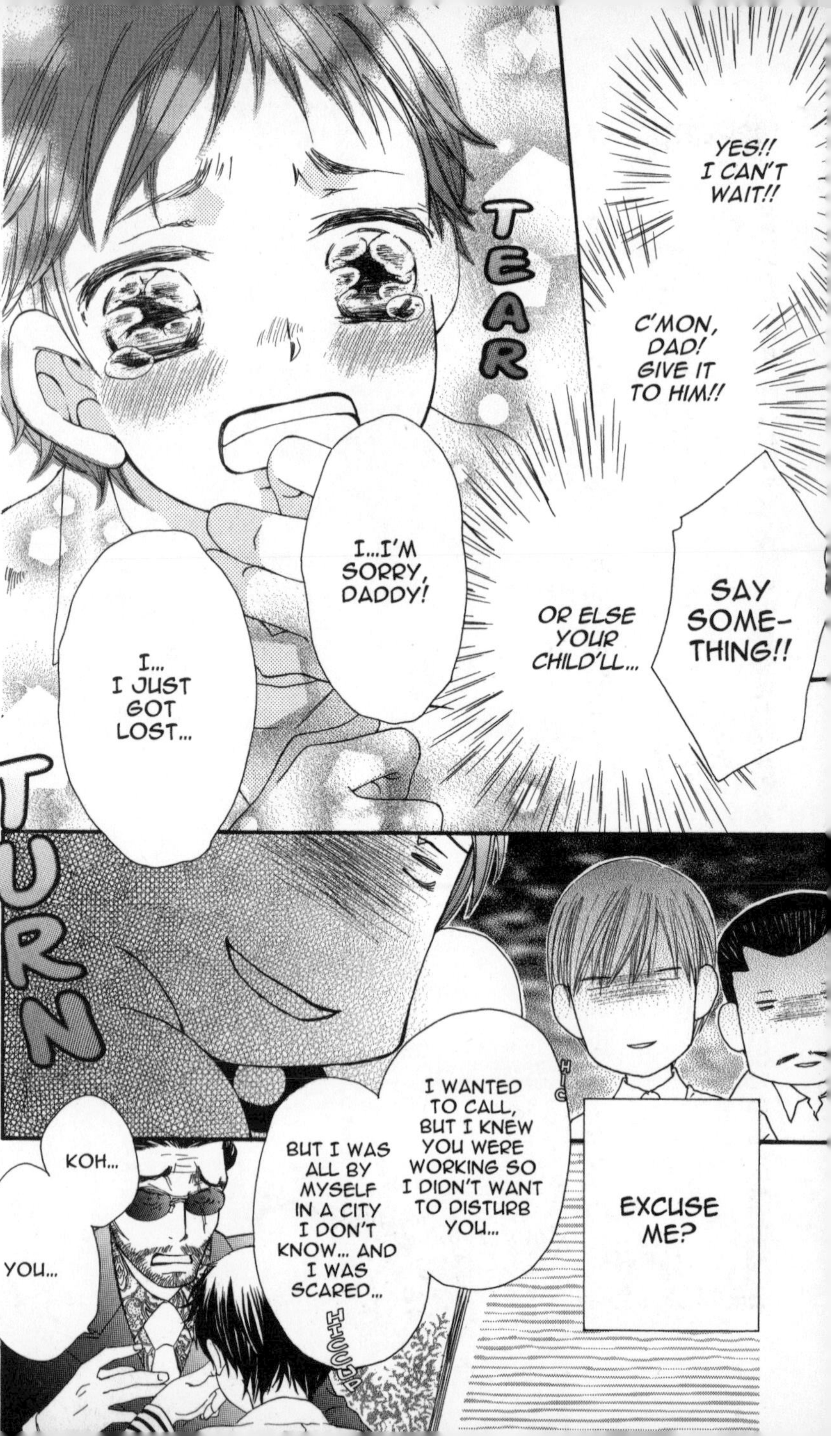
YES!! I CAN'T WAIT!!
C'MON, DAD! GIVE IT TO HIM!!
SAY SOMETHING!!
OR ELSE YOUR CHILD'LL...
TEAR
I...I'M SORRY, DADDY!
I... I JUST GOT LOST...
TURN
EXCUSE ME?
I WANTED TO CALL, BUT I KNEW YOU WERE WORKING SO I DIDN'T WANT TO DISTURB YOU...
BUT I WAS ALL BY MYSELF IN A CITY I DON'T KNOW... AND I WAS SCARED...
HIC
HICCUP
KOH...
YOU...

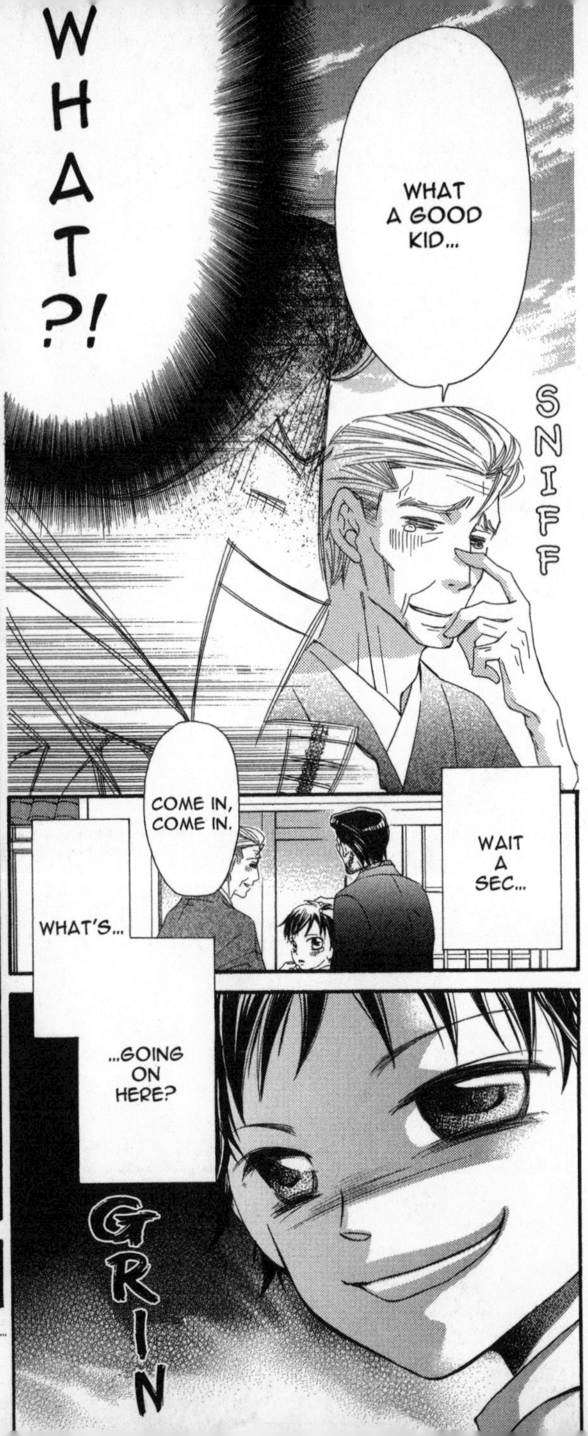

WHAT A GOOD KID...
SNIFF
WHAT?!
COME IN, COME IN.
WAIT A SEC...
WHAT'S...
...GOING ON HERE?
GRIN

WELL, I GOT TO A GOOD BREAK WITH THE SIX CHAPTERS AND BECAUSE IT WAS A HOLIDAY, I DECIDED TO GO HOME AND SEE THE "REAL" RAKUTO IN KYOTO.

↖ (SEE VOLUME 1.)

HE WAS TWO YEARS OLD!

I STOLE... ER, I MEAN I ***TOOK*** HIS NAME WHEN HE WAS BORN, SO IT WAS A REMINDER THAT IT'S BEEN TWO YEARS SINCE I STARTED *WILD ONES*...

HE WALKS AND RUNS AND TALKS A LOT! IT'S AMAZING HOW QUICKLY THEY GROW!!

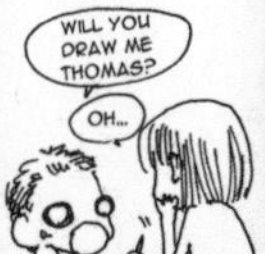

WILL YOU DRAW ME THOMAS?
OH...

I DID MY BEST WITH THOMAS, BUT HE WAS A LOT MORE IMPRESSED WITH THE FIREWORKS I DREW AFTERWARDS. THAT LEFT ME WITH MIXED FEELINGS...

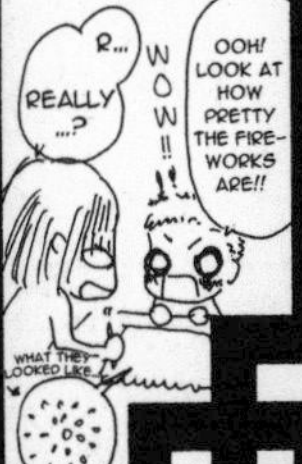

OOH! LOOK AT HOW PRETTY THE FIRE-WORKS ARE!!
WOW!!
R... REALLY ...?
WHAT THEY LOOKED LIKE

BY THE WAY, THE REAL AYA IS ALREADY IN ELEMENTARY SCHOOL...

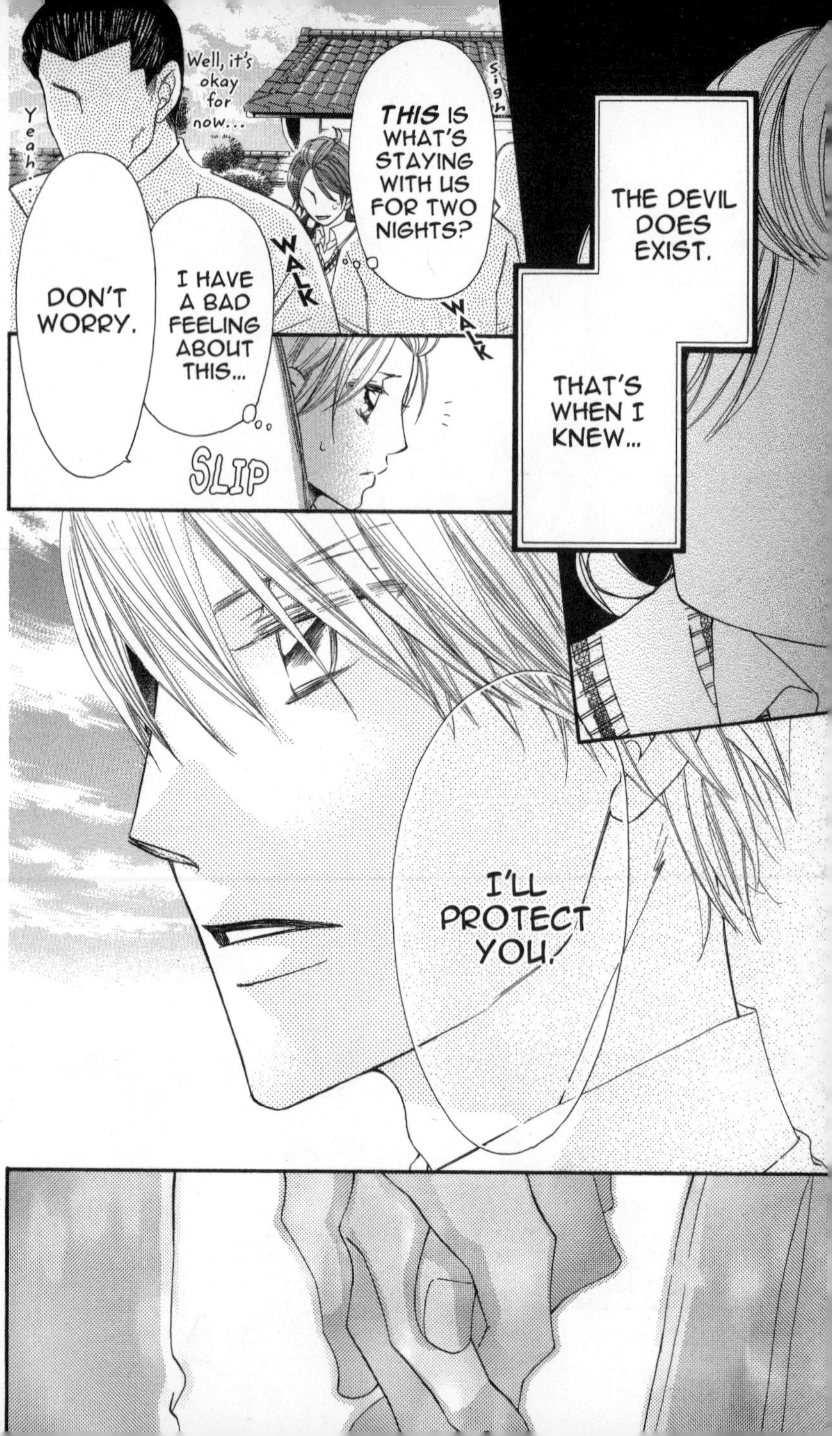
THE DEVIL DOES EXIST.
THAT'S WHEN I KNEW...
Sigh
THIS IS WHAT'S STAYING WITH US FOR TWO NIGHTS?
WALK
WALK
Well, it's okay for now...
Yeah...
I HAVE A BAD FEELING ABOUT THIS...
DON'T WORRY.
SLIP
I'LL PROTECT YOU.

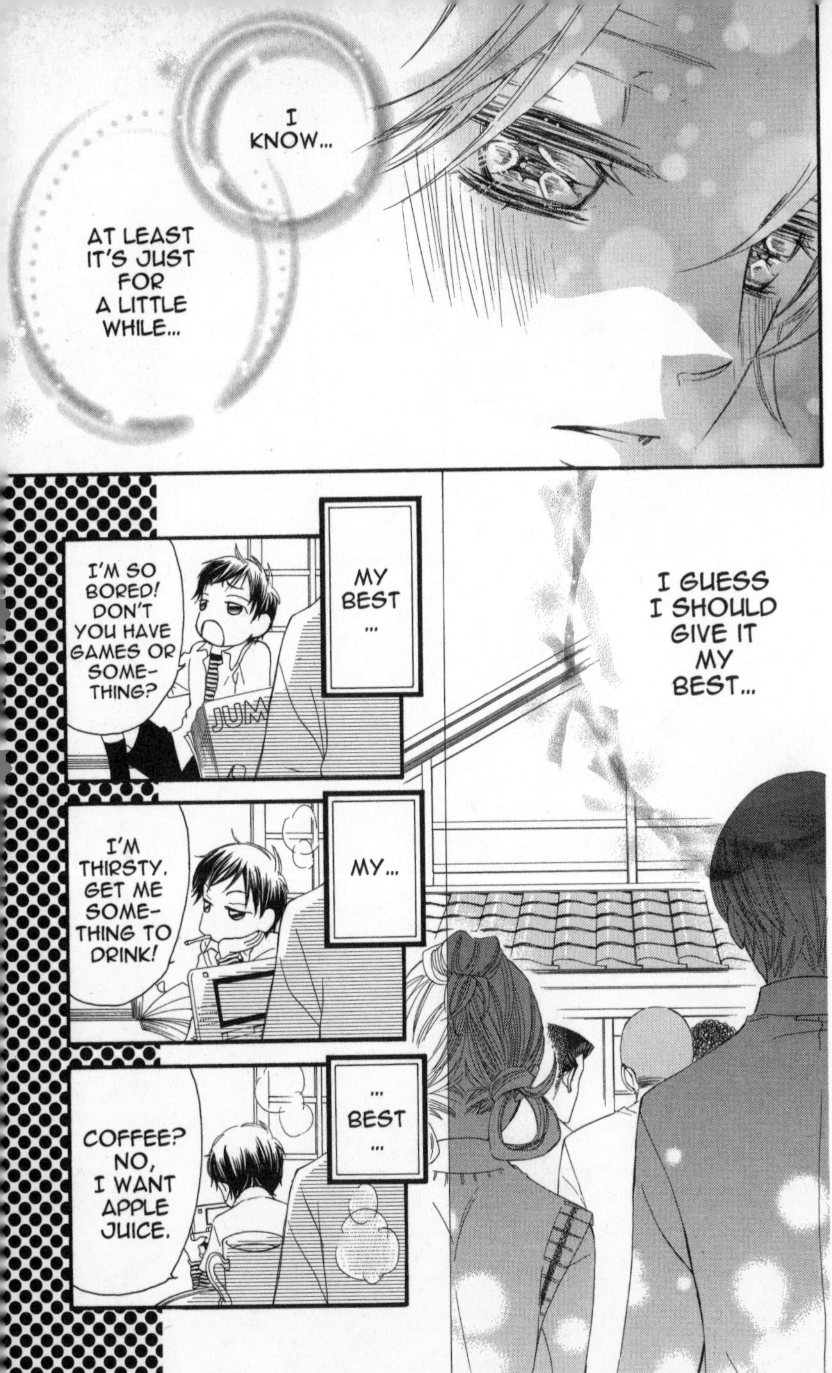
I KNOW...
AT LEAST IT'S JUST FOR A LITTLE WHILE...
I GUESS I SHOULD GIVE IT MY BEST...
MY BEST ...
I'M SO BORED! DON'T YOU HAVE GAMES OR SOME-THING?
MY...
I'M THIRSTY. GET ME SOME-THING TO DRINK!
... BEST ...
COFFEE? NO, I WANT APPLE JUICE.

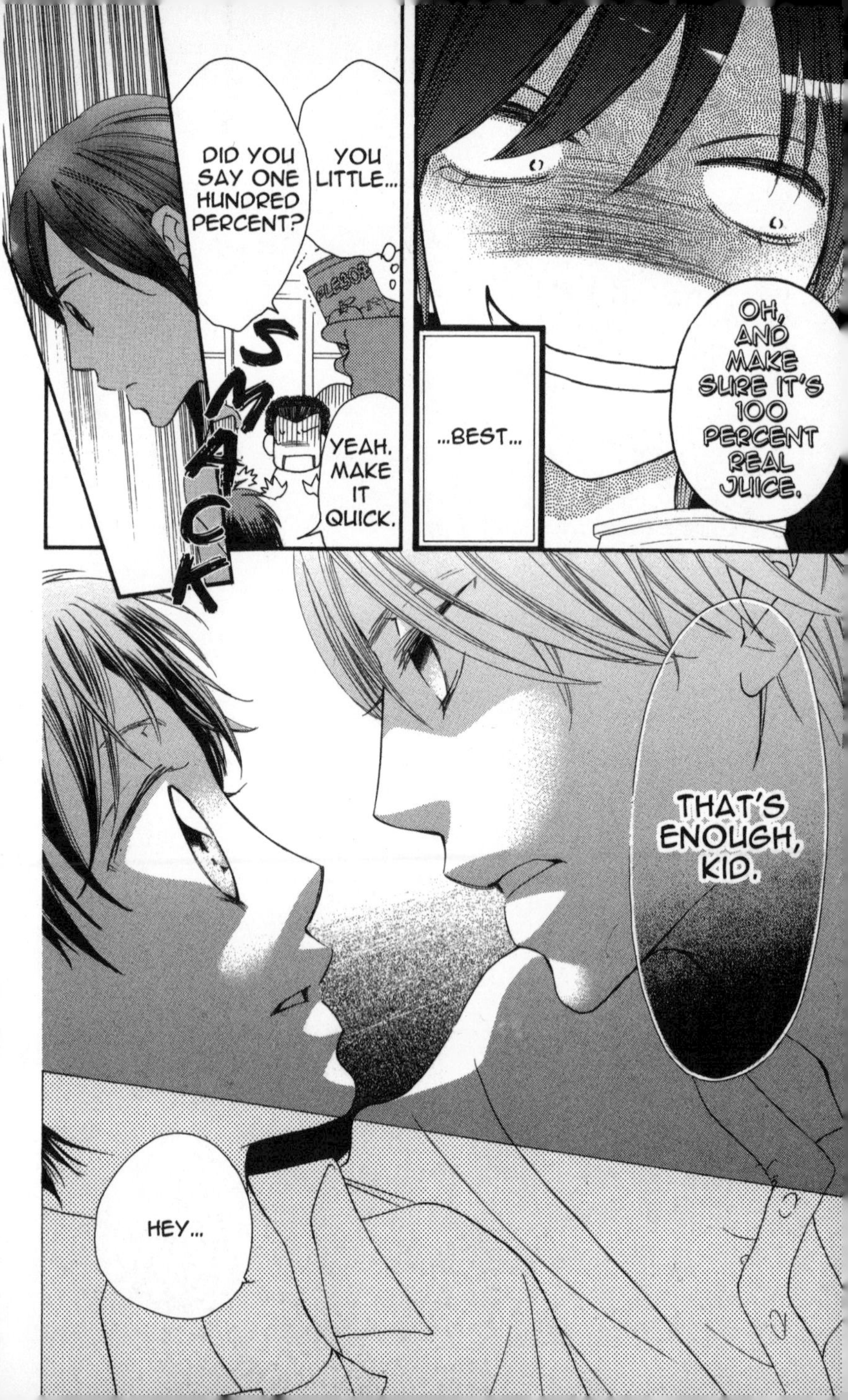
OH, AND MAKE SURE IT'S 100 PERCENT REAL JUICE.
...BEST...
YOU LITTLE...
DID YOU SAY ONE HUNDRED PERCENT?
YEAH. MAKE IT QUICK.
SMACK
THAT'S ENOUGH, KID.
HEY...

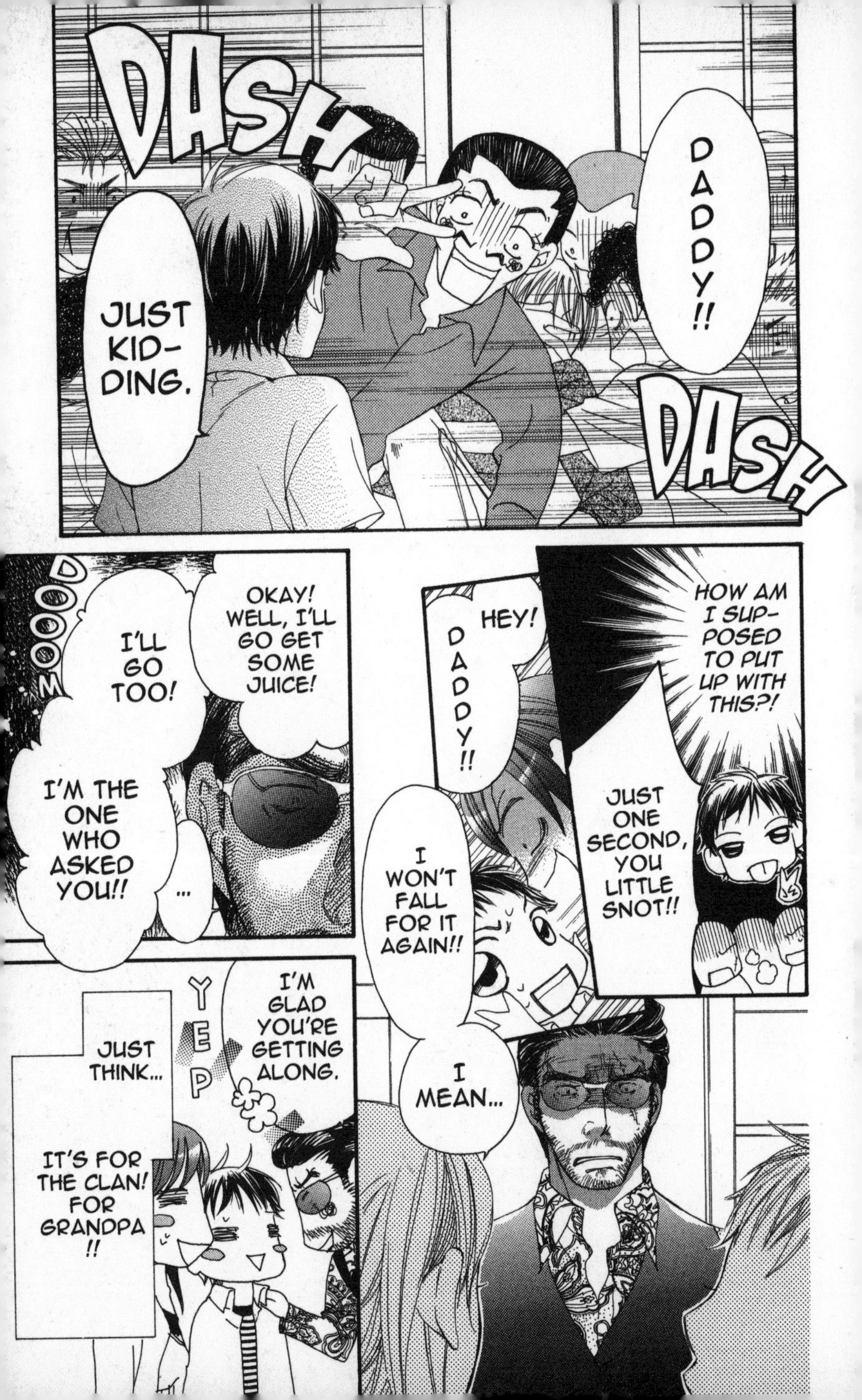
DADDY!!
DASH
DASH
JUST KID-DING.
HOW AM I SUP-POSED TO PUT UP WITH THIS?!
JUST ONE SECOND, YOU LITTLE SNOT!!
HEY!
DADDY!!
I WON'T FALL FOR IT AGAIN!!
OKAY! WELL, I'LL GO GET SOME JUICE!
I'LL GO TOO!
DOOOOM...
I'M THE ONE WHO ASKED YOU!!
...
I MEAN...
I'M GLAD YOU'RE GETTING ALONG.
YEP
JUST THINK...
IT'S FOR THE CLAN! FOR GRANDPA!!

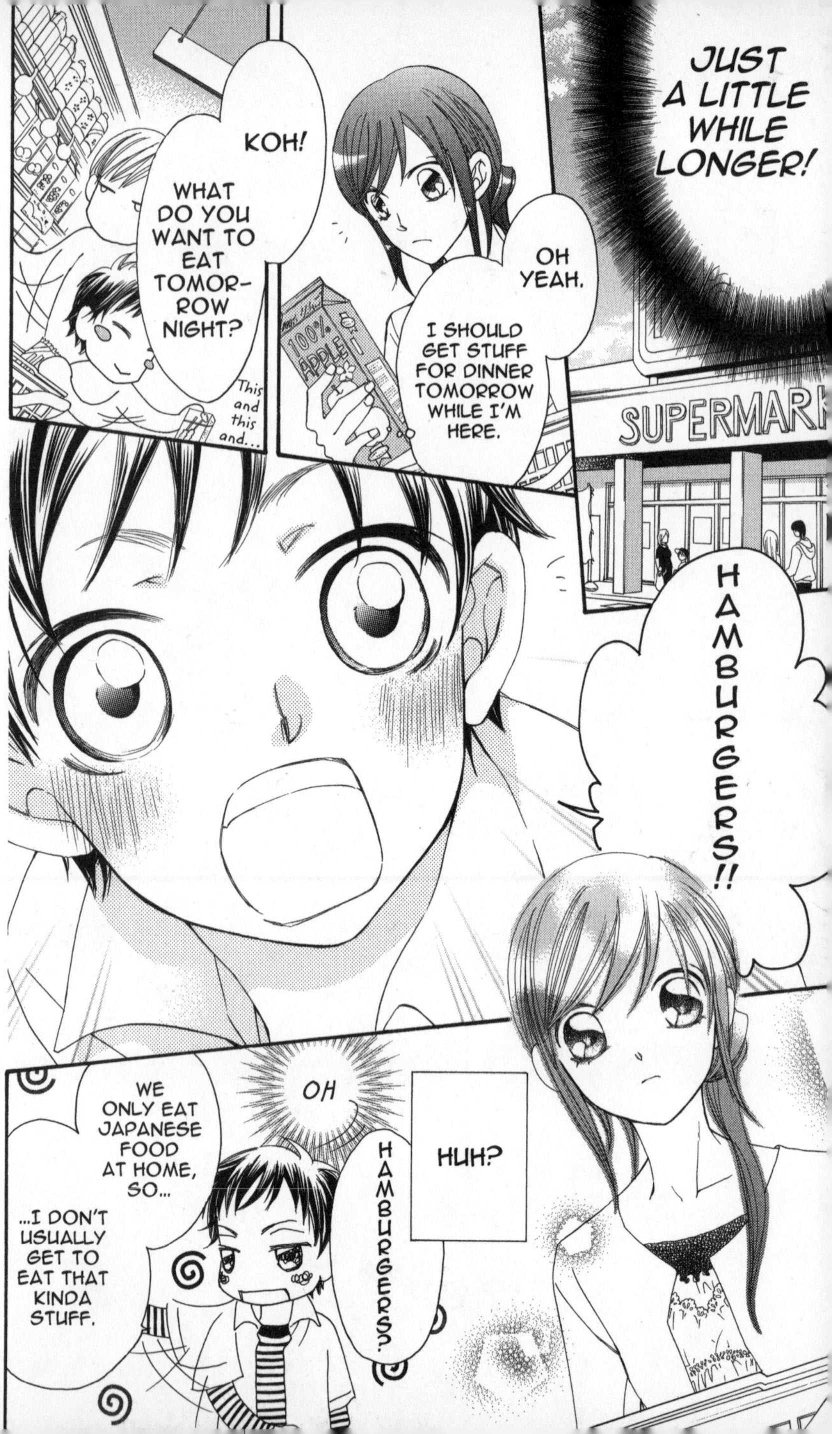
JUST A LITTLE WHILE LONGER!
SUPERMARK
OH YEAH.
I SHOULD GET STUFF FOR DINNER TOMORROW WHILE I'M HERE.
100% APPLE
KOH!
WHAT DO YOU WANT TO EAT TOMORROW NIGHT?
This and this and...
HAMBURGERS!!
HUH?
HAMBURGERS?
OH
WE ONLY EAT JAPANESE FOOD AT HOME, SO...
...I DON'T USUALLY GET TO EAT THAT KINDA STUFF.

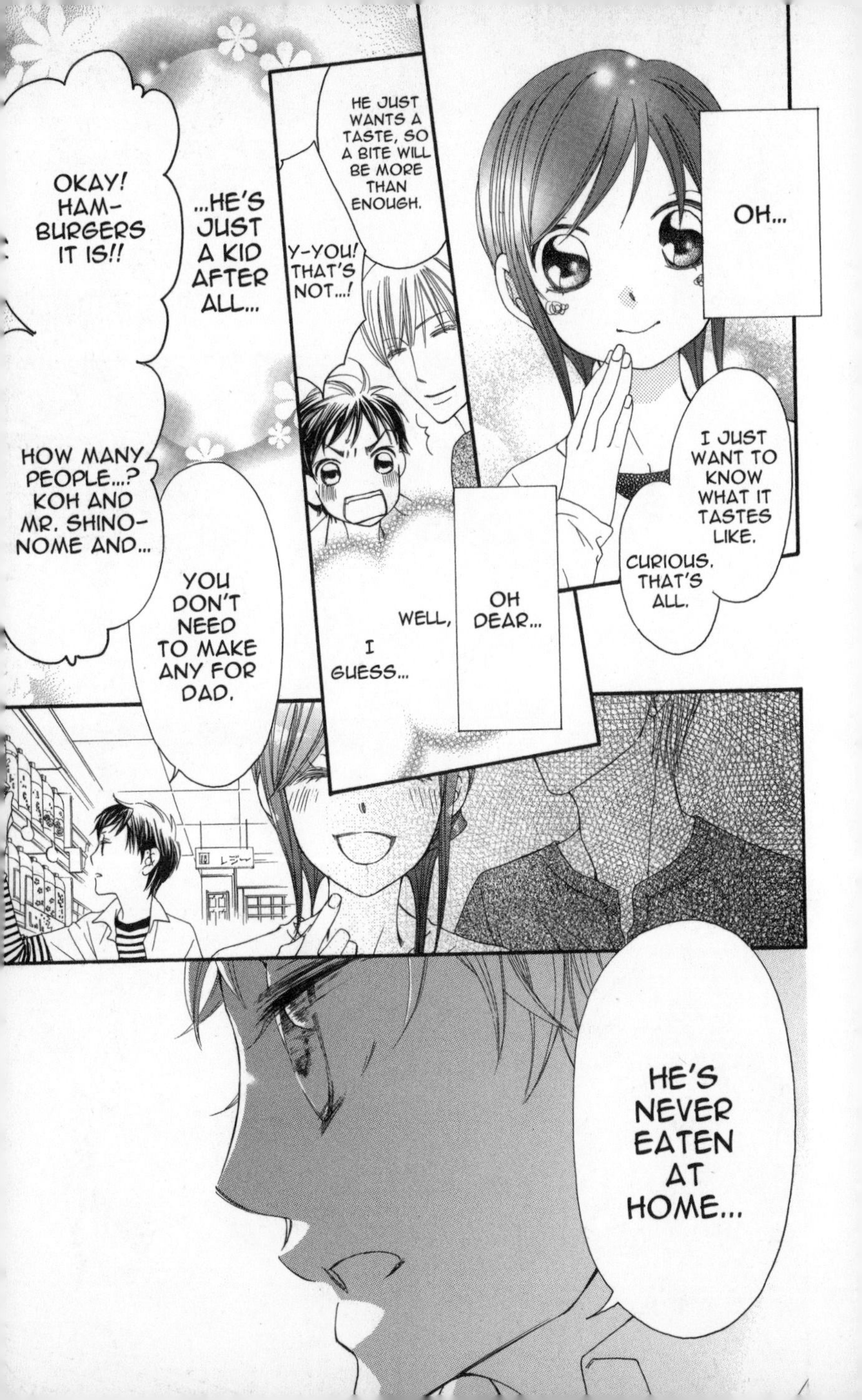
OH...
I JUST WANT TO KNOW WHAT IT TASTES LIKE.
CURIOUS. THAT'S ALL.
HE JUST WANTS A TASTE, SO A BITE WILL BE MORE THAN ENOUGH.
Y-YOU! THAT'S NOT...!
OH DEAR...
WELL, I GUESS...
...HE'S JUST A KID AFTER ALL...
OKAY! HAM-BURGERS IT IS!!
HOW MANY PEOPLE...? KOH AND MR. SHINO-NOME AND...
YOU DON'T NEED TO MAKE ANY FOR DAD.
レジ
HE'S NEVER EATEN AT HOME...

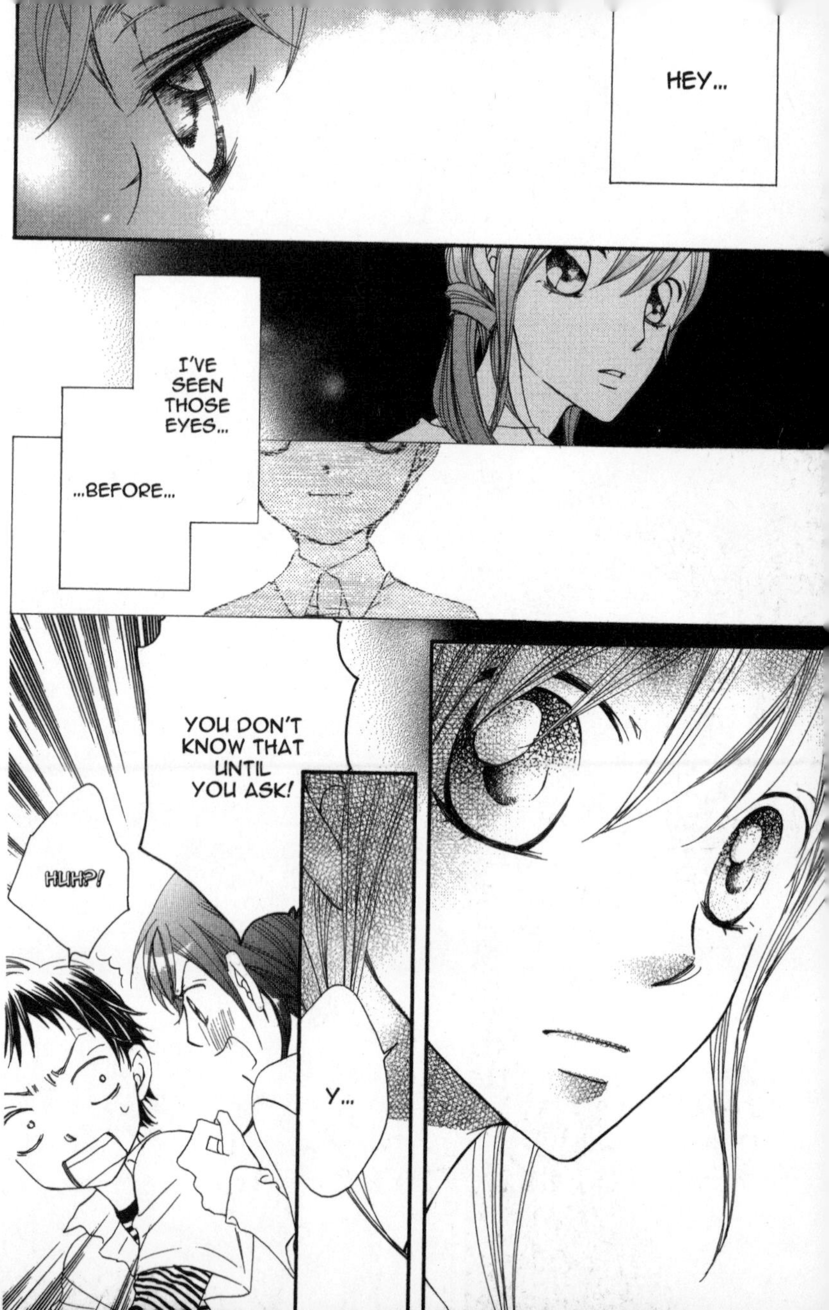
HEY...
I'VE SEEN THOSE EYES...
...BEFORE...
YOU DON'T KNOW THAT UNTIL YOU ASK!
Y...
HUH?!

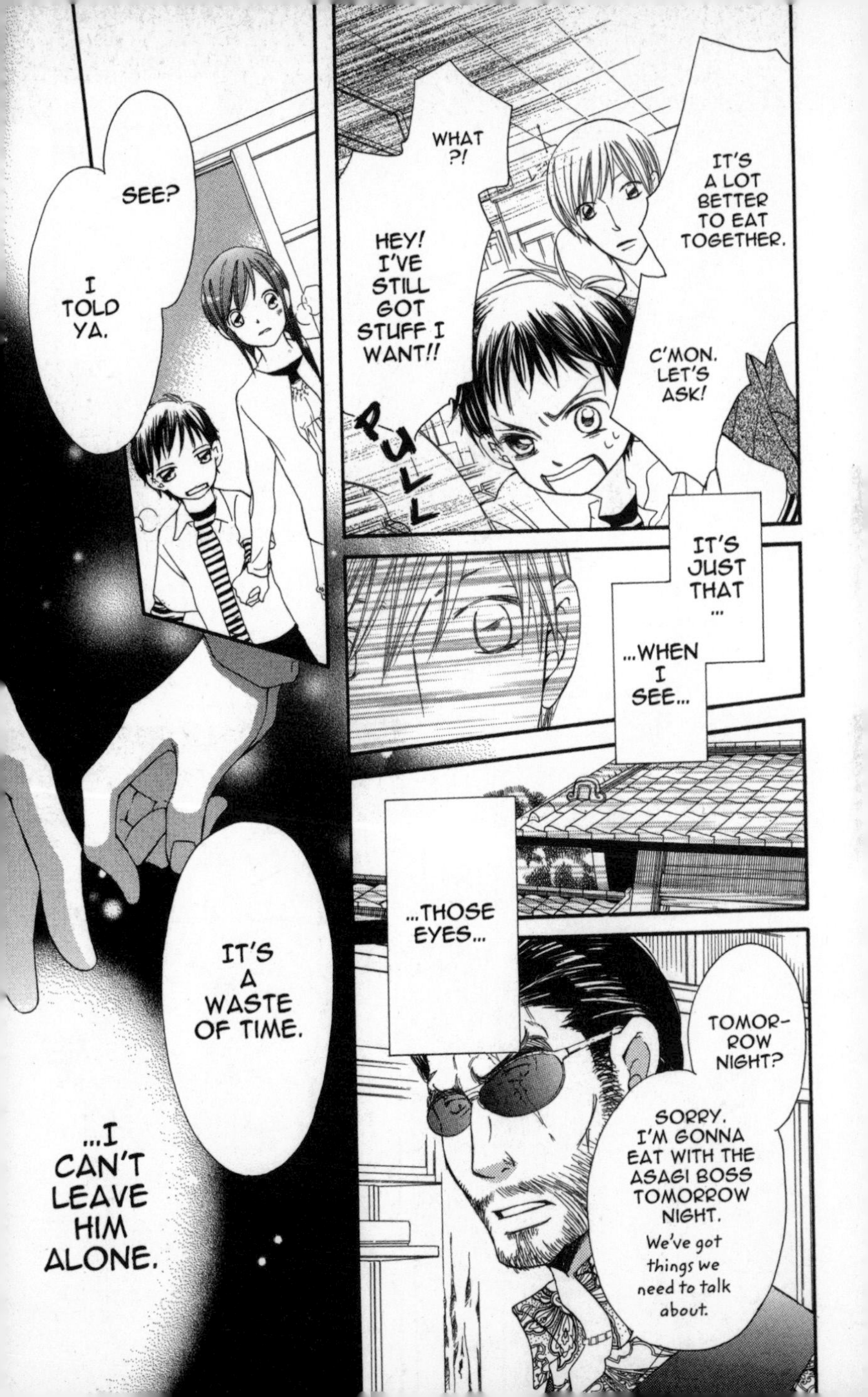
IT'S A LOT BETTER TO EAT TOGETHER.
WHAT?!
C'MON. LET'S ASK!
HEY! I'VE STILL GOT STUFF I WANT!!
PULL
IT'S JUST THAT...
...WHEN I SEE...
...THOSE EYES...
TOMOR-ROW NIGHT?
SORRY. I'M GONNA EAT WITH THE ASAGI BOSS TOMORROW NIGHT. We've got things we need to talk about.
SEE?
I TOLD YA.
IT'S A WASTE OF TIME.
...I CAN'T LEAVE HIM ALONE.

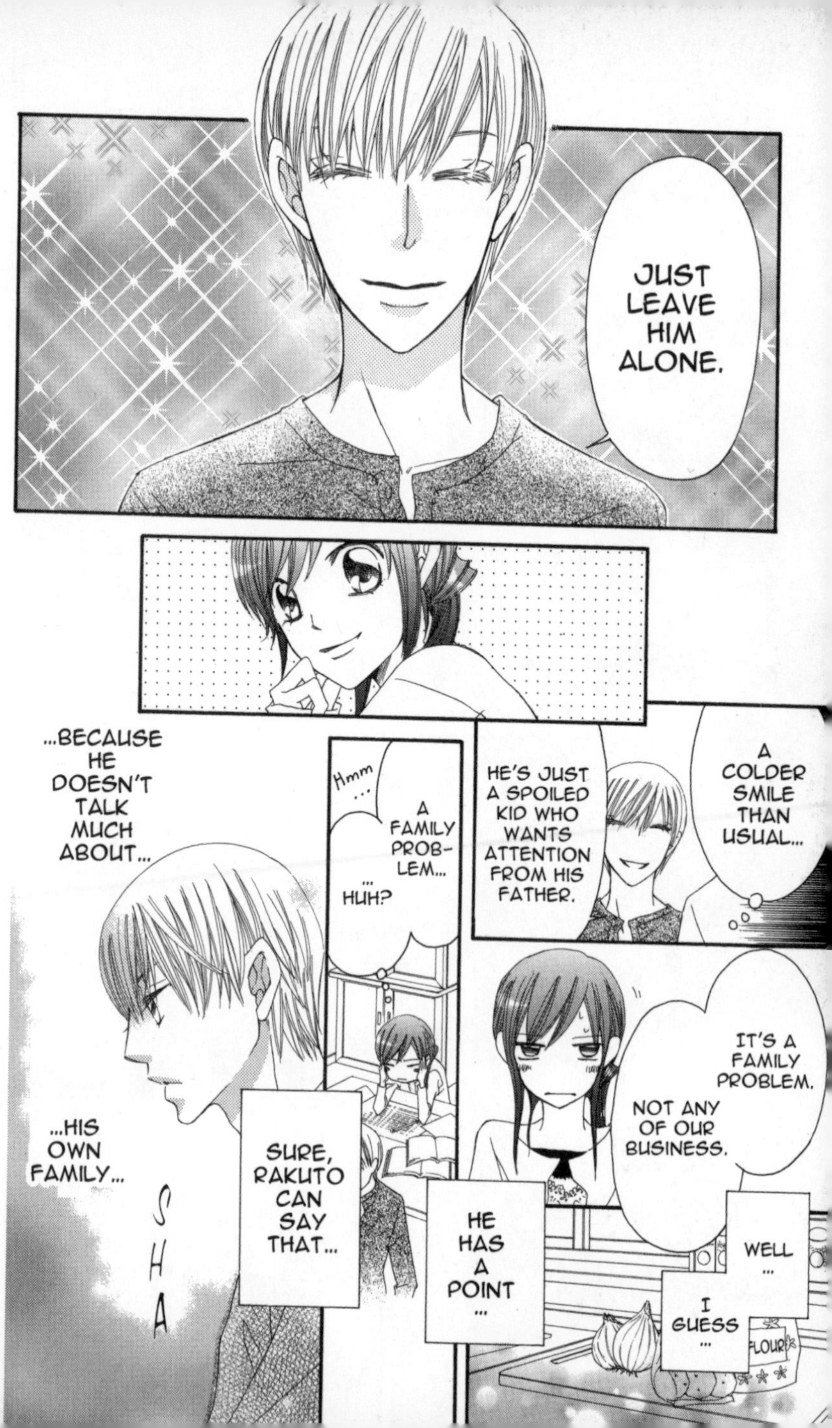
JUST LEAVE HIM ALONE.
A COLDER SMILE THAN USUAL...
HE'S JUST A SPOILED KID WHO WANTS ATTENTION FROM HIS FATHER.
IT'S A FAMILY PROBLEM.
NOT ANY OF OUR BUSINESS.
WELL...
I GUESS...
HE HAS A POINT...
Hmm...
A FAMILY PROBLEM...
...HUH?
SURE, RAKUTO CAN SAY THAT...
...BECAUSE HE DOESN'T TALK MUCH ABOUT...
...HIS OWN FAMILY...
SHA

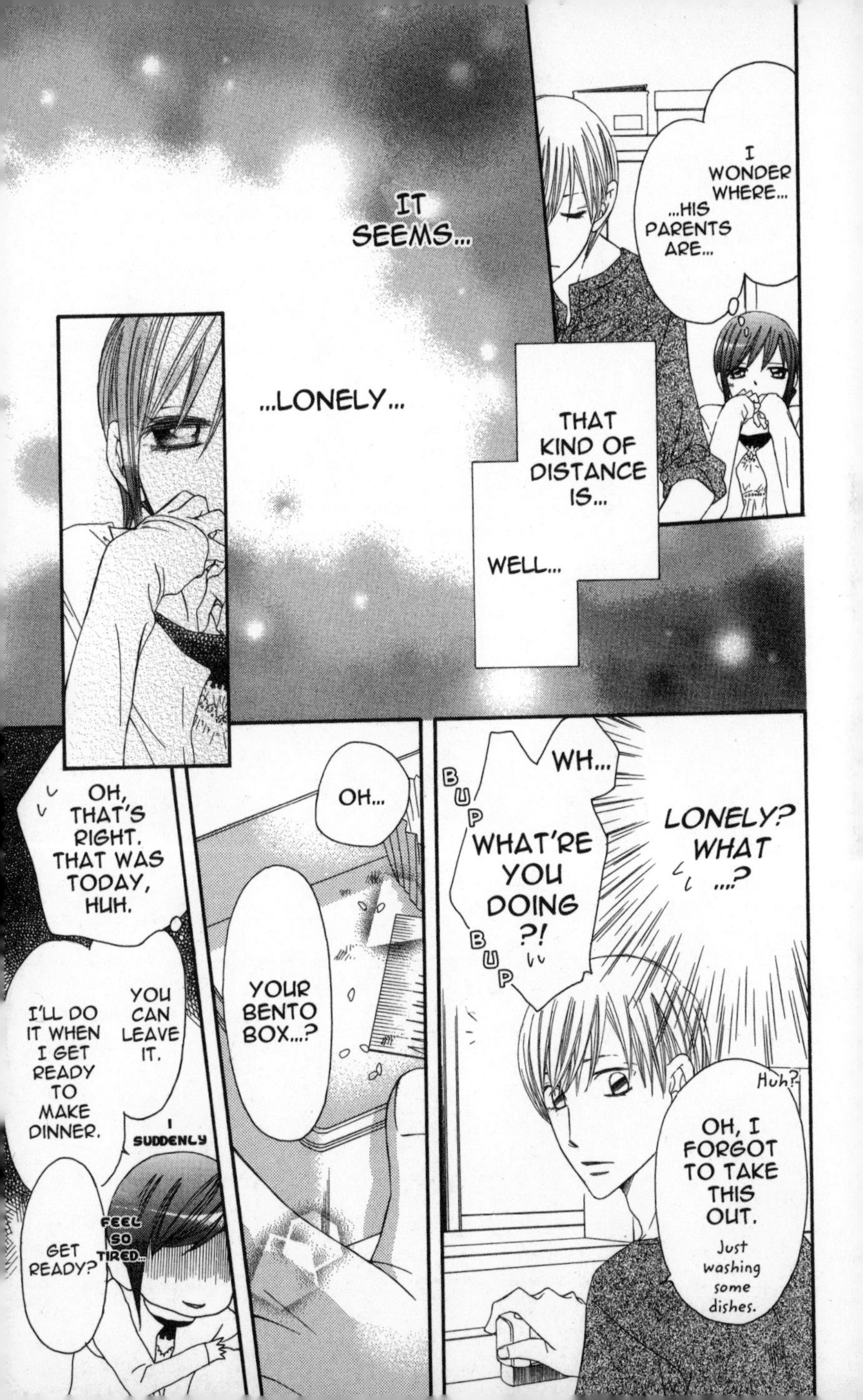
I WONDER WHERE... ...HIS PARENTS ARE...
THAT KIND OF DISTANCE IS...
WELL...
IT SEEMS...
...LONELY...
LONELY? WHAT ...?
WH... WHAT'RE YOU DOING ?!
BUP BUP
Huh?
OH, I FORGOT TO TAKE THIS OUT.
Just washing some dishes.
OH...
YOUR BENTO BOX...?
OH, THAT'S RIGHT. THAT WAS TODAY, HUH.
YOU CAN LEAVE IT.
I'LL DO IT WHEN I GET READY TO MAKE DINNER.
I SUDDENLY FEEL SO TIRED...
GET READY?

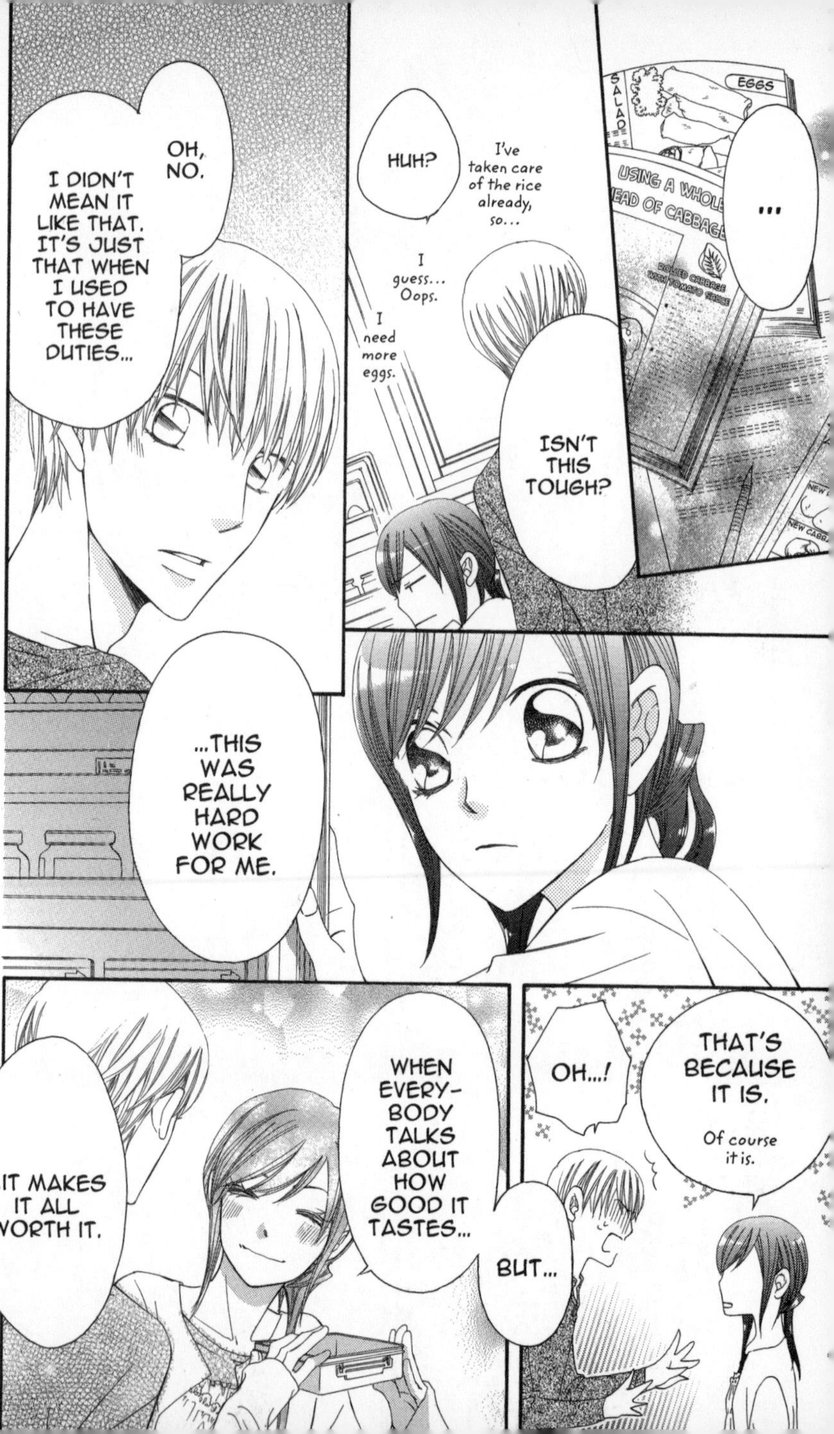
SALAD
EGGS
USING A WHOLE
EAD OF CABBAGE
ROLLED CABBAGE WITH TOMATO SAUCE
...
I've taken care of the rice already, so...
I guess... Oops.
I need more eggs.
ISN'T THIS TOUGH?
HUH?
OH, NO.
I DIDN'T MEAN IT LIKE THAT. IT'S JUST THAT WHEN I USED TO HAVE THESE DUTIES...
...THIS WAS REALLY HARD WORK FOR ME.
THAT'S BECAUSE IT IS.
Of course it is.
OH...!
BUT...
WHEN EVERY-BODY TALKS ABOUT HOW GOOD IT TASTES...
...IT MAKES IT ALL WORTH IT.

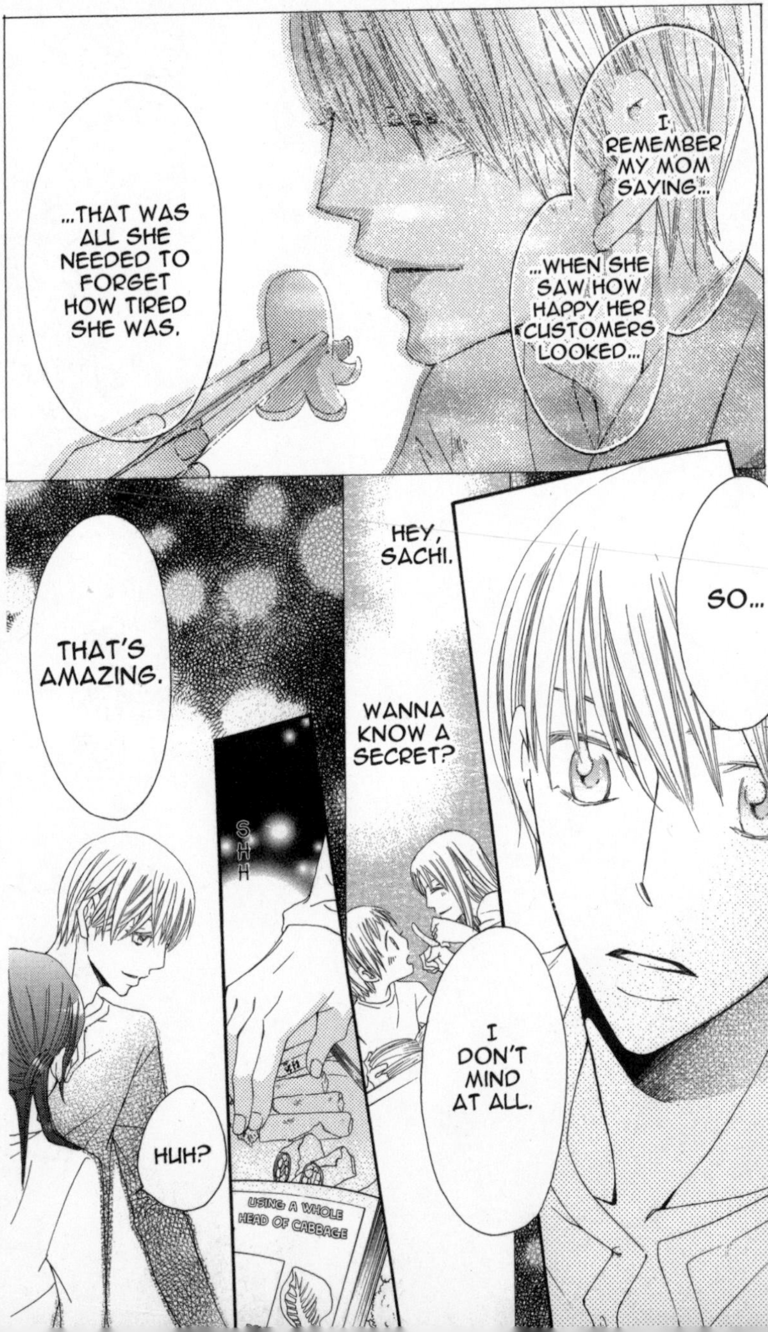
I REMEMBER MY MOM SAYING...
...WHEN SHE SAW HOW HAPPY HER CUSTOMERS LOOKED...
...THAT WAS ALL SHE NEEDED TO FORGET HOW TIRED SHE WAS.
SO...
I DON'T MIND AT ALL.
HEY, SACHI.
WANNA KNOW A SECRET?
SHH
USING A WHOLE HEAD OF CABBAGE
THAT'S AMAZING.
HUH?

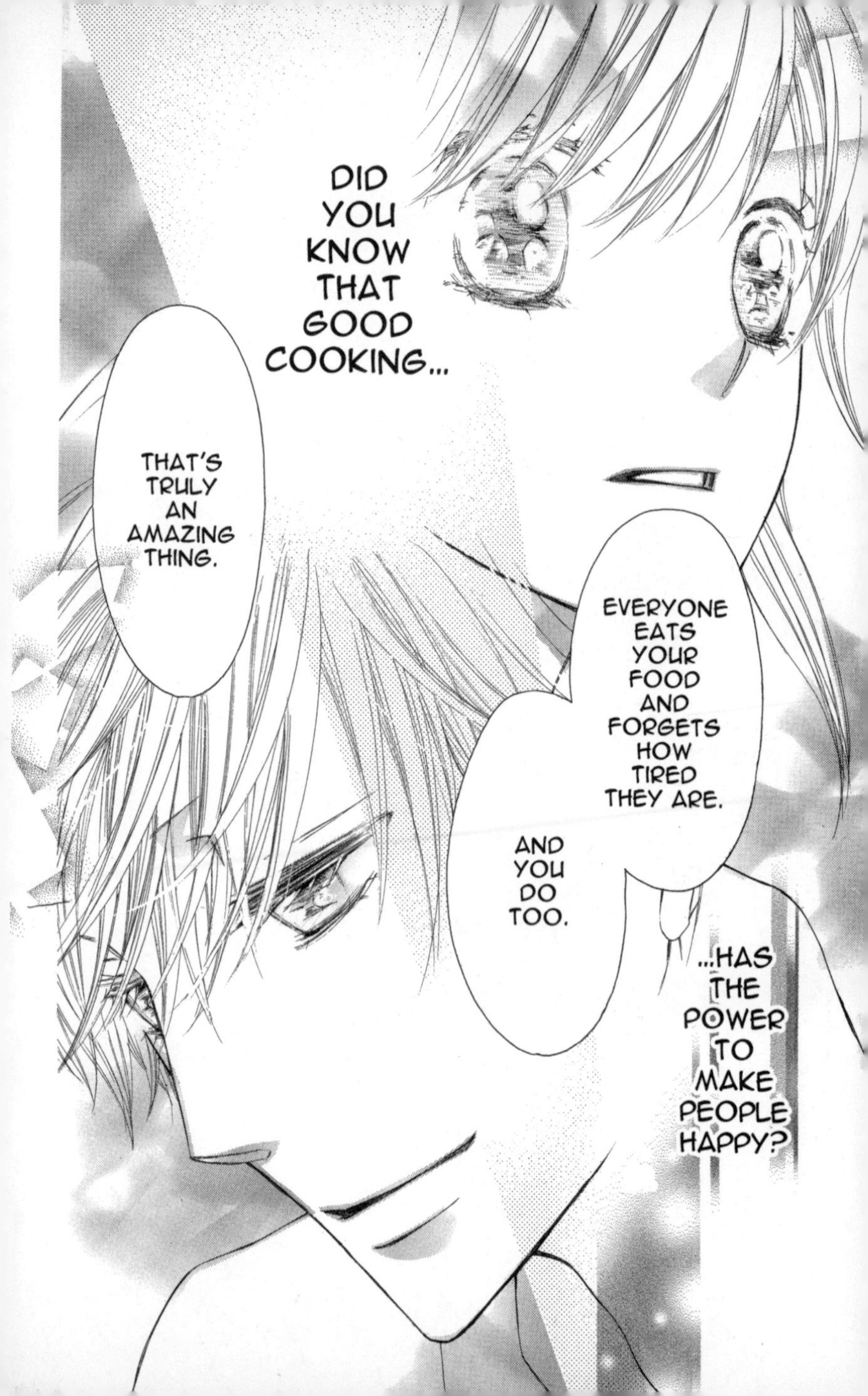
DID YOU KNOW THAT GOOD COOKING...
...HAS THE POWER TO MAKE PEOPLE HAPPY?
EVERYONE EATS YOUR FOOD AND FORGETS HOW TIRED THEY ARE.
AND YOU DO TOO.
THAT'S TRULY AN AMAZING THING.

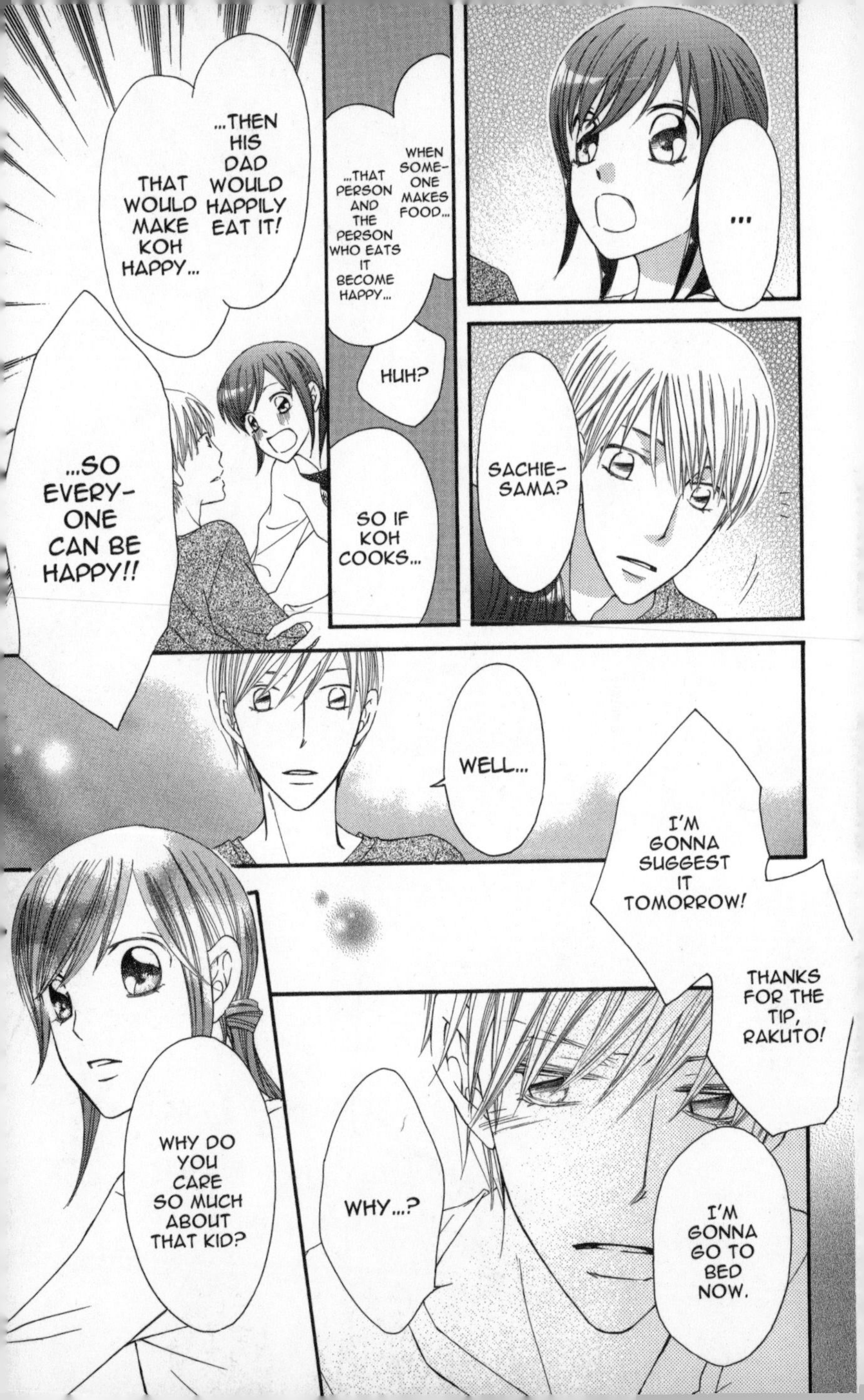
...
SACHIE-SAMA?
WHEN SOME-ONE MAKES FOOD...
...THAT PERSON AND THE PERSON WHO EATS IT BECOME HAPPY...
HUH?
SO IF KOH COOKS...
...THEN HIS DAD WOULD HAPPILY EAT IT!
THAT WOULD MAKE KOH HAPPY...
...SO EVERY-ONE CAN BE HAPPY!!
WELL...
I'M GONNA SUGGEST IT TOMORROW!
THANKS FOR THE TIP, RAKUTO!
I'M GONNA GO TO BED NOW.
WHY...?
WHY DO YOU CARE SO MUCH ABOUT THAT KID?

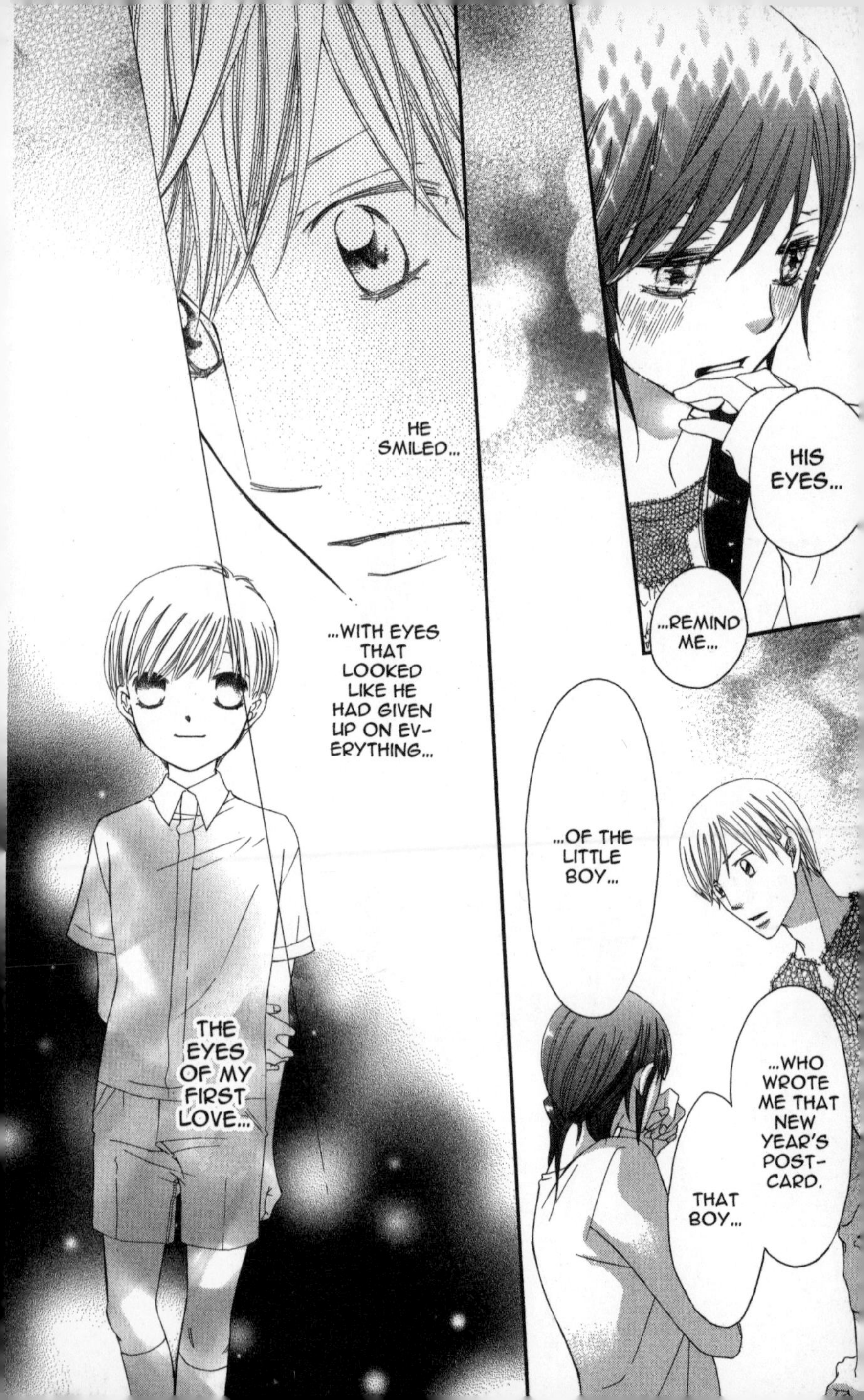
HIS EYES...
...REMIND ME...
...OF THE LITTLE BOY...
...WHO WROTE ME THAT NEW YEAR'S POST-CARD.
THAT BOY...
HE SMILED...
...WITH EYES THAT LOOKED LIKE HE HAD GIVEN UP ON EV-ERYTHING...
THE EYES OF MY FIRST LOVE...

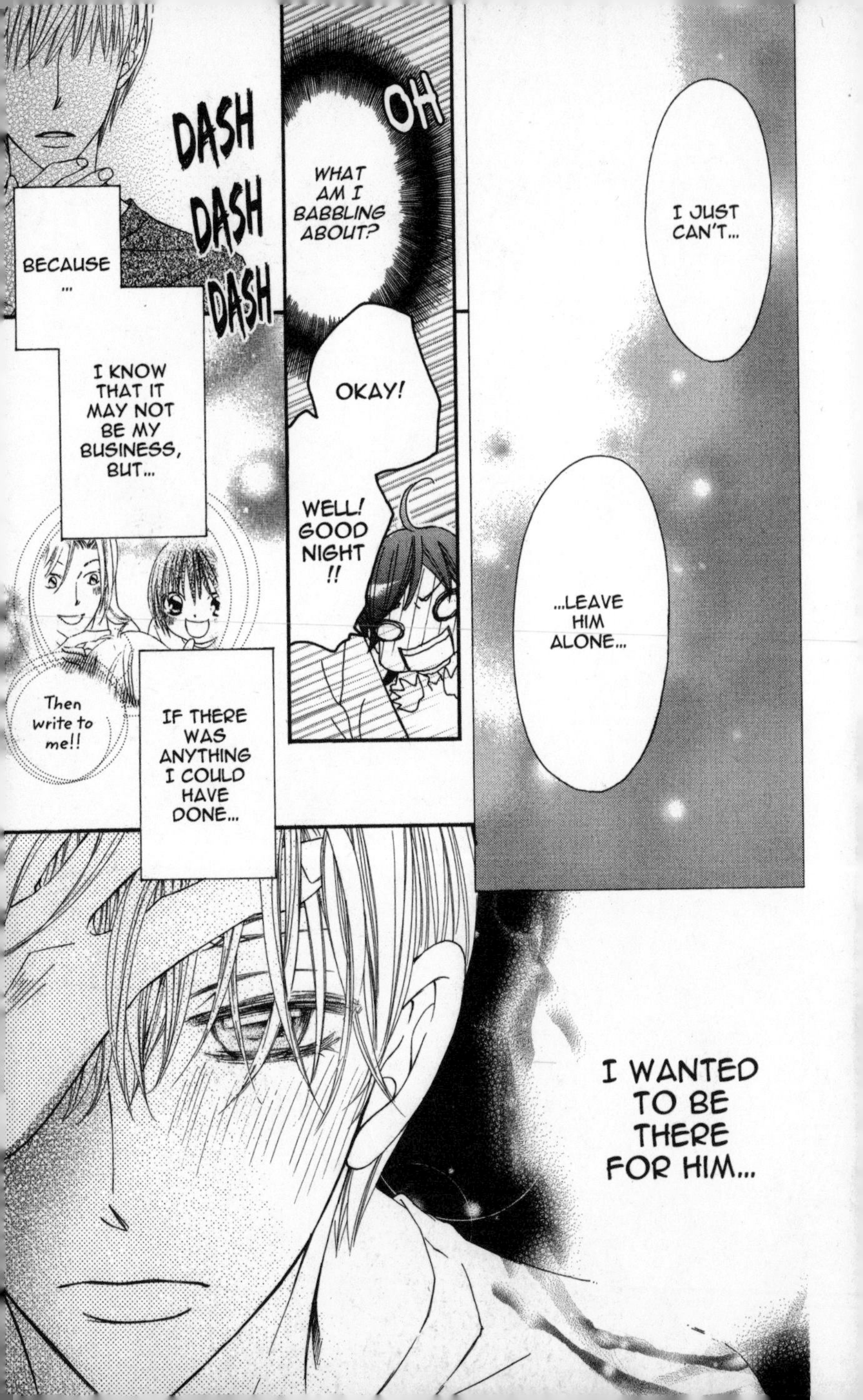
I JUST CAN'T...
...LEAVE HIM ALONE...
OH
WHAT AM I BABBLING ABOUT?
OKAY!
WELL! GOOD NIGHT!!
DASH DASH DASH
BECAUSE...
I KNOW THAT IT MAY NOT BE MY BUSINESS, BUT...
Then write to me!!
IF THERE WAS ANYTHING I COULD HAVE DONE...
I WANTED TO BE THERE FOR HIM...

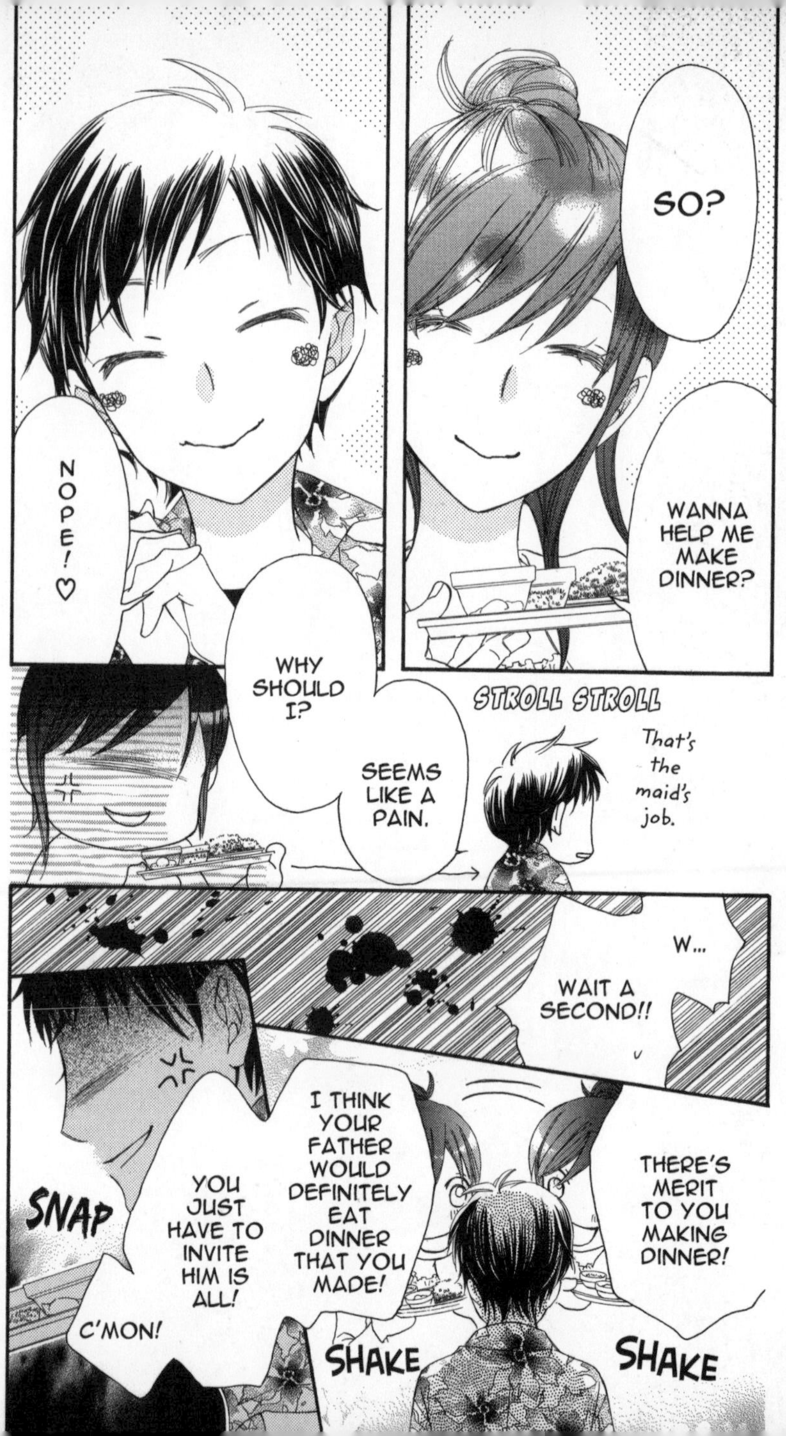
SO?
WANNA HELP ME MAKE DINNER?
NOPE! ♡
STROLL STROLL
That's the maid's job.
WHY SHOULD I?
SEEMS LIKE A PAIN.
W...
WAIT A SECOND!!
THERE'S MERIT TO YOU MAKING DINNER!
I THINK YOUR FATHER WOULD DEFINITELY EAT DINNER THAT YOU MADE!
YOU JUST HAVE TO INVITE HIM IS ALL!
SNAP
C'MON!
SHAKE
SHAKE

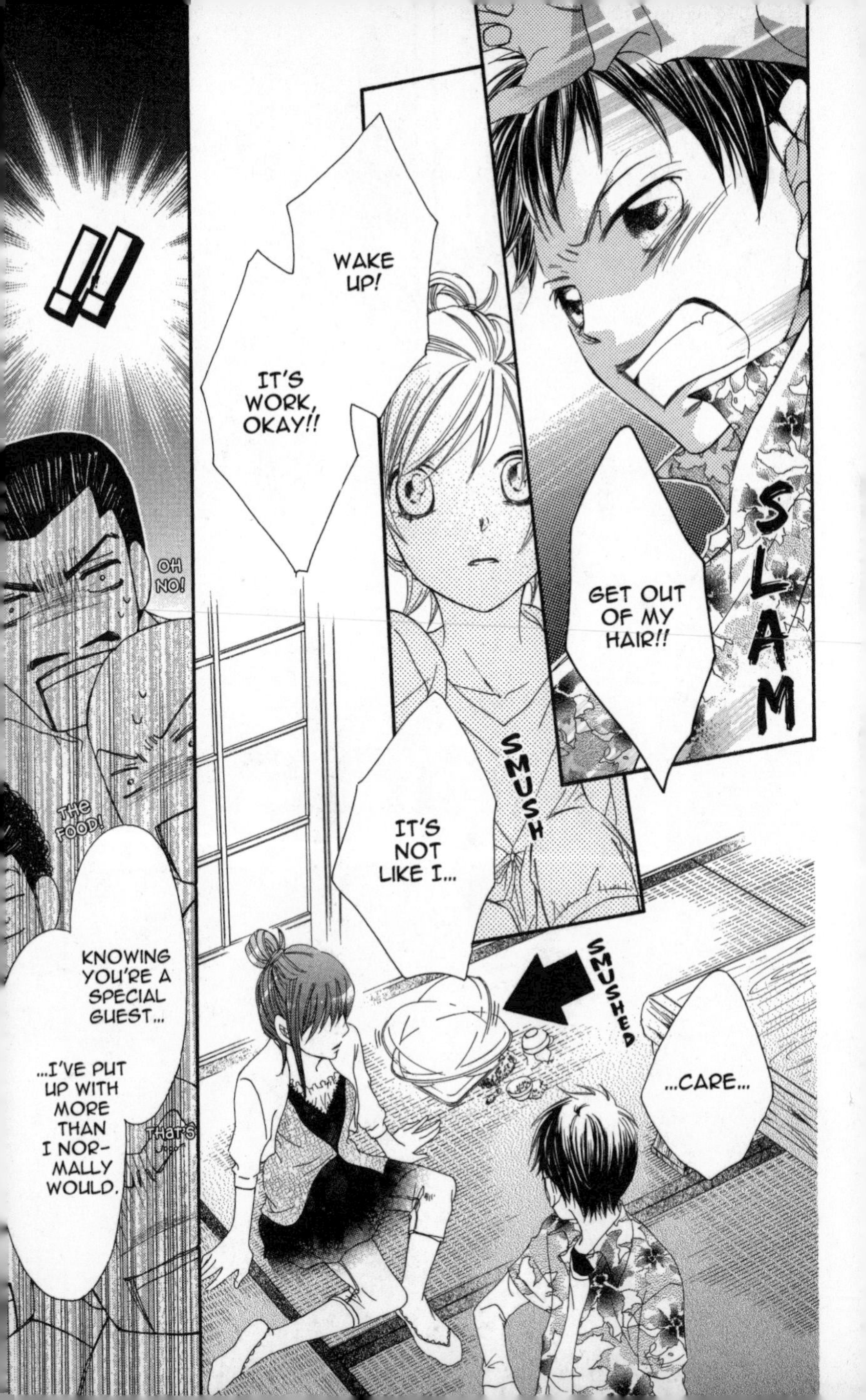
GET OUT OF MY HAIR!!
SLAM
WAKE UP!
IT'S WORK, OKAY!!
SMUSH
IT'S NOT LIKE I...
...CARE...
SMUSHED
!!
OH NO!
THE FOOD!
KNOWING YOU'RE A SPECIAL GUEST...
...I'VE PUT UP WITH MORE THAN I NOR-MALLY WOULD.
THAT'S

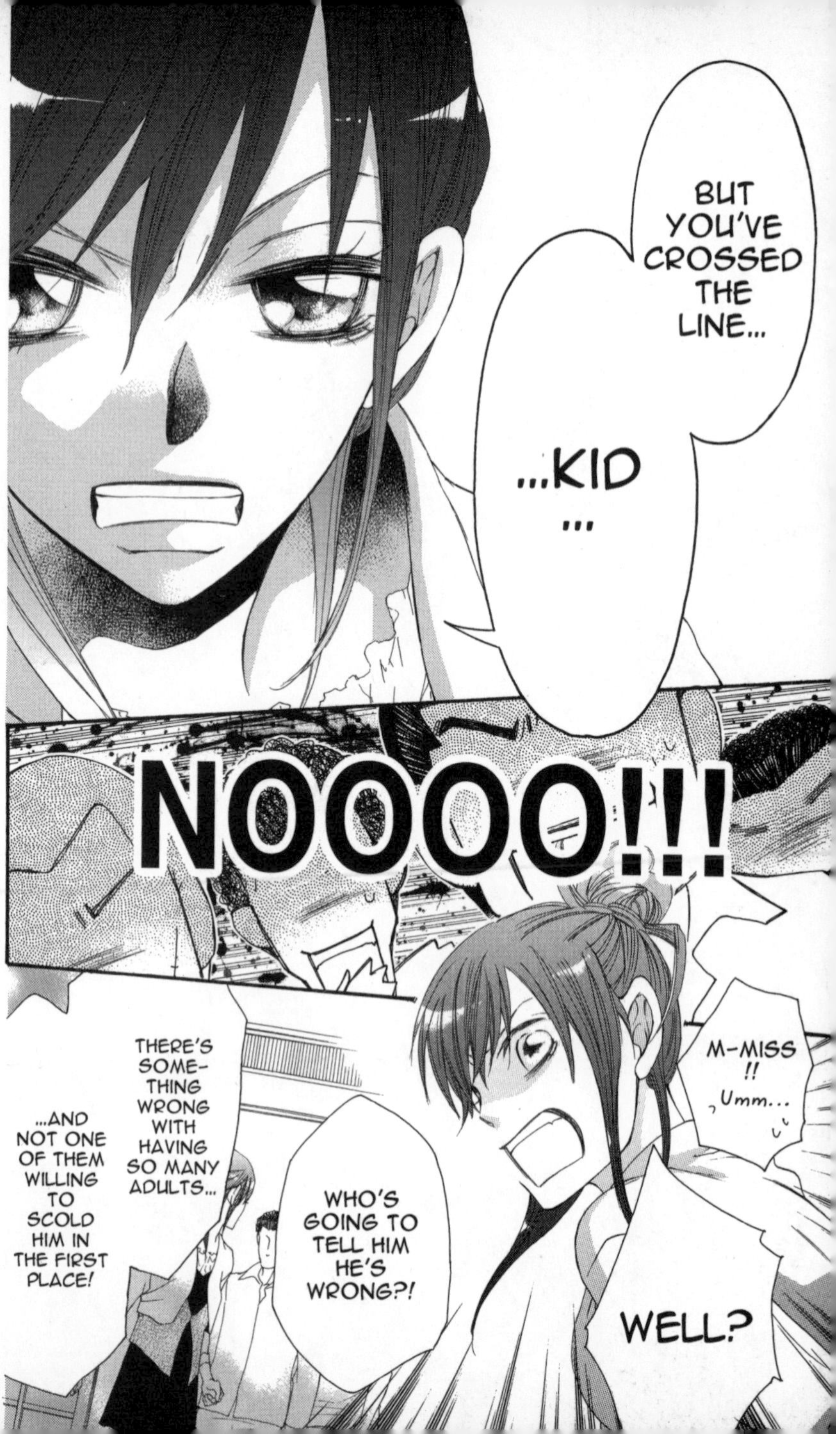
BUT YOU'VE CROSSED THE LINE...
...KID ...
NOOOO!!!
M-MISS !!
Umm...
WELL?
WHO'S GOING TO TELL HIM HE'S WRONG?!
THERE'S SOME-THING WRONG WITH HAVING SO MANY ADULTS...
...AND NOT ONE OF THEM WILLING TO SCOLD HIM IN THE FIRST PLACE!

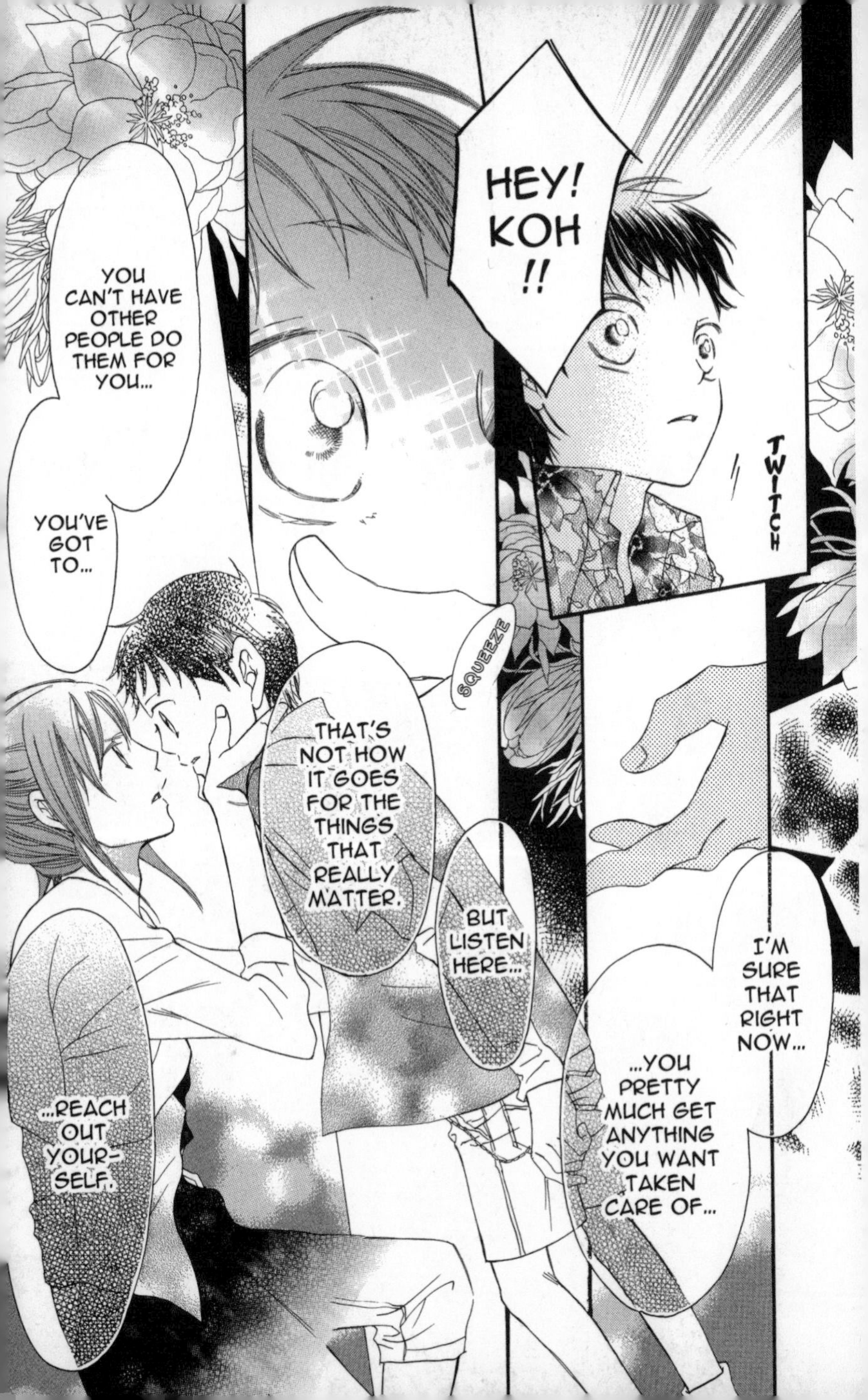
HEY! KOH!!
TWITCH
I'M SURE THAT RIGHT NOW...
...YOU PRETTY MUCH GET ANYTHING YOU WANT TAKEN CARE OF...
BUT LISTEN HERE...
THAT'S NOT HOW IT GOES FOR THE THINGS THAT REALLY MATTER.
SQUEEZE
YOU CAN'T HAVE OTHER PEOPLE DO THEM FOR YOU...
YOU'VE GOT TO...
...REACH OUT YOUR-SELF.

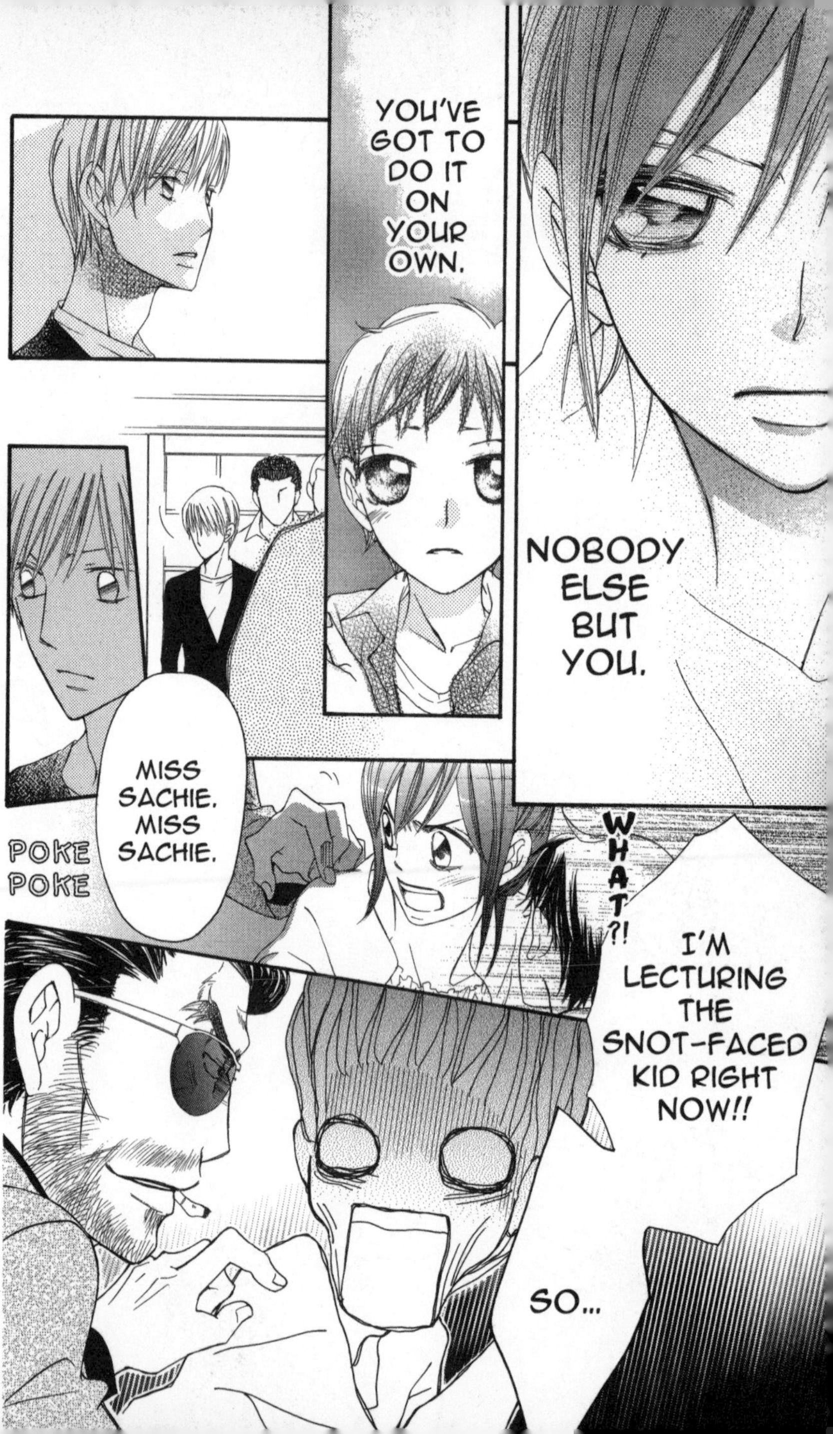
NOBODY ELSE BUT YOU.
YOU'VE GOT TO DO IT ON YOUR OWN.
MISS SACHIE. MISS SACHIE.
POKE POKE
WHAT?!
I'M LECTURING THE SNOT-FACED KID RIGHT NOW!!
SO...

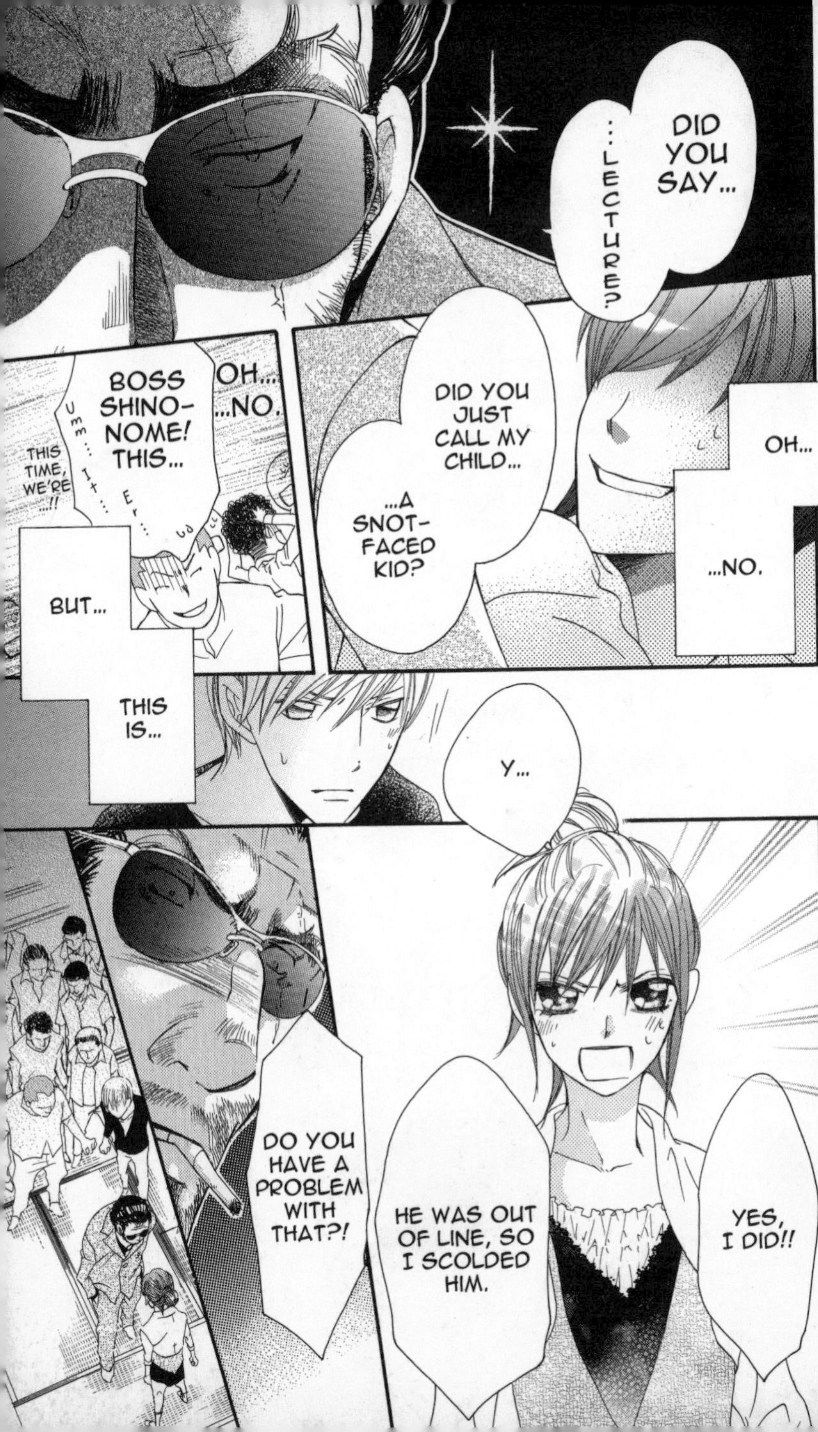

DID YOU SAY...
...LECTURE?
DID YOU JUST CALL MY CHILD...
...A SNOT-FACED KID?
OH...
...NO.
OH...
...NO.
BOSS SHINO-NOME! THIS...
Umm... It... Er...
THIS TIME, WE'RE ...!!
BUT...
THIS IS...
Y...
YES, I DID!!
HE WAS OUT OF LINE, SO I SCOLDED HIM.
DO YOU HAVE A PROBLEM WITH THAT?!

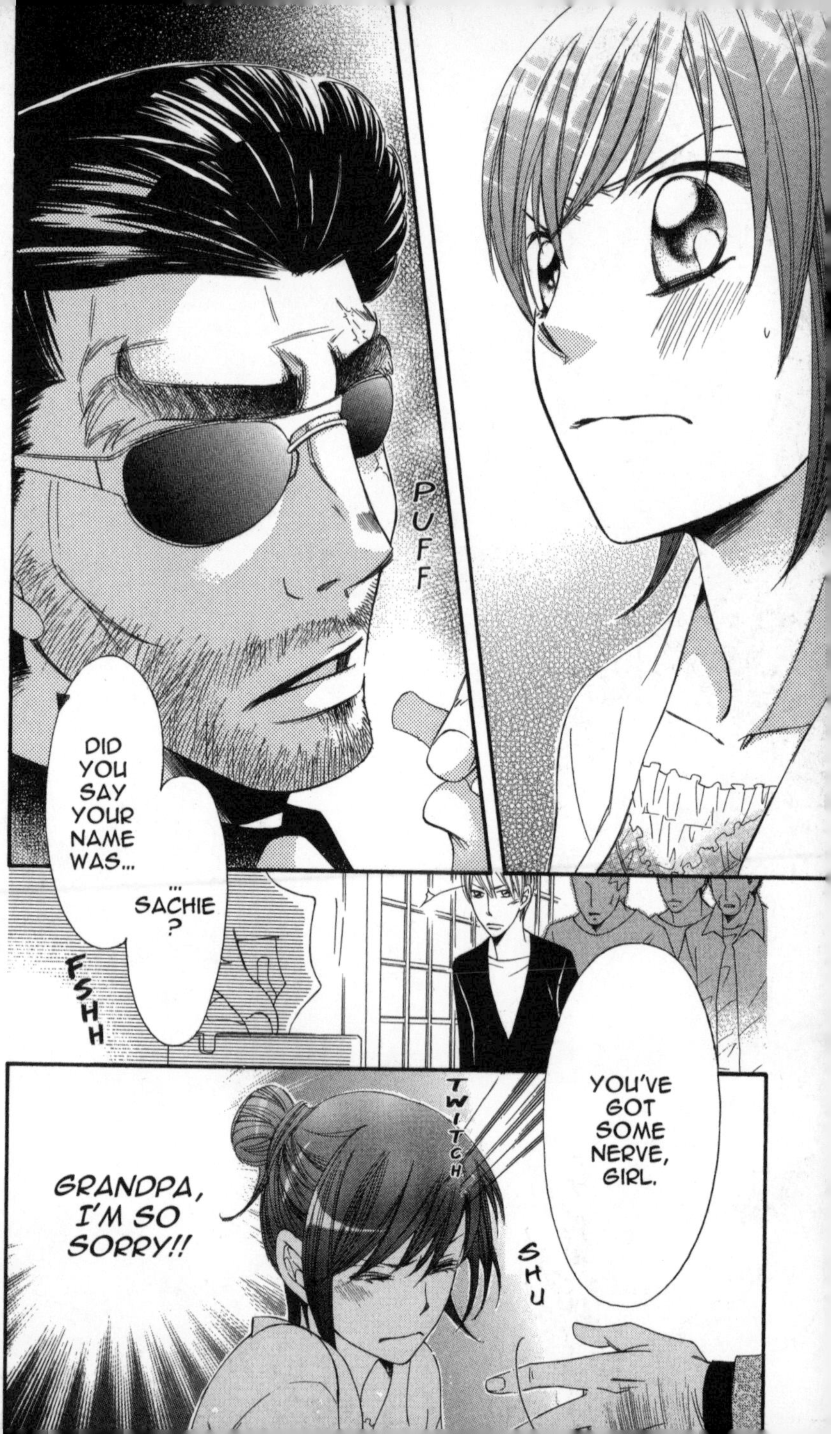
PUFF
DID YOU SAY YOUR NAME WAS...
...SACHIE?
FSHH
YOU'VE GOT SOME NERVE, GIRL.
TWITCH
GRANDPA, I'M SO SORRY!!
SHU

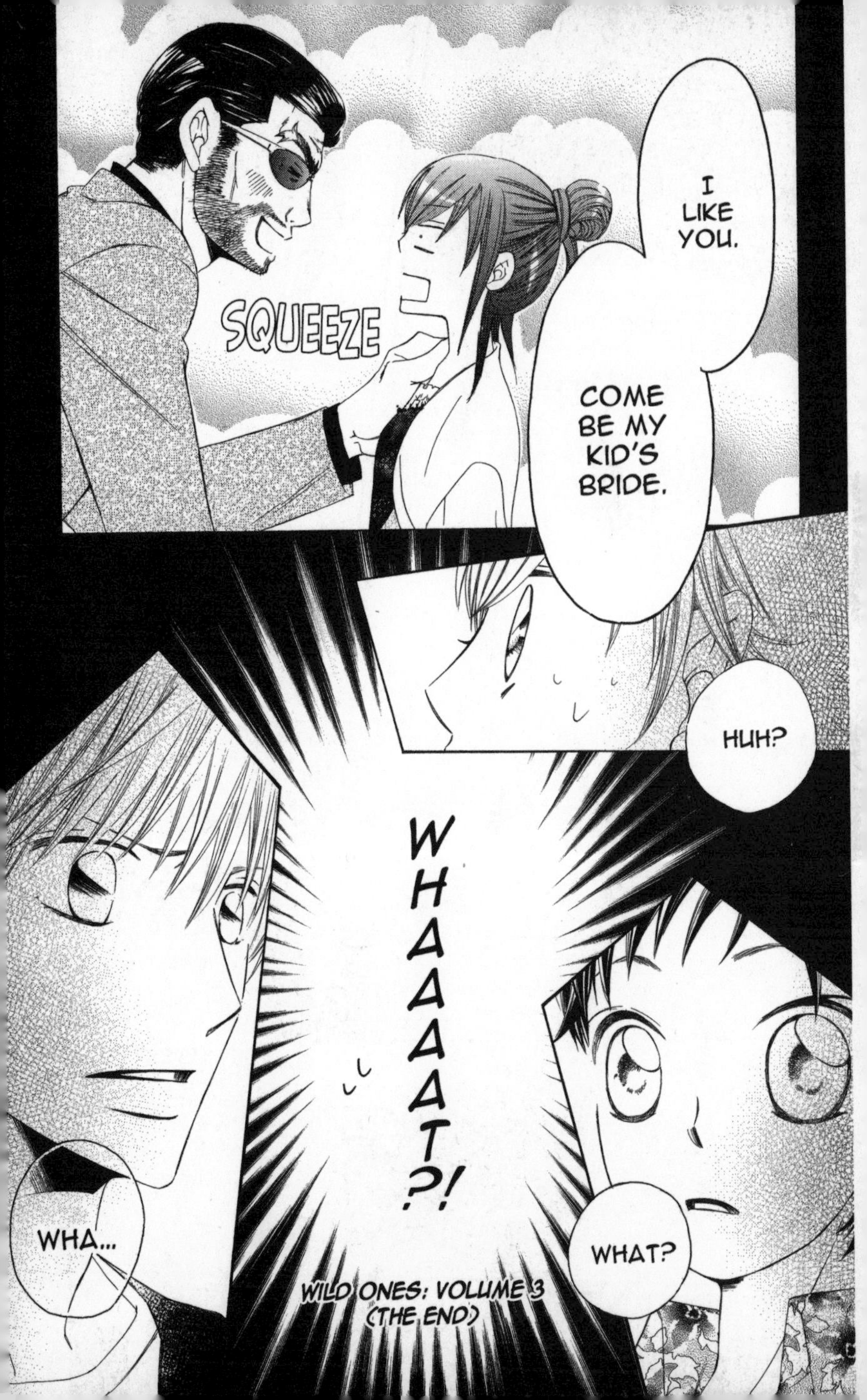
I LIKE YOU.
COME BE MY KID'S BRIDE.
SQUEEZE
HUH?
WHAAAAAT?!
WHAT?
WHA...
WILD ONES: VOLUME 3 (THE END)

THANX!!

Shibata-san
Nagao-san
Igari-san
Yamazaki-san
Kochi-san
Miyazaki-san
And...
Mo-chan!!

I have different people help me each time, so the amount is pretty incredible... This manga is only possible because of the help of so many people.
Thank you so much! Until next time!!
8/2006
Kiyo Fujiwara

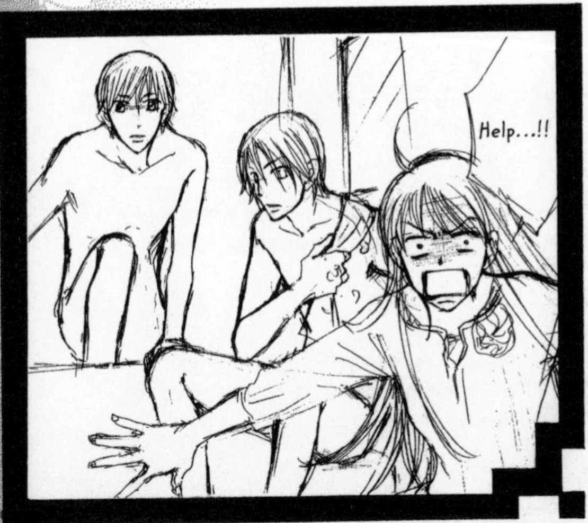

Help...!!

◁| This was during the drafting stage...

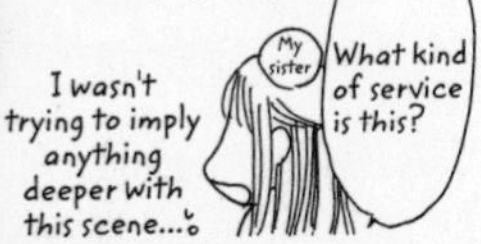

What kind of service is this?
My sister
I wasn't trying to imply anything deeper with this scene...

Wanna be part of the *Wild Ones* gang? Then you gotta learn the lingo! Here are some cultural notes to help you out!

HONORIFICS

Sensei – honorific title used to address teachers as well as professionals such as doctors, lawyers and artists. (On page 51, the author refers to manga artist Marimo Ragawa as "sensei" to show respect.)

Sama – the formal version of "san"; this honorific title is used primarily in addressing persons much higher in rank than oneself. "Sama" is also used when the speaker wants to show great respect or deference. (On page 22— and for pretty much the rest of the series—Rakuto calls Sachie "Sachie-sama" in addition to "princess.")

NOTES

Page 43, panel 5 – Yakuza
Yakuza refers to Japanese organized crime in general or more specifically to its gang members.

Page 47, panel 3 – Onsen
A Japanese hot spring. *Onsen* water is believed to have healing powers derived from its mineral content.

Page 51, panel 5 – Mangaka
A manga artist. Marimo Ragawa is the *mangaka* famous for the series *Baby & Me*.

Page 53, panel 3 – Hanami
Hanami literally means "flower viewing," and it traditionally refers to having a picnic party while admiring the beauty of cherry blossoms.

Page 89, panel 1 – Go
A strategic board game for two players. Black and white stones are placed on the board, where a stone can be captured and removed if surrounded by stones of the opposing color.

Page 149, panel 1 – Bento
A home-made lunch box that may contain rice, meat, pickles and an assortment of side dishes. Often the food is arranged in such a way as to resemble objects like animals, flowers, leaves, and so forth.

Page 157, panel 5 - Men
One of the five strikes in kendo.

Kiyo Fujiwara made her manga debut in 2000 in *Hana to Yume* magazine with *Bokuwane*. Her other works include *Hard Romantic-ker*, *Help!!* and *Gold Rush 21*. She comes from Akashi-shi in Hyogo Prefecture but currently lives in Tokyo. Her hobbies include playing drums and bass guitar and wearing kimono.

WILD ONES
VOL. 3
The Shojo Beat Manga Edition

STORY AND ART BY
KIYO FUJIWARA

Translation & Adaptation/Mai Ihara
Touch-up Art & Lettering/HudsonYards
Cover Design/Hidemi Dunn
Interior Design/Yuki Ameda
Editor/Amy Yu

Editor in Chief, Books/Alvin Lu
Editor in Chief, Magazines/Marc Weidenbaum
VP, Publishing Licensing/Rika Inouye
VP, Sales & Product Marketing/Gonzalo Ferreyra
VP, Creative/Linda Espinosa
Publisher/Hyoe Narita

Arakure by Kiyo Fujiwara
© Kiyo Fujiwara 2006
All rights reserved.
First published in Japan in 2006 by HAKUSENSHA, Inc., Tokyo.
English language translation rights arranged with HAKUSENSHA, Inc., Tokyo. All rights reserved. The stories, characters and incidents mentioned in this publication are entirely fictional.

Printed in Canada

Published by VIZ Media, LLC
P.O. Box 77010
San Francisco, CA 94107

Shojo Beat Manga Edition
10 9 8 7 6 5 4 3 2
First printing, June 2008
Second printing, July 2008

www.viz.com

store.viz.com

PARENTAL ADVISORY
WILD ONES is rated T for Teen
and is recommended for ages
13 and up. This volume contains
suggestive themes.
ratings.viz.com

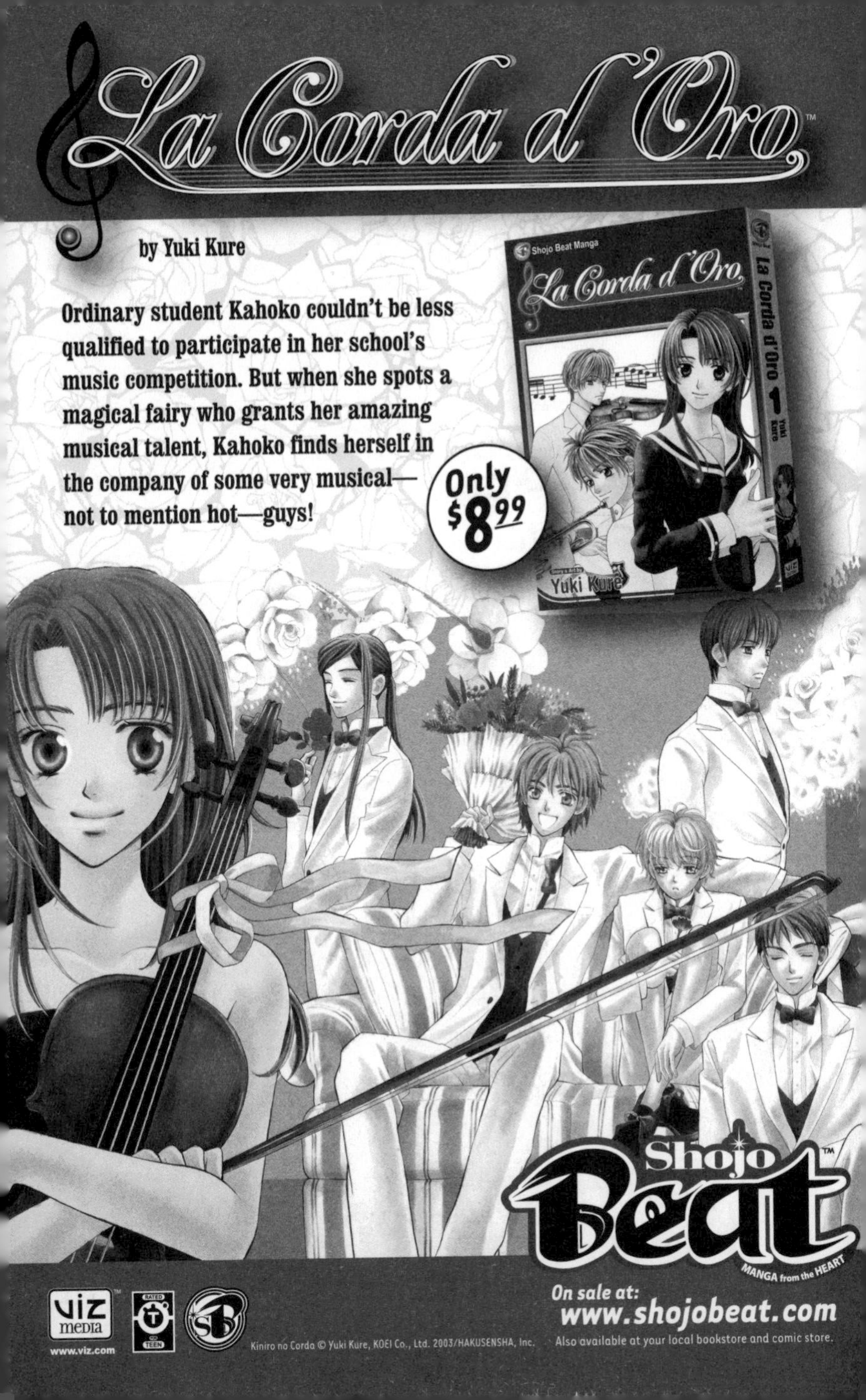
La Corda d'Oro™
by Yuki Kure
Ordinary student Kahoko couldn't be less qualified to participate in her school's music competition. But when she spots a magical fairy who grants her amazing musical talent, Kahoko finds herself in the company of some very musical—not to mention hot—guys!
Only $8.99
Shojo Beat Manga
La Corda d'Oro
La Corda d'Oro 1
Yuki Kure
Shojo Beat™
MANGA from the HEART
On sale at:
www.shojobeat.com
Also available at your local bookstore and comic store.
viz media
www.viz.com
RATED T TEEN
Kiniro no Corda © Yuki Kure, KOEI Co., Ltd. 2003/HAKUSENSHA, Inc.

Skip·Beat!

By Yoshiki Nakamura

Kyoko Mogami followed her true love Sho to Tokyo to support him while he made it big as an idol. But he's casting her out now that he's famous! Kyoko won't suffer in silence— she's going to get her sweet revenge by beating Sho in show biz!

Shojo Beat

MANGA from the HEART

Only $8.99

On sale at:
www.shojobeat.com

Also available at your local bookstore and comic store.

www.viz.com

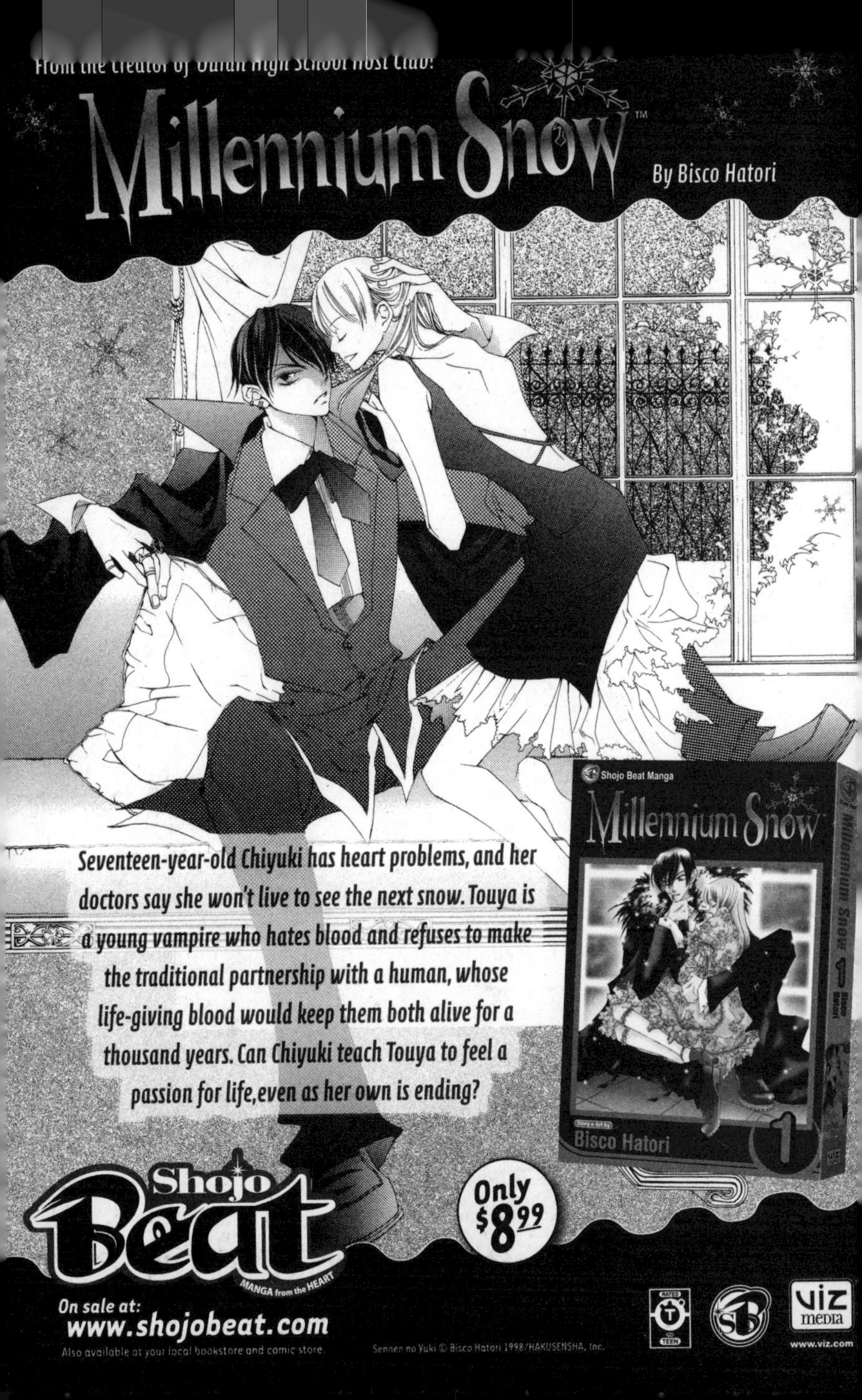
From the creator of Ouran High School Host Club!
Millennium Snow™
By Bisco Hatori
Seventeen-year-old Chiyuki has heart problems, and her doctors say she won't live to see the next snow. Touya is a young vampire who hates blood and refuses to make the traditional partnership with a human, whose life-giving blood would keep them both alive for a thousand years. Can Chiyuki teach Touya to feel a passion for life, even as her own is ending?
Shojo Beat Manga
Millennium Snow
Story & Art by
Bisco Hatori
1
Shojo Beat
MANGA from the HEART
Only $8.99
On sale at:
www.shojobeat.com
Also available at your local bookstore and comic store.
Sennen no Yuki © Bisco Hatori 1998/HAKUSENSHA, Inc.
RATED T TEEN
VIZ media
www.viz.com

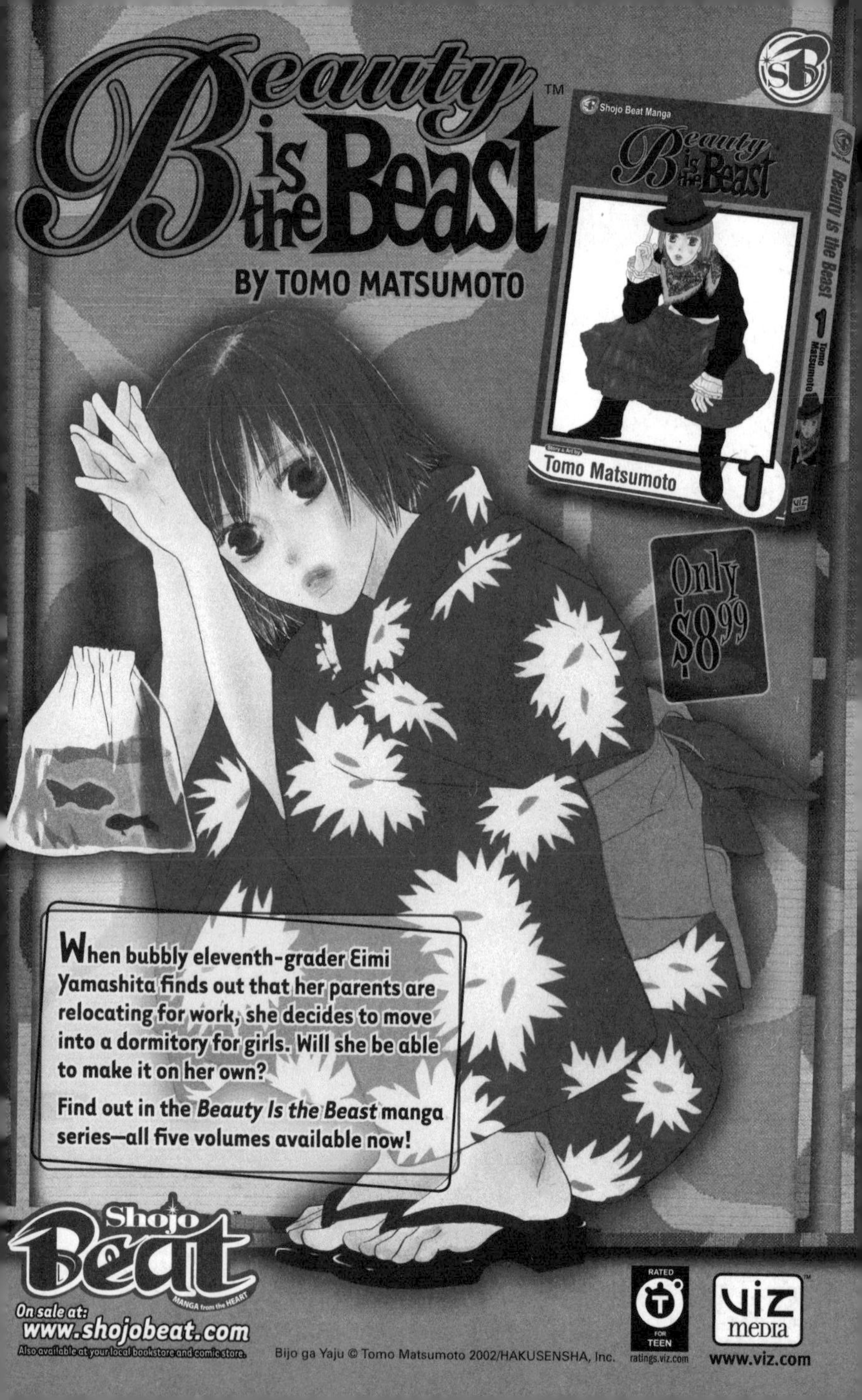

Beauty is the Beast™
BY TOMO MATSUMOTO
Shojo Beat Manga
Beauty is the Beast
Tomo Matsumoto
1
Only $8.99
When bubbly eleventh-grader Eimi Yamashita finds out that her parents are relocating for work, she decides to move into a dormitory for girls. Will she be able to make it on her own?
Find out in the *Beauty Is the Beast* manga series—all five volumes available now!
Shojo Beat™
MANGA from the HEART
On sale at:
www.shojobeat.com
Also available at your local bookstore and comic store.
Bijo ga Yaju © Tomo Matsumoto 2002/HAKUSENSHA, Inc.
RATED T FOR TEEN
ratings.viz.com
VIZ media
www.viz.com

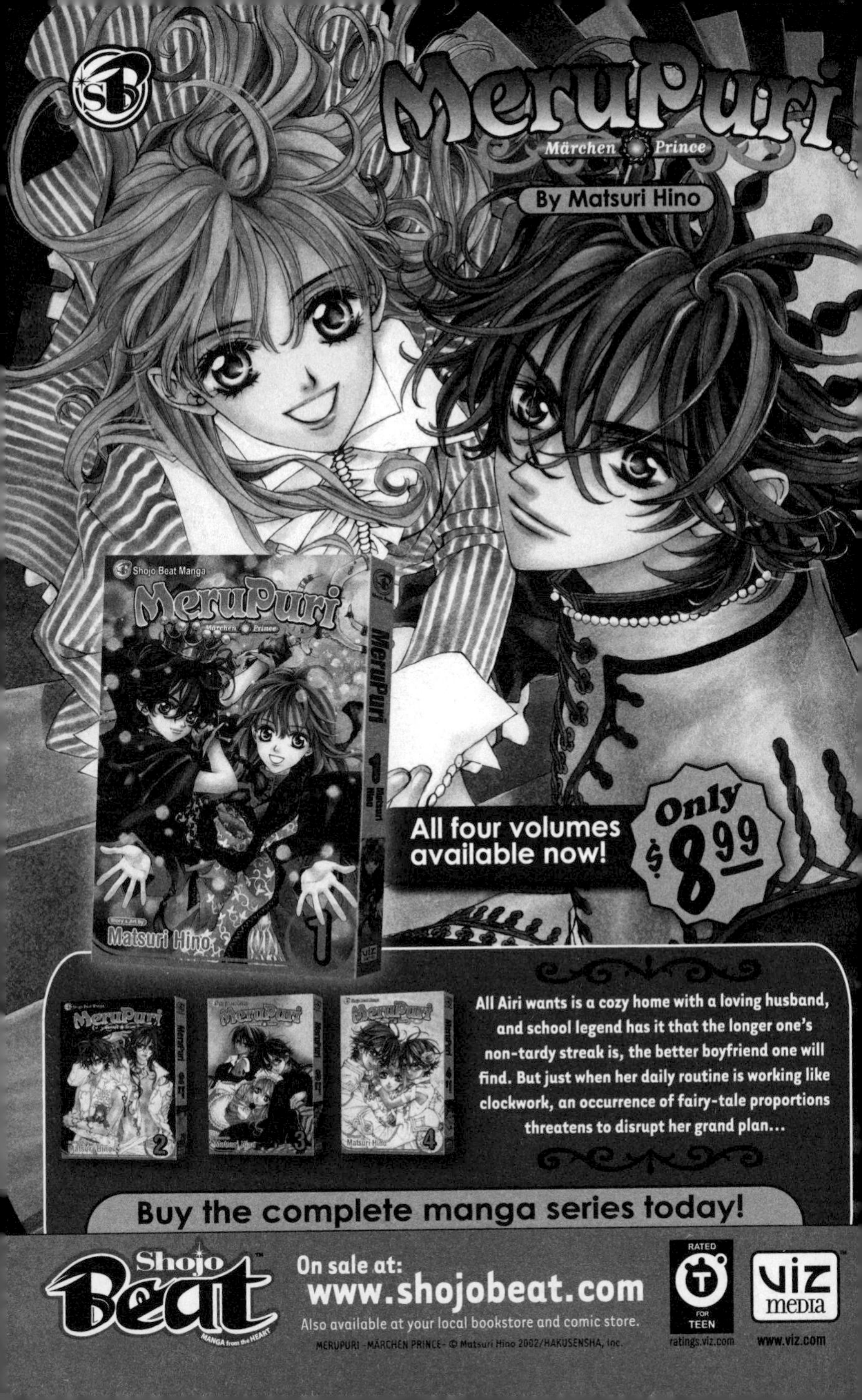
MeruPuri
Märchen Prince
By Matsuri Hino
Shojo Beat Manga
MeruPuri
Märchen Prince
Matsuri Hino
All four volumes available now!
Only $8.99
All Airi wants is a cozy home with a loving husband, and school legend has it that the longer one's non-tardy streak is, the better boyfriend one will find. But just when her daily routine is working like clockwork, an occurrence of fairy-tale proportions threatens to disrupt her grand plan...
Buy the complete manga series today!
Shojo Beat
MANGA from the HEART
On sale at:
www.shojobeat.com
Also available at your local bookstore and comic store.
MERUPURI -MÄRCHEN PRINCE- © Matsuri Hino 2002/HAKUSENSHA, Inc.
RATED T FOR TEEN
ratings.viz.com
VIZ media
www.viz.com